CU00660931

# The ADR Practice Guide

## Commercial Dispute Resol

# The ADR Practice Guide
## Commercial Dispute Resolution

Third edition

### Dr Karl Mackie
Barrister
Mediator and Chief Executive, CEDR
Special Professor, University of Westminster

### David Miles
Solicitor
Partner, Glovers
Mediator and Arbitrator

### William Marsh
Solicitor
Independent Mediator
Director, Conflict Management International

### Tony Allen
Solicitor
Mediator and Director of CEDR
Consultant with Bunkers

Tottel Publishing Ltd, Maxwelton House, 41–43 Boltro Road, Haywards Heath, West Sussex, RH16 1BJ

A CIP Catalogue record for this book is available from the British Library.

ISBN: 978-1-84592-314-3

Typeset by Laserwords Private Ltd, Chennai, India
Printed and bound in Great Britain by William Clowes Limited, Beccles, Suffolk

# Foreword

Mediation – the foremost alternative dispute resolution process – has become a firmly established part of the civil justice scene, in a way and at a speed that is striking. In this jurisdiction this has been achieved in less than 25 years, a twinkling of an eye when set against the centuries-long history of the common law and the courts. Paradoxically, its importance lies not in the fact that it is an alternative to, but in its close relationship with, the work of the courts and tribunals. Opportunities for reasonable settlement are enhanced where appropriate and acceptable to the parties, and, where cases do not settle at mediation, judges can be reassured that the parties' resolve to litigate has been vigorously tested by a skilled intermediary within a confidential process. Mediation should thus be seen as a stage, often but not always the last stage, in the process of dispute resolution.

Its established role is evidenced not just by the increase in use by those involved in commercial disputes, both business and personal, but by the way in which the courts have been involved in considering that role and the ways in which it should be enhanced and encouraged for the benefit of litigants. The fact that the new edition of this book contains a useful and substantial review of the relevant case law, most of which has been emerged since 2000, is further testimony to the growth in significance of ADR.

There remains nonetheless a need for greater awareness about the dynamics of the mediation process among the judiciary, the legal profession and the public at large. I commend this book for providing two benefits that deserve a wide readership. First, it contains a wealth of insight into the inner workings of the mediation process based on the practical skills of four experienced mediators. Secondly, it reviews very fully the legal context into which mediation fits, providing a comprehensive resource for access to the current law and practice relating to ADR.

*Lord Phillips of Worth Matravers*
*Lord Chief Justice's Office*
*Royal Courts of Justice*
*Strand*
*London WC2*
*July 2007*

# Preface

Looking back on our thoughts when we penned the preface to the second edition of this book, we have again travelled a very long journey since we last revised it. The Civil Procedure Rules 1998 had been in force for less than two years, but they had already wrought a fundamental change in the culture of litigation. The first formal recognition of ADR's status as a tool of active case management in CPR, Pt 1, added to what we called the 'dynamic doubt' generated by fears about the new costs sanctions provisions in CPR, Pt 44, had already led to a major surge in the uptake of the use of ADR in general and mediation in particular. CEDR, then the largest provider, enjoyed a 140% increase in mediations in 1999–2000, albeit from a modest base.

Other dramatic changes were also in play, especially over the vexed questions of access to justice and litigation funding, coupled with the shrinking of Legal Aid and the growth of conditional fee agreements as a means of making litigation affordable to many. But the signs of change and progress evident even in 2000 were not to deliver uninterrupted growth of either in civil justice or in the ADR market-place. Despite the 'compensation culture' debate, the trend for issued litigation has until very recently been downward. It is not clear whether this is related to the desire of the Treasury to make civil justice self-funding from hugely increased court fees. Part of it may relate to the enthusiasm for settlement which the CPR has undoubtedly developed.

But after a sharp upward trend in mediations, there seemed to be a lull or even dropping off, as the legal profession found, perhaps to its surprise, that courts were showing little enthusiasm for penalising those who declined to use mediation to settle cases. It was at that point that the Court of Appeal intervened with the decision in the landmark decision of *Dunnett v Railtrack* in which in one bound the courts leapt to imposing a costs penalty (or, more correctly and prosaically, declining to award costs in circumstances where they might have normally been expected) on a successful litigation party solely because they had refused to mediate. This at a stroke required litigants to take ADR seriously, and interest in avoiding such a sanction again led to growth in the use of mediation.

We have to underline that judicial and governmental pressure to mediate underpinned by costs sanctions is only one key route to the growth of ADR. The ideal of course is that its usefulness is voluntarily accepted and that it grows organically because it is embraced as the dispute resolution process of choice by many in a wide number of cases. To underpin the use of a consensual process by threat of adverse consequences risks breeding resentment and resistance. At least there is a distinction to be made between pressing parties to engage, but giving them the freedom to stay engaged or not once they have arrived into the process, leaving the responsibility on the mediator to persuade them to continue or not. But this tension about ADR use, and whether or how to ensure that it is fully used, remains unresolved after nearly 20 years of commercial mediation in the UK and nearly ten years after the CPR.

The most dramatic evidence of change in relation to the status of ADR in the civil justice system since our 2000 edition is the list of decided cases at the front, and the very substantial Part B of this new edition devoted to the legal framework of ADR. The first two editions of this book had no such index of cases, nor were there more than twelve or so English cases referred to in its text, most of which covered matters of general principle and pre-dated the CPR. There were nearly as many European, Australian and US decisions mentioned. In the last seven years, both higher and lower courts have made a number of significant decisions about the way ADR fits into the dispute resolution scene, and we have had to take full cognisance of that fact this time. We have tried to produce a comprehensive guide to the law and practice of ADR as it has emerged through the development of the CPR (already subject to their 43rd amendment in eight years, and with several such amendments having been of considerable significance to ADR) and the now quite substantial body of case-law. Because ADR jurisprudence is still undoubtedly evolving and has by no means reached a state of finality, we have tried to trace the arguments as they have developed from case to case, rather than just stating the bald current principles as they currently stand. We hope that this will assist any who have to argue the next generation of cases before the courts.

For large legal questions and doubts still remain. Can and should courts mandate parties to engage in ADR? Are such orders really in breach of art 6 of the European Convention on Human Rights? Is mere discussion and negotiation properly to be regarded as 'ADR'? Should the courts be prepared to penalise parties for not using mediation more systematically before issue of proceedings? As we write, the pre-action protocols are being reviewed yet again, perhaps to be embodied in one overarching protocol, and as the monitoring of pre-action conduct was one of the revolutionary concepts embodied in the CPR, we can expect further shifts in the balance of responsibility in the conduct of litigation. Above all, the current civil justice system remains bedevilled and frankly pilloried by its enormous cost. As mediation is a process which grew in response to the desire to reduce the cost of conflict, it too must be seen to deliver such an objective, and prove that it in fact does do so.

As with the previous editions, however, we have also aspired to make this a practical handbook to furnish useful guidance to those who have to deal with ADR professionally. We are well aware that this book has a wide spectrum of interested readers, including mediators (both newly accredited and experienced), lawyers representing parties in both transactional and litigation work, academics teaching the theory and practice of ADR to undergraduates and graduates (a very welcome if tardy development in UK university law departments), business and commercial consumers of the civil justice system, maybe even lay clients with an interest in the field, and policymakers in government. We hope that this wide readership will find the mix we offer – of theoretical and practical, legal and inter-personal, with some precedents based on a further seven years of experience of drafting – useful and stimulating. It can be daunting for a professional to engage for the first time in a new and unfamiliar process. We hope that a reading of this book will dissipate such fears and enable everyone to make sound choices in advance of, and to participate effectively in, the mediation process.

We have each contributed different parts of the book, but we share responsibility for the whole. Sometimes we have covered the same ground, but we have tried to do so in a way that sees the same issues from different perspectives the conceptual, the legal and the practical, mirroring the three perspectives that we encounter in various proportions in every dispute we mediate – the commercial, the legal and the personal.

The book remains in three parts. Part A deals (as before) with the conceptual framework of ADR, and Part B with the much fuller topic of the legal framework, including new chapters on costs and funding and the European perspective. Part C has been completely recast to give a practical guide to mediation, being the prime ADR process in the UK. We have removed the specialist chapters on less well-used processes such as mini-trial, on practice development, and on specialist fields such as construction and personal injury and clinical negligence mediations. This is partly out of deference to the publication of *Mediators on Mediation* by our colleagues and friends Christopher Newmark and Anthony Monaghan (Tottel 2005) a volume to which we all contributed in different ways, and which captures not just the mediation process from the viewpoint of a number of noted mediators, but also looks at specialist fields in a way that seemed unnecessary to replicate. Given also the appearance of the *EU Mediation Atlas: Practice and Regulation* by Jayne Singer, published by CEDR, CMS Cameron McKenna and Lexis Nexis in 2004, which gives a comprehensive snapshot of the state of mediation around Europe, the UK mediation profession (if we begin to use that style) has in the last few years certainly tried to offer a comprehensive suite of literature to its potential readership.

*Preface*

We have reduced the content of the Appendices, with just a few key documents included for handy reference with the text, reflecting on the fact that websites offer far more by way of precedents now than was the case at the time of the last edition of this book.

The law is, as far as we can make it, up to date as at 31 July 2007.

*Karl Mackie*
*David Miles*
*Bill Marsh*
*Tony Allen*
*July 2007*

# Contents

*Contents*

# Table of Cases

*PART A*

# THE CONCEPTUAL FRAMEWORK OF ADR

*Chapter 1*
# ADR in civil and commercial disputes

## 1.1 The roots of ADR

There are many positive reasons for adopting Alternative Dispute Resolution (ADR) processes as a means of trying to resolve civil disputes. However, it is probably true that initial enthusiasm for ADR stemmed primarily from a negative source – dissatisfaction with the delays, costs and inadequacies of the litigation process, particularly in the United States where ADR first developed. UK lawyers for many years had tended to dismiss ADR as a phenomenon specific to the United States. Companies in the United States were seen as more litigious. They were faced by claimants whose cases were funded by lawyers paid by substantial contingency fees. Trials were in courts where liability and damages were often determined by a jury, and there was no prospect of recovering legal costs from an opponent in the event of victory. Indeed, much of the same features distinguish the civil justice system in the United States from the United Kingdom even today.

However, by the late 1980s and early 1990s, a more considered recognition grew that ADR was playing an increasingly useful part in the industrialised common law world in overcoming some of the disadvantages of a highly expensive and often rigid adversarial system. The pace of business life picked up sharply through this period, driven by new technology, increasing domestic and global competition, and more active and critical consumers. Individual consumers of the litigation system were also more ready to critique it, and to protest at the cost, delays, stress and unsatisfactory outcomes to which the system was prone. The legal system lagged behind these developments, and ADR was one of the key responses which sought to meet such business concerns in the new environment. Such experience has also now moved beyond the United States to Australia and New Zealand, followed by the United Kingdom and mainland Europe and indeed continues to develop globally.

The late 1990s saw the civil justice system in England and Wales go through an enormous revolution on a scale not seen since the great reforms of the 1870s. This again was in response to the perceived need for fundamental change, highlighted with unanswerable persuasiveness by

*ADR in civil and commercial disputes*

Lord Woolf's monumental report, *Access to Justice* and then implemented in a remarkably short time by the Civil Procedure Rules 1998 (throughout this book referred to as the CPR) and the Access to Justice Act 1999. These changes represented not merely a consolidation and a rationalisation of a messy system, but truly a change in the culture of litigation itself. As the Lord Chancellor in 1998, Lord Irvine of Lairg, said in his foreword to the CPR:

> 'We should see litigation as the last and not the first resort in the attempt to settle a dispute';

and he confirmed the intention of the CPR by noting that:

> '...the changes introduced in April [1999] are as much changes in culture as they are changes to the Rules themselves.'

Those who had been active in ADR development in the United Kingdom during the 1990s contributed to the debate over the Woolf reforms and to the call for ADR to be included in the reforms. They were to see the success of their efforts in the final report and rules. ADR was specifically recognised for the first time at the heart of civil justice procedure as a tool of active case management, the means by which the courts were to attain the overriding objective set out in CPR, Pt 1. This is set out in full in **Chapter 4**.[1]

ADR came of age in England and Wales when the CPR came into force on 26 April 1999. No longer was it a sign of weakness to propose ADR, but a sign of sophistication entirely consistent with the spirit of the Woolf's reforms as embodied in the CPR. It led to a major increase in the use of ADR, with more and more lawyers and business people learning the skills required to mediate or represent clients at mediation.

But it is still salutary to remember the essential advantages of ADR as they always were and still remain, namely to extend the range of options on offer to businesses or litigants who find themselves in deadlocked negotiations with others, whether before, during or outside litigation. ADR offers many of the beneficial features of the litigation system without some of its inherent disadvantages (which may be seen to exist even after and despite the CPR). It offers structured formal third-party intervention, but without either a requirement to fit into the rigid routines of traditional litigation or the high risks of a legally binding judgment from a judge imposed upon the disputants. It offers flexible outcomes, makes speedy resolution possible and restores ownership and control of the outcome to clients where they seek it or find this helpful. ADR's focus on helping

---

1 See **4.2.1**.

parties to settle out of court led to the 'alternative' description being given to this approach. However, the label is frequently criticised as misleading, and with some justification. ADR techniques may have begun outside the system as an alternative to litigation or arbitration, but they can and frequently do accompany and complement such processes. Indeed, ADR is often most powerfully used against the backdrop of existing litigation or arbitration. In that sense, Robert Turner as Senior Master once memorably remarked that formal trial litigation itself becomes the true 'alternative' dispute resolution process.

ADR can also be used for situations where litigation is not really a viable alternative at all. For example, it works well where a family business wants to develop more consensus on its future shape but is struggling to do so by direct discussions between those concerned; or a joint venture between multinational companies which needs to be re-negotiated to meet changes in both participation and commercial pressures, when there is really no 'dispute' as such to litigate. As ADR theory and practice has developed, stress has been laid on choosing techniques to match the needs of the dispute and the joint interests of the parties. Thus, 'Appropriate' dispute resolution is often canvassed as an alternative component of the ADR acronym. The term 'Amicable' has also been proposed, particularly in the construction industry, to stress the non-adversarial objectives and processes of ADR. However, this fails to reflect the fact that many thoroughly non-amicable disputes are amenable to ADR. And of course, it is certainly true that ADR leads to 'Accelerated' dispute resolution in most cases.

In this book, we seek to provide an introduction to and assessment of the major techniques and practices of ADR in commercial disputes, with particular reference to the law and practice in England and Wales, but not forgetting that ADR is particularly amenable to dealing with cross-border and cross-jurisdictional disputes. Indeed, there are signs that London may become a forum of choice for international ADR just as much as it has been the forum of choice over many years for the litigation and arbitration of international commercial disputes. The intention of this book is to enable parties and professional advisers to recognise where various techniques and processes are appropriate and when and how they can be used. At the same time we focus most of our attention on mediation. This has emerged, not unexpectedly, as the best known and most used technique of the ADR family, assuming for a moment that arbitration, as a purely adjudicative process, falls outside the scope of that family. Indeed, mediation practice is so prevalent that many commentators treat the two terms, mediation and ADR, as interchangeable. However, it is important to understand the differences between different ADR processes, and the broader meaning of ADR, not only for historic reasons, but also to assist advisers to understand the possibilities available in designing an approach to suit particular disputes.

The problems with litigation, certainly until the CPR were implemented, are well known and need not be dealt upon further here. Injunctive procedures or other means of emergency relief available in special cases, such as freezing orders and search orders (formerly *Mareva* and *Anton Piller* orders respectively) can swiftly be obtained, and only from a judge. However the more typical scenario is for litigation to involve parties in delay, cost, distraction from day-to-day management, disproportionate worry and uncertainty and loss of control of the claim, once conduct has been handed over to the lawyers. Such problems tend to exist in whatever jurisdiction litigation is conducted, albeit to varying degrees. Most businesses can readily quote horror stories about efforts to achieve satisfactory 'justice' in a business dispute, particularly across frontiers. It is this common international phenomenon that has encouraged ADR to spread across the globe. Despite the initial attempts made in the United Kingdom and elsewhere to dismiss ADR as essentially American, meeting very particular American needs, many countries first evolved elements of ADR in order to escape some of the difficulties of litigation, but without labelling them as ADR as such. Examples are administrative tribunals, Ombudsman systems, family and labour conciliation agencies and laying duties on judges to conciliate. Thereafter, many countries have promoted the use of specifically identified ADR processes as methods of resolving the general class of civil and commercial actions, and the promotion of ADR as a more systematic business and professional discipline has burgeoned.

The legal profession has often been held responsible for the problems of the litigation system by both non-lawyers and reforming lawyers alike. Indeed, the thrust of the Woolf's reforms has been to take overall control of the litigation process away in large measure from the lawyers and give it, perhaps with a degree of optimism (certainly as lawyers then saw it) to the court. Cynical commentators claimed that lawyers controlled the system to generate revenue for themselves in the same way that other businesses seek to generate income from the ventures they control. More often, and perhaps more justly, blame was attributed to the system itself, about which the average litigant or litigator could do little. The effect of the CPR and the Woolf reforms in altering the system to give greater satisfaction will continue under close scrutiny for years to come. Certainly, in respect of the costs of litigation, the reforms do not seem to have achieved their objective, though proceedings may be faster and fewer. But wherever the blame truly lies, the overall result of litigation process remains negative for many parties.

Furthermore, the strength of ADR does not depend upon conferring or apportioning such blame. It seems reasonably universal that civil justice systems tend to be expensive and slow. Such systems require judges to find the truth of the matter – by adversarial or inquisitorial means – based on the evidence laid before the court. Since the parties have a great deal at stake in the decision reached, there is a natural tendency to produce the best arguments and evidence (and therefore seek to hire the best advocates), while doing the utmost to undermine the opposing side's evidence and arguments. It has never taken much by way of imagination or pressure of interests, business or otherwise, for parties to extend this dynamic by adding an element of gamesmanship through use of procedural ploys or manoeuvres so as to wear down, undermine or even bankrupt the other side. In turn, such ploys confirm and strengthen hostility and intensify the emotion and the stakes in the dispute and its outcome. The Woolf reforms certainly sought to minimise the potential for abuse of the system by such procedural games.

Quite apart from any procedural drawbacks to the litigation process, there are substantive or jurisprudential questions that also need to be considered in estimating the value of the litigated result in the common law system. The judge's duty is not to make a determination on grounds of truth or justice in the abstract, nor on what makes for commercial sense or improved business relationships, nor, in personal injury cases, on the basis of sympathy for claimants or willingness to raid the deep pocket of an insurer. Outcomes are determined by the evidence and arguments put before the court, in accordance with technical legal principles. Furthermore, questions of whether business or personal circumstances have changed since the start of the dispute, or may well change for the parties in the future are usually irrelevant. The essential judicial task is to decide issues according to law, which is almost always an exercise in examining the past and allocating blame. Was there a contract? What were its terms? Was a contractual term broken? By whom? Was the defendant in breach of duty or negligent? What damage flowed from breach?

The litigation process in England and Wales can be said to work tolerably well, and perhaps with even greater efficiency under the CPR, mainly because of the good sense of the judges and its users. But the system is not in itself guided by a creative search to establish problem-solving remedies or commercial solutions for difficult issues. Many disputes are not clear-cut, yet judges must reach a determination on the balance of probabilities, often determined on a rather narrow view taken of aspects of a case or the legal principles involved in liability or quantum of damages. It is not surprising that many litigants feel aggrieved when they lose and sometimes even when in theory they win. This sense of grievance is potentially multiplied in terms of cost, delay, uncertainty of outcome and potential for manoeuvre created by the appeals process.

What about arbitration? Designed initially as a process whereby commercial people determined their own disputes, it boasted considerable advantages. Parties can agree simplified procedures, and an arbitrator can be appointed who possesses specific knowledge in a given technical area.

Arbitration might thus be regarded as the alternative to litigation, in which the parties achieve a legally binding adjudication in accordance with law, but without the full trappings of litigation, and without its publicity or its judges, who may have no particular qualifications in the subject matter of the dispute.

Sadly, many commentators, including many members of the arbitration community, feel that arbitration has been 'hijacked' by lawyers, and that its promise has not been fulfilled. Arbitrations can now be just as procedurally complex and lengthy as court trials, leading to an award which can be just as uncertain as that of a judge. There is the additional disadvantage of having to pay for the arbitrator, whereas a trial judge does not yet attract an hourly rate, even with the increased court fees. There are also arguments about whether arbitrators have proved to be sufficiently robust when dealing with lawyers trained in the adversarial and over-complex procedures of the courts. If post-CPR judges demonstrate their mettle as invited so to do by the reforms, arbitration may be the last haven for the adversarial approach, despite the reforms introduced by the Arbitration Act 1996 which has improved matters considerably. Whatever the merits of this debate and its historical twists and turns, it must be said that arbitration remains intrinsically susceptible to these problems because it carries the essential character of litigation – a procedure designed to find for or against parties on the basis of evidence and legal argument.

It is important to note, however, that arbitration as a dispute resolution approach does still represent a viable alternative to full litigation procedure, principally in freeing the parties to determine their own procedure, elect their own judge, proceed in privacy and avoid appeals to the courts in many circumstances. It can thus have significant advantages for certain parties, particularly in international cases where parties seek to avoid becoming involved in domestic courts. However, arbitration's location at the adjudicative end of the dispute resolution spectrum, stretching from negotiation through to litigation, puts it close to litigation both in form and content. Its separate historical development in the United States has led it often to be described there as a form of ADR. In the United Kingdom and elsewhere, arbitration is usually excluded from the range of ADR techniques. We follow that convention in this book and do not discuss arbitration any further in detail.

## 1.2   What is (and isn't) ADR?

As a field that has evolved for differing motives and with different emphases, there are many ways of defining ADR. The most common classification is to describe ADR as a structured dispute resolution process with third-party intervention which does not impose a legally binding outcome on the parties. Mediation is the archetypal ADR process falling within this classification. Europe's largest service provider, the Centre for Effective Dispute Resolution (CEDR) published a revised definition of mediation in 2004, as being:

> 'A flexible process conducted confidentially in which a neutral person actively assists the parties in working towards a negotiated agreement of a dispute or difference, with the parties in ultimate control of the decision to settle and the terms of resolution.'

While it is a good definition of mediation, it is not a perfect definition of ADR. Some techniques outside standard arbitration and litigation can be useful in resolving disputes although they may be binding in certain forms. For example, an Ombudsman may give decisions which can be binding on a commercial party but not a consumer. A Disputes Panel or adjudicator in the construction industry can make an adjudication which is said to be legally binding if neither party chooses to challenge it within a specified period of time. A trade union-management arbitration may be treated by the parties as binding in honour only. Are these, involving third party neutrals in differing ways, ADR procedures?

Furthermore, is the involvement of a third party neutral in some way an essential ingredient of ADR? It has been suggested that ADR encompasses round-table conferences at which parties and their legal teams attend to discuss settlement but without having a third-party neutral to chair such a meeting. While this may be a perfectly sound way to attempt settlement (though we as authors and mediators would unsurprisingly argue that such a process would benefit from being run as a mediation), we do not think that merely bilateral negotiating processes are strictly ADR processes, even if they fall into the compendious description in the glossary appended to the CPR, which suggests, without creating a legal definition, that ADR is: 'a collective description of methods of resolving disputes otherwise than through the normal trial process'.

Like many areas of practice, definitions are not watertight and conclusive. What is more important is to recognise the intention behind the development of ADR. This is to avoid the inflexibility of traditional procedures and institutions for resolving disputes, and to focus instead on analysing how the parties might be assisted to achieve a similar or better result than might have been achieved by arbitration or litigation, with the minimum of direct and indirect cost. Embracing the concept of 'appropriate' or even 'additional' (in the sense of complementary) dispute resolution helps to dispel the feeling that ADR is somehow an 'alternative' culture and not quite mainstream. Indeed, ADR should be a *primary* option for parties faced with a dispute, a view clearly endorsed by the spirit behind the CPR, the pre-action protocols, and new judicial willingness to make penal costs and interest orders dependent upon pre-action and post-action unreasonableness in the conduct of litigation. One of the most telling recent developments in Australia is the move to describe *litigation* as ADR or Alternative Dispute Resolution, re-branding all extra-litigation dispute resolution processes (which would include what we call ADR in this country) as *PDR* or *Primary Dispute Resolution.*

Alternative Dispute Resolution may be used in the true sense of an alternative to litigation or arbitration. But it is probably used far more frequently now alongside litigation or arbitration to complement and improve the quality of settlement negotiations. Most civil litigation traditionally ended in out-of-court settlement, but very often late in the day, and quite often at the court door, under great pressure of time and in less than ideal negotiating conditions. Classically, it took place just before a trial was due to start, or even during the course of that trial. At that point, the vast bulk of the legal costs had been expended and the clients left bewildered at the sudden forestalling of the daunting process of trial and evidence-giving. Alternative Dispute Resolution as a means of accelerated dispute resolution creates a much earlier settlement event, thus having the potential of saving the parties time, cost and the wastage of concern in anticipating the trial, by offering a much more structured settlement process and better or at least different outcomes than a trial would offer. We shall consider below how this claim can be justified, and the circumstances necessary to achieve these results.

First, we examine the spectrum of dispute resolution processes in a little more detail, whether alternative or mainstream.

## 1.3 The dispute resolution spectrum

The way we have chosen to classify dispute resolution processes here (not all of which do we regard as ADR) is by looking at the degree to which the parties themselves have control over both the process and the outcome.

### 1.3.1 Unilateral action

At one end of the spectrum is the unilateral decision of a party to escape or avoid the conflict, for example a consumer not making or following up a complaint, a company writing off a bad debt, or a motorist deciding not to claim for a minor injury. Unilateral action can of course also be taken, not to avoid a dispute, but to influence events in one's own favour. This includes the use of publicity or economic leverage, or direct action which might be potentially lawful, such as self-defence or the abatement of an alleged nuisance; or unlawful, such as physical retaliation. An extreme version of this within the legal system would be to issue proceedings as a threat or a gag, or as a way of mobilising the state's powers to crush an opponent financially or otherwise. In all such unilateral action, the protagonist has complete control of the process.

### 1.3.2 Negotiation

Negotiation is the next most powerful method for a party in terms of their control of the process, subject only to the constraints imposed by the other party (or their constituents). This is the business method that is used more than any other to resolve disputes, and with good reason. It is the most flexible, informal, party-directed, closest to the parties' own circumstances and control, and can be geared to each party's own concerns. Parties choose location, timing, agenda, subject matter and participants. It need not be limited to the initial topic in dispute: either party can introduce other issues as trade-offs for an acceptable agreement.

The growth of interest in ADR has in turn been fuelled by a wider interest in the 'science' of negotiation, particularly because new theories of negotiation have emphasised the more extensive possibilities for joint gains and interest-based outcomes. It will be useful to examine negotiation in more detail in order to understand why third-party methods may become necessary to resolve deadlocked negotiations or even to make negotiations which are not deadlocked more efficient or productive.[2] A common first reaction from many lawyers or clients, on hearing about the interest-based or business-directed aims of ADR in general and mediation in particular, is to assert that this is what they have always done in their own negotiations. They say, 'I have been mediating all my life', or even 'I don't need a neutral to add to my existing negotiating skills'.

### 1.3.3 Mediation and conciliation

These are the third-party ADR techniques closest to negotiation. *Conciliation* is a term sometimes used as a synonym for mediation, and we discuss the distinction drawn between the two concepts below. Essentially, *mediation* is a process of negotiation, but structured and influenced by the intervention of a neutral third party who seeks to assist the parties to reach a settlement that is acceptable to them, as the definition set out above suggests.[3] The mediator does not make an award, nor, in the purest form of mediation, is there any evaluation of each party's claims. However, the dynamic of third-party involvement is potentially much more subtle than this bald description suggests. The later chapters on mediation articulate the various roles of the mediator in greater detail.

One frequently utilised distinction is between *facilitative* mediation, where the mediator facilitates the parties' own efforts to formulate a settlement;

---

2 See **Chapter 2**.
3 See **1.2** above.

and *evaluative* or *directive* mediation, where the mediator additionally assists the parties by introducing a third-party view over the merits of the case or of particular issues between the parties. Such evaluation can be informally requested, or built formally into the process from the outset. Proximity of a court or arbitration hearing can at times encourage use of this style of approach. Indeed, in a number of legal systems, a duty to mediate, or at least to intervene to promote settlement, is imposed upon the judge who is to hear the case, who may tend to do so by giving the parties an indication of which way the judicial mind is moving. This may take the form of a settlement conference, built into proceedings, which may or may not be presided over by a judge.

In some forms of ADR, evaluative mediation may involve the third party giving to the parties a recommendation, usually in writing, on how they should settle the case. Where this flows out of a less legalistic context (as in UK industrial relations mediation) recommendations may be based upon what the mediator regards as reasonable terms of settlement. In a more legalistic context, such recommendations will usually reflect the mediator's view of the merits. In the most formal of contexts (for example under some forms of construction contract or in court-annexed mediation in some US states), these recommendations may be used in further proceedings. If a party fails to obtain an improved award from the court above what was recommended but not accepted, the recommendation may actually bind the parties, or may affect responsibility for litigation costs.

A distinction is sometimes drawn between conciliation and mediation in terms of whether one process leads to written recommendations or third-party settlement proposals, whereas the other does not. There is no international consistency over which term is to be applied to which type of process, and we do not find it a useful distinction to draw in this book. We will henceforth only refer to mediation as encompassing both possibilities and distinguish, where necessary, between facilitative and evaluative modes of mediation. However, while we do not dwell on these distinctions in terminology, it is important to remember the substantive distinction in terms of process possibilities, and also the need to check in unfamiliar contexts exactly which definitions or mediation styles parties or their advisers have in mind. Whichever approach is taken in mediation, control over the decision as to the final outcome rests firmly with the parties and not with the mediator, however evaluative the mediator is invited to be. The parties also usually ought to control whether to ask the mediator to move from facilitative to evaluative mode.

### 1.3.4  Evaluative processes

Mention of recommendations or opinion moves us on to third-party processes where the parties have less control over the outcome than in facilitative mediation. Rather than involving a third party directly in the negotiation process parties may seek some form of neutral and independent evaluation, perhaps an expert opinion on the case or one of the issues, or a third-party review of the case in terms of likely litigation outcome. This is sometimes described as *early neutral evaluation* or *ENE* – a preliminary assessment of facts, evidence or legal merits designed to assist parties to avoid further unnecessary stages in litigation, or at the very least to serve as a basis for further and fuller negotiations. Processes such as *judicial appraisal* or *expert opinion* also come within this definition.

Again, the categorisation is not watertight, since clearly a process such as evaluative mediation spans the divide between these approaches. It does, however, provide a useful starting point from which to assess what each process really offers.

### 1.3.5   Adjudicative processes

Finally, we enter the adjudicative range of the spectrum, where the processes culminate in some form of imposed decision or judgment being delivered. Within this range are many variations. For example, parties can contract for a third party to provide an *expert determination* of all the issues between them, or to decide certain facts, leaving the parties to negotiate the financial implications of those findings. Or they can invite an *adjudication*, which does not have the exact status of arbitration, usually to avoid the binding finality of an award. The parties may agree to a 'non-binding' arbitration, or to an adjudication, which will only become effective as an arbitral award if one party does not seek to challenge or appeal it within a certain specified time. Adjudication is now extensively used as a means of settling construction disputes, governed by statute.

Also, within this range of adjudicative processes lie the various Ombudsman or grievance resolution schemes, which have evolved as cost-effective and readily identifiable systems of redress in many consumer sectors. Typically an industry, government or a public body involved adopts the approach as a collective solution to a gathering cloud of individual consumer grievances that threaten the reputation of the body involved or are adding pressure for statutory regulation of its affairs. The detailed mechanisms of Ombudsman schemes vary, but often they combine the processes of neutral fact-finding, mediation and adjudication in various tiers through which consumers may pursue their complaints.

Finally, *arbitration* and *litigation* also lie within the range of adjudicative processes. At this end of the spectrum, party control of the process is very limited – indeed, engagement in litigation for the defendant is virtually compulsory if interests are to be protected, though perhaps more control is available in arbitration. Even in litigation, however, there may be elements of process choice. For example, choices may be possible as to forum, or over whether to proceed in a higher or lower track than the value of a claim might permit.

### 1.3.6 Hybrid processes

It is important to note that because most ADR procedures are creatures of contract and of practical utility to suit the parties, there is not the same rigidity of procedure as is imposed by litigation or even arbitration, even though there may be guidelines associated with a particular process or third party. There is no mediation equivalent to the civil procedure manuals of the courts, nor should there be, since much of its potency is derived from its inherent flexibility and freedom from rules. Also, the categories mentioned above are merely the more common process choices. Since the whole thrust of ADR is to adopt the process most suited to the particular problem, it follows that numerous hybrid versions of the basic procedures exist. For example, there is the *mini-trial* or *executive tribunal* which is a more formal version of evaluative mediation; and *med-arb*, a mediation process at the outset which switches to arbitration mode to resolve any issues outstanding from the mediation. *Arb-med* may also be attempted, where the third party makes an arbitral decision but keeps it in a sealed envelope while switching to mediation, only revealing the decision if the mediation does not result in settlement. Party control of ADR choices opens up these and many other possibilities.

## 1.4   Why ADR works

Despite the fact that the most common ADR techniques do not *guarantee* resolution of the dispute, most such techniques do in practice lead to a binding settlement. Further, ADR works where previous negotiations have failed. Indeed, it is usually not resorted to until negotiations reach deadlock. How does ADR achieve these results? It is important to understand the dynamic underlying ADR to understand why and when it is appropriate, and why it works.

### 1.4.1   Creating a focus on settlement

ADR procedures usually require clients with decision-making authority from each party to attend the process with their advisers with a view of exploring and achieving a settlement. This factor alone probably contributes considerably to the success of mediation in particular, and explains why it is the leading ADR process. When direct negotiations seem to be unproductive, with parties locked into entrenched positions or into a serial litigation dance, it can be hard to create even the right context or environment for parties to agree to convene. ADR procedures offer a *formal setting* to bring advisers and clients together for a serious attempt at resolving the problems between them. In many cases, this may be the first occasion in months or even years that the parties have jointly addressed the question of settlement. Thus ADR intensifies the *objective* of settlement by creating a forum for settlement efforts and bringing the right people together for this.

If negotiations have broken down, or been conducted at arms length between advisers (for instance by formal CPR Part 36 offers and counter-offers)[4] the ADR event may be the first or even only occasion before trial when the parties have a serious and credible forum in which to discuss issues and concerns as a joint effort or between clients directly. Certainly since the Woolf reforms, there are signs that a number of parties and lawyers are conferring credibility on ADR processes by integrating them into the range of dispute resolution techniques in mainstream practice. For example, there is significant support in family law for the practice of collaborative law, where focus is given to negotiation by requiring lawyers to pledge themselves to settlement efforts, or, failing resolution, to pass the client on to litigation lawyers.

### 1.4.2    The role of the neutral

It is very difficult to provide a simple analysis of the effect of a third party neutral on ADR negotiating processes. We look at the role of the prime instance of such a third party – the mediator – in **Chapter 15**. Suffice it to say here that the presence of a third party adds to the sense of forum, of objective debate and seriousness of intent. Quite apart from the competences and qualities of the neutral, the very presence of a third party generates a feeling of a hearing or a day in court at which all disputing parties are present, something which is statistically rare in the litigation process. This in turn imposes a form of discipline or structure on the proceedings, with the neutral being able to both permit and control the flow of argument and emotion which will inevitably characterise such occasions. This is less easy in round-table meetings.

### 1.4.3    The qualities of the neutral

Parties are often most sensitive to this aspect of ADR, neglecting the other elements which contribute to the underlying dynamics. But the quality and competence of the neutral inevitably add an important element to the success of ADR. The effective neutral uses the other factors to achieve maximum impact in the process. Thorough understanding of the ADR process is vital, alongside the ability to generate trust and respect with all parties, to facilitate communications, to defuse emotions, and to deploy

---

4 See **Chapter 4, 4.2.7** for an explanation of Part 36 offers.

sound negotiating and problem-solving strategy and tactics so as to assist the parties towards resolution.

### 1.4.4 The structure of the process

Broadly accepted ADR procedures have evolved over time to optimise the opportunities to achieve resolution. In mediation, for instance, the structure of a joint meeting, followed by private meetings with each party and further joint meetings if appropriate, creates scope for making real progress on the case. First, the parties have a chance to hear each other. Then they have the opportunity to communicate more fully, frankly and privately with and through the third party neutral. In a mini-trial, there is a formal setting, in which senior executives can take a more detached view of the previous actions and views of their subordinate managers and lawyers.

## 1.5 ADR in the mainstream of civil justice

As awareness has developed of how ADR can complement arbitration and litigation, and can indeed settle intractable cases, removing them from log-jammed court lists, ADR has been brought increasingly into the mainstream of official dispute resolution. There has also been increasing inclusion of pre-agreed ADR mechanisms in commercial contracts and organisational policy guidelines making it a first process of choice for resolving contractual difficulties. Most importantly now, ADR is integrated into court practice.

The trend towards 'court-annexed', 'court-directed' or 'court-referred' ADR has taken a number of forms. In the United Kingdom, the earliest developments are to be found in Practice Directions in the Commercial Court and then in the High Court generally, requiring pre-trial consideration of ADR by legal advisers. In the CPR, specific provision is made by Pt 26.4 for a stay of proceedings to be considered at the stage of allocation of a claim to the proper track, so that settlement by negotiations or ADR may be tried. Pre-action protocols encourage or require thought to be given to ADR before proceedings are issued. Failing that, cases can be referred to ADR at allocation, and also at later case management conferences or even pre-trial review. Furthermore, the various published Practice Guides, Practice Directions and Protocols in the specialist jurisdictions, such as the Commercial Court, the Technology and Construction Court, the Mercantile Courts and the Queen's Bench and Chancery Divisions, all provide for consideration of ADR at case management and pre-trial review stages, as well as prior to issue of proceedings.[5]

---

5 These provisions are all considered in detail in Part B and particularly in **Chapter 4**.

The pilot scheme pioneered by the Central London County Court has now become a permanent fixture there, and has spread around regional county courts, mostly now directing litigants to a National Mediation telephone helpline. There is a mediation scheme attached to the Court of Appeal for dealing with settlement of appeals already lodged. There is now some use of court staff to mediate small claims cases. All of these initiatives have produced good results in a range of cases. In the employment field, ACAS has a statutory duty to seek to conciliate within the greatly enlarged jurisdiction of the Employment Tribunal and pilot schemes have been set up where tribunal chairman are to mediate. Court-approved mediation in the area of family law (which is outside the scope of this book) has now been endorsed by statute within that highly delicate area of human relations.

## 1.6   International variants

Globally, interesting variations are evident, with most variety being found across the many US State courts and in Australia. The following are some of these variations, some of which are also found in the United Kingdom.

### 1.6.1   Court-directederly neutral evaluation

This involves case appraisal on a summary basis at an early stage of proceedings by a judge, senior lawyer or expert, who expresses an authoritative view derived from such a person's status or experience. This is designed to help the parties settle and may be combined with attempts at mediation, arbitration or continued litigation case management.

### 1.6.2   Case settlement conferences

A court requirement may be placed on trial lawyers (sometimes with clients) to meet formally in order to review the case and attempt to negotiate settlement. This may be outside the court milieu, or be a formal process chaired by a judge, sometimes the trial judge in whose docket the case resides.

### 1.6.3   Court-directed mediation

A mediator is appointed by or at the instigation of the court to help the parties explore and achieve settlement.

### 1.6.4   Advisory arbitration

A court-appointed arbitrator makes an award that becomes binding if one party does not appeal it. There may be costs awards against a party who appeals from the arbitration but fails to improve on the arbitrator's award.

### 1.6.5 Settlement weeks

Certain weeks are designated as periods in which parties with cases filed can seek to mediate a settlement. The court writes to litigants to give notice of the procedure and opportunity.

### 1.6.6 Multi-door courthouse

The court may encourage litigants to have an initial meeting with an information officer who can guide the litigant towards the most appropriate process – mediation, arbitration, small claims, case appraisal, case management or full trial – all of which are made easily available by or through the court itself. The idea developed in the United States as a result of the lecture by Professor Frank Sander of Harvard Law School at the Pound Conference in 1976. There is a good recent instance of such a scheme in Lagos, Nigeria, which is being spread to other cities there.

### 1.6.7 Judge conciliators

In certain parts of Europe and Asia, judges themselves are given the duty to try to settle cases where possible as part of standard litigation procedure.

## 1.7 Summary

All these manifestations of officially encouraged ADR generate their own theoretical and practical issues, but none (except where specifically noted above) has emerged so strongly here as to merit further detailed discussion in a practitioner's guide dealing primarily with the UK and European context. Such issues are best left for debate in relation to the details of a particular scheme. Their existence and growth do confirm the irresistible trend internationally for ADR to be regarded as an integral part of dispute resolution activity and a useful tool by which lawyers and other advisers can extend the services they offer to clients and through which civil justice systems can broaden the processes and remedies they offer to their consumers.

*Chapter 2*

# From negotiation to ADR

Interest in Alternative Dispute Resolution as a structured form of third-party assistance to settlement has contributed to a growth in the understanding of negotiation skills and practice. Why do direct negotiations often fail where third-party mediation can succeed? What does mediation or ADR add to direct negotiations to make them more effective? Does understanding ADR improve negotiating performance?

## 2.1 ADR and negotiation

Lawyers and their institutional clients often latch on to the emphasis in ADR on achieving commercial settlements, in order to claim they have been practising ADR throughout their professional lives, their objective having always been, as they see it, to achieve a good settlement for their client or themselves. However, this under-estimates the differences between direct negotiations and third-party assisted negotiations, even though good ADR builds on good negotiating practices.

To understand ADR's contribution, we therefore need to review how negotiation works and particularly how negotiations (and sometimes ADR) can fail. Indeed, the starting point of ADR may be dispute diagnosis. If we know why direct discussions are not making progress, we can develop ideas of what cure to bring to an ailing negotiation. Equally, understanding of what ADR adds and why it works may in turn help professionals to rethink their core negotiating strategies, so that they can improve results from direct negotiations.

### 2.1.1 Disputes, negotiations, consensus-building

Before reviewing negotiating practice and ADR's curative role, we should not forget the broader context of disputes. Some disputes can be said to follow a breakdown of existing commercial relations or an existing negotiation relationship; for example, an argument over payment for goods or services that the purchaser claims were defective. Other disputes arise where the parties have not had a previous relationship, say a claim for breach of intellectual property rights or breach of a duty of care in tort. There may be attempts at negotiation in the latter type of case or an immediate initiation of legal proceedings. In either case, litigation is only one of the options open to the aggrieved party. They may attempt to exert pressure on the other side through the use of economic pressures (non-payment, boycotting purchases of other products by the offending company) or business contacts (an individual or business association that is a contact common to them both) or through a third party representative. Finally, they may accept a business loss and walk away from the situation rather than choose the time, trouble and expense of legal proceedings.

ADR has been used most in disputes that have entered or are likely to enter legal proceedings, having developed further as part of lawyers' litigation practice than it has in business management practices. However, the other sectors should not be ignored, as ADR can and does make a significant contribution in business disputes that have not entered litigation. Conflict prevention is becoming as important if not more important than conflict resolution. Such areas can represent major potential for practice development amongst ADR practitioners, whether as neutrals or partisan advisers.

Finally, there are settings where negotiations may not be part of the standard practice or culture, albeit that behaviour by one party may cause grievance to others. Typical of these would be the development of consumer action groups protesting against world labour exploitation, or the environmental side-effects of business operations, or the inequity of a business practice in an industry in terms of its impact on small business suppliers or consumers. Another common example would be the impact on interest groups of decisions taken by public authorities or regulators, where there may even have been some attempt at prior consultation, but where negotiation seems an inappropriate term for a 'consult-decide-defend' sequence of public decision-making.

These approaches to decision-making, which frequently generate grievances rather than disputes or overt negotiations, have also begun to be influenced by ADR theory and practice. Consensual decision-making, involving all interest groups in the relevant community, may be more effective for long-term stability than unilateral decisions which lead to campaigns by disaffected interest groups attacking the source of the grievance and lobbying public bodies to amend what they regard as bad law.

The application of ADR to these fields tends to introduce negotiation practice or at least problem-solving approaches to decision-making practice. The environmental and public policy areas have become a growing field of ADR practice in the United States in particular, although usually under the label 'consensus-building' rather than ADR (since there may be no clear initial dispute). The most advanced legal recognition of this has also occurred in the United States, where statute now enables regulatory agencies to draft regulations through negotiating processes and not just by traditional consultation methods. (To add to the terminological complexity, this branch of consensus-building is often described as 'reg-neg', or regulatory negotiation.)

Normally, therefore, ADR intervention either builds on existing negotiations or generates a forum in which negotiations take place. For that reason it is important for ADR specialists to understand negotiating practices.

### 2.1.2 Bargaining in the shadow of the court

The issuing of legal proceedings has a significant impact on all negotiations, and in turn ADR, for three reasons.

First, it sets enforceable *deadlines* for processing and ending the dispute. This may increase the pressure on parties to enter negotiations and certainly to conclude them before the risk of an adverse judgment or of incurring significant cost, if the case is allowed to proceed towards trial. There will often be a pressure on both parties to negotiate just before the stages of procedure which heighten costs or risks. The clearest of these stages is immediately pre-trial, when most civil actions have traditionally been settled, even without ADR.

Secondly, it may alter the *agenda* of the negotiations, adding arguments over likely trial outcomes, costs of preparation, principles of law applicable, jurisdiction, and perhaps publicity issues, to what may have been a dispute framed in other ways by the business parties. Indeed, the fact that one party enters litigation at all may provide a justification to another party for breaking off negotiations or raising the stakes by issuing a counterclaim or making a formal offer to settle which carries costs consequences.

Finally, litigation usually introduces for most business parties a new *principal–agent relationship*. Negotiations get to some extent taken over by litigation specialists, who bring to the case their own judgments and professional agendas of how to manage information flows and settlement opportunities or discussions in the phases leading up to trial. While professional theory suggests that the client takes all decisions about a claim even after proceedings have begun, in practice many business users of litigation will defer to the advice of the professionals, unless they are repeat players such as insurance companies, used to dealing with a stream of litigation.

Litigation therefore is potentially double-edged in its impact. It can speed up settlements or it can prolong, intensify and transform the dispute. Overall, however, most forms of civil litigation at some stage induce pressure for settlement by negotiation between parties or their legal advisors.

### 2.1.3 ADR as 'alternative'

We see, therefore, that the concept of ADR in the context of an overview of disputes is a more complex issue than normally considered. Equally, its potential is richer if used effectively. We can summarise ADR's links to negotiating practice as drawing on four strands:

(i) ADR is often not an alternative to court trial at all, but an alternative to traditional settlement practice within those proceedings. For ADR to be justified, it must prove faster, cheaper or more 'effective' in its outcomes than those that can be achieved by the parties and their advisers working within a litigation system without ADR.

(ii) For disputes which have not entered litigation, ADR must provide an effective alternative to negotiations which would otherwise break down, or to disputes which would otherwise enter litigation without the adoption of ADR.

(iii) In some situations where negotiating practice is not a standard response, ADR approaches may assist in the development of negotiating structures and processes to help parties generate consensus or progress on an issue.

(iv) In its most refined form, ADR may be promoted where it can be suggested that in some sense parties might achieve a better or more efficient outcome through its use, even if they might anyway achieve some form of negotiated settlement without it.

In all these contexts, negotiation practice is a central question. To assist us to understand why ADR works where negotiations fail in the above senses, we outline below three core negotiating strategies and the problems they raise. The strategies are a little caricatured to emphasise their features, but are still broadly accurate. We can then consider how to design and implement ADR to meet some of these problems.

## 2.2 Negotiations: why they work and why they fail

### 2.2.1 Positional negotiating

The classic negotiating strategy, taught to managers and lawyers alike, can be described as *positional* negotiating. The assumption behind this in its elementary version is that negotiations are a competitive game in which you need to distrust or at least be wary of the other side. The aim is to outsmart them by following well-known tactics which strengthen your likelihood of coming away with a greater 'slice of the pie'. Positions need to be carved out in advance or adhered to during negotiations, in order to strengthen your hand.

The aim in positional negotiation is to maximise your outcome. Of course, the other side will have their own positional framework worked out too, unless they are naive negotiators. In negotiations, the key is to be able to test how far up your claim ladder they will go, or even whether there is in the first place a possible overlap of negotiating positions, with their bottom line above your top line.

If there is an overlap in the bargaining range, the negotiators effectively compete to assert the strengths of their case and to undermine the other side's in order to come out higher in the range towards their ideal. If it appears that there is a mismatch of expectations, deadlock may ensue and the parties are forced back to litigation or other means of bringing the other party back towards a realistic position.

The following are typical tactics associated with positional negotiations:

- *Preparation of the 'bargaining range' chart*

  Good preparation of your own positions, as well as a good idea of the likely stance of the other party, helps you as a negotiator to establish your own aspirations, and provides a means of assessing the other side's likely expectations and so the range of potential offers in which you could be working.

- *Aiming high*

  There is evidence that negotiators who start with high aspirations tend to do better. So, think through your best case and work from that. Strongly positional negotiators find ways of starting from more extreme positions.

- *Planning and pacing of concessions*

  In positional negotiating, you know that movement from your high opening position is likely. But how much movement? When? How often? And how will this be presented? Positional negotiating theory has a number of maxims to help negotiators strengthen their outcomes. 'Move small, move slow', 'never give without getting', 'try only to make concessions of high value to them but low cost to you'.

- *Concealing information*

  In a situation where negotiators are looking for means to exploit their advantages, giving the other side fuller information may expose your weak points. Therefore, positional negotiators often withhold information which may otherwise make their side vulnerable to exploitation. A statement by an injured claimant's solicitor that 'my client does not want to have the stress of a trial' will only assist the insurance company defendant's negotiating leverage.

23

- **Making threats or bluffing**

    Threats and bluff are often associated with positional negotiation because of its competitive nature and the need to find means to dislodge other negotiators from the firm positions they have taken (as recommended in classic negotiating training). This could take various forms – raising new heads of damage, hinting at adverse publicity, committing to appeal if there is an adverse decision, suggesting public exposure of the other side's misdeeds, etc.

- **Haggling**

    When a deal becomes more visible after the initial opening phases of positional negotiation, the challenge in the final phase of sewing up the deal is how to score the last few points within the negotiating range by haggling. 'Never give without getting' and 'move small, move slow' become intense features of the process as each side tries to raise or lower the final offer or demand or to extract the most concessions.

- **Agreement somewhere near the middle of the bargaining range**

    The ritual dance of concession-giving in positional negotiating means that parties often work inwards from opening positions and end up (in an evenly matched contest) somewhere near the middle between the 'real' opening positions adopted. Both may come away feeling they have had a tough contest and extracted less than their ideal but perhaps above their worst-case 'bottom line' position.

### 2.2.2 Principled negotiating

The classic world of positional bargaining was turned upside down by the work of the Harvard Negotiating Project, crystallised in the international best seller on negotiation *Getting to Yes* by Roger Fisher and William Ury.[1] Their theory of principled negotiating (sometimes referred to by other writers as problem-solving or collaborative negotiating) suggests that one can avoid the gamesmanship and competitiveness inherent in positional bargaining. The key is to look for the settlement that will satisfy both sides' interests by keeping a clear sight on one's best alternative to a negotiated agreement (BATNA) and on options for mutual gain. While the goal of positional negotiating is victory, the goal of principled negotiating is a wise outcome reached efficiently. Negotiations become more difficult if both parties are trained in positional bargaining, whereas negotiations become

---

1 2nd edn, published by Random House.

easier if both sides approach a negotiation with a principled negotiating style. There are four key principles that underlie this approach.

- *2.2.2.1 Separate the people from the problem*

  It is easy in competitive negotiations to mix up aggression over the issues with attacks on the people on the other side. Principled negotiating stresses the need to be 'hard on the problem, and soft on the people'; in other words, to be firm in searching for ways of meeting one's interests while simultaneously working towards good relations with the other party. Good relations make it easier to solve problems.

- *2.2.2.2 Focus on interests, not positions*

  This is one of the essential differences between principled bargaining and positional bargaining. In the latter, the negotiator sets demands based on apparent interests: for example, 'we need to claim £ 1/2m for this loss'. As a result, negotiations become a process of digging in and justifying this position, with the other side countering it with rejection or a lower offer or counter-demand, making it difficult to move from these stated needs. In principled negotiation, the key question is 'Why? What are the interests that underlie such a demand?' By focusing on these underlying needs instead, the way is opened to problem-solving, to more fluid discussions and opportunities to generate other options such as staggered payments, new contract arrangements, offers of free publicity or whatever else might be appropriate to meet the real needs of a party. The classic example quoted on this by Fisher and Ury is of the mother discovering two sisters arguing over an orange. When she asks each of them why they want the orange, one says she needs the peel to bake a cake at school, the other wants to eat the flesh. Both needs can be met when interests are discovered. With a purely positional approach, the assumption is that each should have half; in fact not fully meeting the interests of either. Structured settlements in personal injury litigation are a good example of the evolution of a legal outcome that can better meet the interests of both parties than traditional one-off lump sum damages, and periodical payments may do the same. The Fisher and Ury approach was heralded many years earlier by perhaps the first US management consultant, Mary Parker Follett, who distinguished 'integrative' bargaining (mutual gains, sometimes by enlarging the pie) from 'distributive' bargaining (slicing the existing pie).

- *2.2.2.3 Invent options for mutual gain*

  By focusing on interests, it becomes easier to explore a range of ways of meeting the real needs of each party. However, the need to problem-solve, brainstorm, and look for ways of 'expanding the pie' is also an explicit requirement of principled negotiating. Out of this can come 'win-win' opportunities, rather than the 'win-lose' or 'lose-lose' outcomes typical of positional bargaining. Even if both sides give up important things in reaching an agreement, 'lose-lose' can become a sense of shared contribution to a chosen outcome. Thus, this approach encourages negotiators to search for a variety of options before deciding which option best meets the interests of the parties jointly.

- *2.2.3.4   Insist on objective criteria*

  Part of the principled aspect of this approach to negotiation is a search for rational standards by which settlement terms can be judged, rather than relying on purely subjective demands made by negotiators. Is there an objective criterion against which to match an offer – for example, the price paid by other customers, the market rent, or the level set by legal precedents? Objective criteria can be applied to process as well as substantive factors, as in the traditional ploy to prevent arguments between children cutting a cake – 'you slice, he chooses'.

## 2.2.3   Pragmatic negotiating

Principled negotiating theory has provided a very powerful counter-weight to the classic instruction manuals of the positional negotiator, and has helped to reshape practice in many negotiation settings. However, many experienced negotiators believe the real world of negotiating remains more complex and requires often a mix of positional and principled approaches. Even in those settings where it is possible to 'expand the pie' and search for 'win-win' options, at some stage it is necessary to slice any pie and allocate rewards. 'Claiming' value then takes precedence over 'creating' value. Similarly, being open about one's interests and preferences may in some situations leave one vulnerable to exploitation by a competitive negotiator. The negotiator's dilemma is therefore inherent in the tension of balancing the openness needed for effective problem solving in any situation with the avoidance of misuse by the other side of information they have been given. Even a matter as basic as telling the other side how much you are really willing to settle for will tend to preclude them from offering you more.

Skilful negotiating therefore requires a sense of balance in the approach adopted and an ability to lean towards one direction or another in any negotiation or stage of negotiation. Typically, principled negotiating practice is easier to adopt when the negotiations are with parties with whom there is a longer-term relationship or greater trust. Positional negotiating may come to the fore in one-off deals such as in claims for damages from a party unlikely to be encountered again, such as in the sale of a house or in a motor accident. Similarly, certain types of negotiator are more inclined to adopt competitive, positional practice and it can be risky or simply too difficult to try to change their approach towards a preferred practice of principled negotiating.

It is important, however, to stress caution to hardened positional negotiators who are inclined to dismiss principled approaches. Principled negotiating can still be applied to one-off deals or with parties one distrusts, and can yield better, perhaps unexpected, results in many cases. Would-be mediators should in particular work hard at learning this approach, as it underlies good mediation practice. The theory of principled negotiation first set out in *Getting to Yes* has subsequently been further elaborated by negotiation scholars in focusing particularly on how to manage difficult people, the mind-skills of communication and working with 'difficult conversations', and finally by addressing the neglected role of emotion in understanding how to work well with people as well as problems.

## 2.3 Designing ADR to overcome barriers to settlement

Having reviewed the negotiating and dispute contexts in which ADR can play a part, we are now in a better position to understand how and why ADR can add value to current negotiating practice. ADR interventions, whatever their exact design, always change the dynamics of a negotiation or dispute in some way. Bringing in a neutral third party itself adds a new figure to the equation, at least temporarily shifting the attention of the parties from their conflict and the personalities in it towards the contributions of the neutral and the third party procedure. Good ADR design is about using intelligent analysis or intuition to determine exactly when, how and why such neutral intervention should be applied, whether formulated in initial ADR contract clauses or as a one-off intervention in an existing conflict. A deep knowledge of good negotiation techniques can be vital to this.

ADR design is not an exact science, nor does it offer a universally applicable fixed procedural remedy such as litigation. Rather it is often as much a question of people judgment and process analysis as of issue analysis. Hence the justified prevalence amongst ADR techniques of the flexible approach of mediation, which leaves individual mediators free to choose from a range of tactics and techniques to assist settlement in any particular case. However, mediators also must assess within a mediation why previous negotiations have failed and therefore decide which approaches will best help the parties reach a settlement that they can accept. We need, therefore, to consider the underlying causes of inefficient negotiations and settlement failures, and the implications of these for the design of ADR techniques or approaches.

### 2.3.1 Problems inherent in implementation of negotiating strategies

#### 2.3.1.1 Positional negotiating

Of the three core approaches described in the preceding section, the one with perhaps the greatest inherent chance of breakdown is competitive or positional negotiating (borne out in an empirical study of US litigators by Gerald Williams[2]). The essence of the game is to hold out for maximum gain whatever the cost to the other side. Delay, insistence on positions, minimal concession giving, refusal to acknowledge weaknesses or uncertainties in their case, all may work to the advantage of hard bargainers in a certain percentage of cases. However, in others, particularly where matched with competitive negotiators on the other side, this approach will grind negotiations to a halt, as neither side will budge and both will sense that the stakes are rising.

In litigation proceedings, this gamesmanship will take parties 'up to the wire' as they engage in bluff to force the other party to duck out before the next phase of risks and costs imposed by the adjudication system. Indeed, one might argue that the strict theory behind adversarial litigation procedure is premised on competitive negotiating. The objective is to win by presenting one's best case rather than for the adjudicator to investigate the truth or justice of the dispute, as more typically occurs in an inquisitorial approach. This is to some extent a caricature of each system, but it does reflect inherent tendencies found in them.

At the extreme, competitive negotiators will be unable even to open up negotiations. A mere request to negotiate may be perceived by them as receiving or conveying a sign of weakness. The result may be that no real negotiations take place until immediately before the threat of an imposed decision by the adjudicator, generating a settlement on the steps of the court which perhaps may force one side suddenly to offer a large concession. The problems of this approach are self-evident. Costs, delays and lack of trust are driven up to high levels, in a way that tends to epitomise 'lose-lose' approaches. Ultimately the parties will martyr themselves (either literally or at least to professional fees) rather than give way. If it is the lawyers who are responsible for this sort of negotiating approach, there is a serious risk that it will disaffect or disempower the client.

At its broadest level, the encouragement to use ADR represents a challenge to the ethos of adversarial negotiating practice among litigators and businesses. Even within the traditional culture however, positional negotiators have some sense of a need to consider the costs of total intransigence. Designing an ADR approach for this circumstance means finding ways to assist the parties to explore the bargaining range without loss of face.

---

2 Legal Negotiation and Settlement: G Williams: West Publishing 1983.

A contract clause or court direction requiring an ADR process early in any dispute will help parties overcome any feeling that the suggestion of negotiations may undermine their claims. The absence of such a clause or direction often makes it much more difficult for such negotiators to agree to ADR in the early stages of a case. ADR intervention becomes a delicate matter of indicating to all parties that an ADR procedure is a neutral effort to save all parties costs rather than an indication of any side's unwillingness to fight on. Discussions with an ADR provider organisation may also assist in neutrally brokering entry to the process.

Mediators faced by parties locked in a competitive strategy are usually able to take some, but by no means all, of the gamesmanship out of the negotiation. To begin with, they can channel communications and offers or counter-offers in a less competitive or confrontational way than the parties may have done. They can create a safe space for parties to test their approach, options and potential offers and bargaining range. As shuttle diplomats, mediators can extend and defuse the 'haggling' stage, making it easier for parties to review offers without the antagonism or face-saving requirements generated in direct, face-to-face negotiations. For example, parties will often reveal to a mediator that they are willing to move their position if the other side will move, or they may tell a mediator what they say they will *really* settle for, if the other side will also indicate their position. Usually such offers will be given initially to the mediator in confidence so that the potential for useful further bargaining can be assessed. The mediator can think whether the parties have come close enough in their offers, and help them progress in the light of that assessment. Disclosing such an offer openly to the other side at the outset will be seen to risk appearing as a willingness to compromise their overt claims.

Most commercial mediations may go through a stage like this where a financial settlement is involved. Mediators therefore need to know how to work with positional bargainers and to know how to detect whether there might be further movement possible that has not yet been revealed, even to the mediator. Competitive negotiators may use gamesmanship in mediation as well as elsewhere. Good mediators, however, should also explore the potential for principled negotiation, and for more creative options than positional negotiators would normally have reviewed, thus adding further value to the process.

### 2.3.1.2 Principled negotiating

Impasse between principled negotiators is likely to reflect inability to agree on the standards to apply as criteria for settlement terms, or failure to find adequate means of solving a problem in a way that meets their interests, or perhaps mismatched personal styles or communications. In these circumstances, mediation is again the most likely ADR route to breaking a deadlock, although in some cases a technical expert in a facilitative role may also help the parties towards a deal. Amongst the tactics a neutral could adopt would be:

- to help the parties re-evaluate their commitment to standards for decision-making;
- to help the parties identify and collect information on the case relevant to sensible decision-making;
- to assist them with further efforts at brainstorming solutions;
- to rework earlier options canvassed in negotiations to see if a new formula might be prompted to emerge to overcome the deadlock;
- to provide a more detached style or free up communication blockages.

### 2.3.1.3   Pragmatic negotiating

In the real world, mediators are rarely dealing with one or other of the pure models of positional or principled negotiating. Mediators will find they are working in most cases partly in the mode of problem-solvers, helping the parties search for options or appropriate standards to justify settlement terms, but also partly working with positions and attempts to secure the best slice of cake that the parties perceive to be available.

In each negotiating strategy, mediators may also provide a fresh influence on intractable negotiations or an independent review of the case with each party. This may not be an expert or formal evaluation but rather a broad-brush or common-sense appraisal of the strengths and weaknesses of their case. Mediators not only work through the issues relating to possible terms of settlement, but also consider with each party how they see their BATNA (Best) as well as their WATNA (Worst Alternative to a Negotiated Agreement). This helps parties to step back, re-assess their positions and revisit their negotiating options.

### 2.3.1.4   Unskilled negotiators and strategy mismatch

Negotiations can break down not only because of difficulties inherent in negotiating style but merely because the negotiators lack basic skills or training in effective negotiating. Many professionals and managers learn their negotiating tactics by trial and error or by sitting beside the senior partner in a negotiating team. This may not equip them effectively for certain types of negotiations or for more complex or multi-party cases. Thus, one can meet ineffective competitive negotiators who threaten and bluster, but are unable to cope with subtler shades of bargaining; or with principled negotiators who have learned the value of reasonableness but who interpret it to mean only the way they see the case.

30

A particular form of this occurs where there is a mismatch of strategies adopted by the parties to the negotiation. Neither side may be sufficiently flexible or perceptive to understand why they seem to be failing to communicate. This difficulty may be further exacerbated by difference of style and effectiveness between a client and his or her professional advisers. Mediation intervention can again work if the mediator creates a safer environment through which each side can explore their case more thoroughly and communicate more effectively. To achieve this a mediator needs to bring communication skills and mental flexibility to the negotiation.

### 2.3.2 Problems inherent in the structure of negotiations

#### 2.3.2.1 Principal–agent tensions

Negotiations are not always conducted directly by the principals. They may have effectively handed over the negotiating to their professional advisers or may have left negotiations to someone lower down the corporate hierarchy. In some negotiations, this can create a further likelihood of impasse or delayed settlement. The middle manager may not want a realistic settlement, as it may expose his own failings on a project. The litigation lawyer may commit to a legalistic approach, and be less used to taking a purely commercial attitude. Incentives can also be different. There may be little direct financial incentive for opposing lawyers to settle a case early when they are charging on an hourly rate or have a Conditional Fee Agreement based on hours worked.

Mediation can assist in these cases by ensuring that those with decision-making authority are required to be present during a mediation and hence involved directly in focusing on settlement options and the real costs of any alternatives. Also, a good mediator may in the course of a mediation identify the need to involve a more senior manager in discussions, or to review commercial settlement options as well as strict legal principles. Agent motivations may even need to be brought into the open or brought into the calculus of settlement structures. Equally, the lawyer may have a client who is difficult or holds unrealistic expectations, and therefore may welcome the influence on the client of an independent neutral.

#### 2.3.2.2 Litigation and the bargaining context

The timing and nature of settlement discussions may be profoundly affected by the way the court system works in a particular jurisdiction. Are there pre-action requirements to explore settlement? Do judges have a duty to conciliate or not? Is disclosure of documents a formal part of its procedure? How is information collected and assessed? What is the extent of delays in the courts, and so forth? Such variations are likely to impact on the timing of settlement discussions and on pressures to settle. The development of court-annexed ADR schemes is a result of the recognition that, when left to their own devices, parties may not work up sufficient enthusiasm for ADR without court prompting. This may be either because of taking a competitive approach, or belief that tactical advantage is held at a particular stage of proceedings. This mirrors the view taken by Lord Woolf in his reforms that case management needed to be transferred to the judges because of shortcomings in the way litigation had generally been conducted between parties and their lawyers.

### 2.3.2.3  Resistance to negotiations

Related to the above, the balance of power between parties may induce one party to delay settlement, for example to avoid immediate cash payments. ADR clauses, summary judgment procedures, more efficient litigation systems, interim payment requirements and other procedural features may also be necessary to generate movement towards negotiation or ADR.

Also, as discussed above[3] there are occasions such as consumer and environment disputes or public policy-making procedures, where there has been no previous culture or practice of negotiated consensus. In these settings, ADR specialists may perform a lobbying role, encouraging parties to adopt consensus-building approaches. Mediation or facilitation in this area can require more complex and protracted judgments over tactics and process. Questions will arise (among other issues) over the following:

– how to identify interest groups to be represented in negotiations;
– managing spokespersons and their constituency relations;
– the role of expert evidence and procedures for reaching consensus;
– the provision of neutral funding resources to assist groups without special funding;
– identifying effectively neutral 'host' organisations who can sponsor the process.

### 2.3.3  Problems inherent in the psychology of conflict

It is well established in common sense and in psychological research on conflict that once parties begin to slide into conflict, they then act, perceive and think about their situation in ways that make it harder to settle the dispute. Ethnic, national and religious conflicts exemplify this phenomenon over centuries. Lawyers too, faced at a first interview by an angry client, may find it awkward to engage such clients in immediate discussions on the weaknesses of their case or on the advantage of opening settlement discussions, with or without ADR.

---

3  See 2.1.1.

The impact of conflict on parties is to reduce their interest in communicating openly with the other side. Communications that do take place are interpreted in ways that devalue offers made or actions taken, in order to fit the hostile perception and judgments brought into the situation. A maxim of positional negotiation that reflects this is the phrase 'always make them work hard for a concession'. In other words, concessions easily won are immediately devalued by the competitive recipient. Thinking grows more rigid about the situation and team members who suggest concessions or the need to re-evaluate the situation can become outcasts and be regarded as betraying the true interests of the group. The concept of *reactive devaluation* dominates the assessment of each side's communications, 'if the other side say that, I shall assume that it is wrong or has an illicit motive!'

Bringing such disputes to lawyers or litigation does not necessarily trigger a more reasoned approach into the situation. The litigation itself, and the lawyers involved, may be used as an extension of the parties' search for weapons to defeat the other side and confirm their own views, rather than to resolve a dispute wisely; hence some of the criticism of lawyers' role in divorce proceedings.

Mediators have a particularly challenging task in resolving such problems. A primary need is for mediators to conduct themselves in a way that ensures that all sides continue to see them as truly neutral rather than partisan. In this way they can cautiously open up lines of communication, or can help a party move beyond recriminations into thoughts for the future, or can serve as a lightning rod on which each side can finally vent their long-held grievances and hostility with regard to the other party. Mediation thus provides emotionally a form of 'day in court' for such cases and can help release the pressure in a way that cannot be guaranteed by the litigation process. Mediations in more complex versions of these cases will very often lead the parties towards new institutions, policies, practices, dispute resolution procedures or other approaches which help establish new structures for the future that can begin to turn party energies towards a more constructive future.

At a simpler level, a concession offered through a mediator may appear to have been given more reluctantly and formally (and hence appear more worth winning) than if a party offered it directly. And if it is conveyed as a 'mediator's proposal', it can avoid the tendency to devalue it, had it appeared to be suggested by the opponent.

### 2.3.4   Judgments of risk

In addition to the psychology of conflict, the psychology of judgments made under risk or uncertainty is relevant to negotiation or mediation. Apparently, faced with a loss, more people will prefer to take a risk and gamble to recover their losses even if the predicted loss will be even higher, instead of cutting their losses. One form of this is the attitude to 'wasted costs' or the phenomenon of 'throwing good money after bad'. If I have spent £50,000 so far on litigation, I may prefer to spend another £100,000 to pursue the chance of succeeding at trial rather than waste the first £50,000 by withdrawing from the action. This is so even though the fact that I have spent £50,000 has no real impact on the probability of success and that it may be more rational to take the early loss. Combined with a sense of anger at the other side, this is a powerful cocktail to encourage continuation of the conflict rather than a realistic resolution.

The converse phenomenon is that a party faced with a choice between a certain positive outcome now and a doubtful but better one in the future will very often prefer to accept what is available, even in the teeth of advice to the contrary from an adviser. The party's agenda will rarely be the same as the lawyer's and, with complications over conditional fee funding, there is even a potential for conflict between lawyer and client. So, a party may feel that their private interest or target has been met, and simply want to be disentangled from the claims process and its attendant risks and strains forthwith. Mediators have to be alive in such cases to the confusion over ownership of the dispute which such internal pressures can create.

Mediators may help parties and their advisers think through the risks more carefully by neutral questioning and summarising of party positions and principles. Alternatively, a party may be willing to accept a non-binding view or reality-test from a credible third party as a way of finding a more tangible justification for cutting their losses earlier.

### 2.3.5 Genuine and good faith disagreements

Finally, barriers to settlement may arise from a genuine clash of judgments on the facts of a case or on the principles that should determine terms of settlement or the outcome, or other legal rights which apply. The psychology of conflict, however, suggests that all parties will generally justify their positions in such terms. Parties and their lawyers inevitably find ways to justify their reasoning as they follow the natural psychological path of seeking confirmation of their own view of the case.

Mediation may help strip away some of the other barriers to settlement that are not at the core of the dispute, such as poor negotiating skills, communications and team member problems. However, most mediators also have to deal with good faith disagreements. To some extent these can again be tackled by the mediator by reviewing the case with each side, communicating alternative view points, exploring strengths and weaknesses and probing for settlement opportunities. Mediators can informally challenge existing stances and help the parties to re-assess their case.

But where there is a defined and critical issue that divides the parties, other ADR options may have to be considered. For instance, the mediator may have to allow witnesses to be called and to question them so that the parties can reach a considered view on their credibility. Alternatively, the mediator may have to give a formal evaluation of the merits of the issues dividing the parties (if qualified to do so) or call in an expert to give such a neutral appraisal. If it is clear from the start that there is a core disagreement along these lines, a mini-trial or neutral evaluation format may need to be adopted in preference to, or supplementary to, mediation.

## 2.4   ADR organisations and dispute systems design

In overcoming the various barriers to negotiated settlements, it may be necessary to work to more than one design. While parties themselves or an appointed neutral may be quite capable of doing this, there are many disputes where an ADR organisation's input may be more powerful. For instance, there may be an informal 'mediation' required even to get all parties to consider utilising an ADR process at all, followed by a further phase of refining and agreeing the details of procedure or the neutral(s) to be appointed. Involving the individual neutral from the beginning of this whole process has the advantage of allowing the parties to develop a relationship with, and trust in, the neutral, and (where relevant) the ADR provider through which the mediator was appointed.

However, it has the major disadvantage that, in the sensitive early stages, a mediator's preference for certain aspects of procedure may sow seeds of distrust regarding the mediator's neutrality or effectiveness. Also, early discussions on the design of the process may reveal the need for a different kind of neutral (in terms of skill, credibility or expertise) than first considered. Finally, it is common experience amongst ADR organisations that parties locked in antagonistic conflicts find it initially difficult to agree on anything, least of all the name of a neutral. The fact that one side puts forward a name confirms the other side's presumption of bias (another instance of reactive devaluation)!

The essential thrust in ADR design is to take gradual steps towards proce- dural agreements while retaining maximum flexibility. Attempts to impose too rigid a set of rules or terms of reference in difficult disputes can often merely serve to provide grounds for further argument between parties already deadlocked on key substantive issues. Furthermore, too great an enthusiasm for design may end up with parties reinventing a litigation system.

It follows, then, that there is a substantial and critical process of diagnosis required of the dispute resolution professional at many stages during the life-cycle of a dispute. Only by identifying the barriers to settlement in a

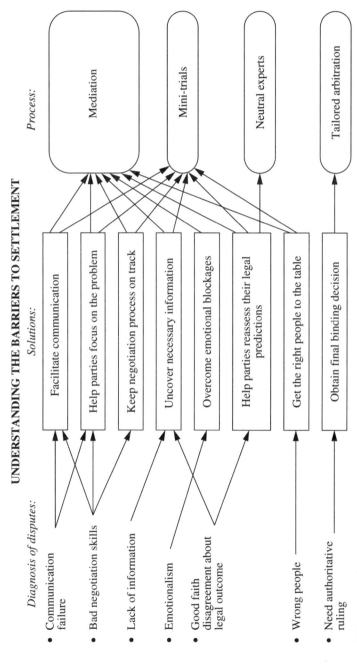

UNDERSTANDING THE BARRIERS TO SETTLEMENT

*Diagnosis of disputes:*

*Solutions:*

*Process:*

- Communication failure
- Bad negotiation skills
- Lack of information
- Emotionalism
- Good faith disagreement about legal outcome
- Wrong people
- Need authoritative ruling

Facilitate communication

Help parties focus on the problem

Keep negotiation process on track

Uncover necessary information

Overcome emotional blockages

Help parties reassess their legal predictions

Get the right people to the table

Obtain final binding decision

Mediation

Mini-trials

Neutral experts

Tailored arbitration

This chart is derived from a chart developed by Professor Eric D Green, Boston University School of Law and J.A.M.S/ENDISPUTE, © 1993 case can serious attempts then be made to overcome or circumvent them. In the absence of such a diagnosis the dispute must inevitably become harder to resolve.

It also follows that each different diagnosis will imply the need for a different remedy or, in procedural terms, that the different processes of negotiation, ADR, arbitration and litigation can all prove effective if applied at the right time. The key to the successful understanding and use of ADR techniques is to recognise what they contribute to a dispute, and then to be able to apply the right technique at the right time. Many of the problems of litigation arise not just from its inherent procedural flaws, but from the fact that it is treated as a universal procedural remedy and applied to cases for which it is sometimes highly appropriate and sometimes highly inappropriate. Or, to quote the old adage, 'if all you have is a hammer, everything will look like a nail'.

The diagnostic process is illustrated in the diagram at the end of this chapter, showing some of the main barriers to settlement and suggesting ADR techniques which might be appropriate to handle them. The extension of choice provided by ADR puts an onus on dispute professionals to approach all disputes with much closer diagnostic scrutiny, and a much more creative range of procedural options. It also should allow advisers and clients to approach ADR and settlement discussions in a more open and positive way. After all, they can help design and influence the ongoing process, and choose a process which has no risks of imposed decision. Understanding the ADR options and how best to implement them are therefore increasingly important for professionals who work in the context of negotiation and dispute management.

*Chapter 3*

# An overview of the dispute resolution landscape

As we have seen in the first two chapters, there are a number of ways to classify ADR methods, both in terms of the extent of party control and also in terms of its relationship to negotiating techniques. We have touched upon some of the forms of processes that have developed to meet the needs which these various approaches illustrate, and given some early ideas as to how to select procedures appropriate to cases. The diagram at the end of **Chapter 2** is a useful guide, but only a very rough tool.

This chapter looks in more detail at the ways in which specific ADR processes operate, summarising the main practice points associated with these techniques, and identifying some variations. There is an important array of options, and it is important for professionals to ensure that they select the dispute resolution forum that will be the best one to overcome barriers to settlement in their particular case. Mediation will only be looked at in outline in this chapter, as it has become by far the most significant ADR process both in the United Kingdom and worldwide, and will be examined in considerable detail in **Chapters 11 to 15**.

## 3.1 Finding the most appropriate process

ADR processes are classified in broad terms only, and then again can vary in detail and emphasis according to the cultural or professional background of the neutral. Many ADR specialists hold the view that ADR processes should remain flexible to avoid the descent into rules and rigidity that have undermined the reputation and effectiveness of traditional litigation or arbitration.

Many ADR techniques have only been systematised in the last 20 years or so, and their variations, strengths, terminology and procedures are still evolving with experience. There is nevertheless a surprising unanimity of practice that has grown up around the globe. As a result, ADR has become an especially useful technique for dealing with cross-border disputes where there is at least a minimum level of ADR awareness and training in each country. Advisers operating in an international context should, however, check that terms and processes are being used to mean the same thing, as variants do occur.

We shall adopt a slightly different classification of dispute resolution processes for this chapter, based on the three primary distinguishing features of the dispute resolution landscape, which give to each ADR method its characteristic central driving force. These are:

-   negotiation;
-   mediation;
-   adjudication.

## 3.2  Negotiation processes and variants

While strictly not an ADR technique itself, there being no third-party intervention, negotiation underlies much ADR practice, as we have seen in **Chapter 2**, and negotiated outcomes are seen as the objective of the main ADR techniques. Indeed, mediation is often referred to as 'assisted negotiation', though we would argue that it has much wider ramifications. We shall revert to that in the next section.

Interest in commercial ADR has emerged from and fed back into a growing literature on negotiating science in the last 30 years. The development of principled bargaining, allied with a sense of the interdependence of business, consumer and public relationships, have stimulated a search for third-party ADR mechanisms to reduce the adversarial tendencies of many commercial or litigation negotiating practices. As a by-product, many professionals who have trained in ADR methods report that the principles they have learned often improve their direct negotiating practice. Third party techniques can also be adapted to support negotiations, even where not led by a mediator.

### 3.2.1  Facilitation of discussions

Some third party interventions occur at a much lower level than formal mediation or adjudication, in essence to attempt to facilitate or broker the start of negotiations at all. Interventions by ADR providers or even the mere suggestion of mediation by one party frequently stimulates parties to open or re-open discussions and reach their own directly negotiated settlements. Such techniques might be described as 'facilitation', 'using good offices' (in a diplomatic setting) or 'conciliation', though there tends to be little systematic theory or language in this sector of dispute resolution.

### 3.2.2   Evaluation for guidance

Parties may seek the view of a third party on aspects of their case or on technical issues, which helps them to address their differences and clarify negotiating positions. This kind of approach may contribute to the parties' negotiating material but does not seek directly to influence the path or even the process of negotiations (as in mediation), nor to offer any binding judgment. The following are techniques of this kind:

#### 3.2.2.1   Neutral fact-finding

This involves an investigation and report of what the facts of a case must have been in the view of an independent third party.

#### 3.2.2.2   Expert appraisal

Where there is an issue of quality or professional assessment, an expert assessment can give a stronger foundation or objective criteria for subsequent negotiations.

#### 3.2.2.3   Early neutral evaluation

This is a technique used in certain US state courts, and offered (though rarely taken up) by the English Commercial Court and the Technology and Construction Court, where senior lawyers or judges evaluate the likely outcomes of a case on the basis of a summary brief: this is expected to lead to more realistic negotiations between the parties. It can also involve jointly obtaining the respected opinion of an expert or a senior lawyer on points at issue. There are some parallels with evidence-gathering from single joint experts as ordered fairly frequently under CPR Pt 35, albeit that the expert does not remove the responsibility for the ultimate decision from the judge on core issues at trial.

#### 3.2.2.4   Executive amicable settlement procedure

Many commercial dispute clauses attempt to deal with the 'wrong people problem' in negotiation by deliberately moving the required negotiation to the senior executive or director level before external dispute resolution. Not only is a broader corporate view taken of the problem then, but in theory senior executives will be less personally involved in the personal antagonisms or career or budget sensitivities that may have afflicted middle managers dealing directly with the dispute.

### 3.2.3  Preventative dispute resolution techniques

Many of the ADR third party processes can be said to help settle disputes earlier and more informally and thereby prevent dispute escalation. However, thought should also be given to the many 'better management' approaches that can either reduce conflict or handle it more constructively to prevent a formal dispute emerging in the first place. Such systems could include:

– Training in *principled negotiation* (positional negotiation training may increase the rate of conflicts over time!).
– *Team working,* education and consultancy (how to collaborate better, solve problems in group working, etc).
– Application of *quality management systems* to customer or supplier relations ('Total Quality Management', Six Sigma or ISO 9000).
– *Partnering* (a term used in the construction industry to refer to team-working arrangements between the various parties to a construction project, with early joint education, regular meetings, funds for contingencies and other mutual support systems).
– *Reg-Neg* (a term used in the United States to refer to an approach used by administrative agencies of negotiating new regulations with interest groups fully and in advance of their introduction.

A number of these efforts at improving direct negotiations also involve third parties as educators or consultants. More formal third party approaches to the same end might include:

– *Project Mediator* (a process involving the early appointment of a disputes specialist and facilitator with a standing role on a major construction contract to oil the wheels of communications between the parties).
– *Advisory mediation* (a term used by the UK industrial relations agency ACAS to refer to the appointment of a facilitator-mediator to work with an employer and employees to devise agreed negotiating or employment procedures that will enhance relations between the parties).

### 3.2.4  Negotiating skills and third-party intervention

Advisers or neutrals working in more formal third party resolution processes should at least be aware of the range of techniques to facilitate better direct negotiations, even if not themselves skilled in those. In their role as, say, mediators, they must have a thorough sense of how negotiations succeed or fail. They may also wish to draw on some of these techniques during mediation (for example, expert appraisal) in order to overcome obstacles or to propose methods of future working relations between the parties. Similarly, advisers should seek to become experienced in how to optimise for their clients the value of having a third-party process, and how best to work with different styles of mediators.

### 3.2.5   Managers as dispute resolvers

Equally, managers should be better informed about the dispute landscape to enhance their own range of techniques. In particular, managers and advisers should have an ability to recognise when to initiate third party intervention before conflicts escalate. Mediation and other approaches are too often only employed as a last resort, or once arbitration and litigation also become options. In fact, many public and private sector negotiations will have dragged on or festered for months or years before this stage. Alert managers should be able to trigger constructive intervention before this level of aggravation and inefficiency is reached.

## 3.3   Mediation processes and variants

Mediation is the central and most frequently adopted ADR technique around the globe. Its uses stretch from the highest level of international diplomacy to the humblest of inter-personal problems. We deal in full detail with it in Part C,[1] and confine ourselves here to a summary of its essential shape, with the major procedural variants found in practice.

### 3.3.1   Normal mediation procedure

Mediation involves the appointment or intervention of a neutral third party which seeks to help the parties in dispute to reach a negotiated agreement. The mediator becomes actively involved in the negotiation process but has no power to adjudicate or impose an award. Typically, mediations in civil disputes are conducted on a confidential basis and 'without prejudice' to other legal rights or remedies of the parties in the event that they do not reach an agreement to settle their differences.

A typical non-family civil dispute mediation goes through four basic phases.

#### 3.3.1.1   Preparation

This includes drawing up a mediation agreement, appointment of mediator and delivery of written submissions and document bundles to the mediator

---

1 **Chapters 11–15**.

and other parties, plus any pre-mediation contact by the mediator with the parties, either by telephone or sometimes in a pre-mediation meeting.

### 3.3.1.2   Opening joint session

Introduction by the mediator and brief presentations by each party of their case at a round-table meeting.

### 3.3.1.3   Private meetings (or 'caucuses')

'Shuttle diplomacy' by a mediator, who seeks in confidential sessions with each party to clarify privately the nature of their case and their settlement interests, and to help the parties to design their own acceptable settlement. Exploration of the issues and underlying interests will shade into bargaining, with exchanges of offers from party to party, sometimes across the table, or more often by the mediator taking proposals from one party to the other.

### 3.3.1.4   Conclusion

A joint meeting to agree or sign written terms of settlement, which are usually a legally binding contract or consent order; or to terminate the mediation process. Termination may occur at a range of levels. Negotiations may have completely broken down; agreement may be reached on further information needed before negotiation can start again; agreement may have been reached on some issues, leaving a narrower range to be litigated or discussed later; the parties may agree to adjourn and reconvene at a later date in mediation; or the mediator may offer to follow up separately with each party.

### 3.3.2   Main variants in mediation procedure

### 3.3.2.1   Joint and private meetings

Mediators often differ in how much they rely on joint meetings or private meetings and on how flexible they are in mixing the two. In UK family mediation, for instance, separate meetings with one or other party are rare. In public policy or environmental mediation, meetings are sometimes held in public in front of an audience of stakeholders. Confidentiality is the norm in commercial mediation. This refers to both confidentiality as between all parties in the mediation and third parties outside the mediation: and also confidentiality of communication between mediator and a party in a private session unless the mediator is authorised by that party to disclose information to the other party or parties.

### 3.3.2.2   Facilitative/evaluative mediation

There is a spectrum of styles of approach among mediators, in theory at least. At one end is the facilitative approach, where the mediator avoids giving opinions and judgments, and merely assists parties to clarify their communications, interests and priorities. At the other end is said to be the evaluative approach, where the mediator expresses opinions on the merits of issues in dispute in order to generate movement towards settlement. There is a tendency to characterise the facilitative approach as soft and the evaluative as hard. The truth is much more complex. Facilitative mediations will very often entail robust reality-testing by the mediator, which is all the more telling because of the mediator's neutral status and facilitative role. The giving of an appraisal or an opinion over settlement range (sometimes provided for in a mediation agreement at the parties' and mediator's option) may need very soft presentation by a supposedly evaluative mediator.

There is also a tendency to characterise the two approaches as the only two possibilities for mediators. In reality, there are endless shades of grey among mediators, not least derived from differing personalities and styles. Furthermore, wherever a mediator works on this spectrum in the course of a mediation, decisions over the outcome will always remain the parties' ultimate responsibility.

As we shall see in our later discussion on mediation practice, the above distinction is often too simplistic to catch the richness of mediation practice. However, it can be a useful framework for parties in terms of choosing an appropriate mediator (known to be facilitative or evaluative in style) or deciding what they need from mediation to overcome obstacles to settlement between them and the other party (or between them and their own advisers).

### 3.3.2.3   Conciliation

This term has traditionally been used to refer to a process similar to mediation but distinguished from it by virtue of the fact that in mediation the third party is more active in putting forward terms of settlement or an opinion on the case. For example, the UK's statutory industrial relations agency, ACAS, distinguishes conciliation from mediation where third parties issue a written recommendation. Unfortunately, there is no international unanimity on which term connotes the more active process. Increasingly, the term *mediation* has been adopted as the generic term for third-party facilitation in commercial disputes whether or not the third party is active. We therefore do not use the term conciliation again in this book.

### 3.3.2.4  Mini-trial or executive tribunal

This is a more formal type of mediation practice and associated clearly with an evaluative approach. Formal, but abbreviated, presentations of their best legal case are made by each party to a panel of senior directors from each company with (usually) a neutral chairman to manage proceedings. After the presentations, the executives adjourn and attempt to negotiate a settlement on the basis of what they have heard. The neutral adviser is there to facilitate negotiations or to mediate, if the parties' negotiations stall. The neutral adviser may be asked to give a view on the likely outcome if the case went to trial or arbitration in order to facilitate settlement. The executive tribunal is a powerful approach for major corporate disputes. It is not used anything like as frequently as mediation, however.

### 3.3.2.5  Consensus-building

This expression is often used as a substitute for mediation (or facilitation) in environmental or public policy dispute resolution processes; for example over planning the location of a new chemicals factory in a community, or setting new environmental standards. It refers usually to a more protracted process in which a third-party consultant seeks to identify the various interest groups connected with a development, and to facilitate consultation, discussions or negotiation between them. The aim is thereby to achieve a 'wiser' and more consensual outcome than in the normal public policy approach involving either lack of adequate consultation or consultation without full participative decision-making. It helps to combat the NIMBY ('not in *my* back yard') phenomenon on the one hand and on the other hand the defective political process of decision-making that can be summed up as 'Consult-Announce Decision-Defend Decision-Amend Decision'. This is when those consulted realise that the decision does not meet their interests and battle politically or through the courts to amend it.

Consensus-building approaches have been most widely used in the United States and Australia and fall within variations on assisted negotiation as well as mediation.

### 3.3.2.6  Med-arb

Sometimes parties wish, for reasons of cost or time, to avoid the possibility that a mediation may not achieve final determination of a dispute if the parties fail to agree. They therefore contract to give the mediator power to convert into an arbitrator role and make a legally binding award, in the event that mediated negotiations do not lead to settlement of all issues.

This technique, called med-arb, is not widely used but interest in it is growing, for example in the US construction industry, and some jurisdictions have legislated to deal with the potential legal problems for arbitrations conducted under these circumstances.

The main theoretical arguments against med-arb are two-fold. First, the process appears to run counter to traditional rules of natural justice that a party should hear the evidence and arguments put forward against it and have a chance of reply. Private meetings in the course of a mediation undermine this principle unless the mediator is allowed to reveal everything said in private. Alternatively it has to be accepted that the mediator has to put out of mind any unilateral information in handing down an arbitral award, a very difficult thing for the mediator to do.

Med-arb also theoretically undermines the power of the mediation process, because each party may feel reluctant to be as open with the mediator on their offers or vulnerabilities, if there is a chance that the mediator will become an arbitrator of their case.[2]

Despite these major theoretical drawbacks, there appears to be growing support internationally for med-arb practice. Parties are said to value the more robust commercial approach involved, and there are many cases where little really sensitive information is revealed in private sessions. However, as yet it is not commonly used in the United Kingdom and parties should be warned of the theoretical disadvantages. Perhaps if they do use it, they should afford themselves a contractual opportunity to opt out of the arbitration phase that would otherwise follow the mediation phase, although this still undermines the robustness of the mediation process.

A variation on this promoted by the American Arbitration Association is MEDALOA, mediation followed by "last-offer arbitration" (see below for a description of this form of arbitration).[3] Another variant is "arb-med", where the arbitrator writes an award but leaves it in a sealed envelope only to be opened if having then converted to a mediator role, mediation does not lead to settlement.


## 3.4 Adjudicative processes and variants

In determining which appropriate dispute resolution method to adopt, consideration must of course be given to the option where a third party hands down a judgment. Some of these techniques are associated with the discipline of ADR, although the traditional alternatives of litigation or arbitration are commonly held to be outside ADR, though in the United States

---

2 See 3.4.3.
3 For a case in which an adjudicator took on the note of mediator but was prevented from reventing to adjudicator see *Glencot Development and Design Co Ltd v Ben Barrett & Son (Contractors) Ltd* [2001] CILL 1721.

it has been more common to regard arbitration as one of the new 'alternatives'. It is also important to stress the difference between adjudication as a broad conceptual category of techniques involving imposed decisions (as used in this section) and adjudication as a specific ADR process.

Adjudications by definition imply non-negotiated outcomes, involving decisions handed down by a third party, usually on a win-lose basis. However, some of these assumptions may be modified by party control of parts of the procedure, or by way of substantive legal principles (for example, as the concept of contributory negligence reduces the damages awarded to a claimant).

### 3.4.1 Litigation and court trial

The civil litigation system in many common law jurisdictions has increasingly become a settlement system. Typically, over 90 per cent of claims issued in such systems do not proceed to trial, and further cases do not proceed to judgment. However, ADR has been perceived as a valuable complement to this system, not just because it helps prevent some cases going to trial, but because it is said to speed up the process of settlement and thereby reduce the cost and management time allotted to litigation. Finally, the litigation system is geared to a specific range of legal principles, legal remedies and historical analysis of cases. ADR techniques offer potentially more flexible, creative and future-orientated outcomes.

It will, of course, frequently be necessary to decide that litigation is the appropriate route to take either in general or as an initial step to:

- establish a legal precedent;
- establish, or (as defendant) avoid, the opening of floodgates to a class of claims;
- make a public statement on the importance of an industry practice;
- achieve summary judgment;
- enforce judgments, awards and agreements;
- compel and examine documents and witnesses;
- obtain rapid injunctive relief;
- force another party into taking settlement discussions seriously, or the prospect of facing a judgment.

Also relevant to the choice of litigation as a primary approach would be questions which can vary substantially according to the case and jurisdiction involved:

–   the speed of getting to trial;
–   the costs involved;
–   the likely recovery of such costs;
–   the likelihood of recovering any judgment;
–   the quality and relevance of any judgment;
–   the management time and energy likely to be used;
–   the risks of publicity and the value and potential damage to commercial relationships and public image.

Four other major aspects of litigation practice should be noted in considering dispute resolution options:

(1)   Common law jurisdictions (and civil law perhaps to a lesser extent) are increasingly seeking ways to improve the efficiency, speed and price of access to the courts. This will have some impact on the use of alternatives.

(2)   As part of these attempts at reform, courts and legal systems are increasingly adopting active case management systems, amply demonstrated by the reforms embodied in the CPR in England and Wales.

(3)   Also as part of these reforms, courts are increasingly attempting to integrate ADR methods into court procedures by way of court-annexed ADR or multi-door courthouse concepts. Thus lawyers and parties may be advised to consider ADR, or be informed of the options, or directed to use it subject to rights of opt-out or costs sanctions.

(4)   In several civil law countries and other jurisdictions (for example Japan) judges have a duty to seek to bring the parties to a pre-trial settlement. The nature and thoroughness of this duty to effect conciliation varies, but will often involve the judge giving the parties a preliminary view of the case rather than employing facilitative mediation. Some countries are using the 'new wave' of ADR development to reintroduce judicial mediation as a more structured approach. Where there is a distinct judicial profession distinct from private client practice, as in many civil law jurisdictions in Europe and, for example, in Quebec, judges are increasingly taking the role of mediators.

### 3.4.2   Arbitration

Arbitration has been the traditional private alternative to court, with parties contracting to be bound by a third party private award that is normally legally enforceable as a court judgment.

As a dispute resolution approach, the advantages claimed for arbitration are that it is private, and that parties can tailor procedures and time-scales to their needs rather than be bound by fixed court systems. Finally, the parties can choose their decision-maker, who may have specialist background knowledge to bring to bear on the case. Over the years, however, arbitration's reputation has suffered, mainly because it has become increasingly costly and proceedings have become as protracted as court timetables. Also parties are not always as free to choose their arbitrator as they would wish, and often become upset on 'losing' their case 'unjustifiably' due to what they consider a poor quality arbitrator, as compared with judicial standards.

A vigorous debate has taken place in the arbitration world on how to address such issues. The reforms in the Arbitration Act 1996 and UNCITRAL Model Law have made appreciable improvements. We look at some special types of arbitration in the next section, but otherwise leave arbitration as being outside the scope of this book.

### 3.4.3 Tailored arbitration

A number of variations of arbitration are worth noting in terms of the landscape of dispute resolution.

#### 3.4.3.1 Documents only arbitration

A simplified arbitration based solely on documentary, and not oral, evidence or argument, used in a number of consumer arbitration schemes.

#### 3.4.3.2 'Amiable Compositeur' or 'ex aequo et bono'

An additional arbitration approach found in civil law systems where awards can be guided by considerations of equity and fairness and not according to strict legal rules, used more often in consumer cases, but not recognised in common law systems.

#### 3.4.3.3 'Hi-Lo' arbitration

A process where parties agree on a limited range of figures within which they will accept an award, ie with a minimum and maximum. The arbitrator may or may not be informed of the agreed range. Not widely used as an approach.

#### 3.4.3.4 Final-offer/last-offer/pendulum/baseball arbitration

A process where parties agree that their last offers will be placed before an arbitrator who can only choose one side's offer or the other side's claim figure. It is mainly used in industrial relations contexts with the rationale that it will help parties decide to put forward only reasonable figures.

### 3.4.4 Expert determination

In some instances the parties may be divided only by a technical question, for example the valuation of a company or the reasons for collapse of a bridge. In such cases a common approach is a contractual agreement to appoint an expert to make a determination of the question in issue. Being a valuation, this approach has been treated by the courts as having different legal characteristics and remedies from an arbitral award, although the distinction between the two is not always clear.

### 3.4.5 Adjudication

This expression is often used in a technical sense in construction contracts to refer to the statutory procedure enacted for that industry. It is intended as a procedure that will bind parties to a decision soon after a dispute notice is given. Parties usually have an option to reject the decision and initiate litigation or arbitration proceedings within a certain time period or after substantial completion of the construction contract.[4]

### 3.4.6 Dispute review board

This is a standing adjudication panel system used in major construction contracts. The Board is generally appointed at the outset of the project and stays in close touch with it, adjudicating disputes as they arise. A well-known example of this was the dispute review board appointed to resolve problems arising out of the Channel Tunnel and the Hong Kong airport construction projects.

### 3.4.7 Ombudsman

The ombudsman system has evolved as a successful approach to delivering prompt responses to citizen or consumer complaints, so as to protect public sector or industry reputations. An ombudsman office is established as an independent agency to review and adjudicate on complaints. Usually fact-finding and adjudication are involved, often heavily based on documentation, though sometimes there are also efforts at mediation during the inquiry stage. In the United States, and a few English companies, corporate ombudsmans are also used to adjudicate on or investigate employee or member complaints within particular organisations.

## 3.5 Dispute resolution systems: old or new?

The range of available dispute resolution processes continues to grow as both society and the commercial world evolve, together with re-thinking of

---

4 Where the contracting parties in a construction dispute do nor agree their own dispute resolution procedure, adjudication is impliedly included by virtue of the Housing Grants Construction and Regeneration Act 1996, ss 108 and 114(4).

the field of dispute resolution of which ADR is a creative part. For companies, public sector organisations or sectors faced with recurring disputes, the landscape of dispute resolution offers the opportunity to apply some systems management thinking to their problems. Can a dispute procedure be devised which delivers greater benefits, such as reduction of cost or delay, improved relations, minimum management diversion or other criteria?

Use of one of the major landscape features – negotiation, mediation or adjudication – may suffice, but there is also the option of adopting a *multi-step procedure,* for instance *negotiation + mediation + adjudication* (litigation or arbitration) or a *multiple choice system,* for instance the *multi-door courthouse,* with adequate means of guidance to the parties. These approaches can be embodied in contractual terms.

It is certainly not beyond the wit of those in dispute and those engaged in ADR to devise yet more useful adaptations to the existing landscape features to meet individual needs. The principles have already been discussed at the conclusion of **Chapter 2**. For example, ADR is increasingly becoming the tool of choice for dealing with cases that might be regarded as untriable, perhaps because of the sheer complexity of issues, involvement of huge numbers of parties or multi-jurisdictional problems. While settlement of the whole dispute is the ultimate hope, there is much that ADR technique and its deployment in the hands of a skilled facilitator can achieve along that road in what might be called 'mega-litigation'. Designing how to make the issues in such a case manageable and how to deal with classes of party in a consistent but personally sensitive way is crucially helpful. There is a critical balance between trying to tackle the outcome globally and breaking it into comprehensible components.

Such processes will usually spread over weeks and months, rather than the more typical finite mediation process confined to a day or two. A true project management approach is required, with the facilitator (or quite often two facilitators) working in close conjunction with each party's team. A particular example of such an approach was exemplified in the mediation of the retained organs litigation in England and Wales, in which the mediation design and delivery process was spread over a period of about two years. This is described in greater detail in **Chapter 11**, together with several other instances of project design.[5] Future editions of this book will undoubtedly need to reflect further learning from engagement by ADR providers and advisers in the wide range of such processes that is beginning to develop.

We now turn to Part B to consider the legal framework of ADR. In Part C we examine the practical framework for the principal ADR process, mediation.

---

5 See **11.6.1**.

*PART B*

# THE LEGAL FRAMEWORK OF ADR

# Chapter 4

# ADR and the Civil Procedure Rules 1998

## 4.1  The path to the Civil Procedure Rules 1998

The single most significant spur to the development of Alternative Dispute Resolution within civil justice in England and Wales was Lord Woolf's reforms proposed and implemented in the 1990s. In his historic interim and final *Access to Justice* reports of 1995 and 1996, he identified expense, slowness and complexity as the problems still besetting the civil justice system, despite numerous earlier proposals for reform. He took the view that the basic principles that should underpin an accessible civil justice system were that it should be:

- *just* in the results delivered;
- *fair* and seen to be so, by ensuring equal opportunity to assert or defend rights, giving adequate opportunity for each to state or answer a case, and treating like cases alike;
- *proportionate*, in relation to the issues involved, in both procedure and cost;
- *speedy* so far as reasonable;
- *understandable* to users;
- *responsive* to the needs of users;
- *certain* in outcome as far as possible;
- *effective* through adequate resources and organisation.

His aim was to change the whole approach to civil litigation from a wasteful adversarial mind-set to one of co-operative problem-solving by encouraging settlement rather than trial of disputes.

Encouraging the development of ADR was one of the ways in which Lord Woolf felt these aims could be achieved. In Chapter 18 of his 1995 Interim Report, he decided not to recommend that ADR should be compulsory, resisting the urge to import US approaches into the courts wholesale, noting that there were appreciable practical differences in each jurisdiction, such as jury trial of civil actions and easily accessed appeals. Treating arbitration, mediation and the work of ombudsmen as the primary forms of ADR process then, he advocated court encouragement of the use of ADR rather than court-annexed schemes. He was also clear that in deciding 'on the future conduct of a case', a judge should be able to take into account a litigant's unreasonable **refusal to attempt** ADR. He did not then contemplate retrospective costs sanctions for past unreasonable litigation conduct.

However, in his Final Report of 1996, he reversed that view and recommended[1] that courts should take into account unreasonable refusal of a court's proposal that ADR should be attempted when considering costs orders. He even suggested sanctioning unreasonable behaviour **in the course of** ADR, not something that was implemented. By that time too he was expressing less certainty about not providing for compulsory referral to ADR. The debate which he initiated on these two topics continues, as we shall see. He also specifically recommended that solicitors for clinical negligence claimants and those seeking judicial review should consider ADR; that the topic of ADR should be considered at case management conferences; and the courts and the Lord Chancellor's Department should raise the profile of ADR.

The new approach to litigation advocated by Lord Woolf, with its profound implications for the whole of the civil justice system, had actually started to emerge just before the *Access to Justice* interim report was published. In a January 1995 Practice Direction issued by the Lord Chief Justice and the Vice-Chancellor, introducing what was said to be the first of a wide range of procedural reforms and improvements, Lord Bingham CJ said,

> 'the aim is to try and change the whole culture, the ethos applying to the field of civil litigation'.

As part of this change, the courts in England and Wales had begun to devise an express duty on lawyers to consider using ADR. A consistent source of encouragement since the mid-1990s has been the Commercial Court, which issued its *Practice Note: Commercial Court; Alternative Dispute Resolution* in 1994,[2] requiring lawyers to bring ADR to their client's attention. The Practice Note required legal advisers in all cases to:

'(a)    consider with their clients and the other parties concerned the possibility of attempting to resolve the particular dispute or particular issues by mediation, conciliation or otherwise; and

(b)    ensure that parties are fully informed as to the most cost-effective means of resolving the particular dispute.'

---

1 Recommendation 42.
2 [1994] 1 All ER 34.

Whilst this stopped short of making engagement in ADR a mandatory step in the court process, it did make it virtually mandatory for lawyers to **consider** ADR with both client and other parties. The Commercial Court's subsequent track record shows that parties have taken this judicial encouragement very seriously, making the Commercial Court probably the most effective forum in which gentle but firm judicial persuasion to try ADR has operated well. From the start, the court's judges have required a high level of understanding among commercial practitioners about ADR and its practical application to commercial cases. Take-up in this sector has consequently been at an increasingly high level, as satisfaction levels have increased with experience. The judges have developed various types of order as their contribution to this development. These are discussed in more detail in **Chapter 5** below.

The Commercial Court's approach was subsumed in general terms across the High Court by the 1995 Practice Note (Civil Litigation: Case Management)[3] issued by the Lord Chief Justice (touched upon above), introducing a case management role for judges in all civil cases for the first time. A slightly different approach was adopted. Legal advisers conducting cases were required to lodge a checklist at least two months before trial. This included questions as to whether the advisers had discussed the possibility of using ADR, both with their client and with the other side, and whether they considered that some form of ADR might assist in resolving or narrowing the issues.

In response to Lord Woolf's particular concerns about clinical negligence claims, Queen's Bench Practice Direction 49 was issued on 16 November 1996, dealing with cases in the specialist Clinical Negligence list in the Queen's Bench Division. This required the parties to state at the first summons for directions 'whether ADR has been considered and if not why not and if ADR has been rejected why this is so'.

This lacked the specific requirement for mutuality of approach characterised by the Commercial Court. The ADR enquiry by the court was arguably a little too early in the process of exchange of expert opinions. ADR was not made mandatory.

There can be no doubt that what has followed, culminating in the Civil Procedure Rules 1998 (CPR) and the Access to Justice Act 1999, has radically and irrevocably changed the face of civil litigation and the culture in which it operates. As a result, ADR has been brought firmly into the mainstream of dispute resolution in England and Wales, and has become a significant topic for debate in the Court of Appeal, as the rest of Part B of this book shows. There are signs of parallel reforms in the closely

---

3 [1995] 1 All ER 385.

related jurisdictions of Scotland, Northern Ireland and the Irish Republic. Following a Green Paper issued in 2002, the European Commission published a Draft Directive and Code of Conduct for mediation in 2004 as part of its developing policy over ADR, given its growth in significance throughout the enlarged European Community, with many of the newer states actively engaged in embodying ADR into their reformed civil justice systems. These are considered in more detail in **Chapter 10**.

## 4.2  The Civil Procedure Rules 1998

The CPR came into effect on 26 April 1999. They represent the most extensive overhaul of the civil justice system since the Judicature Acts 1873–75, and embody throughout the aspirations for change already articulated by Lord Woolf (then Master of the Rolls and later Lord Chief Justice) and Lord Bingham (then Lord Chief Justice).

The significance of the CPR goes far beyond a mere rationalisation of High Court and County Court procedure into one coherent and reasonably readable set of procedural rules for most types of claim, convenient though this may have been. It has been the change of culture in litigation to a higher level of inter-party co-operation, as clearly demanded and intended by Lord Woolf, that the CPR were designed to deliver and which has been substantially achieved. Such a change is entirely congruent with the culture in which ADR will flourish. Co-operative problem-solving is welcomed, and arid confrontation, procedural warfare and aggressive positioning all face the risk of being penalised by costs sanctions. It is, perhaps, this fundamental culture change that is the greatest surprise and the greatest achievement of the civil justice reforms. The results of the revolution in relation to costs and funding (which we also discuss in outline below)[4] remain less clearly positive.

We set out below some of the specific ways in which the CPR have sought to achieve this culture change, commenting on the inter-relationship between the CPR and ADR processes.

### 4.2.1  The overriding objective and active case management

For the first time in this (and maybe any) jurisdiction, the court set itself an overriding objective, to be found at the very head of the CPR 1998 in Pt 1. It is a guide for all court users – lawyers, judges and the public as a whole – as to the essential purpose of the civil litigation process against which to test any issue that may arise. The overriding objective is such a

---

4 See **Chapter 8**.

novelty and so fundamental to the effect of the CPR and the place of ADR within the new scheme of things, that we set out the key provisions in full (and we have emphasised certain important phrases):

'**CPR 1.1** (1) These Rules are a new procedural code with the overriding objective of *enabling the court to deal with cases justly.*

(2) Dealing with a case justly includes, so far as practicable:

(a) ensuring that the parties are on an equal footing;

(b) saving expense;

(c) dealing with cases in ways which are proportionate to the amount of money involved, the importance of the case, the complexity of the issues and to the parties' financial position;

(d) ensuring that it is dealt with expeditiously and fairly;

(e) allotting to it an appropriate share of the court's resources.'

The court is placed under an obligation to further the overriding objective by **actively managing cases**, a phrase which is defined in CPR Pt, 1.4(2) to include:

'**CPR 1.4** (2) (a) encouraging the parties to co-operate with each other in the conduct of the proceedings[5];

(b) identifying the issues at an early stage;

(c) deciding promptly which issues need full investigation and trial and accordingly disposing summarily of the others;

(d) deciding the order in which issues are to be resolved;

(e) **encouraging the parties to use an alternative dispute resolution procedure if the court considers that to be appropriate and facilitating the use of such procedure;**

(f) helping the parties to settle the whole or part of a case;

(g) fixing timetables or otherwise controlling the progress of the case;

---

5 Tellingly, this is a new illustration of active case management which heads the list in the final version of the CPR but which did not appear in the first draft.

(h) considering whether the likely benefits of taking a particular step will justify the cost of taking it;

(i) dealing with as many aspects of the case as it can on the same occasion;

(j) dealing with the case without the parties needing to attend court;

(k) making appropriate use of technology; and

(l) giving directions to ensure that the trial of a case proceeds quickly and efficiently.'

Part of the change in culture produced by CPR Pt 1 was achieved simply by transferring control over the pace and conduct of litigation from the legal profession to judicial case management. A further very significant engine for change is its emphasis on requiring a co-operative approach to the conduct of litigation.

It is a highly significant demonstration of the culture change which the Woolf reforms aimed to achieve that the delineation of active case management in CPR Pt 1.4(2), set out above is fully congruent with the aims and objectives of ADR. Indeed, the management obligations laid on the court might themselves (with minor modifications) describe what a mediator seeks to do. The specific mention of ADR at para 1.4(2)(e) was the first official recognition of ADR in the court rules in England and Wales, and is perhaps the best indication of its arrival in the mainstream of civil justice. Commenting retrospectively in 2005 on ADR's place in civil justice in the appeal case of *Burchell v Bullard*,[6] Lord Justice Ward spoke of:

'not only the high rate of a successful outcome being achieved by mediation but also its importance as a track to a just result running parallel with that of the court system. Both have a proper part to play in the administration of justice. The court has given its stamp of approval to mediation and it is now the legal profession which must become fully aware of and acknowledge its value.'

### 4.2.2 Pre-action conduct and the protocols

The CPR introduced three more related concepts which have revolutionised thinking and practice over strategy, timing and tactics among litigators.

#### 4.2.2.1 Pre-action conduct

Under CPR Pt 44.5, the court became entitled to take into account in determining what costs orders to make in any case the reasonableness of

6 [2005] EWCA Civ 358 at para 43.

*pre-action* conduct as well as what it has always examined, namely post-action conduct of each party. This most fundamental change enshrined in the CPR was prefigured by Lord Woolf's remark in Chapter 7 of his Final Report, where he said that his recommendations were intended, among other objectives, to'make the court's powers to make orders for costs a more effective incentive for responsible behaviour and a more compelling deterrent against unreasonable behaviour'.

If proceedings are, in a court's opinion, unjustifiably or prematurely issued, even an apparently 'successful' party may be penalised in costs. Until the CPR, judges were extremely reluctant to penalise perceived pre-action misconduct, or indeed post-action 'misconduct' by a party who broadly won the litigation. The interest of the judges in how parties behave prior to issue of proceedings has been increasing, chiefly through the development of pre-action protocols to define reasonable pre-issue conduct.

### 4.2.2.2   The pre-action protocols

The CPR append pre-action protocols which give guidance as to what best practice is before proceedings are issued. The protocols, initially drafted by sector practitioners rather than either the Executive or Judiciary, in effect define in broad terms what constitutes reasonable pre-action conduct, providing a yardstick against which the judge can later, if necessary, assess the reasonableness of a party's approach to pre-action behaviour. The first to be published covered the specialist sectors of personal injury and clinical negligence. These have been followed by protocols relating to construction and engineering, defamation, professional negligence, judicial review, disease and illness, housing disrepair and possession actions over rent arrears, with others still coming. Until 2006, each took a slightly different approach to pre-action disclosure of positions and evidence, and also to pre-action negotiation. The Practice Direction to the protocols made it quite clear that actions of all kinds should be conducted in the spirit which informs these protocols and, in April 2003,[7] were amended to provide[8] that the letter of claim should:

> 'state (if this is so) that the claimant wishes to enter into mediation or another alternative method of dispute resolution, and draw attention to the court's powers to impose sanctions for failure to comply with this practice direction',

with a reciprocal requirement required in the letter of response.

The 41st amendment to the CPR, effective as from 6 April 2006, introduced a standardised approach to ADR for each of the protocols and their Practice

---

7  30th amendment to CPR.
8  in para 4.3(f) and (g).

Direction, largely (it is believed) at the initiative of the judiciary. All of them now embody a common requirement:

'The parties should consider whether some form of alternative dispute resolution procedure would be more suitable than litigation, and if so, endeavour to agree which form to adopt. Both the Claimant and Defendant may be required by the Court to provide evidence that alternative means of resolving their dispute were considered. The Courts take the view that litigation should be a last resort, and that claims should not be issued prematurely when a settlement is still being actively explored. Parties are warned that if the protocol is not followed (including this paragraph) then the Court must have regard to such conduct when determining costs.'

Each protocol goes on to summarise methods appropriate for each sector which might be adopted. Common to each sector and to the Practice Direction (which covers disputes where there is no applicable protocol) are the following:

– Discussion and negotiation;
– Early neutral evaluation by an independent third party;
– Mediation – a form of facilitated negotiation assisted by an independent neutral party.

Each protocol and the Practice Direction concludes with the statement:

'It is expressly recognised that no party can or should be forced to mediate or enter into any form of ADR.'

As we shall see in **Chapters 5** and **6,** this bald statement is not perhaps quite as emphatic or clear as it may seem to be, and may yet both be a source of controversy, and also be subject to amendment.

### 4.2.2.3   Pre-action offers to settle

Offers to settle, dealing with both monetary and non-monetary proposals, can now be made before issue of proceedings by any party, and which, if not accepted, can have adverse costs and interest consequences for the offeree. The details are more fully set out under **4.3.6** below, which deals with Pt 36 offers and payments into court. While so-called *Calderbank* letters[9] were used to try to achieve a similar effect, their true effectiveness was much more doubtful than the much clearer regime now established under the CPR.

---

9 Derived from the important family case of *Calderbank v Calderbank* [1975] 3 All ER 333.

Even when not followed by a payment into court as required by CPR Pt 36.10(3), a pre-action offer which broadly complies with all other CPR Pt 36 requirements may be effective in shifting costs liability where that offer is not beaten.[10] Pre-action offers to mediate may also, if ignored, give rise to costs sanctions against a refusing party.[11]

For these three reasons, there is now serious pressure on parties to consider settlement through ADR or otherwise before proceedings are issued. The importance of generating such pressure derives from the objectives of the protocols, which (as their Practice Direction[12] sets out) are:

'(1)   to encourage the exchange of early and full information about the prospective legal claim,

(2)   to enable parties to avoid litigation by agreeing a settlement of the claim before the commencement of proceedings,

(3)   to support the efficient management of proceedings where litigation cannot be avoided.'

They are intended to generate sufficient exchange of information before issue to improve the chances of settlement without the need for proceedings, and thus to maximise costs savings. However, compliance is seen inevitably to lead to the 'front-loading' of work and thus additional costs. While it is true that the numbers of issued cases have reduced markedly since the CPR came into effect,[13] overall costs seem not to have reduced much if at all, and this may be one period in the life of disputes where the cost-saving dividend from front-loading still remains to be secured.

### 4.2.3   Stays for ADR and settlement at allocation stage: the multi-track and fast-track

The one moment when the CPR specifically raise the possibility of ADR is at the allocation stage, when the court decides, assisted by the comments of the parties, into which track the claim should be allocated. This process is triggered by filing and serving a defence to the claim, at which point the parties must file an allocation questionnaire, the claimant normally either paying an allocation fee or being struck out. Pt 26.4 provides that:

'(1)   A party may when filing the completed allocation questionnaire make a written request for the proceedings to be stayed while

---

10  *Stokes Pension Fund Trustees v Western Power Distribution* [2005] EWCA Civ 854.
11  *Burchell v Bullard*, above fn 5.
12  At para 1.4.
13  For instance, from roughly 9,800 Chancery and 107,000 Queen's Bench proceedings in 1998 to 5,800 Chancery and 15,300 in 2004, and from 2.01 million county court money claims in 1998 to 1.87 million in 2004.

> the parties try to settle the case by alternative dispute resolution or other means.
>
> (2) Where –
>
> (a) all parties request a stay under para (1); or
>
> (b) the court, of its own initiative, considers that such a stay would be appropriate, the court will direct that the proceedings be stayed for one month.
>
> (3) The court may extend the stay until such date or for such period as it considers appropriate.'

Though this is the first reference to a time when the courts might order ADR after inter-party discussion, experience from the courts suggests that this is happening less at allocation stage than at case management conferences and pre-trial reviews. The Allocation Questionnaire sent out by the court asks at Question A: 'Do you wish there to be a one month stay to attempt to settle the case?'

The form's guidance notes talk about the parties being "able to negotiate a settlement" but there is no specific mention of ADR as the group of processes to be used, as there is in CPR Pt 26.4.

As we shall see later, it is important that by the time of mediation, each party should have sufficient information available to be able to advise and consider settlement safely and responsibly. Allocation stage is relatively soon after issue of proceedings, with only the additional clarity as to the issues brought by the exchanges of statements of case. Especially, if a protocol has been properly followed or the spirit of the protocols fully observed, settlement by negotiation or mediation should be tried before issue of proceedings. Little will have changed by allocation stage apart from the formal definition of issues in the Statements of Case, though this may be the time that a party keen to mediate has the first opportunity to seek an ADR Order against a party reluctant to engage in mediation. If a case is not ready for mediation by allocation stage, then mediation can and should be left until later. In fast-track cases, dealing with claims up to £15,000 in value, there may well not be a directions hearing. In multi-track cases, there will usually be at least one case management conference and a pre-trial review, both of which would almost certainly be good occasions to see whether ADR has anything to offer.

It should be noted that Pt 26.4 provides for the court *of its own motion* to order a stay where it thinks it appropriate, regardless of the wishes of either party. An instance of judicial intervention at the earliest is to be found in the case of *C v RHL*,[14] in which Colman J was asked to grant

---

14 [2005] EWHC 873 (Comm).

an anti-suit injunction to stop international proceedings in relation to a share sale dispute. Instead, he suggested that the overall interests of all parties would be served by referral to mediation, commenting that: 'That procedure provides scope for the kind of commercial solution to these disputes which it is beyond the power of the court or of the ICC arbitrators to engender.'

He consequently made an ADR in Commercial Court form. These will be discussed in more detail in **Chapter 5**.

There is no essential need for existing proceedings to be stayed for ADR. If a party or the court believes that a request for ADR is another party's ploy to gain time by delay, the timetable for the case can if desired continue unabated, with costs continuing to be incurred meanwhile. It is only where all parties agree to engage in ADR in good faith that there is little point in expending more time and cost on forwarding litigation when there is a good chance that ADR will settle it.[15]

### 4.2.4 Case management and ADR

A provision was introduced into the CPR by the 41st amendment in October 2005 which reflects the options for the court to make directions about ADR at allocation where there is no allocation or case management hearing. Paragraph 4.10 of the Practice Direction made in relation to CPR Pt 29 provides that:

> 'Where the court is to give directions on its own initiative without holding a case management conference and it is not aware of any steps taken by the parties other than the exchange of statements of case, its general approach will be:
>
> (1) to give directions for the filing and service of any further information required to clarify either party's case,
>
> (2) to direct standard disclosure between the parties,
>
> (3) to direct the disclosure of witness statements by way of simultaneous exchange,
>
> (4) to give directions for a single joint expert on any appropriate issue unless there is a good reason not to do so,
>
> (5) unless para 4.11 (below) applies, to direct disclosure of experts' reports by way of simultaneous exchange on those issues where a single joint expert is not directed,

---

15 For a case where proceedings were stayed (partly) for failure to observe the TCC Pre-action protocol, see *DGT Steel Cladding Ltd v Cubitt Building* [2007] EWHC 1584 (TCC).

(6) if experts' reports are not agreed, to direct a discussion between experts for the purpose set out in rule 35.12(1) and the preparation of a statement under rule 35.12(3),

(7) to list a case management conference to take place after the date for compliance with those directions,

(8) to specify a trial period; and

(9) **in such cases as the court thinks appropriate, the court may give directions requiring the parties to consider ADR. Such directions may be, for example, in the following terms:**

**"The parties shall by [date] consider whether the case is capable of resolution by ADR. If any party considers that the case is unsuitable for resolution by ADR, that party shall be prepared to justify that decision at the conclusion of the trial, should the judge consider that such means of resolution were appropriate, when he is considering the appropriate costs order to make.**

**The party considering the case unsuitable for ADR shall, not less than 28 days before the commencement of the trial, file with the court a witness statement without prejudice save as to costs, giving reasons upon which they rely for saying that the case was unsuitable."'**

This makes it possible for a procedural judge to make such an Order in fast-track cases where there is normally no Case Management Conference. Implicitly, such a direction can be also be made at a Case Management Conference where the parties actually attend, as is the norm in clinical negligence cases for which Master Ungley developed the wording of this Order. Its wider use was approved by the Court of Appeal in *Halsey v Milton Keynes NHS Trust*.[16] The Order does not define what type of ADR is to be used.

### 4.2.5 The specialist jurisdictions and Court Guides

The CPR are not the sole source of procedural wisdom for court users. Several specialist jurisdictions have published their own guides, sometimes establishing procedures appreciably different from the mainstream provisions of the CPR, the Admiralty and Commercial Court Guide being the prime example. This disapplies CPR Pt 26.4 (which provides for a stay of proceedings while settlement by ADR or otherwise is explored), but reproduces and extends much of what was in the Commercial Court Practice Direction about ADR. Part G of the Guide deals with the topic of

---

16 [2004] EWCA Civ 576; [2004] 4 All ER 920 at para 32: see **Chapter 6** for a full discussion of its significance.

ADR. Adjournment for ADR is preserved; the Commercial Court judges will in appropriate cases invite the parties to consider ADR and may make orders to encourage its deployment, setting out a draft order in Appendix 7. Para G1.4 provides that:

> '**G1.4** Legal representatives should in all cases consider with their clients and the other parties concerned the possibility of attempting to resolve the dispute or particular issues by ADR.'

The Practice Guides issued by the Chancery Division,[17] the Queen's Bench Division,[18] the Technology and Construction[19] and Mercantile Courts[20] all specifically raise such a possibility in various ways and at various stages to suit such specialist types of case.

### 4.2.6 Small claims track cases

The small claims track developed from the most successful innovation in the civil justice system in the late 20th century, namely the County Court small claims procedure. With legal costs virtually never being awarded whoever wins, it has been kept as a simple and accessible forum for low value disputes. The current jurisdiction is up to £5000 for money claims except personal injury, but the ceiling for personal injury is much lower at £1000. Claims higher than that level will normally be fast-track and will attract a costs award for the successful party in addition to damages. Court schemes for mediating small claims track cases were piloted in Exeter and Manchester County Courts, and the Manchester model, using an in-house staff mediator, has been deployed across a number of court areas.

### 4.2.7 Part 36 offers and settlement procedures

The CPR extend the long-standing right of a defendant to seek to transfer a potential costs liability from defendant to claimant by making a payment into court, in effect 'without prejudice except as to costs', in several important ways. By virtue of CPR Pt 36, both claimants and defendants can now make a formal offer to settle either before or after proceedings are issued, indicating what they would be prepared to pay or accept, and also specifying any acceptable non-monetary terms for a settlement agreement. Defendants do not have to pay the amount offered into court to await judgment. If the offer is accepted, the defendant has 14 days to pay the amount, and in default the claimant can enter judgment for the amount of the offer.[21] Claimants who do better at trial than a defendant's Pt 36

---

17 Chapter 17.
18 Chapter 6.6, re-issued in January 2007 with specific contact details for the National Mediation Helpline.
19 See Section 7.
20 Appendix A(1) questions 32–35 and A(3) question 10.
21 See CPR 44th amendment, effective from 6 April 2007.

offer will normally be awarded their standard costs in addition to their remedy, and (if the defendant has behaved particularly unreasonably) possibly indemnity costs. Claimants who do less well than a Pt 36 offer will normally (but not always) have to pay both sides' costs from the date of the Pt 36 offer. Defendants who reject a claimant's Pt 36 offer and do worse at trial can expect penal interest at anything up to 10 per cent above current base rate to be awarded on damages and costs, the latter probably being awarded on a indemnity basis. However, there have been a number of cases in which the courts have departed from these normal expectations, giving rise to uncertainty for advisers in being able to predict accurately what costs orders a judge might make.[22]

Part 36 procedure has almost certainly led already to more settlements, both before and after issue of proceedings. Mediations are often preceded by such offers and very often followed by them if a case does not settle. The mediation throws up more information upon which to assess the right level for such a proposal to be made. Nothing obliges a Pt 36 offer to match what was offered at a mediation, and this adds an extra dimension to negotiations at a mediation.

Part 36 offers and their specific impact on the mediation process are considered in more detail in **Chapter 8**, in the context of costs and funding issues.

### 4.2.8  Costs

Lord Woolf regarded the problem of costs as 'the most serious problem besetting our litigation system'. As we have seen in relation to the pre-action protocols, the CPR give permission for judges to take unreasonable pre-action conduct into account in determining costs orders even against otherwise successful parties. The same range of tools is available to deal with post-issue unreasonableness. These include summary orders for costs on interim hearings, payable immediately; full information about costs expended and anticipated to be prepared and exchanged at every case management occasion; and orders for costs to be based on conduct, which is specifically said in Pt 44.3(5) to include:

'(a)  conduct before as well as during the proceedings and in particular the extent to which the parties followed any relevant pre-action protocol;

(b)  whether it was reasonable for a party to raise, pursue or contest a particular allegation or issue;

(c)  the manner in which a party has pursued or defended his case or a particular allegation or issue;

---

22  See for instance *Ford v GKR* [2000] 1 All ER 802, *Painting v University of Oxford* [2005] EWCA Civ 161 for cases on either side, and *par excellence, Dunnett v Railtrack* [2002] EWCA Civ 303; [2002] 2 All ER 850.

(d)  whether a claimant who has succeeded in his claim, in whole or in part, exaggerated his claim.'

The other key feature to the new costs regime is the requirement of *proportionality* between the costs incurred and claimed by the receiving party and the subject matter of the litigation. Costs payable on the (usual) standard basis which are disproportionate to the amount or importance of the litigation will be disallowed. CPR Pt 44.5(1) provides that, in deciding how much should be allowed for costs, the court must have regard to all the circumstances in deciding (when applying the standard basis for assessment) whether costs were proportionately and reasonably incurred and were proportionate and reasonable in amount. It is only when costs are to be assessed on an indemnity basis that proportionality is ignored. This emphasis picks up on the provisions of CPR Pt 1.1(2)(c) and the overriding objective. Dealing with cases justly is said to include adopting ways which

'are proportionate to the amount involved in the case, to the importance of the case, to the complexity of the issues and to the financial position of each party'.

The net effect of these linked provisions, put bluntly, is that a party can 'succeed' in litigation, but because of either unreasonable or disproportionate conduct of the claim may not 'win' in terms of obtaining all or most of the legal costs of winning. In an extreme case, the court even has jurisdiction to order the 'winning' party to pay costs to a 'losing' party.[23]

The courts have already demonstrated their willingness to make tougher costs orders, sometimes much to the surprise of the party which might have thought it had 'won', especially under the pre-CPR regime. The net result for mediators will be to provide ample grounds for testing whether success at trial might or not be of doubtful worth. The attractions of settling a case on a party's own terms will increase in proportion to the uncertainty of the litigated outcome, and uncertainty over the exercise of wide judicial discretion is found in the costs aspect of the CPR more than any other.

The implications of the court's costs jurisdiction for mediation practice are considered in more detail in **Chapter 8**.

## 4.3   Choices in litigation and ADR: which is truly alternative?

Translated into the ADR field, all these issues have important implications. The choice and timing of methods to resolve a dispute is extensive. The

---

23 As happened over costs prior to a Pt 36 offer in *P4 v Unite Integrated Systems* [2006] EWHC (TCC) 2924, in a case where, had the successful defendant not refused mediation, Ramsey J would have awarded all costs against the unsuccessful claimant.

spectrum stretches from the informality of direct negotiations, through the flexible semi-formality of mediation in which parties choose whether or not to settle, to processes requiring third-party adjudication like arbitration and litigation at the other end. A careful decision has to be made now whether all proper avenues have been explored before issuing proceedings. Should negotiations be tried first? Should both claimant and defendant make a Pt 36 offer first? Even if Pt 36 offers have been tried and failed to produce a settlement, is it not right to try ADR then, before proceedings are started? Is it negligent, or at least risky, *not* to do so, bearing in mind the court's likely approach to costs? Parties are certainly writing letters to each other 'without prejudice save as to costs', indicating willingness to mediate a case before issue if all other ways of settling have failed to produce a settlement, indicating that later reference will be made to that letter if their opponent spurns the invitation. The Pre-action Protocols and their Practice Direction specifically warn that adverse costs consequences may follow if reasonable attempts are not made to settle before issue of proceedings.

Furthermore, the choice is not one to be made solely at the start of the claim and before issue of proceedings. It needs continually to be re-visited and re-made later in the litigation process. For example, when new information comes to light following disclosure of documents or witness evidence, there may be an increased desire either to settle, or alternatively, to move away from settlement. Each time a choice of tactic has to be made, ADR must be one of the options to be considered. It should, therefore, be addressed with the client prior to the issue of proceedings and at regular stages during the process of litigation. There is nothing new or 'alternative' about the principle. It is simply an inherent feature of the lawyer – client relationship. What is new is the range of techniques available.

## 4.4    Court schemes and ADR research

In parallel with the reforms in civil procedure, efforts have been made to investigate the effectiveness of ADR through a number of pilot schemes, two of which involved associated academic research to appraise effectiveness in a number of ways. We look very briefly at three of these schemes, though we recommend study of the published reports for detailed understanding of the findings.

### 4.4.1   The Central London County Court scheme

The Central London County Court is the premier County Court trial centre for civil cases in London, and can take cases from anywhere in the country, including transfers of High Court cases. In 1996, the judges agreed to set up a pilot scheme which offered voluntary mediation in any defended case in the court involving claims of over £3,000. The scheme was appraised by Professor Hazel Genn over two years. Her report was published by the Lord Chancellor's Department in July 1998 (Research Paper 5/98, available free from the LCD). The scheme has continued with increased take-up and apparent benefit.

The model used was time-limited (three-hour) mediations at the court between 4.30 and 7.30 pm. During the pilot period, take-up was low, but the report's findings indicated that mediation provided a satisfying way of settling disputes, reducing conflict and cost where it succeeded, with positive feedback from both parties and lawyers. Professor Genn's report addresses these issues in detail, but perhaps most tellingly she identified the need to:

> 'focus on the value that mediation adds to normal settlement negotiations between solicitors, rather than simply setting up mediation in opposition to trial. The experience of the profession is that most cases are not, in the end, tried. Mediation *can* add value to the normal claims settlement process in civil disputes. It offers a cathartic pseudo 'day in court' to parties; it gets cards on the table and all the parties around the table; and, with the help of a skilled mediator, it introduces some authoritative objectivity into the assessment of the strengths and weaknesses of the parties' claims.'

The scheme outlasted its pilot period and remains in place. It is being used as a model for other schemes regionally.

A further pilot scheme was also established at Central London County Court, authorised under the CPR, which enabled cases to be referred compulsorily to mediation unless one or both parties persuade the court to let them opt out of the mandated mediation. It mirrored a similar scheme in Ontario where over 3,000 cases were mediated within a two-year period. The Central London opt-out scheme lasted for one year and gave rise to numerous applications to opt out. It is understood that almost all applications to opt out were refused. However, throughput was not high, and though the settlement rate was surprisingly higher than the voluntary scheme, the amount of judicial time required to police it in its short life was probably regarded as disproportionate. The compulsory scheme is reviewed exhaustively in Twisting Arms: court referred and court linked mediation under judicial pressure, by Professors Hazel Genn and Paul Fenn and others. Published in 2007 by the Ministry of Justice.[24]

Court schemes of varying designs have been established in a number of major County Courts in England and Wales,[25] with further developments

---

24 Ministry of Justice research series 1/07.
25 These include Birmingham, Manchester, Leeds, Newcastle, Exeter, Cardiff, Swansea and Guildford.

such as a National Mediation Helpline and Mediation Awareness Weeks being initiated by the Department for Constitutional Affairs.

### 4.4.2 The NHS pilot scheme and research report

In April 1995, a little before the Central London pilot scheme began, the National Health Service Executive initiated a pilot scheme to assess mediation as a tool for dealing with clinical negligence claims. Such claims are highly technical, usually funded on both sides out of the public purse, and have a relatively low success rate for claimants. Yet by 1995, there was a burgeoning interest in claiming against health professionals which has shown little sign of waning ever since.

This was a highly imaginative step, as there was virtually no track record for mediation of clinical negligence in the United Kingdom at the time that the pilot was set up. The investigation went in parallel with the implementation of new complaints procedures following the Wilson report. These were introduced in 1996, in the hope that they would provide the 'soft' remedies of apology, explanation, reassurance and so on, often regarded as fundamentally important to dissatisfied patients, though excluding consideration of monetary compensation, which was left to the litigation process.

Again, take-up of the offer of almost free mediation in the two Health Regions covered was very low, for reasons explained in Professor Linda Mulcahy's report on the pilot *Mediating medical negligence claims: an option for the future?* (published by the Stationery Office in January 2000, though completed in late 1998). Yet the findings on those cases investigated were very positive. High levels of satisfaction were found among both parties and lawyers, as contrasted with high levels (about 70 per cent) of considerable dissatisfaction among parties with traditional litigation, even where they had obtained compensation. The report concluded that:

> 'there are considerable benefits to mediated settlement and that plaintiffs [sic] in particular have much to gain . . . .
>
> It clearly has the potential to encourage more appropriate and effective resolution of disputes.'

### 4.4.3 The Court of Appeal Mediation Scheme

Perhaps, the most surprising initiative has been the Court of Appeal Mediation Scheme, initially established on a voluntary basis in 1997. How can ADR really assist in cases where a judicial decision has already been made, which now is sought to be reviewed on technical grounds by a higher court? The simple answer is that many appeals are subject to compromise already, and mediation can assist parties to reappraise their risks in the light of permission to appeal having been granted by a single Lord Justice on the basis that such an appeal has a 'real prospect of success'.[26]

By April 2000, nearly 40 cases had been through the scheme, with a settlement rate of about 45 per cent, perhaps not surprisingly lower than settlement rates of cases before trial at first instance. A further 13 per cent settled before the appeal was heard. Again there were clear signs of success.

In her report *Court-based initiatives for non-family civil disputes,* published in 2002, Professor Hazel Genn pointed out the limitations of the scheme. It was revised and relaunched in 2003, with moderate fees being payable by both parties to fund external administration by a contracted ADR provider and payment of fees to mediators on a panel chosen by the Court itself. These changes produced a markedly more successful scheme since then, with over 70 mediations in its first three years and a settlement rate of just above 50 per cent, and higher in some sectors like personal injury.

## 4.5   An ADR jurisprudence

Two main questions have occupied the courts in thinking about judicial intervention in relation to ADR since the CPR. These are:

(1)   Can and should the courts *order* parties to undertake ADR; and

(2)   Can and should the courts *impose costs or other sanctions on* parties who unreasonably refuse to engage in ADR?

The first option, if legitimate, makes it possible for judges to try to ensure that parties use ADR before proceedings are concluded by judgment, with settlement probably saving appreciable costs for the benefit of the parties. The second option, if legitimate, is too late to influence conduct of that particular case before trial, but might be seen as having the force of precedent to advisers generally, in warning them of what might happen to them if they act unreasonably in subsequent litigation. The problem behind these questions is the same: how should courts take steps to achieve the overriding objective by use of this particular tool of active case management, especially in the light of the view that ADR is a purely voluntary process. Ordering a party into ADR perhaps offends the concept of voluntary choice, whereas penalising someone for not voluntarily choosing to engage in ADR sounds like a contradiction. There is also the question of a litigant's right to access to the courts. Each of these questions will be discussed in turn in the following chapters.

---

26  See CPR, Pt 52.3(6).

# Chapter 5

# The courts and ADR Orders

## 5.1 Mediation as a necessarily voluntary process?

In the Preface to the second edition of this book, published in 2000, we commented on the irony that the development of a consensual informal process has had to be fostered by a degree of compulsion or pressure generated within the orthodox legal system. This was written well before the leading cases of *Dunnett v Railtrack*[1] and *Halsey v Milton Keynes NHS Trust*[2] began to transform thinking about ADR among civil practitioners. We said then that: 'one of the inherent benefits of ADR has always been the concept of voluntary engagement in the process.' 'Engagement', is of course, an ambiguous word, embracing both **encouraging engagement** in ADR at the outset as well as **continued engagement** in ADR, once started. None of the authors would ever seek to challenge the second gloss, but views have perhaps shifted some way in relation to the first. We would strongly argue that parties must be free without penalty to disengage from mediation once started, if they decide in good faith that it no longer serves their interests. What is much less certain is whether external judicial pressure upon parties to engage less than entirely voluntarily in mediation necessarily reduces the effectiveness of the process in any way. We noted in the previous chapter the apparent contradiction about ordering parties to engage in a 'voluntary' process. We think that a valid distinction should be drawn between compelling parties to engage in mediation, which might perhaps be regarded as justifiable, as contrasted with compelling them to continue in mediation once started, let alone requiring them to reach a settlement, which is certainly unjustified. If so, has this distinction been drawn by the courts when confronted with these issues?

After all, ADR is a compulsory part of civil procedure in many common law jurisdictions around the globe, even where there is also provision for judge-chaired settlement conferences shortly before trial. It remains a significant issue for the English civil justice system and its approach to ADR to decide whether the more mature deployment (for better or worse) of integrated ADR in other jurisdictions suits England and Wales or not. International experience does make it clear that there

---

1 [2002] 2 All ER 850; [2002] EWCA Civ 303
2 [2004] 4 All ER 920; [2002] EWCA Cia 576.

is no **necessary** jurisprudential or practical principle requiring that engagement in ADR at the outset must be voluntary. Indeed, it was in 2004 that CEDR consciously removed the word 'voluntary' from its standard definition of mediation (which adequately cross-references the position).[3]

English courts and rule-makers have so far shied away from truly mandatory ADR. Dyson LJ in *Halsey v Milton Keynes NHS Trust* quotes the 2003 White Book as follows:

> 'The hallmark of ADR procedures, and perhaps the key to their effectiveness in individual cases, is that they are processes voluntarily entered into by the parties in dispute, with outcomes, if the parties so wish, which are non-binding. Consequently the court cannot direct that such methods be used but may merely facilitate and encourage.'[4]

No distinction is drawn in that passage between voluntary entry and voluntarily continuing to participate in ADR, and the reference to non-binding outcomes as a justification is a little opaque, as almost all mediation parties normally seek agreed outcomes that bind all participants. So, whether this passage is based on detailed research and understanding of the field is open to question.

The second thread of objection to compulsion stems from a view that to impose mediation on unwilling parties might, as a matter of principle, be in breach of Article 6 of the European Convention on Human Rights. To order parties to mediate, it is said, deprives them of their right to 'a fair and public hearing within a reasonable time by an independent and impartial tribunal established by law'.[5] This issue will be discussed in more detail in **Chapter 10**.

However, judges in the Commercial Court have been making self-styled ADR orders since the mid-1990s which put considerable pressure on parties to engage in ADR against the background that they might later regard reluctance or failure to have done so in good faith as a reason for a costs penalty. The orders do not usually spell out such risks. The wording is firm and persuasive, but the orders remain tactfully silent over the consequences of refusal. Some judges have been prepared to be somewhat more assertive where parties have been shown to dally in co-operating over administrative arrangements for a mediation for ulterior reasons, for instance by not agreeing a mediator.

---

3 The new CEDR definition is set out at 1.2 above.
4 Civil Procedure 2003, para 1.4.11, quoted at Para 9 of Dyson LJ's judgment in *Halsey*: [2004] 4 All ER 920; [2004] EWCA Civ 576.
5 See Article 6(1).

## 5.2 The Commercial Court ADR Order

The starting point for any review of ADR Orders must inevitably be the draft Order contained in Appendix 7 of the Admiralty and Commercial Court Guide, which has been used by the Commercial Court since 1995, well before the CPR. As we shall see, this is still acknowledged as the classic template for such orders.

This takes the following shape:

'(1) On or before [Day 1] the parties shall exchange lists of 3 neutrals or identifying one or more panels of individuals who are available to conduct ADR procedures in the case prior to [Day 4].

(2) On or before [Day 2] the parties "shall in good faith endeavour to agree a neutral individual or panel from the lists so exchanged or provided".

(3) Failing such agreement [by Day 3], the Case Management Conference will be restored to enable the court to facilitate agreement on a neutral individual or panel.

(4) The parties **shall take such serious steps as they may be advised** to resolve their disputes by ADR procedures before the individual or panel so chosen by no later than [Day 4]

(5) If the case is not finally settled, the parties shall inform the court by letter by [Day 5] [a specified stage of the proceedings] what steps towards ADR have been taken and (without prejudice to matters of privilege) why such steps have failed. If the parties have failed to initiate ADR procedures the Case Management Conference is to be restored for further consideration of the case.

(6) [Costs].'

### 5.2.1 Good faith

There is a good deal of unfamiliar language in this form of Order, such as 'shall in good faith endeavour' and 'take such serious steps as they may be advised', with even the court offering to 'facilitate agreement' if the parties cannot agree on a neutral. In fact, no one seems to have found much difficulty in understanding what these concepts might mean, however difficult they might be to enforce.

In the Central London County Court, where their scheme has been run since 1996, a typical order made at a case management conference commences: 'The parties and legal representatives do now give serious consideration to using the mediation scheme at the court with a view to early settlement.'

In another County Court, the wording used has been that 'there be a stay of proceedings to attempt a mediated settlement until' a specified date.

There has been some reluctance among judges to accept that there can be an enforceable duty to do things 'in good faith', as opposed to enforcing an obligation 'to use best endeavours'. Some of this debate emerges in **Chapter 9** relating to the enforceability of ADR contract clauses. With a wide costs discretion, what is strictly enforceable as a matter of law may become less significant when sanctions can be imposed for unreasonable conduct. A dramatic illustration of this approach is to be found in *Rowallan Group Ltd v Edgehill Portfolio No 1*,[6] a decision of Lightman J, when he imposed indemnity costs on a claimant in summarily dismissing his claim under CPR, Pt 24 for, among other things, arranging for issue of proceedings *during* the mediation with no prior letter before action, so as to 'get in first', and then asking the mediator to enquire at the mediation whether the defendant's solicitor would accept service.

### 5.2.2 Stay of proceedings

It should be noted that the normal form of this order does not specifically provide for a stay of the proceedings. What happens in practice very often is that the ADR form of words is embedded within the main timetable for an action, to minimise any delay if ADR does not settle a claim. This will sometimes provide for the completion of certain stages (such as amendment of statements of case, disclosure, exchange of statements of witnesses of fact or some or all expert evidence) before the ADR timetable starts. It may then perhaps provide for a stay at that stage (though by no means in every case) of between one and three months, and then for further directions in default of settlement, going so far as to fix a trial date or a trial window. Some orders are simply made on the basis of a stay for a fixed period to try ADR and adjournment of all other directions. Much depends upon the stage reached in the proceedings. It would appear that as many if not more orders are made at case management conferences or on specific directions as are made at allocation stage under CPR Pt 26.4.

In one Queen's Bench claim in which the judge ordered a defendant to pay into court £10,000 as a condition of setting aside judgment in default of defence, the judge additionally ordered that the action be stayed for 28 days from the payment into court 'for the parties to explore ADR'. Exchange of witness statements of fact was ordered to take place thereafter.

---

6 [2007] EWHC 32 (Ch).

Typically a stay is ordered until a specified date, but occasionally a court will order a stay 'until the conclusion of the mediation', perhaps a rather difficult moment to define precisely. One Technology and Construction Court Order made by the assigned judge at his first consideration of the case observed that:

> 'Mediation is not an alternative trial. Resolution of the differences between the parties seems to be a reasonable prospect by mediation without enlarging on the numbers participating and it should be attempted after close of pleadings.'

The judge ordered that, following service of the Reply, there would be a stay for eight weeks, which was not to affect later dates already set in agreed directions. In the same order, the judge, as is the practice in the TCC, set the trial date.

A stay may not actually be specified, but if a period is embedded in a timetable when only ADR is required of the parties (as sometimes happens), that really is as good as ordering a stay, since there are no other procedural deadlines during that period.

Liberty to apply in respect of the stay is often specifically ordered, though the CPR probably preserve an implied right to apply anyway.

### 5.2.3  Choice of mediator and mediation machinery

The standard order appears to mandate 'good faith' choice by the parties, with the court facilitating any difficulty in reaching a decision. Some courts have been prepared to adopt a more robust approach, ordering that in default of agreement an ADR provider should have power to nominate a mediator. This happened in *Kinstreet Ltd v Balmargo Corp Ltd,* an unreported decision of Mrs Justice Arden in July 1999, in which she also made an ADR order in the teeth of opposition from at least one of the parties. In one multi-party Commercial Court case in which the standard order was made, the parties failed to agree and on reference back to the court for 'facilitation', the same judge ordered that the mediator with the support of the majority of parties from a slate of three mediators was to act.

In one unreported Chancery claim, the judge ordered 'the parties to try to settle this case by mediation' specifying a date by which this was to have occurred and for a report back to the court. It provided that CEDR was to administer the mediation and was to be 'responsible for the appointment of the mediator after consultation with the parties'.

In a major multi-party claim between a company in liquidation and its former employees, an interesting representative order was made 'in order that a process of mediation may be undertaken as soon as practicable in respect of actions ... suitable for mediation' ... between employer and employees. The lead solicitors for each side were ordered to make contact with CEDR to instruct them to administer the mediation, and apply jointly for the appointment of a mediator from CEDR's panel. A list of ten actions in which the liquidator and employees were willing to submit to mediation was to be exchanged and four actions identified for mediation. In an interesting postscript to the order, it was provided that:

> 'whereas any ensuing mediations can only continue on a voluntary basis and subject to the terms of such mediation agreements as may be entered into the Lead Solicitors ... in consultation with the mediator as appropriate shall in good faith attempt to agree a timetable, venue and procedures for mediation ...'

going on to make it clear that the mediation order was not to affect the operation of existing orders or the progress of the court action, thus not staying the action pending ADR.

Some County Courts have made orders that 'the parties try to settle this case by mediation' and identified a provider who was required to produce a list of potential mediators to facilitate agreement of a nominee by the parties. In default of agreement of a mediator by a specified time and date, the provider was to appoint a mediator, with the parties being bound by that appointment. In one such court a powerful extra paragraph was added which provided:

> 'Pursuant to the overriding objective and their duty to the court, both parties shall co-operate to implement the terms of this Order expeditiously and purposefully and without pre-conditions or qual-ifications. In the event of a party's default, the other party may apply forthwith for the defaulting party's Statement of Case to be struck out for judgment to be entered on that party's claim and for costs.'

In another unreported District Registry Queen's Bench order which had stayed a claim involving a building dispute for six weeks 'in order for a formal ADR to take place', after providing that 'the expertise of the mediator should be preferably that of an engineer/surveyor' with a knowledge of the particular technical field 'rather than a lawyer' the Order continued:

> 'Any proposals in the mediation shall be without prejudice, but if as a consequence of one party's failure to co-operate and thereby sabotage the ADR, then either party can make an application to the judge with a view to lifting the stay.'

The sanction visualised for non-co-operation over setting up a mediation ordered by the court is thus to be able to get on with the proceedings without further delay, perhaps even being able to obtain an early termination through striking out, though courts have generally been slow to do this since the CPR. However, a party who is shown at trial to have failed to co-operate over participating in a mediation will, as we shall see in **Chapter 6**, face serious risks of a costs sanction even if he wins the case on the merits.

The main point to make about the appointment provisions of the standard order is that, in this respect at least, they sound mandatory. Parties 'shall' find a mediator and set a date within a determined period. Is even this degree of mandating at risk of infringing ECHR Article 6 rights?

### 5.2.4 Costs of seeking an ADR order

Orders on applications for an ADR Order have normally been for costs in the case, though there is no reason why a party who has obstructed the other's proposal for ADR, whether made before or after issue of proceedings; should not be penalised if an ADR Order is made, either by an immediate costs sanction, or perhaps by having costs reserved to the trial judge.

### 5.2.5 Non-compliance with an ADR Order

If a party fails to co-operate over setting up a mediation despite an ADR Order in Commercial Court form, the parties are ordered to report what steps towards ADR have been taken and (without prejudice to matters of privilege) why such steps have failed. If the parties have failed to initiate ADR procedures the Case Management Conference is to be restored for further consideration of the case.

This is an enquiry as to why parties did not enter into mediation, and, as will be shown in **Chapter 6**, may give rise to costs sanctions. However, this falls well short of an enquiry as to why the mediation failed to settle the case, and whether a party failed to act reasonably at the mediation. The Commercial Court ADR Order thus underlines the important distinction between court persuasion to mediate (buttressed by sanctions), and the general restraint shown by courts from seeking to peer behind the veil of confidentiality governing a mediation, which makes the content of mediation debate and reasons for terminating it confidential even from the judge at any later stage of the same litigation.

However, the Commercial Court has apparently not found it necessary to sanction failure to comply with ADR orders made by them. Colman J, the prime mover behind the Commercial Court ADR Order, has commented that the court finds that parties simply do not ignore such orders, whatever their true status as 'Orders of the Court' might be. He was unable to recollect any instance of a case where a party ignored the procedural judge's order to mediate and returned to explain why. There have been cases where mediation was tried and did not produce a settlement, but the court will not go behind such a report. Parties have ignored judicial recommendations in other courts, however, so the true status of the order and the court's response to it has become significant, as we shall see.

## 5.3 The effect of the CPR on Commercial Court ADR Orders

When ADR orders were devised by the Commercial Court judges, there was no defined overriding objective for civil justice, as there has been since 1999. CPR Pt 1 has now identified ADR as one of the court's tools of active case management available to achieve that objective. The Commercial Court was never slow to encourage its use, and has continued to do so in largely unaltered form. But the new status of ADR as being of significance for the whole civil justice system led to the courts discussing what this meant in terms of ordering ADR more widely.

Matching the profession's general response to the CPR, there was a marked increase in the take-up of ADR immediately after their introduction, with a marked drop in the number of cases issued in the courts. Practitioners doubtlessly feared that they might indeed be criticised, and possibly face costs sanctions, if they did not try ADR. Courts began to assume that mediation would save costs and order it accordingly in various ways. In *Muman v Nagasena,*[7] a dispute over control of a Buddhist temple, the court imposed a stay until mediation had been tried. In *Guinle v Kirreh and Kinstreet v Balmargo,*[8] Mrs Justice Arden was dealing with three complex inter-related disputes. Several parties sought an ADR order; several opposed mediation. She formed the view that mediation would save huge costs. She rejected criticism that the obligation 'to take such steps as the parties might seriously be advised' to settle was meaningless, agreed that there was no need for a stay of the hearing for ADR to take place, claimed jurisdiction to make such an Order and 'directed' ADR in the terms of the Commercial Court Appendix 7 form. She cited CPR Pt 1 and noted that dealing justly included proportionality of cost, bearing in mind that one party (if unsuccessful) would not be able to afford the costs of trial. Whether there is any material difference between a direction and an order in this context is debatable.

---

7 [2000] 1 WLR 299: the court specified use of the CEDR Scheme for the National Council for Voluntary Organisations.
8 Unreported, 3 August 1999, Ch 1994 G 2999.

Courts also began to give warnings and issue advice at the conclusion of cases that parties should seriously consider ADR or run the risk of costs consequences, though such advice fell short of an order. Lord Woolf was a member of the Court of Appeal in *Dyson & Field v Leeds City Council*,[9] in which, citing CPR 1.4(2)(e) for the first time in a reported appeal, Ward LJ said that the court 'should encourage the parties to use an alternative dispute resolution procedure to bring this unhappy matter to the conclusion which it now deserves sooner rather than later'.

A claimant had successfully appealed against a judge's unexplained preference for the defendant's expert, but a re-trial was required. The Court of Appeal made it clear that they would look very unfavourably on a repeat appearance before them if the insurer rejected their recommendation to mediate, in effect requiring future mediation of the remaining issues to avoid a re-trial. Lord Woolf himself gave the lead judgment in *Cowl v Plymouth City Council*,[10] delivering powerful strictures on both parties' failure to use an available ADR process rather than the delay and cost of fiercely contested judicial review proceedings. He produced the first general warning to practitioners when he said: 'Today sufficient should be known about ADR to make the failure to adopt it, in particular where public money is involved, indefensible.'

Lord Woolf was both openly trying to influence advisers in later cases as to what the courts would expect of them, and implicitly giving guidance to procedural judges as to what they should expect of parties in terms of knowledge about ADR, and their willingness to engage in it effectively.

As we shall see in the next chapter dealing with costs sanctions, if one case can be said to have changed the course of ADR development more than any other in England and Wales, it is *Dunnett v Railtrack*.[11] No actual ADR Order was made, simply a recommendation by the single Appeal Court judge (who allowed Mrs Dunnett to appeal after losing her claim against Railtrack) that the parties should mediate through the Court of Appeal Mediation Scheme, then available *pro bono*. That recommendation took on something close to the status of an Order in its effect, and the Court of Appeal responded by depriving Railtrack of its costs.

Blackburne J followed the effect of *Guinle and Kinstreet* closely in *Shirayama v Danovo*[12] in making an ADR Order against the implacable opposition of the claimant in a dispute between the owners of County Hall

9 Unreported, 22 November, 1999 CCRTF 1998/1490/B2.
10 [2001] EWCA Civ 1935; [2002] 1 WLR 803.
11 [2002] 2 All ER 850; [2002] EWCA Civ 303.
12 [2003] EWHC 3006 (Ch).

and the Saatchi Gallery, a tenant of part. He decided in a later judgment in the same case that he could not order the attendance of a specified person at such a mediation against his will.

## 5.4   Halsey v Milton Keynes NHS Trust and the status of ADR Orders

It was not until the conjoined appeals in *Halsey v Milton Keynes General NHS Trust* and *Steel v Jones and Halliday*[13] that the Court of Appeal took the opportunity to review the status of ADR Orders generally and the proper approach to judicial compulsion in relation to ADR. The actual facts of the case themselves concern whether costs sanctions should be imposed for ignoring an inter-party request to mediate, and thus will be considered in the next chapter. But the court took the opportunity to express views about ADR Orders too, which, while strictly *obiter*, were intended to give guidance and establish the working framework within which decisions about ADR could and should be made. The court invited interested bodies to intervene with submissions, and these were received from CEDR, ADR Group, the Chair of the Civil Mediation Council and, at a late stage, the Law Society.

The court considered that to oblige truly unwilling parties to mediate would impose an acceptable obstruction on their right of access to the court, in violation of Article 6 of the European Convention on Human Rights. It is not clear whether this was fully argued. It was certainly a last-minute submission made in the name of the Law Society, and the only case cited – *Deweer v Belgium*[14] – dealt with waiver of court access through an agreement to arbitrate. We examine the human rights argument in **Chapter 10** in more detail, but ordering a party to try a settlement process, which is emphatically *not* an adjudicative process, from which he can withdraw without penalty once started is a strange breach of Article 6.

Even supposing that this view was wrong, the Court of Appeal in *Halsey* took the view that mediation is best engaged in voluntarily.

> 'If the court were to compel parties to enter into a mediation to which they objected, that would achieve nothing except to add to the costs to be borne by the parties, possibly postpone the time when the court determines the dispute and damage the perceived effectiveness of the ADR process.'[15]

---

13  [2004] 4 All ER 920; [2004] ECWA Civ 576.
14  [1980] EHRR 439; ECHR Ag 1000042.
15  See para 10.

Hitherto the judgment talks of parties in the plural, suggesting that it would be wrong for the court to direct ADR when every party to litigation wants to litigate. But after saying that judges should test out expressions of opposition to ADR and not take it at face value, para 10 of the judgment ends:

> 'But if the parties (or at least one of them) remain intransigently opposed to ADR, it would be wrong for the court to compel them to embrace it.'

What the court does have (the judgment continues) is power to encourage parties into ADR, and not to compel them. It goes on to approve the Commercial Court form of ADR Order, and interpret it as 'the strongest form of encouragement', though falling short of actually compelling them to 'undertake an ADR [sic]'.[16] If such an ADR 'Order' (or robust encouragement, as it should perhaps correctly be called) were to be ignored, a judge for that reason alone can impose a costs sanction on the party refusing.

Where does this leave the Commercial Court ADR Order and the earlier cases decided in the light of it? Those who had opposed ADR in the *Guinle/Kinstreet* case and in *Shirayama* case certainly must have left the court feeling that they had no alternative but to engage in mediation in accordance with the Commercial Court ADR 'Order' made 'against' them. Railtrack ignored a recommendation to mediate in *Dunnett* and were penalised. The *Dunnett* case remains untouched by the *Halsey* case, as do any cases in which a proper ADR Order was made. Indeed, the advice to mediate in the *Dunnett* case emanated from a single Lord Justice when giving permission to appeal, and never purported to be an ADR Order at all. In practical terms, therefore, the true status of such ADR orders becomes academic. They are ignored at the costs peril of the refusing party, be they a true order of the court or a mere robust encouragement. Certainly, no one has ever sought to commit a refusing party for contempt, or to have their statement of case struck out.

Is there a fair distinction between cases where all parties oppose mediation or only one of two or more? Reverting to the overriding objective in CPR, Pt 1, the answer should be 'No'. If ADR is a proper means of reducing court time and party expense, then the fact that both parties oppose its use might well be criticised as in breach of the requirements to save expense, to deal with matters expeditiously and to allot an appropriate share of the court's resources. Where one party objects and others agree, why should the opposing party have a veto? It is certainly right that a costs sanction should be reserved for ill-judged refusals of that kind, but meanwhile the case has had to grind on to a conclusion despite the wishes of other parties. What is wrong in a judge intervening to make an ADR 'Order' even if one party objects? Even where a mediation does not settle a case, issues are

---

16  In para 30.

tested and narrowed, reality checked, determination to litigate reviewed and refined, and any unsettled case can be assumed to be worth trying by the judge, who can then be sure that the parties require a decision. Yet, in *Nokia v Interdigital Technology*,[17] in which the parties expressed interest in mediation but one wished to limit its scope to UK intellectual property issues while the other would only mediate if worldwide issues were included, Pumfrey J declined to make an ADR Order, suggesting that the only sanction left to the court was to penalise unreasonable refusal to mediate at the end of the trial. This is surely a surprising position, especially where parties had at least agreed in principle to mediate, but disagreed as to the scope of the dispute to be discussed. The overriding objective requires active case management and facilitation of settlement attempts in order to avoid trial where possible, not simply to be resigned to a trial and a costs argument at its conclusion. Not to require use of a process which can start out on a narrow basis and easily be enlarged to embrace wider issues was, in the authors' view, an opportunity missed.

To summarise the fate of the ADR Order, it appears to be alive and well, despite the ambiguity of its status. Its future deployment depends on whether procedural judges have the will to use it at the right time and in the right circumstances. Many senior judges had never been to a mediation because it was simply not available as a process when they were in practice. Time is changing this. But the need for judicial training over such matters remains paramount, especially while assertions made to judges by lawyers about mediation and its suitability are not necessarily based upon sound experience or training either. As Dyson LJ said in *Halsey*:

> 'The value and importance of ADR have been established within a remarkably short time. All members of the legal profession who conduct litigation should now routinely consider with their clients whether their disputes are suitable for ADR.'[18]

Treating parties as a judge's clients for the purposes of that statement, it holds true for them as well as lawyers representing parties, just as the overriding objective directs all professionals engaged in civil justice. The underlying problem is that the pace of ADR development still depends upon professional people with little direct personal experience of its value.

## 5.5 Other ADR Orders and forms of judicial encouragement

Besides the Commercial Court Order, the court in *Halsey* notes with approval the encouragement given by the Queen's Bench, Chancery,

---

17 [2005] EWHC (Pat) 2134.
18 In para 11.

Commercial Court and Technology & Construction Court Guides, characterising these as 'a less strong form of encouragement'.

The other form of order specifically considered is the Order used in clinical negligence cases, devised by Master John Ungley and his colleagues dealing with such work. This provides that:

> 'The parties shall by [Day 1] consider whether the case is capable of resolution by ADR. If any party considers that the case is unsuitable for ADR, that party shall be prepared to justify that decision at the conclusion of the trial, should the judge consider that such means of resolution were appropriate, when he is considering the appropriate costs order to make. The party considering the case unsuitable for ADR shall, not less than 28 days before the commencement of the trial, file with the court a witness statement without prejudice save as to costs, giving reasons upon which they rely for saying that the case was unsuitable.'

The court in the *Halsey* case commended the fact that:

> '(a)  it recognises the importance of encouraging the parties to *consider* whether the case is suitable for ADR, and
>
> (b)  it is calculated to bring home to them that, if they refuse even to consider that question, they may be at risk on costs even if they are ultimately held by the court to be the successful party;'

and suggests that it might be used more widely, especially in personal injury cases. Indeed, this wording has now found its way into the CPR Pt 29 Practice Direction, as we saw in **Chapter 4**.[19]

What this form of order does is to relieve the procedural judge from any responsibility for determining the suitability of a given case for ADR, leaving it to the parties to assess that on the merits and taking the risk (if they refuse) that the trial judge will take a contrary view if the case proceeds to judgment. As we assert in **Chapter 6**, however, it is very hard to define what makes a case unsuitable for mediation. Even in the *Halsey* case, mediation was regarded as not inherently unsuitable. Many, if not most, cases will at some point in their life cycle be suitable for mediation. The better questions are whether it is ready for mediation and whether the cost benefit of mediating makes sense. It is of course open to a party (as indeed is happening) to ask the procedural judge to specify the form of ADR to be used, this usually being mediation.

---

19  At 4.2.4.

## 5.6 The effect of encouraging ADR in the pre-action protocols

The remaining question is to consider what effect judges may feel that the consolidated provisions in the pre-action protocols relating to ADR might have. Will ignoring the recommendation to try ADR there be treated similarly to ignoring an ADR Order or judicial recommendation? There is no guidance on this as yet, but some initial comments are worth while.

The approach is very similar to the Ungley Order, in that it is provided that:

> 'the parties should consider whether some form of alternative dispute resolution procedure would be more suitable than litigation, and if so, endeavour to agree which form to adopt. Both the Claimant and Defendant may be required by the Court to provide evidence that alternative means of resolving their dispute were considered.'

In such situations, the duty to consider ADR clearly lies on both parties equally, and it is also made clear that costs sanctions await parties who ignore the protocol requirements. It goes on to provide that 'claims should not be issued prematurely when a settlement is still being actively explored'.

This is slightly strange. Surely, what is intended is that claims should not be issued if parties ought still to be exploring settlement. A bilateral contracting-out from settlement discussions ought not to be an excuse to prevent sanctions.

The concluding comment that 'it is expressly recognised that no party can or should be forced to mediate or enter into any form of ADR' reflects the court's current reluctance to compel parties into ADR. Ironically, there is no such power to compel ADR at the pre-action stage. It is arguable that someone keen to mediate before issue should have the right to seek a pre-issue ADR Order against a refusing party, comparable to a pre-action disclosure. The only current remedy is to issue proceedings, paying the substantial court fee on issue, and seek an ADR Order at allocation stage.

We suspect that the main problem over enforcement of these protocol duties will lie in the breadth of the definition of what constitutes ADR at that stage. Besides any methods particular to that sector, every protocol and the Practice Direction lists the following:

'– Discussion and negotiation;
– Early neutral evaluation by an independent third party;

– Mediation – a form of facilitated negotiation assisted by an independent neutral party.'

This revisits the very nature of ADR. As Dyson LJ said in the *Halsey* case,

'The term "alternative dispute resolution" is defined in the Glossary to the CPR as a "collective description of methods of resolving disputes otherwise than through the normal trial process. In practice, however, references to ADR are usually understood as being references to some form of mediation by a third party ... The cases in which the question of displacing this rule have been discussed have usually been concerned with refusal of mediation by the successful party. The two appeals before this court fall into this category. In what follows we shall concentrate on the cost consequences of a refusal by the successful party to agree to mediation.'[20]

Mediation then remains the focus, with ADR being used synonymously with mediation, except that when considering whether use of other settlement methods might excuse refusal of mediation he says: 'But it is also right to point out that mediation often succeeds where previous attempts to settle have failed.'

Will judges accept that the protocol requirements to try to avoid litigation will be met by parties who say that they have had a quick but fruitless discussion or negotiation? Of course, such processes resolve the vast majority of cases settled before issue, but will judges expect another ADR process prior to the issue of proceedings to be tried first when discussions had failed?

There is an unarguable qualitative difference between discussion and negotiation on the one hand (including round-table conferences) and a more formal but less adversarial process such as mediation. The whole concept of having the added value of a third-party neutral to engage actively with the parties so as to assist them to resolve their dispute, allowing them to determine whether terms are acceptable, is far beyond discussion or negotiation. A quick chat on the telephone or between solicitors in the absence of clients could easily satisfy an incurious or uncritical judge in deciding whether the protocol requirements have been met. All such discussions are 'without prejudice', so how will a judge satisfy himself over the adequacy of compliance if discussion or negotiation are claimed to satisfy the protocol requirement? Will it be sufficient for parties to say 'we had a discussion' or 'we negotiated' for the litigation to be allowed to continue, or might a judge legitimately say, 'but you should also have used

---

20  See para 5.

mediation'? We point out the important differences in status between mere 'without prejudice' discussions and the more securely confidential process of mediation in **Chapter 7**.[21] We must await answers to these questions. Certainly, there has been little evidence of robust enforcement of protocol requirements by procedural judges hitherto since their introduction along with the CPR.

## 5.7   The future of ordering ADR

So the courts in England and Wales remain reluctant to compel parties into mediation, whether before or during litigation. As we write, this approach has been challenged in a lecture by a senior Chancery judge.[22] We can safely anticipate that, as an understanding of what mediation really is and can achieve develops within the judiciary, so will their approaches to firm encouragement or even requirement of ADR of parties in their decisions.

---

21  see 7.2 and particularly 7.3.
22  'Mediation – an approximation to Justice': the SJ Berwin Mediation lecture by Sir Gavin Lightman in July 2007.

*Chapter 6*

# The courts and costs sanctions for refusing ADR

## 6.1 The new approach to costs in the CPR

The previous chapter discussed the first question posed at the end of **Chapter 4** as to how and when the courts should order or otherwise encourage parties to enter into ADR. This chapter looks at the second of those questions, namely whether and when a court should impose costs sanctions on a party who refuses to mediate. We already know that to ignore an ADR order or other similar encouragement given by a judge might of itself justify a sanction against even a successful party who refuses mediation. The crucial issue considered in this chapter is what happens if one party spurns an invitation to mediate made by another party without any ADR order. The issue comes into closest focus when considering this in relation to refusal by a successful litigant, who would otherwise normally expect to be awarded costs.

CPR Pt 44 provides:

> '44.3 (1) *The court has discretion as to:*
>
>     (a) *whether costs are payable by one party to another;*
>
>     (b) *the amount of those costs;*
>
>     (c) *when they are to be paid.*
>
> (2) *If the court decides to make an order about costs:*
>
>     (a) *the general rule is that the unsuccessful party will be ordered to pay the costs of the successful party; but*
>
>     (b) *the court may make a different order.'*

So, the pre-CPR presumption that costs follow the event is noted, but the court's power to depart from it is accorded similar prominence. Indeed, perhaps the main feature of litigation under the CPR has been judicial willingness to depart from costs orders that would have been regarded as normal before the CPR, both generally and in relation to Pt 36 offers, and by no means only in relation to refusal of ADR. With the weaponry of unreasonable conduct, exaggeration and disproportionality available, plus willingness to apportion costs according to the success on different issues tried by the court, costs outcomes have, if anything, become harder to predict than before the CPR. The net effect of this issue-responsive approach to costs awards has been to generate a much greater chance that unsuccessful parties who might have been condemned to pay all the costs before the CPR can now aspire to rescue some of that costs exposure. In effect, success has become a relative matter, and quite frequently neither party can really claim to have won completely at trial.

With the overriding objective requiring encouragement of ADR as a means of fulfilling the overriding objective, then it must be arguable that refusal to mediate by a successful party might be regarded as being unreasonable conduct worthy of sanction. The rest of this chapter sets out the ways in which the courts have developed their thinking in this area, and seeks to draw principles from what has happened to both wholly and partly successful parties when mediation has been proposed and refused.

The impact of costs and funding issues is examined in greater detail in **Chapter 8**.

## 6.2 Early developments in post-CPR case-law

There was simply no basis before the CPR for threatening costs sanctions for failure to mediate. The earliest relevant decisions, as we saw in the last chapter, represent attempts by the court to order that ADR should take place, usually relying upon CPR Pt 1. In *Dyson and Field v Leeds City Council*[1] the Court of Appeal gave the first indication that a court might consider depriving a party of a costs award which they might otherwise have expected. They firmly indicated that the parties should try ADR before the expense of the retrial which they had reluctantly ordered was incurred. Even in 1999, Ward LJ was identifying the delicate balance between carrot and stick which has dominated judicial thinking on this topic:

'I would add that the court has powers to take a strong view about the rejection of the encouraging noises we are making, if necessary by imposing orders for indemnity costs or indeed ordering that a higher rate of interest be paid on any damages which might at the end of the day be recoverable. With that warning of dire consequences but essentially with a note of encouragement, I would allow this appeal and remit the matter back to the County Court.'[2]

A hint of what might develop emerged in the Technology and Construction Court case of *Paul Thomas Construction Ltd v Hyland and Power*,[3] where

---

1 (1999) Unreported, 22 November 1999.
2 *Dyson v Field*, above fn.1 at [18]–[19]. For a similar more recent encouragement to use ADR by the Court of Appeal on ordering a retrial, see *Burne v A* [2006] EWCA Civ 24.
3 Unreported, 8 March 2000, TCC.

Judge Wilcox found that the conduct of the claimant in both declining to co-operate without payment of a substantial sum, and then issuing High Court proceedings and seeking summary judgment and an interim payment under CPR Pts 24 and 25 was unreasonable and not in the spirit of the CPR and the Pre-action Protocol Practice Direction, and awarded the defendant indemnity costs, thus adding to the pain of a procedural defeat for a claimant who was probably owed something. Recalcitrance over refusing to enter discussion was certainly part of the reason for the sanction, even if not strictly for refusing ADR.

*Cowl v Plymouth City Council,*[4] also noted in **Chapter 5**, was more of a discussion as to the duty of parties to try ADR and to regard litigation as the last resort. No costs sanctions were threatened, merely a reminder was given, in this case to both parties, that to waste costs on proceedings was unacceptable.

## 6.3   The landmark case of *Dunnett v Railtrack*

The generality of Lord Woolf's warnings in November 2001 in the *Cowl* case moved with startling speed to a very specific penalty imposed in February 2002 in *Dunnett v Railtrack*[5] on a successful litigant for refusing to mediate. The facts and framework of this case need explanation. Mrs Dunnett had been told by contractors for Railtrack that they could not padlock a gate in the fence between her paddock and a railway line. When the newly installed gate was left open by strangers and her horses were killed by an express train, she sued for the loss of her horses and her psychiatric injury. She lost in the County Court, partly perhaps because her lawyers wrongly framed the case. She appealed in person and in giving her permission to appeal, Schiemann LJ suggested that mediation be attempted. Railtrack rejected this out of hand, despite the fact that the Court of Appeal then offered a free mediation scheme, and they also (unsuccessfully) opposed an extension of time sought by Mrs Dunnett.

The Court of Appeal expressed regret that mediation had not been attempted before trial, noting that this had not been suggested by the Cardiff County Court. They then considered Railtrack's rejection of Schiemann LJ's suggestion, and whether the fact that Railtrack had made Pt 36 offers – first of £2,500 after permission to appeal had been given, and later to bear their own costs if the appeal were withdrawn – made any difference to their position. Brooke LJ, giving the only judgment, decided that the offers were irrelevant and on the facts declined to make any order as to costs. In doing so, he made the following important observations:[6]

---

4  [2001] EWCA Civ 1935; [2002] 1 WLR 803.
5  [2002] 2 All ER 850; [2002] EWCA CIV 3003.
6  In paras 14 and 15.

'Skilled mediators are now able to achieve results satisfactory to both parties in many cases which are quite beyond the power of lawyers and courts to achieve. This court has knowledge of cases where intense feelings have arisen, for instance in relation to clinical negligence claims. But when the parties are brought together on neutral soil with a skilled mediator to help them resolve their differences, it may very well be that the mediator is able to achieve a result by which the parties shake hands at the end and feel that they have gone away having settled the dispute on terms with which they are happy to live. A mediator may be able to provide solutions which are beyond the power of the court to provide.'

He went on:

'It is to be hoped that any publicity given to this part of the judgment of the court will draw attention of lawyers to their duties to further the overriding objective in the way that is set out in Part 1 of the Rules and to the possibility that, if they turn down out of hand the chance of ADR, when suggested by the court, as happened on this occasion, they may have to face uncomfortable costs consequences.'

Railtrack undoubtedly 'won' both below and on appeal. They even 'won' in relation to their modest Pt 36 offer, made despite their firm denial of liability. No ADR Order had been made, nor did any protocol require use of ADR as best practice. They rejected mediation because they felt that engagement would necessarily have meant that they had to offer something more, a view firmly rejected by the court as a 'misunderstanding' of the purpose of ADR, pointing to the fact that mediation could deliver outcomes impossible to obtain from a court. Was it right for them to be sanctioned? There have been many who have criticised the decision since.

We believe that the court was right, and that the criticism is misplaced. Changing the perspective slightly, all that Railtrack had to do was to attend a free Court of Appeal Scheme mediation, perhaps without an external lawyer, to meet with Mrs Dunnett, listen to the concerns and emotions she chose to air, express regrets without admitting legal liability, and see if there was any other way in which their future relationship as neighbouring landowners with conflicting interests might be improved. They could then have decided whether anything they heard within the confidentiality of the mediation process justified improving on any previous offer within a confidential settlement and, if no consensus emerged through the good offices of the mediator, continuing with the appeal with nothing changed by the mediation. What was to be lost in not doing that? They discovered all too quickly that by not making a modest investment in a mediation, they lost their costs of the appeal.

The *Dunnett* case had a disproportionate effect on legal thinking about ADR, best traced from CEDR's published case numbers statistics. In the year following the CPR, CEDR's caseload increased by 140 per cent. In the following two years the numbers first plateaued and then reduced by about 20 per cent. In each of the two years after the *Dunnett* case, the annual upward trend was just over 25 per cent. One cogent interpretation of these figures is that with judges having shown little sign of ordering ADR or sanctioning failure to use it after the CPR, it took the shock of the *Dunnett* case to compel advisers to realise that to ignore recommendations and invitations to mediate might be risky. The *Dunnett* case was probably the first and certainly the most notorious decision to show that even a successful litigant who correctly called their legal risk might yet face a costs sanction if perceived by a judge to have acted unreasonably in relation to the process choices made.

There are several points to note about the case, though. First, Mrs Dunnett was undoubtedly the weaker party, represented for free by the Bar Pro Bono Unit against a major corporation well able to afford the consequence visited on them as an example to others. Secondly, the reason for the decision was based firmly on ignoring a judge's recommendation to mediate, and not on a mere offer on Mrs Dunnett's own initiative. Though believed to be so at the time (many unwilling parties cited the *Dunnett* case as the reason for mediating in the months that followed, often merely when the other party had proposed it), it is not an authority for saying that there may be costs consequences for ignoring another party's proposal to mediate rather than a judge's order. Thirdly, the order simply deprived the successful party of their costs, and did not completely reverse the normal costs expectation; Railtrack was not ordered to pay Mrs Dunnett's costs, such as they were.

## 6.4 Other cases where sanctions were imposed

The Court of Appeal thereafter adopted the *Dunnett* case line in several subsequent cases. An insurer which broadly won its appeal in a personal injury case, reducing a damages award of £260,000 by just over £60,000, had its costs reduced by £5,000 for failing to accept judicial advice to mediate.[7] In *Leicester Circuits Ltd v Coates Brothers* plc,[8] the defendants in a commercial dispute withdrew from a mutually agreed mediation the day before it was due to be held. At the trial a month later, the claimants won, but the defendants successfully appealed and sought their costs of the appeal and in the court below. The Court of Appeal accepted the claimants' criticism of the defendants' withdrawal from mediation, and only awarded the defendants their costs below up to eight days before the mediation

7 *Neal v Jones Motors* [2002] EWCA Civ 1757.
8 [2003] EWCA Civ 333.

date and then costs of the appeal, requiring them to bear their own costs for the remainder of the time before trial and the three-week trial itself.

The defendants sought to justify withdrawal from mediation as being merely akin to a negotiation that failed. Judge LJ responded: 'The whole point of having mediation, and once you have agreed to it, proceeding with it, is that the most difficult of problems can sometimes, indeed often are, resolved.' The Court of Appeal regarded the issue as being whether there had been a realistic prospect of successful resolution through mediation, a test with particular significance in one of the major first instance decisions on this topic, *Hurst v Leeming*, which is discussed below, and which promulgated a similar test. Judge LJ took a firm view in the *Leicester Circuits* case in commenting: 'It hardly lies in the mouths of those who agree to it to assert that there was no realistic prospect of success.'

The *Dunnett* case was (perhaps for the first time) cited to the Court of Appeal in *Leicester Circuits*. Judge LJ quoted from Brooke LJ's judgment, particularly his assertion that the parties themselves have a duty to further the overriding objective. The key passage in Judge LJ's single judgment on costs reads:

> 'It seems to us that the unexplained withdrawal from an agreed mediation process was of significance to the continuation of this litigation. We do not for one moment assume that the mediation process would have succeeded, but certainly there is a prospect that it would have done if it had been allowed to proceed. That therefore bears on the issue of costs.'

In a decision obverse to the *Paul Thomas* case,[9] the Court of Appeal in *Virani Ltd v Manuel Revert y Cia SA*[10] ordered that an unsuccessful defendant who had refused to mediate or negotiate before losing at trial and again on his appeal (despite advice from the single Lord Justice) should pay the successful claimants' costs on an indemnity basis.[11]

In *Royal Bank of Canada v Ministry of Defence*,[12] the Ministry of Defence (MoD) won on most but not all issues in a dispute over the validity of notices served under the break clause of a lease, but they had declined several invitations to mediate. The claimant drew attention to the Government's public pledge of March 2001 to use mediation in suitable cases wherever an opponent agreed to it. Lewison J found that the case was suitable for

---

9 See **6.1.** above.

10 [2003] EWCA Civ 1651: the costs award is only reported in the LawTel report and not in the full transcript of the judgment on the merits.

11 See also *Stansbury v Bristol Rugby Club* (unreported, 9 Dec 2002) a decision of Eady J where again indemnity basis costs were awarded against the losing defendant who refused mediation.

12 [2003] EWHC 1479 (Ch).

ADR, criticised the MoD's failure to abide by the pledge, and declined to award costs to the MoD.[13]

Apart from the mutually agreed mediation in the *Leicester Circuits* case, and the Government Pledge factor in the *Royal Bank* case, the other cases cited above all involved ignoring a judge's recommendation to use ADR. The decisions in which mediation was proposed by one party and ignored by others, without any judicial pressure are the ones where controversy has been heightened. These were almost all first instance decisions, until the whole topic was reviewed in the second leading case of *Halsey v Milton Keynes General NHS Trust* in 2005.

## 6.5 Cases where sanctions were not imposed on a refusing party

One of the early decisions where a sanction was not imposed has been claimed as theirs by both proponents and opponents of sanctions to mediate. In *Hurst v Leeming*,[14] Lightman J established a demanding test for those who refused to mediate to avoid a sanction, but decided that the defendant had met it. The case involved a last-ditch claim against a barrister by a bankrupt solicitor acting in person over a partnership dispute, after he had sued most other available parties. Lightman J persuaded the claimant that his case was hopeless and had to be discontinued, thus exposing the claimant to the normal liability on discontinuance for the defendant's costs. However, the claimant argued that because the defendant had declined to mediate as required by the Professional Indemnity Pre-action Protocol, the decision in *Dunnett* meant that he should be given relief from such a costs order. The defendant produced a number of reasons to excuse that refusal. Those rejected by Lightman J were:

- that heavy costs had already been incurred;
- the serious allegations of professional negligence;
- the fact that the defendant believed he had a watertight case;
- the fact that the claimant's case had already been fully refuted.

The test he defined was that if mediation can have no reasonable prospect of success, a party may refuse mediation with impunity. Lightman J found that on the facts of this case the defendant 'quite exceptionally' was justified in declining mediation, largely because of the almost obsessive approach of the claimant and his determination to extract a large sum of compensation through the mediation process and finding that he 'was

---

13 The pledge aspect of this case is criticised in *Halsey v Milton Keynes NHS Trust* at para 35: the real issue is one of suitability.
14 [2001] EWHC 1051 (Ch); [2003] 1 Lloyds Reports 379.

unlikely to accept any mediation which did not achieve that result'. He summarised the position by saying that:

> 'by reason of the character and attitude of Mr. Hurst, mediation had no real prospect of getting anywhere. That is not a view which is easily sustainable in any case, but on the facts of this case, it is sustained.'

He went on:

> 'Refusal is a high risk to take. For if the court finds that there was a real prospect [of mediation success] the party refusing to proceed to mediation may, as I have said, be severely penalised. Further, the hurdle in the way of a party refusing to proceed to mediation on this ground is high, for in making this objective assessment of the prospects of mediation, the starting point must surely be the fact that the mediation process itself can and does often bring about a more sensible and conciliatory attitude on the part of parties than might otherwise be expected to prevail before the mediation, and may produce a recognition of the strengths and weaknesses by each party of his own case and of that of his opponent, and a willingness to accept the give and take essential to a successful mediation. What appears to be incapable of mediation before the mediation process begins often proves capable of satisfactory resolution later.'

The language used by Lightman J suggested that the burden lay on the person seeking relief from a costs sanction, though this view was later rejected by the Court of Appeal in the *Halsey* case. Indeed, it was always the unsuccessful claimant who was seeking relief from the normal rule that costs followed the event. The case comments powerfully on mediation as an intrinsically better way to resolve disputes. Most significantly, Lightman J declined to excuse refusal to mediate where the refusing party (even rightly) thought he had a watertight case. This echoes the positions of Railtrack, the insurers of Jones Motors, and (eventually) Coats Industries Plc in their respective cases. This question is re-examined by the Court of Appeal in *Halsey*.

But even assuming that the burden truly was laid on Mr Hurst rather than Mr Leeming to secure costs relief, how did the court come to excuse refusal? Did it have more to do with the claimant's myopic intransigence than fault on the defendant's part? There was no evidence of any willingness on the part of the successful defendant to compromise, and no settlement offers were apparently made at any time. The refusal to mediate flew in the face of protocol requirements, and the overriding objective, though not in the face of any judicial recommendation. So how did the defendant escape a sanction? The answer may lie in looking at the conduct of the party seeking relief, namely the unsuccessful Mr Hurst who proposed mediation. It was his obsession that was, in the court's view, likely to lead to impasse at any mediation, to an extent that forgave refusal to engage in that process. Contrast this with how Mrs Dunnett, Mr Neal, Leicester Circuits and Mr Virani might have felt aggrieved at the refusal to mediate. Each of them apparently offered to engage in the mediation process in good faith, whereas Lightman J ultimately felt that Mr Hurst deserved no such relief.[15]

So the unsuccessful party seeking relief from costs must deserve such a benefit and not forfeit it in the light of the way they conducted their litigation. In *SITA v Watson Wyatt: Maxwell Batley Pt 20 defendant*,[16] the judge declined to penalise a Pt 20 defendant who declined mediation offered by the Pt 20 claimant largely because the way in which the claimant sought to 'browbeat and bully' the defendant into the process by 'self-serving invitations (demands would be a more appropriate word) to participate in the mediation'. The judge found that the claimant would never have contemplated being persuaded that their case had no merit. He also found that the timing of proposed mediation excused the defendant, a perhaps less convincing excuse to experienced mediators. But an almost equitable requirement of seeking costs relief with clean hands seems to emerge which is consolidated by the leading case of *Halsey v Milton Keynes General NHS Trust.*[17]

## 6.6 *Halsey v Milton Keynes General NHS Trust* and inter-party offers to mediate

The appeal in the *Halsey* case was conjoined with *Steel v Joy and Halliday*, which was a dispute between two insurers over how to apportion liability for the damages caused by successive torts, which will be considered separately in relation to the principles which emerged from the joint judgment. The *Halsey* case itself involved very different facts. Mrs Halsey alleged negligence against the hospital in which her husband had died. Her solicitor wrote several times before issuing proceedings in forthright terms, first seeking £5,000 costs for preparing and attending the inquest, then seeking £7,500 damages and costs, then seeking mediation. The Trust denied the claim. Later, the claimant's solicitor wrote to the Department of Health, warning about the high cost of proceedings in the light of the Trust's refusal to mediate as being 'an unnecessary waste of both costs and resources'. The claimant wrote three or four more letters pressing for mediation, with the Trust still saying that 'on such a low quantum claim, we do not consider this to be a cost-effective use of NHS resources'.

---

15 Another case where the Court of Appeal declined to impose a sanction is *McCook v Lobo* [2002] EWCA Civ 1760.

16 [2002] EWHC 2401 (Ch) (Park J); [2004] EWCA Civ 576. Mediation actually settled the main dispute between SITA and Watson Wyatt.

17 [2004] EWCA Civ 576; [2004] 4 All ER 920.

All attempts to persuade the Trust into mediation foundered, and the claim proceeded to trial, where it was dismissed. The claimant unsuccessfully sought relief from an adverse costs order, relying in particular on the *Dunnett* and *Hurst* cases, and then appealed against the order for costs which was made against her. Having heard the witnesses, the trial judge found that the claimant would not have walked away from a mediation without a monetary settlement.

So far the case is on all fours with both *Hurst* and *SITA*, with a claimant found to be intransigent in demands and unrealistic in openness to a simple non-monetary outcome, and thus perhaps did not require special consideration of principle. Wherever the burden lay over excusing a refusal to mediate, a court had both evidence and authority upon which to excuse the Trust. But the Court of Appeal wanted to take the opportunity to lay down some general principles about how to handle refusals to mediate, and whether and when costs sanctions for doing so might be imposed.

Having discussed ADR Orders,[18] the Court of Appeal turned to cases where no specific judicial recommendation had been made to use ADR. In the light of CPR, Pt 44.3(4), it found that the burden on altering the normal expectation that costs would follow the event lay upon the party seeking relief. Thus the unsuccessful party who proposed mediation must satisfy the court that the successful party who refused should be penalised, the test being that *the successful party acted unreasonably in refusing to agree to ADR.*[19]

The Court set out six factors which might be relevant in testing out reasonableness in this context, and which were not seen as exhaustive. Each will be discussed in turn.

### 6.6.1 The nature of the dispute

The court adopted a passage from the 1999 Commercial Court Working Party Report to suggest that there are 'many cases which do not lend themselves to ADR procedures', citing clarification of law or construction as a precedent to govern future business interests, and allegations of fraud as examples, with the court adding the need for injunctive relief, resolution of a point of law and precedent. While saying initially that 'even the most ardent supporters of ADR acknowledge that the subject-matter of some disputes renders them intrinsically unsuitable for ADR', the judgment concludes by saying 'In our view, most cases are not by their very nature unsuitable for ADR', a slightly grudging double negative. Indeed, neither the *Halsey* (a clinical negligence claim) nor the *Steel* case (a personal injury and insurance claim) was found to be inherently unsuitable for ADR.

---

18 See the discussion of this aspect of *Halsey* in **Chapter 5**.
19 At para 13 of Dyson LJ's judgment.

We believe that indeed very few cases are intrinsically unsuitable for mediation, an attitude which embarrasses proponents and infuriates opponents or those with limited knowledge of ADR. If a case could conceivably be settled, it can be mediated. Of course, mediation provides neither peremptory orders nor precedents. It has frequently been used to help parties negotiate a solution after a peremptory order (whether injunction or freezing or search order) has been obtained; and to help parties avoid the risks of an adverse precedent even in areas of entirely novel law.[20] Practitioners need to be alive to the fact that this factor is capable of challenge, and may not ultimately be regarded as persuasive.

The court decided that if a public body such as the NHS ignored the Government Pledge to mediate, based as it is on agreeing to use ADR if a case is suitable for it, this would not of itself justify penalising it for refusing to mediate. This casts some doubt on the decision of the *Royal Bank* case, though suitability for ADR was rather assumed in that case, and the *Halsey* case itself was not found to be inherently unsuitable for ADR. The overriding test remains whether it was unreasonable to refuse ADR on the facts of a given case.

### 6.6.2 The merits of the case

This factor was of significance on the facts of both the *Halsey* and *Steel* cases, where defendants rejected mediation because they reasonably believed (rightly, as it turned out in both cases) that they had a good prospect of success at trial, and said they thought that mediation would be a waste of time and resource. The court in the *Halsey* case felt that it would be harsh to penalise a party who wanted to bypass mediation for trial and who ultimately got their risk assessment right. They inserted their own gloss on Lightman J's remarks in the *Hurst v Leeming*, rephrasing it as 'the fact that a party [unreasonably] believes he has a watertight case is no justification for refusing mediation', inserting the bracketed word. If a party reasonably believes he has a watertight case, this may well be sufficient justification for refusing to mediate.

One or two points need to be made. First, a similar line might have been taken by the defendants in the *Dunnett* and *Neal* cases, had it not been for

---

20 For instance, the retained organs group litigation, involving highly novel and disputatious law, and in which far more claimants emerged satisfied by the Alder Hey group mediated settlement than the National group of claimants, who did not settle and had their claim litigated. The National group trial judgment – to be found at *A & B v Leeds Teaching Hospitals NHS Trust* [2004] EWHC 644 (QB) – eliminated the claims of nearly half the 2,000 claimants and also set lower standards for damages for those who won, at the expense of very substantial costs liabilities (regardless of who had won), and with further issues needing to be litigated to ascertain who had actually won or lost. Eventually further mediations settled both damages and costs. A fuller account of this litigation is given in **Chapter 11**: see **11.6.1**.

the judicial recommendations to mediate which were ignored. Secondly, few cases have no risks attached. If such a case exists, it would surely be normal for either the claimant or defendant to seek summary judgment under CPR Pt 24. The true distinction in most cases is not between water-tight and border-line, as suggested here in *Halsey*, but between the various shades of grey that normally surround most litigation issues. If mediation is rejected and a party wrongly calls their risk and does not win at trial, they may face additional costs sanctions for not mediating, as happened in the *Paul Thomas* case and perhaps in the *Virani* case.[21] Deciding whether to reject mediation becomes just another part of the risk analysis.

It is worth recording that mediation can lead to virtual capitulation by one or other side, with expressions of regret but no admission of fault and other non-monetary benefits delivered. In the *Halsey* case itself,[22] counsel was noted to have urged the court to remember that:

> 'the claimant might have been persuaded in the course of the mediation to drop her claim: all she really wanted was an expla-nation of how her husband had died in hospital. This possibility cannot be dismissed out of hand, although there is no evidence to support it.'

Indeed, the trial judge had rather found Mrs Halsey's intentions as being to the contrary. But counsel had a fair point, which will be discussed further in considering the last of the six factors as to whether mediation had a reasonable prospect of success.

### 6.6.3 Other settlement methods have been attempted

Dyson LJ commented[23]:

> 'The fact that settlement offers have already been made but rejected is a relevant factor. It may show that one party is making efforts to settle and that the other has unrealistic views of the merits of the case. But it is also right to point out that mediation often succeeds where previous attempts to settle have failed.'

It is not quite clear whether it is the party with 'unrealistic views on the merits' is the one proposing or rejecting mediation. Is the court suggesting that a party might be forgiven refusing mediation who said 'I have made a Part 36 offer which has been rejected: I cannot be criticised for not mediating, since my opponent rejected it unreasonably'? Mediation may be the perfect occasion to clarify such issues face to face.

---

21 See 6.3 above.
22 See para 52.
23 At para 20.

The point about mediation succeeding where other methods have failed is however undoubtedly true. It is a rare mediation with no prior negotiation or Pt 36 offer. It would be surprising if the addition of a mediator who can talk privately to both sides were not to enhance bilateral discussion in which parties usually find it hard to negotiate in a principled way and to abandon adversarial posturing. What is not discussed is whether discussion or negotiation can be regarded as discharging any duty to seek settlement. The amendments made in the 41st edition of the CPR to the pre-action protocols seems to hint at this. We agree with the Court of Appeal in *Halsey* that mediation may well help to settle what discussion fails to settle.

This factor is finally consigned to being in truth part of whether mediation has a reasonable prospect of success.

### 6.6.4   The costs of mediation would be disproportionately high

This factor featured in the *Halsey* case, where the NHS wanted to avoid the cost of what they regarded as being a probably wasted mediation investment. An adverse cost benefit must always be a theoretical justification for refusing to engage in a non-compulsory activity. But with inexpensive and even *pro bono* court and private provider schemes developing, and bearing in mind that the level and cost of representation at a risk-free confidential mediation lies entirely within the choice of each party, this must be a relatively rare justification for refusal on its own.

### 6.6.5   Delay

The court thought that late mediation might perhaps prejudice trial dates and be properly rejected for that reason. In practice the authors know of no instance where this has happened. Fixing a mediation, which can be done very quickly without any need to stay proceedings, should never mean the vacation of a trial date. Late mediations do occur and frequently lead to settlement and appreciable cost savings if held before trial briefs have been delivered and before cancellation fees are chargeable by expert witnesses. Frustratingly for mediators keen to see maximum savings in cost and time, the lateness of the mediation is usually because the parties' advisers have been dilatory in contemplating the use of mediation or in making the arrangements.

### 6.6.6   Whether mediation has a reasonable prospect of success

This factor has its origins in Lightman J's judgment in *Hurst v Leeming*. However, the court in the *Halsey* case declined to accept without qualification his test as to the circumstances in which refusal to mediate might be excused, namely 'whether, viewed objectively, mediation had any real prospect of success'. While Lightman J was prepared to assume that many intractable disputes could be mediated successfully, even when parties did not think so, the Court of Appeal felt that it was difficult for a court to decide this objectively with hindsight. They also felt that it did not allow for the fact that an unreasonable party might try to justify refusing to mediate when it was his own unreasonableness that meant that mediation had no reasonable prospect of success. This is of course exactly what Mr Hurst tried and failed to do, in Lightman J's opinion.

Where this factor comes into play, the court decided that it is for the unsuccessful party to show that mediation had a reasonable prospect of success (not that it *would have* succeeded), consistent with their view that it was for an unsuccessful party to shift the normal expectation that costs follow success in litigation and to show that rejection of mediation was unreasonable. Dyson LJ comments that such a burden will not be unduly onerous for an unsuccessful party, though the unsuccessful parties in both *Halsey* and *Steel* failed to do so. As we have seen, Mrs Halsey did not satisfy the court that she might have accepted an explanation and no money. It is worth looking at the conjoined appeal of the *Steel* case to see application of the six factors at work, to consider whether this optimism is justified, and to introduce some debate as to what constitutes success in mediation.

## 6.7   *Steel v Joy and Halliday*: a case study on applying the *Halsey* factors

Mr Steel was injured in separate accidents in 1996 and 1999, involving different defendants and insurers, D1 and D2, both of whom admitted liability to the claimant. The claims brought against each were consolidated, as the triable issue related to the relative contribution made by each defendant to the exacerbation of a previous condition. D1's negligence accelerated his condition by 7–10 years, as would have D2's negligence on its own, but taken with the first accident, it only caused 3–6 months of extra disability. D1 argued that D1 and D2 should share the whole claim, whereas D2 only accepted liability for the 3–6 month exacerbation. D1 proposed mediation to C and D2 two months before trial, but D2 asserted that this was a point of law requiring a judge's decision and declined. When warned of possible costs consequences they replied 'We are not prepared to compromise on the point of law and therefore mediation would be pointless'. They did win their point of law, and D1 sought not to have to pay their costs as they had refused mediation. The judge took the view that mediation so late in the day could probably have achieved little on this topic. The Court of Appeal agreed, applying their six core points, and found:

(1)   that D2 wanted the point of law decided by the court, and they were entitled to do so without fearing penalty;

(2)    that D2 reasonably (and rightly) believed that their case was watertight and that D1's case had no merit;

(3)    there was no suggestion that previous settlement negotiations were relevant; there were none;

(4)    mediation would have created disproportionate cost, set against a two-hour trial of the issue;

(5)    it was late in the day and substantial costs had already been incurred, though there was no suggestion that mediation would have delayed the trial;

(6)    D1 had not shown that mediation had a reasonable prospect of success.

Overall, the Court of Appeal found that D1 had not proved that D2 had acted unreasonably in refusing to mediate, and confirmed the judge's costs order.

It has always been a perfectly proper reason for litigating rather than mediating, when a point of law needs decision. Precedent is what courts are there to provide, and mediation cannot possibly give rise to legally binding precedent. This is not to say that cases built around liability issues cannot be mediated; quite the reverse. If the party seeking a precedent is content to live with the outcome, win or lose, there is no risk factor at stake. If it would welcome a favourable precedent but dislike an unfavourable one, risk abounds and settlement may be wise. Mediations have often settled where parties decide on reflection to buy up their risk of an adverse precedent, even where the law is entirely novel.[24] So points of law do not by themselves make mediation unlikely to succeed. In the *Steel* case, D2 was actually arguing that the law was settled and that D1 was seeking to overturn good clear law, a view which the Court of Appeal shared in rejecting D1's arguments.

It is easy enough for a party who has won to say that they refused mediation on this ground as justifying refusal to mediate. The challenge is to predict the legal outcome correctly before trial and decline to mediate on that basis, and it was for getting that right that D2, perhaps understandably, escaped sanction in the *Steel* case. The penalty for getting it wrong is substantial. To chance losing the point of law and to face possible indemnity costs, as happened in the *Virani* case (where the Court of Appeal sanctioned a party who refused to mediate because it thought it would win a point of law) is risky indeed.

What of the other reasons in the *Steel* case? Counsel for D2 mentioned a likely figure of £20,000, sensibly characterised by Dyson LJ as 'surprisingly

---

24  The retained organs litigation again comes to mind: see note 18 above.

high'. As suggested in relation to the *Halsey* case above, D2 could have attended at a mediation for perhaps two hours with a senior claims manager (many of whom are well qualified to handle their party's case in the informal and without prejudice surroundings of a mediation) and without legal representation; or perhaps D2's panel solicitor would not have charged D2 too much for attending. The level and thus the cost of representation at mediation is within the unfettered choice of each party. There is usually no need to bring two solicitors, plus leading and junior counsel, to a mediation. Fees for mediator and provider (if any) would have been split unless otherwise agreed, either on a fixed fee or an hourly rate basis. Parties need stay no longer than they wish at a voluntary process. So a mediation need cost each party no more than its share of the hourly rate of the mediator and the representation it chooses to arrange, if any.

Mediation shortly before trial is a very different matter from having to consider vacating a trial date for a mediation, something which never arose in the *Steel* case. Mediating late in a case's life can still save enormous costs, especially in a large case, when the parties can enjoy the expensive luxury of having all the evidence in place. It will certainly be cheaper than court-door settlement, which is a hugely wasteful exercise. Any case which settles there or very shortly before trial could almost certainly have been mediated successfully at least two or three months earlier. It is almost always because preparation had not been done in good enough time that settlement occurs so late, and only rarely because entirely new material has suddenly emerged at the last minute to change the risk perspective.

Why did the court find that D1 had failed to show that mediation had a reasonable prospect of success? They relied in effect on the fact that D2 felt there was no room for compromise in the law, and that to engage in mediation when D2 was simply unwilling to shift would be waste of time and money, because there would have been no settlement.

## 6.8   What amounts to 'success' in mediation?

We return to the question begged by the sixth factor in the *Halsey* case, namely 'what is success' in the context of a mediation. The assumption made by the courts hitherto has been that mediation succeeds where it settles cases and that if settlement does not emerge from mediation it has 'failed', and was therefore not worth doing. Many, if not most, cases settle at mediation. If they did not, the process would soon fall into disrepute. Settlement often emerges much to the surprise of the parties, who have assumed from the way adversarial litigation has been conducted that there was no willingness on a opponent's part to perceive a risk of failure and to make concessions accordingly. The process offers opportunities to restore open and direct communication between the parties themselves, rather than at arms length through their lawyers, which the litigation process rather prevents. Misunderstandings can be sorted out, the priority and weight of each case made clear and tested both mutually and in private with the help of a skilled and neutral mediator, risks re-appraised and choices made over whether to shift or stick on positions. Outcomes unavailable from a court judgment can be discussed and mobilised if felt to be of value, and future interests considered and met rather than just allocation of blame or rights over past history, free of any necessity to use blame as the sole basis for decision-making.

These are rightly regarded as valuable characteristics of the mediation process, and serve to remind judges that it is difficult to predict what value can indeed emerge from a mediation which a refusal to mediate might forfeit. Can it properly be said that mediation is only a success if it brings litigation to an end by payment even of a discounted sum of damages? While claiming that its record of settlement justifies its widespread use even in the teeth of resistance on the part of those legal professionals who have not previously experienced it, we suggest that mediation offers far more to a modern civil justice system. It may lead to withdrawal of a case against a party, settlement in full of a claim, or a settlement into which a proper discount has been built for the risks of litigation after frank appraisal across a table and in private of those risks by each party. A neutral mediator will make frank communication possible within a safe environment, will act both as a sounding-board in each side's risk debate, and as a confidential facilitator of negotiations where each party may prefer to posture in front of each other, but may be prepared to admit greater flexibility in private to the mediator. The mediator will always have a better idea of whether settlement is achievable than either side separately. It is extremely rare for a mediation not to narrow issues, or to make things worse. The norm is for mediation to save time at a trial or to bring settlement forward. The process also makes non-monetary benefits available both from the very engagement in the process and from devising non-monetary outcomes.

What it also does where settlement does not occur, is to ensure that any case which then proceeds to trial does so having been tested in the fires of neutrally conducted debate. A judge can assume that if the parties have not settled at mediation and found that the benefits made available privately have not satisfied their needs, they at least have decided that the best place for resolution is a judicial decision in the court-room, and that the case is worth fighting. Court door settlements will be less likely, cases prepared for trial will stand up, and court resources will not be wasted. A judge who finds that one party has made a serious misjudgment about the risks they faced can make costs decisions accordingly.

Might brief and inexpensive mediations in *Dunnett, Halsey* and *Steel* cases have been worth considering from this perspective? We would argue that they would have, if timed and priced right. Railtrack, as

Mrs Dunnett's continuing neighbour, might have found a way to co-exist with her despite the disaster. Mrs Halsey may well have continued as a mollified potential patient of her local NHS Trust, mollified quite apart from what had happened to her husband. Even the two insurers for D1 and D2 might have had other reasons for jointly reviewing their risks over this and other cases. D2 would doubtless have articulated the strength of its case on the law of successive torts, and we shall never know whether they might have persuaded D1 to withdraw their arguments without the need for trial. It is not impossible. So, subject always to cost benefit, is there such a strong case for excusing refusal to mediate? Again, we would suggest not.

## 6.9   Applying the principles in *Halsey*

Since the *Halsey* case confirmed that, subject to the considerations discussed in the judgment, courts have a discretion to impose costs sanctions for refusal of an inter-party offer to mediate, judges in a number of later decisions have grappled with whether to impose such sanctions. Cases have fallen on both sides of the line, and in the important case of *Burchell v Bullard*,[25] it was only the fact that the defendant's refusal to mediate before issue of proceedings at the invitation of the claimant pre-dated the decision in the *Dunnett* case that spared the defendant from a costs sanction for that refusal.

The *Burchell* case was an appeal only on the costs order made on a claim and counter-claim based on the apportionment of costs appropriate to the relative success of each party. The burden shifted very substantially from claimant to defendant even without further sanction for the refusal to mediate. Reasons for refusal rejected by the Court in *Burchell* included the specious suggestion made that the case was 'too complex', the judges finding that building claims of this type suited mediation '*par excellence*'. Compared with the £185,000 estimated costs of a case where in the end the defendant had to pay about £5,000 to the claimant, the Court regarded the costs of mediation as a drop in the ocean. Interestingly, the decision applied the factors in the *Halsey* case (where the NHS Trust was entirely successful) despite the fact that the defendant was broadly unsuccessful. The significance of *Burchell* is particularly in emphasizing the effectiveness of pre-issue inter-party offers to mediate. As Ward LJ says:

> 'The profession can no longer with impunity shrug aside reasonable requests to mediate. The parties cannot ignore a proper request to mediate simply because it was made before the claim was issued. With court fees escalating it may be folly to do so.'

---

25  [2005] EWCA Civ 358.

The revised pre-action protocols which have followed the *Burchell* case may give new importance to decisions over ADR at this stage of disputes.

In another costs apportionment case,[26] after dividing the costs attributable to the percentage success of each party, the judge added a further 15 per cent to the costs liability of a payer who declined to mediate in a case which the judge found had good prospects of settlement because he felt that the parties were reasonable people keen to do a commercial deal. Cases in which the court declined to penalise refusal to mediate include those where the judge took the view that the atmosphere between the parties was such that mediation was unlikely to succeed,[27] where a claimant with unrealistic views about his case proposed it two months before trial[28] and where the judge was (perhaps surprisingly) prepared to exonerate a refusing party who wanted to fight so as not to pay more than he believed the case was worth, even though the judge found that mediation would probably have settled the case at the level awarded by the judge.[29]

The *Halsey* case was also considered in *Daniels v Commissioner for Metropolitan Police*,[30] a case where the defendant, confronted by a number of similar claims which he regarded (like Ms Daniels' claim) as spurious, refused to negotiate at all or to respond to any claimant's Pt 36 offer. Drawing parallels with the decision in the *Halsey* case as to sanctioning refusal to mediate, the court declined to penalise the defendant for refusing to negotiate. But in *P4 v Unite Integrated Systems plc*,[31] Ramsey J ordered that the defendant, who made a Pt 36 offer of £6,000, 18 months before trial but kept judgment down to £387, should have its costs from the date of the Pt 36 offer, but should pay the claimant's costs up to that date for failing to fulfil disclosure at the pre-trial protocol stage and declining the claimant's proposal to mediate.

Judges are still learning what mediation can achieve, so it is unsurprising that a broad range of exercise of discretion will be found in years to come. Reporting will be patchy and appeals on costs only, as occurred in the *Halsey, Burchell* and *Daniels* cases, are relatively rare.

## 6.10   Where all parties fail to use ADR

In all the cases discussed so far, one party (usually the unsuccessful one) complained about the refusal of the successful party to agree to an

---

26 *Yorkshire Bank plc and Clydesdale Bank Asset Finance Ltd v RDM Asset Finance and J.B Coach Sales* (unreported, 30 June 2004) Judge Hangan QC QBD.
27 *Re Midland Linen Services Ltd* [2004] EWHC 3380 (Ch).
28 *Palfrey v Wilson* [2007] EWCA Civ 94.
29 *Hickman v Blake Lapthorn and David Fisher* [2006] EWHC 12 (QB).
30 [2005] EWCA Civ 1312.
31 [2006] EWHC 2924 (TCC).

invitation to mediate. The courts have on several occasions considered whether to penalise parties where no one has mediated or all parties have ignored court recommendations to try the process. Earlier decisions find the courts being reluctant to find that both parties were at fault and disallow costs accordingly,[32] but several decisions since the *Halsey* case have demonstrated a firmer approach, especially where the court has felt that parties were indulging in unnecessarily vituperative and costly litigation. These have included a dispute over a will with allegations of fraud,[33] a claim for stress at work (in which the court said that with settled principles now such cases should normally be mediated),[34] and an employment dispute between a solicitor and the firm employing her,[35] in which the Court of Appeal declared 'a plague on both your houses' for the 'posturing and jockeying for position taken by each side', resulting in no order as to costs of the appeal.

Again in *Longstaff International v Evans and others*,[36] a case where a mediation had set terms of agreement which later remained unperformed, the parties had agreed to use mediation again, but instead litigated aggressively and put difficult pre-conditions on further mediation. Both the Chancery master and the appeal judge decided that there should be no order as to costs.

## 6.11  A summary on costs sanctions

The following propositions can be derived from the decisions on this topic:

- Any party, successful or not, who ignores a court recommendation to mediate or an ADR 'Order' risks a worse costs outcome than they might otherwise have hoped to achieve, for that reason alone.

- Where an *unsuccessful* or only partly successful party ignores another party's proposal to negotiate or mediate, they may face an additional costs penalty, such as indemnity costs, for their refusal.

- Costs sanctions may be imposed on a *successful* party who declines to use mediation at the behest of an opponent in

---

32 For example, in *Corenso v Burnden Group* [2003] EWHC 1805 (QB); and to an extent *Valentine v Nash* LTL 29 July 2003 (CA), though there one unreasonable party made a tentative application for a costs sanction on an appeal based on an ignored offer to mediate before trial: also *ARP Capita v Ross & Co and the Law Society* [2004] EWHC 1181 (Ch), where each side successively failed to mediate.

33 *Couwenbergh v Valkova* [2004] EWCA Civ 676, in which the court reminded the Legal Services Commission of its role in keeping costs down if possible.

34 *Vahidi v Fairstead House School Trust* [2005] EWCA Civ 765.

35 *McMillen Williams v Range* [2004] EWCA Civ 294.

36 [2005] EWHC 4 (Ch).

mediation, though it is for the unsuccessful party to show that they should be imposed. The court will weigh such issues as are set out in the *Halsey* case (and any other relevant matters) to determine whether to do so.

– Where *both* parties decline or fail to mediate in circumstances where the court thinks they should have done, they may both face costs sanctions.

*Chapter 7*

# The legal foundations of mediation

As with any ADR process, the legal framework for a mediation is primarily created by the agreement signed at the beginning of the process. There is not yet, any Uniform Mediation Act or equivalent legislative framework in the United Kingdom (as exists in the USA) to govern the status of ADR or its participants, including the the mediator, apart (if this is to be counted as ADR regulation) from the Arbitration Act 1996. However, each process, and the agreement relating to it, is underpinned by some important general legal principles, sometimes extended by specific contractual terms normally included in such agreements. Some contractual terms have begun to receive comment and open support from the courts on the basis of public policy. The boundaries of such principles and commentaries need to be understood, however, so that ADR agreements can be drafted and amended sensibly, and areas where uncertainty still exists are appreciated.

We look at the terms of mediation agreements in particular in this chapter, as these have been considered more than any other type of ADR agreement to date in this jurisdiction. There are two specimen mediation agreements in Appendix A.

## 7.1   The status of a mediation agreement

A typical mediation agreement provides:

- for the appointment of the mediator;
- that the parties will 'attempt in good faith to settle the dispute by means of a mediation';
- a definition of the dispute about which the mediation is to take place;
- for a representative of each party to attend with authority to settle;
- for confidentiality of the process and documents produced in relation to it;
- for the mediator to observe a given code of conduct, covering such matters as conflict of interest and exceptions to confidentiality, in relation to possible criminality or danger;

- that the parties will not call the mediator to give evidence in later or continuing litigation;
- that any settlement must be in writing signed by the parties to be binding and enforceable;
- that parties can withdraw at any time, and the mediator can withdraw for defined reasons;
- for the proper law of the mediation contract and the forum for later dispute resolution;
- for the basis on which the costs and fees associated with the mediation will be borne.

Is a mediation agreement a binding and enforceable contract? There is certainly a theoretical basis for challenging this, on the same basis as challenges to the validity of ADR contract clauses, namely that they represent at their heart a mere agreement to negotiate. The validity of ADR contract clauses is discussed in **Chapter 9**, and this debate will not be repeated here. It is sufficient to comment that we are unaware of any attempt being made in the United Kingdom to set aside the effect of a mediation agreement or any of its clauses, and there are a number of cases where the courts have operated on the assumption that mediation agreements are valid and contain enforceable provisions, especially as to the confidentiality of the process,[1] and the requirement that for a settlement agreement to be binding, it must be in writing signed by the parties.[2]

## 7.2 'Without prejudice' status

The success of mediation as a process is substantially founded on the principle that what takes place at the mediation is and remains inaccessible to the courts in subsequent litigation if the mediation does not result in settlement. Putting it another way, mediations do not generate admissible evidence. How is access to such theoretically relevant material as admissions concerning liability and causation of damage and willingness to make an offer effectively denied to trial judges?

The starting point is the 'without prejudice' rule of evidence, which has developed as a mix of public policy and implied or express agreement between parties. The House of Lords made it clear in *Rush & Tomkins v*

---

1 *Instance Bros Ltd v Denny* The Times 28 Feb 2000 and *Venture Investment Placement v Hall* [2005] EWHC 1227 (Ch). The certainty of the procedure commended itself to Colman J in *Cable & Wireless v IBM* [2002] EWCH 2059 (Comm) sufficiently to allow him to enforce an ADR contract clause in that case.
2 See *Brown v Rice & Patel* [2007] EWCA 625 (Ch).

$GLC^3$ that all genuine negotiations, whether oral or written, undertaken in an attempt to settle a dispute are protected from subsequent disclosure in proceedings, whether or not the label 'without prejudice' has been applied to them. They quoted Oliver LJ's rationale for this from his judgment in *Cutts v Head*,[4] a judgement long before ADR and the CPR began to aspire to the same aims:

> '... Parties should be encouraged so far as possible to settle their disputes without resort to litigation and should not be discouraged by the knowledge that anything that is said in the course of such negotiations (and that includes, of course, as much the failure to reply to an offer as an actual reply) may be used to their prejudice in the course of their proceedings.'

Thus, if discussions take place before a mediation agreement is signed, or a mediation takes place without a mediation agreement being signed, the 'without prejudice' rule will protect exchanges between the parties themselves as part of the process and preparation for it from subsequent disclosure, subject to the exceptions of and limitations to the rule. Clearly, such protection applies also to communications through solicitors and counsel for each party. But there is no authority on whether by extension similar protection would be afforded to admissions and offers made or reported to or passed through an independent intermediary such as a mediator in the absence of a further protection such as a specific agreement not to call a mediator as a witness (a common clause discussed below in **7.4**). But it seems highly likely that this protection would be afforded on public policy grounds.

'Without prejudice' protection does not simply limit later disclosure as between those between whom the privileged communication initially passed. In cases involving parties who were not privy to the privileged communications or settlement discussions or the mediation, there cannot be any express or implied contract: restrictions can only be founded on public policy considerations. In the *Rush* case, having confirmed the privileged attached to communications between direct disputants, Lord Griffiths went on:

> 'But it would surely be equally discouraging if the main contractor knew that if he achieved a settlement those admissions could then be used against by him **by any other** sub-contractor with whom he might also be in dispute. The main contractor might well be prepared to make certain concessions to settle some modest

---

3  [1988] 3 All ER 737.
4  [1984] 1 All ER 597.

claim which he would never make in the face of another far larger claim.'

This passage was quoted with approval in *Instance Bros v Denny*,[5] in which Lloyd J had to decide whether privileged communications in 'without prejudice' correspondence, settlement meetings and at a mediation conducted on CEDR's standard terms should be kept from subsequent litigation about wider disputes in the United States between the same or related parties. He granted injunctions to restrain disclosure of all three classes of communication from use in US proceedings.

What are the limitations on 'without prejudice' protection? A mediation agreement itself, despite being created for the purpose of 'without prejudice' discussions, will be admissible to prove its terms. It might be argued that the contents of 'without prejudice' exchanges may be accessible to a judge to prove that there never was a genuine dispute between the parties which could earn such protection. It is unlikely that a mediation would be set up for a non-existent dispute, but the problem is avoided by spelling out the nature of the dispute as a recital in the mediation agreement. Again, an apparently protected 'without prejudice' offer or admission may be admissible to prove not the content of what was asserted but the fact that the assertion was made. A settlement agreement signed at a mediation is admissible to prove whether or not a binding and enforceable contract was made,[6] and a 'without prejudice' document containing a settlement offer but also evidencing an act of bankruptcy is admissible to prove the act of bankruptcy.[7]

In *Brown v Rice and Patel*,[8] a dispute between a trustee in bankruptcy and a purchaser of a property from the bankrupt at an alleged undervalue, the judge admitted evidence to show whether or not a concluded agreement had been reached at the mediation held shortly before trial, regarding such an investigation as permissible as an exception to the 'without prejudice' rule. He found that agreement had not been reached, mainly on the basis that the self-imposed requirement in the mediation agreement that any settlement had to be in writing signed by the parties to be binding had not been met. He took the view that mediation was simply assisted 'without prejudice' negotiation, and therefore subject to the normal exceptions to the 'without prejudice' rule.[9]

---

5  (2000) The Times, 28 February.
6  For further illustrations, see Hoffmann LJ in *Muller v Linsley and Mortimer* [1996] PNLR 74; (1994) The Times, 8 December.
7  *Daintrey, ex parte Holt, Re* [1893] 2 QB 116.
8  [2007] EWHC 625 (Ch): Stuart Isaacs QC sitting as a Deputy High Court Judge.
9  In *Chantrey Vellacott v The Convergence Group plc* [2007] EWHC 1774 (Ch), Rimmer J admitted evidence of offers made by each side during a mediation to assist him in deciding what costs order to make in relation to the mediation work, counsel for both parties having purportedly waived 'without prejudice' privilege.

There are limitations on disclosure of 'without prejudice' exchanges when it comes to deciding to costs issues in later litigation. It was made clear in *Reed Executive Plc v Reed Business Information Ltd*[10] that 'without prejudice' material possibly relevant to unreasonable behaviour giving rise to costs sanctions (in that case over one party's refusal to adopt ADR) can only be seen by the court if it also marked 'without prejudice save as to costs'.

Evidence may also be admissible of unambiguous impropriety in the course of otherwise 'without prejudice' negotiations. Thus, if serious threats are made to compel agreement at a mediation, these may lose protection. Such exceptions are discussed in full by Robert Walker LJ in *Unilever Bros v Proctor & Gamble*,[11] though in doing so he said:

> 'Expansion of exceptions [to the 'without prejudice' rule] should not be encouraged when an important ingredient of Lord Woolf's reforms of civil justice is to encourage those who are in dispute to engage in frank discussions before they resort to litigation.'

Only the clearest impropriety will forfeit the privilege,[12] and any attempt in a mediation to engage in impropriety is likely to be challenged by the mediator or the other party before taking shape sufficiently to be impeached later.

Despite the general applicability of the 'without prejudice' rule, mediation agreements often remind parties specifically of its impact specifically through such provisions as:

> 'all information (whether in oral, written, electronic or any other form) created for the purpose of, or at, or arising out of or in connection with, the mediation will be without prejudice to and privileged from disclosure and inadmissible as evidence in, any existing or future litigation in relation to the dispute or any other proceedings whatsoever, except where such information would in any event have been disclosable in any such proceedings.'

This probably adds nothing to the general law, even as regards proceedings outside the dispute settled at mediation,[13] unless the reasonableness of a compromise reached in a mediation is put in issue in later proceedings by someone with a legitimate interest in those settlement terms.[14]

---

10  [2004] EWCA Civ 887.
11  [2000] 1 WLR 1436.
12  See *Aird & Aird v Prime Meridian Ltd* [2006] EWHC 2338 (TCC).
13  See above fn.3.
14  See *Standard Telephones & Cables v Tomlin* [1969] 3 All ER 201 and above fn.6.

It means that the written case summaries prepared for the purposes of the mediation are privileged. But it does not mean that documents which are disclosable in the ordinary course but which emerge for the first time at a mediation can have any privilege conferred upon them for that reason alone.[15] It also appears to mean that early communications between parties and the mediator before a mediation agreement is signed will become protected by the later signing of the mediation agreement, as well as being automatically covered by 'without prejudice' privilege. As Lloyd J said in the *Instance Bros* case:[16]

> 'Mediation is defined as the attempt to settle the dispute by mediation. The process of getting to entry into the mediation agreement is itself, albeit at a preliminary stage, an attempt to settle the dispute by mediation.'

Such matters were considered in *Aird v Prime Meridian*.[17] In a construction dispute, mediation was agreed and an order made for the experts to meet and produce a joint statement. The claimant's expert thought it was agreed that the joint statement would be covered by mediation privilege, but the order did not make this clear. When he appeared to change his mind over matters in the joint statement after the mediation did not settle the claim, the defendants argued that the joint statement should be made available to the judge under CPR Pt 35.12(3). The trial judge found that it was intended to be privileged, following the view expressed in *Smith Industries v Weiss*[18] that 'without prejudice' protection should only be held to be waived in 'clear and unambiguous circumstances'. However, the Court of Appeal reversed this decision, construing the order and Pt 35.12(3) objectively. In doing so, May LJ commented that mediation confidentiality:

> 'would not apply to documents obviously produced for other purposes which were needed for and produced at the mediation; for example their building contract or the antecedent pleadings in the proceedings.'

This is an unsurprising statement of what anyone in a mediation is likely to expect to be the case. It should make no difference to the fundamentals of mediation confidentiality.

---

15  See the Australian case of *AWA Ltd v Daniels* 24 February 1992 *per* Rogers CJ in the Commercial Division of the Supreme Court of New South Wales, where disclosure was ordered of a document released expressly 'without prejudice' during a mediation which did not settle.

16  At page 33 of the unreported judgement transcript: see EDR Law on the CEDR website at *www.cedr.co.uk*.

17  [2006] EWHC 2338 (TCC) (HHJ Coulson QC); appeal decision at [2006] EWCA Civ 1866.

18  (Unreported, 23 March 2002): Mr R Kaye QC sitting in the Chancery Division.

So when does 'without prejudice' protection first arise in relation to a mediation? Is it only when a mediation agreement has been signed and the process properly started, or does privilege extend back far enough to prevent the court from hearing evidence about who refused to mediate and why? There are inconsistent decisions on this point. In *SITA v Watson Wyatt and Maxwell Batley*,[19] Park J received as evidence a good deal of material which was ordinarily protected as exchanged on 'without prejudice' occasion when considering whether a successful party who declined mediation should be penalised. In *Leicester Circuits v Coats Industries*,[20] a party who pulled out of a mediation very shortly before the due date was penalised in costs, and there was no question raised that the court could not receive evidence of what happened to decide this point. But in *Reed Executive v Reed Business Solutions*,[21] the court declined to see correspondence specifically marked 'without prejudice' in which the parties debated whether to mediate. In *ARP Capita London Market Services Ltd v Ross & Co*,[22] the successful party who had refused to mediate tried unsuccessfully to argue that 'without prejudice' protection applied to antecedent negotiations over whether to mediate. Courts seem ready to admit evidence of failure to mediate for the purpose of assessing whether to impose a costs sanction and not to treat the pre-mediation period as otherwise privileged, unless specifically made 'without prejudice'.[23] The court could of course admit evidence if the pre-mediation transactions were marked 'without prejudice save as to costs'.[24]

The important question, though, is whether mediation is *merely* 'assisted "without prejudice" negotiation', as suggested in the *Brown* case. As we have seen, mediations, unlike normal 'without prejudice' negotiations, are conducted subject to the terms contained in a lengthy agreement which contains a number of significant provisions intended to bind the parties. It is surely over-simplifying the significance and effect of such agreements to regard the process as no more than a 'without prejudice' discussion with a neutral to assist. In the absence of a judicially recognised, or statutorily created, concept of mediation privilege, it can only be synthesised by the mobilisation of contractual obligations and related concepts already known to the law, as this chapter discusses.

---

19 [2002] EWHC 2401 (Ch).
20 [2003] EWCA Civ 333.
21 [2004] EWCA Civ 887.
22 [2004] EWHC 1181 (Ch); Sir Andrew Longmore VC.
23 See also *Framlington Group and Axa Framlington v Barnetson* [2007] EWCA Civ 502, where the Court of Appeal held that where parties might reasonably have contemplated litigation when making 'without prejudice' proposals, privilege will attach. Also see the discussion in *Bradford & Bungley plc v Rashid* [2006] 1 WLR 2006 (HL).
24 See *Reed Executive v Reed Business Solutions* above.

## 7.3 Confidentiality

In addition to any implied or specific term as to 'without prejudice' status, most mediation agreements include detailed provisions as to the confidentiality of the process, requiring signatories to keep confidential and not use for any collateral or ulterior purpose all information in whatever form arising out of, or in connection with, the mediation, including such matters as whether or not the fact that a mediation is to take place or has taken place, what happens at the mediation and the fact and terms of settlement.

As to confidentiality of the fact that a mediation is to take place or has taken place, there has been a shift in thinking, about which those advising parties to a potential mediation need to give consideration. Before the CPR, it was assumed that those intending to mediate might well wish to keep not only the fact of an impending mediation confidential but even the existence of a dispute at all. Now that the CPR and later judicial decisions have made it desirable to claim either willingness to mediate, or credit for having engaged in mediation, mediation agreements often no longer provide that the fact that a mediation is to take place or has taken place is to be confidential. CEDR consciously altered its Model Mediation Agreement to make the default position such that there is no confidentiality as to the fact of a mediation. However, it is always open to parties engaged in particularly delicate situations where confidentiality as to either dispute or settlement attempts is paramount to include a specific provision to achieve that.

The confidential status of dealings between the mediator and the parties prior to the mediation has just been touched in the previous section. The *Instance Bros* case makes it clear that a confidentiality clause in a subsequently signed mediation agreement will apply in full to antecedent negotiations. The CEDR agreement in that case provides that:

> 'every person involved in the mediation will keep confidential and not use for any collateral or ulterior purpose all information (whether given orally in writing or otherwise) produced for or arising in relation to the mediation.'

Lloyd J specifically said:

> 'it seems to me right to regard communications preceding the mediation agreement and during the discussions which led to it as being within the scope of the confidentiality clause. I would regard the use of such material for the United States proceedings as being a collateral or ulterior purpose and therefore in breach of the clause.'

A contractual provision which confirms confidentiality for what happens at the mediation is not merely an evidential rule preventing disclosure of admissions and offers at a subsequent trial. Such a term imposes a positive contractual obligation on all signatories to the mediation agreement (including the mediator and the mediation provider) which is enforceable by positive action for an injunction[25] and/or damages. This distinction is very important. A mediation conducted under an agreement containing a confidentiality clause is a far safer environment than a mere 'without prejudice' discussion or round table conference, where the contents of discussions are simply preserved from being used as evidence before a judge or other decision-maker. The settlement terms are not protected from report after such meetings: indeed, many journals report the outcome of settlement discussions virtually as precedents. Even the content of 'without prejudice' discussions might be publishable, so long as they do not come to the attention of the trial judge. A positive obligation as to confidentiality as to both content and outcome of a mediation may also prevent controversy over whether without prejudice protection extends to the exchanges in question. This can arise where it is perhaps too early in the life of the dispute for the privilege to apply, or where there may not be a justiciable dispute at all, such as in a grievance procedure where parties want or agree to keep discussions from the internal company decision-maker. In 'pre-dispute' facilitations, it is vital to agree the scope of confidentiality before discussions start.

There is no judicially articulated rule of public policy yet enunciated which achieves the same degree of confidentiality, so it will be necessary to continue to make provision for it contractually in the mediation agreement. But there seems to be no judicial enthusiasm in England and Wales for trying to find out what happened behind the closed doors of a mediation: indeed, they recognise that the confidentiality of a mediation is vital to the success of the process.

In *Re D (Minors)*,[26] the Court of Appeal found that statements made to a conciliator could not be introduced by one of the parties as evidence in proceedings under the Children Act 1989 other than in exceptional circumstances, such as where the statement indicates that the maker has in the past caused or is likely in the future to cause serious harm to the well-being of the child. Although the case dealt with children and was specifically stated to be limited to its particular facts, there are one or two very telling points in the judgment of Sir Thomas Bingham, then Master of the Rolls. First, he talked of the law as: '... recognising the general inviolability of the privilege protecting statements made in the course of conciliation.'

---

25 Such an injunction was granted against a party seeking to disclose what transpired at a mediation in both *Instance Bros Ltd v Denny* (2000) The Times 28 Feburary and *Venture Investment Placement v Hall* [2005] EWHC 1227 (Ch).

26 [1993] 2 All ER 693.

More specifically, he was clear that the reason for the protection afforded to such statements is an independent head of privilege which has grown beyond the 'without prejudice' rule and is therefore not subject to the same exceptions. Thus privilege does not attach to a document described as such if it does not contain truly 'without prejudice' material, such as a genuine offer to settle, and he did not question that point. However, he continued:

> 'But we do not accept that evidence can be given of statements made by one party at a meeting admittedly held for the purposes of conciliation because, in the judgment of the other party or the conciliator, that party has shown no genuine willingness to compromise.'

*Re D* was of course a case involving suitability of a parent to have contact with children. But we expect that a similar response might be given by a court invited to hear evidence that a party was intransigent and had no genuine willingness to settle within the confidential confines of a commercial mediation.

Several cases abroad have upheld the confidentiality of what passed within a mediation. In *XvY*, a decision of the Tribunal de Commerce in Brussels in 1999, the confidentiality clause in a CEDR mediation agreement was held to prevent a party from including mention of a mediation in subsequent proceedings. The Tribunal ordered the reference to be struck out and imposed stiff penalties for breach.

As might be expected perhaps, two decisions of the US courts illustrate their determination to penalise breach of mediation confidentiality. In *Parazino v Barnett Bank,* a 1997 Florida appeal case, the claimant who revealed to a newspaper that the bank had made an offer at a mediation which she had refused, hinting that this showed a degree of acceptance of her case, had her entire claim for $100,000 struck out 'with prejudice'. In *Bernard v Calen Group,* a New York appeal case, the claimant's counsel, who had always opposed a court-directed mediation which failed, applied to the judge to end the mediation, quoting what had happened at the mediation (as he saw it) as evidence of the defendants having not engaged seriously in the process. The defendant moved for sanctions, and the court imposed a $2,500 fine (payable personally) on the lawyer.

More recently here, in the leading case of *Halsey v Milton Keynes NHS Trust,* Dyson LJ said:

> 'We make it clear that it was common ground before us (and we accept) that parties are entitled in an ADR to adopt whatever position they wish, and if as a result the dispute is not settled, that

is not a matter for the court.... if the integrity and confidentiality of the process is to be respected, the court should not know, and therefore should not investigate, why the process did not result in agreement.'[27]

Thus, in England and Wales at least, even unreasonable behaviour or failure to engage in good faith in the mediation process is not apparently justiciable at the suit of an aggrieved party in later litigation. Such a purist position has not been maintained in other common law jurisdictions, where attempts have been made to invite judges to peer behind the veil and to penalise those who allegedly misbehaved, or to seek to show that settlement terms were less than fair and reasonable and should be set aside.

Does the privilege, such as it is, apply only for the benefit of the parties, or does the mediator have enforceable protection too? Certainly, where the mediator (and even a mediation provider) is a party to the mediation contract, they have in theory equally enforceable rights, even if enforcing these by action might seem somewhat counter-intuitive for people seeking to minimise resort to litigation. The only recent instance suggesting the contrary (and it seems not to have been argued before the judge) appears in the *SITA* case,[28] in which the defendants settled at mediation with the claimants but failed to persuade the third party into mediation to make a contribution. Having lost the third party proceedings, the defendants sought a costs sanction against the third party and tried to buttress their argument by telling the judge that the mediator had said that they should be able to extract a contribution from the third party. The latter relied on what the mediator purportedly said to excuse their refusal to engage. No one including the judge seems to have considered whether that material should have been laid before the judge at all. On the basis of the above discussion, it should not have been, and the judge should perhaps have declined to admit it on public policy grounds, even though both parties thought it in their interests to introduce it.

As mediators usually confirm to parties at the mediation, there is a deeper level of confidentiality which is normally deployed during the process and which forms another cornerstone for its success. The mediator will normally engage not only in joint meetings with all present, but also in private meetings with all or selected members of each party's team. In such meetings, the mediator will encourage the parties to discuss their

---

27 [2004] EWCA Civ 576 at para 14; [2004] 4 All ER 920. But see *ARP Capita London Market Services Ltd v Ross & Co* [2004] EWHC 1181 (Ch), where Longmore VC was invited to utilise this paragraph of the *Halsey* judgement to prevent investigation into why a successful party had declined to mediate. Eventually Longmore VC decided that the successful party had *not* declined mediation, and ordered the unsuccessful defendant to pay the costs.

28 [2002] EWHC 2025 and 2401 (Ch).

positions, interests and options frankly, on the understanding that nothing disclosed confidentially to the mediator during such discussions will be disclosed to any other party without express permission. By this means, the mediator builds up a truer and fuller picture of possible progress than either party would be likely to do in face-to-face negotiations, where caution over disclosure of true positions is the norm. Indeed, it is this knowledge of the overall picture that chiefly enables the mediator to help the parties to progress towards resolution.

This aspect of the mediation process calls for considerable trust to be reposed in the mediator and for considerable professional judgment and integrity on the part of the mediator. As Colman J once pointed out[29] for a neutral decision-maker to act thus would be a frank breach of the rules of natural justice. But of course a mediator is not a decision-maker, so that natural justice in its normal sense does not impinge on what the mediator does. Regulation of mediators in this respect has to be based purely on contract and potential tortious liability for negligence which causes damage. A mediator's responsibility for acting fairly and confidentially in this way used to be set out in a mix of codes of conduct and model procedure. Now a specific term often appears in mediation agreements to the effect that 'The mediator will not disclose to any other party any information given to the mediator confidentially by a party without the express consent of that party.'

Breaching confidentiality contrary to such a provision would clearly be a breach of contract by the mediator, and possibly negligent. The usual rules, subject to any enforceable exclusion of liability in the mediation agreement protecting the mediator from action, would apply to whether actionable damage had occurred.

Section **7.5** discusses the rare circumstances in which a mediator may be compelled by external authority to disclose information given in confidence.

## 7.4 Mediator immunity from giving evidence

Mediation agreements will usually contain a clause in the following form:

> 'None of the parties to the mediation agreement will call the mediator or any employee, consultant, officer or representative of [the relevant mediation provider] as a witness, consultant, arbitrator or expert in any litigation or other proceedings whatsoever. The mediator will not voluntarily act in any such capacity without the written agreement of all the parties.'

---

29 ADR-an irreversible 'tide' (2003) 19(3) Arbitration International.

In a process where a mediator is the probable repository of confidential information from all those who participate, it is highly undesirable that the mediator might be a compellable witness in subsequent litigation. Such involvement might take several forms. First, where a mediation fails to settle a case, one party might want to call the mediator to verify or corroborate what that party or an opponent said or did, or even as to the state of a party's health or finances, on key issues relevant to the substantive litigation. Given both the contractual and public policy confidentiality of the process as discussed above, it is perhaps unlikely that a judge would receive any such evidence anyway. Secondly, a party might want to call the mediator as to the interpretation of the settlement terms where a dispute arises later over what they are or mean. Thirdly, one party might want to try to bring evidence that an opponent behaved unreasonably over their participation in the mediation process or did not apparently 'attempt in good faith to settle the dispute by means of a mediation', perhaps to buttress an application for a costs sanction. Some mediators such as those operating on behalf of ACAS, are granted statutory immunity. Such immunity is not yet available for commercial mediators in the United Kingdom and the issue therefore has to be dealt with by contract.

A clause in the mediation as above protects both mediator and parties from the mediator being called in this way, at least as regards those who signed it. But will it protect a mediator from being compelled to attend by a judge, or by a party to litigation who was not party to the mediation agreement? After all, the normal rule, founded in public policy, is that a potential witness cannot by agreement bind himself not to give evidence. Judges themselves are not compellable over matters relating to discharge of their judicial functions, but magistrates are, and as mediators do not discharge judicial functions at all, they may be all the more compellable. Nor is a mediator an expert unless called as such about mediation procedure, so that none of the protections for expert witnesses apply.

The only absolute category of a contractually created immunity from giving evidence (also buttressed by common law and indeed public policy) is that of solicitor and client, where the privilege is the client's and not the lawyer's. The relationship of doctor or therapist with a patient is not ultimately sacrosanct, nor that of priest and penitent. The compellability of a spouse was increased by the Police and Criminal Evidence Act 1984, and that of a journalist regarding a source reduced only to some extent by the Contempt of Court Act 1981, s 10. While the court has discretion to respect disclosures made within confidential relationships and to excuse a witness from answering questions about them, this is bound to depend upon the importance of the answers to the issues being tried in the case in question. As Lord Wilberforce said in the House of Lords in *British Steel Corporation*

125

*v Granada Television*,[30] a civil case where a television company was compelled to disclose its confidential source of information to the claimants:

> 'As to information obtained in confidence and the legal duty which may arise to disclose it to a court of justice, the position is clear. Courts have an inherent wish to respect this confidence whether it arises between doctor and patient, priest and penitent, banker and customer, between persons giving testimonials to employees, or in other relationships . . . But in all these cases the courts may have to decide that the interests in preserving this confidence are outweighed by other interests to which the law attaches importance.'

So, in civil cases, it is extremely unlikely that any court would seek to extract confidences from a mediator or party about what transpired confidentially in a mediation, since there is a major public interest in making mediation work well in contributing to the settlement of civil disputes. *Re D*[31] illustrates the likely approach that would be taken generally, with its proviso about child protection.

As already noted, part of the protection for a mediator may lie in the content of what he is invited to testify about, which may itself be protected from judicial eyes by the explicit or public policy content of such evidence. But if a defendant wanted to call the mediator to speak as to the physical condition of a claimant at a mediation in an attempt to show that the claimant was not as disabled as he claimed, or to prove that a party was in truth bankrupt or trading when insolvent, what then? Assuming that the defendant could persuade the judge that the mediator's purported contractual immunity was void as contrary to public policy, is there any other basis on which the judge could decline to receive such evidence?

In practical terms, CPR Pt 32.1 gives a huge discretion to a trial judge as to declining to hear any relevant and admissible evidence:

> '32.1 (1) The court may control the evidence by giving directions as to:
>
> (a) the issues on which it requires evidence;
>
> (b) the nature of the evidence which it requires to decide those issues; and
>
> (c) the way in which the evidence is to be placed before the court.
>
> (2) The court may use its power under this rule to exclude evidence that would otherwise be admissible.'

---

30 [1981] 1 All ER 417 at 455.
31 [1993] 2 All ER 693: see **7.3** above.

However, any judge who tried to exclude relevant and admissible evidence without a principled foundation would be likely to find himself appealed swiftly. Is there a public policy ground that might be deployed to justify declining to hear a mediator on factual matters? None seems to have been articulated so far, possibly because no judge has tried to push matters to that extent.

It seems likely that judges might seek to formulate such a public policy protection in the light of their apparent determination to protect the confidentiality of the mediation process. In an unreported case in the Bristol County Court in 1997, *Bezant v Ushers Brewers,* District Judge Gillian Stuart Brown refused to hear evidence from a mediator who had been subpoenaed to give evidence about what had happened at a mediation; and upheld the binding force of the agreement negotiated at the mediation. The authors are aware of several moves that have been initiated to attempt to call mediators as witnesses, but are not aware of any case hitherto in which a mediator has actually given evidence to an English Court about what happened at a mediation. In *Brown v Rice and Patel,*[32] it appears that a District Judge summoned the mediator to attend to give evidence, but it was conceded at trial by both sides, and not challenged by the judge, that the mediator should not (and possibly could not) be called as a witness.

Article 6 of the draft European Directive published in 2004 proposes that Member States should enact legislation to protect mediators and mediation providers from being compelled to give evidence as to:

–   an invitation by a party to engage in mediation or the fact that a party is willing to engage in mediation;

–   views or suggestions over possible settlement during a mediation;

–   statements or admissions made during a mediation;

–   mediator proposals;

–   the fact that a party was willing to accept a mediator's proposal;

–   documents produced solely for the purpose of a mediation.

All such evidence would be treated as inadmissible. Exceptions are suggested to make such evidence admissible to implement or enforce any settlement emerging directly from the mediation, and for overriding public policy considerations, such as the protection of children or to prevent physical or psychological damage to any person, and (of course) where the mediator and the parties agree. There currently appears little prospect of early implementation of the Directive. Even implementation would not

---

32 [2007] EWHC 625 (Ch).

answer whether a mediator can be called to give evidence of a purely factual nature.[33]

## 7.5 Mediator compellability by external legal authority

As the EC Directive's proposed exceptions to mediator immunity suggest, there are a number of circumstances in which a mediator might be, or feel, compelled by moral considerations to break confidentiality. In the unlikely event that a party disclosed to a mediator information or intentions which might lead to injury or death of others or to the future commission of a crime, then most codes of conduct and mediation agreements relieve the mediator of their normal obligations to keep confidential what they are told. For instance, the duty of confidentiality may be removed if:

- the mediator is required under the general law to make disclosure;
- the mediator reasonably considers that there is a serious impending risk of significant harm to the life or safety of any person if the information relating to that risk is not disclosed;
- the mediator reasonably considers that there is a serious risk of being made personally subject to criminal proceedings unless the information sought is disclosed.

A number of official investigators have considerable powers under the 'general law' to compel co-operation besides the police – HM Revenue and Customs, the Security Services, liquidators, administrators and trustees in bankruptcy under the Insolvency Acts.

There is also the whole question of possible disclosure required by the Proceeds of Crime Act 2002, and allied provisions under the anti-terrorism and drug trafficking legislation. The main risk under the 2002 Act relates to the offence under s 328 of 'arranging' (entering into or becoming concerned in an arrangement), or aiding, abetting, counselling or procuring such an arrangement, which the mediator knows or suspects facilitates the acquisition, retention, use or control of criminal property by or on behalf of another person. 'Criminal property' is defined widely as proceeds or benefits, whether direct or indirect, of any conduct which constitutes a criminal offence in the United Kingdom. It will include tax evasion, benefits obtained through an illegal cartel, bribes paid and even saved costs from failing to comply with a regulatory requirement, failure to observe which is a criminal offence.

33 See further discussion of this and other European issues in **Chapter 10**.

It is probably easy to avoid acquiring actual knowledge as a mediator, but suspicion is a subjective and somewhat slippery concept. A mediator must consider all factors in deciding how to secure protection in the circumstances of any given case. To defend a charge of arranging, the mediator must make an authorised disclosure to the National Criminal Intelligence Service who have seven days within which to confirm that a transaction is untainted and may proceed, hardly of much practical use in a mediation. At the same time, the mediator must not 'tip off' a suspected party or an offence may be committed under s 333 of the Act. The mediator may thus have to adjourn the mediation without explanation so as to fulfil the duties imposed by the legislation.

Some guidance, but no apparent protection for mediators as such, emerged from the Court of Appeal in *Bowman v Fels*,[34] where a solicitor acquired information in the course of litigation which he felt suggested that criminal conduct over VAT avoidance might be involved. The Court held that such disclosure of information during litigation was not intended to be covered by the Act. The proper interpretation of s 328 was that it was not intended to cover or affect the ordinary conduct of litigation by legal professionals. That included any step taken by them in litigation from the issue of proceedings and the securing of injunctive relief or a freezing order up to its final disposal by judgment and included agreement to dispose of the whole or any aspect of legal proceedings on a consensual basis. The originating EU Directive and the 2002 Act did not envisage that any of those ordinary activities fell within the concept of 'becoming concerned in an arrangement which ... facilitates the acquisition, retention, use or control of criminal property'. The Court disapproved of the decision to the contrary of Dame Elizabeth Butler-Sloss in *P v P (Ancillary Relief: Proceeds of Crime)*.[35] They went on to say that even if s 328 did apply to the ordinary conduct of legal proceedings, it did not override legal professional privilege or a solicitor's implied duty to the court not to disclose information gained from documents disclosed by another party to adversarial litigation and not read in open court.

Whether this decision affords any protection to a mediator is open to doubt. Perhaps the only comfort to mediators, whether they are solicitors themselves or not, is that there will almost certainly be someone else under precisely the same duty of disclosure in a mediation as they themselves are. This is a topic that can only be dealt with superficially here, and in view of its huge importance to mediators in terms of potentially disastrous outcomes, they must be advised to acquaint themselves with their responsibilities under this legislation and ensure that they err on the side of caution

---

34 [2005] 4 All ER 609; [2005] EWCA Civ 226.
35 [2003] EWHC Fam 2260 ; [2004] Fam 1.

in discharging them. Even if a mediator feels up to asking an awkward question on such matters, they might be well advised not to insist on hearing the answer.

## 7.6   Authority to settle

Most mediation agreements provide that someone should attend for each party who possesses full authority to settle the dispute to be mediated. This is sometimes done by requiring the nomination of an identified 'Lead Negotiator', who must attend with such authority.

Such a term in the agreement reduces to the absolute minimum any risk that the person who attends the mediation does not have actual and ostensible authority in law to bind the party represented as his or its authorised agent. It is highly desirable, if not essential, though at times ignored, that each party should be represented at the mediation by someone with full authority to settle the dispute. Making this an express term of the mediation agreement helps to emphasise the importance of this principle to those representing each party.

Possessing authority does not of course mean that a settlement will be agreed. This may be because of a disagreement in good faith over an acceptable outcome. Sometimes, however, for a variety of reasons, a party may send a negotiator with limited or fettered authority, who is not authorised to deal at the level proposed, however much that level looks sensible. A company might send a manager or director; a partnership might send one or more partners. Either might send simply a lawyer, whether in-house or external, with a degree of authority to settle. The authority may extend up or down to a certain financial limit, or may require the representative to discuss the matter with others before concluding a settlement. This situation is by no means ideal. If a deal is struck after 12 hours of mediation, and final agreement is subject to a phone call to someone who has not been present, the latter may object to some proposals. Not having been present to hear all the debate and watch the deal slowly emerge, the absentee is not well placed to judge its terms properly from within the context of the mediation.

If this happens, then the parties and the mediator simply have to work within that constraint. What might arise is whether there is any remedy in the hands of the aggrieved party for the fact that their opponent has actually breached the terms of the mediation agreement, by not disclosing any limitation on authority before signing the agreement and in effect warranting full authority to settle, or by disabling themselves from being able 'in good faith to settle the dispute' by means of the mediation. While there has been considerable litigation to seek remedies for such matters in the United States and Australia, no such litigation has to our knowledge been determined in the United Kingdom. As such disclosure has to emerge from the confidential confines of the process itself, there will be difficulty in initially adducing evidence of it. It is unlikely to fall into the 'unambiguous impropriety' exception to the 'without prejudice' rule, even if a way around any specific confidentiality clause can be found. Furthermore, even if liability can be established, there may be problems over proof of damage. But where the United States and Australia go first, the United Kingdom often follows, so we may expect points of this nature to be litigated in the future.

Four further situations relating to authority to settle are worth bearing in mind.

### 7.6.1   Insured parties

Where the liability of one or more parties is to any extent covered by insurance, the insurer's consent will be required to any settlement, perhaps depending on the level of self-insurance or excess on the policy. If insurers carry the whole or the majority of the risk themselves, they will attend the mediation and control it as they would any litigation, having been subrogated to the rights of their insured. This is obviously the optimum solution. If the insurers are unable or unwilling to attend, the lines of settlement authority should be clearly set up in advance, but it is less than ideal not to have the decision-maker present in person.

If there is a dispute between the insurer and party as to indemnity, the insurer ought to attend the mediation as an additional party, enabling the subsidiary dispute between insured and insurer to be settled at the same time. At least the presence of the insurer will allow the insured to settle the main dispute with the insurer's authority, leaving the indemnity problem between them to be sorted out later. Similar considerations apply to reinsurance contracts. In whichever capacity they attend, they should be bound into the other contractual provisions relating to 'without prejudice' status, confidentiality and mediator immunity.

### 7.6.2   Groups of companies and partnerships

Where a party is one of a group of companies, care should be taken to ensure that authority to settle is present on behalf of all those companies in the group who are likely to be involved in the settlement. This may well be a wider group than those who are party to the dispute. The same principle applies to appropriate channels of authority and consent in respect of a partnership. Again, with both companies and partnerships it is unlikely that the whole main board or all the partners will attend, giving rise to the need for care to be taken over authority to settle.

### 7.6.3   Public bodies

Complications may well arise with public bodies. Given the decision-making structures of national or local government, it is unlikely that any individuals will be able to attend a mediation with completely unfettered authority to settle. More likely, those who attend will be authorised to agree settlement terms subject to obtaining final approval from the relevant Minister or an appropriate committee, typically a finance committee. Although not ideal for the reasons given above, mediation can and does still operate effectively in these circumstances. It may be helpful, however, to obtain a commitment in advance that the appropriate committee will meet within a specified and short period following the mediation, so that the matter is not left unresolved for too long. Further, the track record of the person attending the mediation and the Lead Negotiator in securing approval of a recommended settlement is relevant. The mediator might even be asked to attend that meeting to assist in explaining (and if necessary justifying) the settlement terms.

### 7.6.4   Parties under legal incapacity

It is clearly impossible for a binding agreement to be made at a mediation which affects the rights of a party to a dispute who does not possess legal capacity to contract. This may well arise in mediations relating to personal injury and clinical negligence claims, where there may be claimants who are infants or who have suffered serious brain damage, or in wills and trusts cases involving infant beneficiaries. This is not to say that such cases cannot be effectively dealt with by mediation. Terms that are agreeable are worked out and agreed, conditional upon court approval. Application is then made to the court for approval by the judge.

For this reason, as we suggest in **Chapter 12**, it is wise for the counsel who is to advise on the reasonableness of any provisional settlement for this purpose, to be actually present at the mediation, so as to take a full part in the debate which leads to the terms to be referred to the court. The counsel can then give due explanation to the judge from direct knowledge over any appreciable discount for litigation risk.

## 7.7   The enforceability of settlement agreements

Mediations are intended to be the channel through which parties in dispute can bring their dispute to an end. This may not happen for good reason, requiring the litigation to continue. But, if settlement is reached, the parties need to know that this has indeed happened and the terms on which it has happened, and they also need to know that the terms are enforceable, if this is what they intended.

As to the first major point, a balance has to be struck within the mediation process to enable it to be non-binding until clear terms of settlement are agreed. As we have seen, the content of discussions during mediations remains privileged if no settlement is reached. As a further means of creating a secure environment for exploring settlement, most mediation agreements specifically provide that any settlement reached through a mediation must be recorded in writing and signed by the parties before it is binding. This is a self-imposed formality: without it, an oral contract properly supported by consideration would suffice to settle a mediated dispute, except where other legal requirements are imposed, such as over sale of land. It is a means of ensuring certainty over whether, and on what terms, agreement has been reached. It also acts as a reassurance that there is no unwitting or under-evidenced agreement.

Where a case already in litigation is settled through mediation, the norm is either for a settlement agreement to be signed at the conclusion of the mediation, which includes a term requiring the parties to lodge an agreed consent application within a specified time which reflects the agreed terms; or for the parties to agree and sign the terms of a Tomlin Order containing the agreed terms which can itself be lodged to secure the formal stay of proceedings on terms which allow for the immediate enforcement of the order if default occurs. Our experience is that default is very much a rarity, perhaps because parties have close control over the negotiated outcome and feel more satisfied with what they have negotiated instead of having an outcome imposed. Either way of recording settlement terms if signed by all parties constitutes sufficient writing to satisfy the mediation agreement's requirement.

In cases where no litigation proceedings have been commenced, so long as the parties ensure that the normal requirements for a binding contract are observed, the settlement agreement will be enforceable just like any other contract. In England and Wales it cannot be made into a court order unless proceedings are formally commenced. If such a settlement agreement is breached, then, depending on its terms, proceedings can be commenced for breach of contract as usual.

Courts are reasonably relaxed over allowing matters far outside the scope of the action before it to be included in settlement agreements lodged in the form of schedules to Tomlin Orders. Indeed, one of the reasons for using a Tomlin Order is that confidential terms can be set out in the schedule, which are not open to public view. However, where there has been mistake, fraud or illegality, settlements in Tomlin Order form can be challenged just like any other contract.

Special formalities are required for settling disputes relating to Employ-ment Tribunal cases in a way which is effective to exclude the Tribunal's jurisdiction. Unless such requirements relating to compromise agreements are met, the Tribunal's jurisdiction will not be ousted, whether the mediation takes place before or after the issue of an application to the Tribunal. Compromise agreements must either have involved action by a conciliation officer from the Arbitration and Conciliation Service in negotiating the settlement terms, or

- must be in writing;
- be related to the particular complaint at issue and not a general settlement of past and future issues; and
- be based on advice from a 'relevant independent adviser'[36] with suitable professional indemnity insurance, who has no connection with the other party to the dispute.

Observation of the required formalities will however only oust the **Tribunal**'s jurisdiction; contractual claims in the **civil courts** will be barred if the settlement agreement is otherwise valid.

Judges rarely intervene on their own initiative because they disapprove of the content of a settlement. One instance of an attempt to do this arose in *Thakrar v Thakrar*,[37] in which the Court of Appeal refused to allow the Tomlin Order to be sealed and granted permission to appeal to administrators, apparently based on concerns that a court dealing with this issue on the merits would be unlikely to approve a payment which might appear to be a preference over unsecured creditors. The effect of this refusal was reversed in *Thakrar v Ciro Citterio Menswear Plc (in administration) and others*,[38] when in further proceedings for a declaration that the company was bound by the mediation agreement, the Vice-Chancellor found the settlement to have been unconditional as to its effect, and declined to find that it was in any way illegal. He further found that a genuine compromise made on the advice of lawyers of a dispute, involving a doubtful question of fact which might or might not render a transaction illegal, should be upheld by the court, and did so, finding that the settlement agreement negotiated within the mediation and embodied in the draft Tomlin Order was both unconditional and enforceable.

Mediators and parties need to bear the need for a written agreement in mind where for instance a cooling-off period is agreed (useful for consumer disputes and where parties are unrepresented), or if some other condition

---

36 A qualified barrister, solicitor or legal executive; or a union official or advice centre adviser certified by their organisation as competent – for full details see *Harvey on Industrial Relations and Employment Law*.
37 [2002] EWCA Civ 1304.
38 [2002] EWHC 1975 (Ch).

has to be met before an agreement is reached. Even settlements on such terms should be written down and signed for them to be binding.

Although the possibility of a written settlement agreement being over-ridden by waiver, estoppel, or a collateral contract was discussed in the *Brown* case,[39] none of these was in the event found to have modified the requirement for writing signed by the parties imposed by the mediation agreement. With no such formality in evidence, the judge found that there was no binding agreement on the facts of that case.

## 7.8  The need for greater legal protection for ADR processes

There is almost certainly no special kind of mediation privilege in English law, merely reliance on the contractual terms in mediation agreements and the effect of the normal rules of procedure and evidence. If judges make incursions into such matters as the confidentiality of what occurs at a mediation, it may well be that mediation and other ADR processes will need the kind of definition of its parameters and protection for its status that legislation has provided in other common law jurisdictions, and that the EU Draft Directive proposes.

---

39  [2007] EWHC 625 (Ch).

*Chapter 8*

# Litigation costs and funding in relation to mediations

Unlike a number of other common and civil law jurisdictions, litigation in England and Wales involves not only decisions about what remedies are available to dispose of the substantive issues in any given dispute, but also about who should bear the costs of the dispute, whether or not proceedings have been issued. The costs at stake can often match or outstrip the sums in dispute. Thus, at the end of any hearing, whether a trial or application, the judge will be required to decide what costs order to make in the light of the substantive decision, and there may be lengthy argument on what the appropriate order should be. When settling cases too, whether before issue or trial, similar regard has to be given to negotiating an acceptable basis for the payment of costs. Thus, almost without exception during a mediation, the issue of where the burden of costs is to lie will arise. This can prove a serious obstacle to settlement, even when the dispute itself has been sorted out. Some major areas of dispute have virtually no costs jurisdiction, such as employment tribunals, and this too has implications both for funding and the way settlements are crafted at mediations.

Related to costs considerations are questions of funding. Clearly, a party that can afford to litigate has greater power of choice over whether to settle, both within and outside mediations, than a party under financial constraints. Since the large-scale reduction in scope and availability of Legal Services Commission (LSC) funding in civil claims (formerly known as Legal Aid), other means have been developed to enable those who are neither poor nor rich enough to fund their litigation to do so. Use of Conditional Fee Agreements (CFAs) in which a successful party can recover a success fee and any litigation insurance premium from the unsuccessful party has been authorised by the Access to Justice Act 1999. The problems that arise from their use are now emerging at mediations, hence the need for some review of their effect and how mediators might help parties to deal with these.

These are complex topics and cannot be covered in full detail, but we now set out an outline of the significant ways in which costs can impinge upon mediation practice, particularly for non-lawyer readers of this book.

## 8.1 Costs: some definitions

The legal costs of conducting litigation include:

- the legal costs of the solicitors in conducting the case for their client, both before and after issue of proceedings;
- fees payable to the court on issue of proceedings or applications made during the case, and on filing allocation and listing questionnaires;
- any barrister's fees incurred in advising, settling statements of case, and the brief fee and refresher fees for representation at interim hearings and trial;
- any expert's fees for giving reports on and attending at trial to give evidence;
- other incidental expenses;
- Value Added Tax.

These will be referred to as 'the costs of the claim', whether incurred by a claimant in making a claim or a defendant or third party in defending a claim, and will include costs incurred both before and after the issue of proceedings. Note that, normally, the successful claimant may have some expectation of recovering pre-issue costs, but defendants do not have any expectation of costs reimbursement in investigating a claim before issue unless and until proceedings are issued.

A sub-division of the costs of the claim will be those costs and expenses incurred in preparing for and attending at a mediation on behalf of any party. These will be referred to as 'the costs of the mediation'. A further sub-division which will be dealt with later in this chapter are the fees and expenses payable to the mediator either directly or to and through any mediation services provider in respect of the mediator's services in preparing for and conducting a mediation and any agreed follow-up. These will be referred to as 'the mediation fees'.

The above are definitions developed for the purpose of this book. It is also necessary to define and distinguish several more terms which appear in the CPR, and without which the concepts related to costs of any claim cannot be understood. There are two bases upon which such costs are awarded by a judge or agreed on settlement. The *standard basis* is the norm, and when it is applied, costs are allowable if they are proportionate to the matters in issue, with any doubt over the reasonableness of what is sought being decided in favour of the *paying party*. In practical terms, where a party is awarded or agreed to receive standard basis costs, these will rarely cover all the receiving party's liability to its own lawyers for their costs of the claim. That party may still be left with a liability for anything between 20–30% of its costs of the claim. Conversely, the *indemnity basis* for paying costs is close to 100% of the receiving party's costs of the claim. Proportionality is disregarded on this basis, and any doubt over reasonableness will be resolved in favour of the *receiving party*.

Where agreement proves impossible over what should be paid, the court can be invited to rule on allowable costs of the claim through the elaborate and quite costly procedure of *detailed assessment*, when a costs judge will rule on disputed costs issues between the parties. In cases where the hearing of an application or a trial takes no more than one day, the judge will normally make a *summary assessment* of the costs involved at the conclusion of the hearing.

## 8.2 The basis for costs awards under the CPR

As was explained in **Chapter 6** in relation to costs sanctions for declining ADR, the CPR have encouraged judges to make orders in relation to the costs of the claim in a much more issue-sensitive manner than before. CPR Pt 44 provides for such orders to take into account the behaviour of each party both before and after the commencement of proceedings in deciding what order to make. The central provisions of CPR Pt 44 are as follows:

44.3 (1)  The court has discretion as to:

(a)  whether costs are payable by one party to another;

(b)  the amount of those costs;

(c)  when they are to be paid.

(2)  If the court decides to make an order about costs:

(a)  the general rule is that the unsuccessful party will be ordered to pay the costs of the successful party; but

(b)  the court may make a different order. . . . . . . . .

(3)  . . . . . . . . .

(4)  In deciding what order (if any) to make about costs, the court must have regard to all the circumstances, including:

(a)  the conduct of all the parties;

(b)  whether a party has succeeded on part of his case, even if he has not been wholly successful;

(c)  any payment into court or admissible offer to settle made by a party which is drawn to the court's attention (whether or not made in accordance with Part 36).

139

(5)   The conduct of the parties includes:

(a)   conduct before as well as during the proceedings and in particular the extent to which the parties followed any relevant pre-action protocol;

(b)   whether it was reasonable for a party to raise, pursue or contest a particular allegation or issue;

(c)   the manner in which a party has pursued or defended his case or a particular allegation or issue;

(d)   whether a claimant who has succeeded in his claim, in whole or in part, exaggerated his claim.

Since the CPR, the courts have in practice frequently made orders departing from the traditional rule that the costs follow the event. The leading case in relation to mediation is *Dunnett v Railtrack*,[1] where a successful appellant was refused costs for declining mediation recommended by the court. However, there are many instances of cases which have nothing to do with mediation where the judge has exercised discretion against parties who had apparently won, yet did not obtain all their costs;[2] or where an offer on Pt 36 was not beaten, and yet the defendant did not secure the traditional consequences of victory.[3] Certainty over costs outcomes has been further eroded by the concept of proportionality, which can be used to disallow costs on the standard basis which are found to be disproportionate to the matters in issue. There is however little evidence of widespread disallowance of standard basis costs by costs judges as being disproportionate. While there is little published evidence of costs sanctions being imposed because of unreasonable litigation conduct before issue of proceedings, whether for failure to observe the pre-action protocols or otherwise, the Court of Appeal in *Burchell v Bullard*[4] indicates that such powers are there and may be exercised.

The result of this flexibility of approach in making costs orders has been a considerable degree of unpredictability about costs outcomes, something about which mediators might test out during the mediation process where there is a possibility that a party might not recover all their costs as a result of perhaps unreasonable or extravagantly conducted litigation.

## 8.3   Transferring the potential costs burden: CPR Part 36

As we saw in **Chapter 4**,[5] Pt 36 of the CPR enlarged the possibilities for parties to encourage settlement of proceedings by imposing significant

1 See **Chapter 6**; and also see the discussion in *Burchell v Bullard* (See 6.9).
2 For example, *Mars v Teknowledge* TLR 8 July 1999.
3 For example, *Ford v GKR Construction Ltd* [2000] 1 All ER 802.
4 [2005] EWCA Civ 358.
5 See 4.2.7.

costs penalties on parties who fail to improve on a formal offer to settle made by their opponent. If a *defendant* makes a written offer to settle for a certain sum, or on both monetary and non-monetary terms, giving the claimant 21 days to accept it, the claimant must decide within that time whether to accept or reject the offer. If accepted, the claim is concluded on the terms set out in the offer, and the claimant is also automatically entitled to his costs of the claim on the standard basis. If the claimant rejects the terms of the offer and does better than the offer at trial, he will normally receive at least standard basis costs for the whole claim, or even (if the defendant's conduct of the case is open to criticism) indemnity basis costs. If, however, the claimant fails to obtain judgment on terms better than those formally proposed in the defendant's Pt 36 offer, he may well only be granted costs up to the date of that offer, and be ordered to pay both (or all other) parties' costs from the date of that offer to the end of the trial. In such a circumstance, whatever lesser sum of damages is awarded will be available to offset the claimant's costs liability to the defendant. If the claimant loses altogether, he will face a judgment for the defendant's costs and be liable to his own solicitor for all his own costs, unless he and his solicitor entered into a lawful CFA, under which the solicitor agreed not to charge his client any costs unless the claim was won. Conditional Fee Agreements and insurance against liability for the defendant's costs are considered in more detail below. Defendants no longer have to pay the amount of their Part 36 offer into court to await the outcome of the trial. If they fail to pay the offered sum within 14 days of acceptance of the offer, judgment may be entered for the unpaid sum and Pt 36 costs protection will be lost.[6]

Part 36 introduced for the first time the right for *claimants* to make offers to settle. A claimant may serve a written offer to settle on the defendant, usually somewhat less than the full amount of the claim, indicating perhaps an acceptance of litigation risk. If the defendant agrees to settle on that basis within 21 days, again the claim is ended on those terms plus standard basis costs payable by the defendant to the claimant. If the claimant does better than his own Pt 36 offer at trial, he may be awarded indemnity costs and interest at a penal rate of up to 10 per cent above base rate on such damages and costs and for such period as the court may order. Part 36 offers can be made either before or after issue of proceedings, and will normally have the same consequences.

In every case, the trial judge must not be told of the fact or terms of any Pt 36 offer until after judgment has been given on the substantive issues at trial. But no such secrecy need be used with a mediator, as the mediator makes no judgments. A mediator should always enquire what Pt 36 offers to settle, if any, have been made by any party before the mediation. Nothing

---

6 See CPR 44th amendment, effective from 6 April 2007.

is likelier to inflame negotiations than unwittingly conveying a worse offer than that party proposed before the mediation by a Pt 36 offer or otherwise.

Part 36 thus creates incentives to settle by allowing proposals to be made without prejudice except as to costs, which, if refused, can shift or increase liability for the costs of the claim. Part 36 procedure allows a claimant or defendant to concede confidentially that they may not win wholly and protect themselves from liability for the cost of unreasonably prolonged litigation. Such offers frequently precede mediations and, where a mediated settlement does not emerge, will frequently be made or increased shortly afterwards, based on reappraisal of risks made during the mediation process. Where a Pt 36 offer was made but rejected before a mediation, the party who made the offer may argue at the mediation that the party who declined it remains at risk on costs, because the Pt 36 offer remains at a challenging level. Occasionally, a mediation leads to settlement on the basis that the terms of an earlier Pt 36 offer are accepted late, with some compromise on costs since the date of that offer. This has to be done by mutual agreement, since a party who does not accept a Pt 36 proposal within the 21 days following the offer has no right to accept it after that period, except by agreement or court order.

## 8.4 The impact of litigation funding on mediation

A successful party in an English lawsuit will want to recover as much of his costs outlay (in other words, his funding commitment to his own lawyers) from the unsuccessful party as he can. The extent to which this is possible depends on the way the case has been funded.

### 8.4.1 Normal funding

The simplest arrangement is where each party and lawyer contract for the party to pay the lawyer's costs of the claim, usually on an agreed hourly rate or sometimes a fixed fee. Every solicitor is required by professional practice rules[7] to set out the terms of engagement to each client when instructed at the outset. The rate or fee may be the same whether the case is won or lost or there may be a discount from the rate if the case is not won. Both sides will normally operate on this basis in a commercial claim. At the conclusion of the case, whether by trial, acceptance of a Pt 36 in due time or settlement, both parties will be liable to pay their lawyer's costs of the claim in full on that agreed basis, but the successful party will hope to recover a large proportion of those costs from the unsuccessful party. As we have seen above, if the court orders that costs are recoverable on the standard basis, then the successful party will almost certainly still

---

7 Solicitors' Code of Conduct 2007, Rule 2.

have to pay a proportion of his own lawyer's costs of the claim. If an indemnity costs order has been secured against the unsuccessful party, then the successful party may well recover virtually all his costs liability to his lawyer. Where a claim is discontinued, the claimant will normally be liable to pay the defendant's costs of the claim on the standard basis.

### 8.4.2 Legal Service Commission funding

Legal Services Commission funding, formerly known as Legal Aid, is only available in very limited types of case. These include clinical negligence claims and claims against the police and other professionals. The financial limits are set very low, so that relatively few people are financially eligible. Claims brought on behalf of children may well attract LSC funding, as they are normally without means.

Where a claimant (or, rarely, a defendant) has LSC funding for a claim to be brought or defended, that party will normally be protected from any adverse costs order against the opposing party even if he loses or fails to beat a Pt 36 offer. When a Pt 36 offer is made, however, or evidence emerges which casts doubt on the assisted person's prospects of success, his legal advisers are obliged to report such matters to the LSC who may withdraw funding if it seems no longer reasonable to continue it. Occasionally defendants will draw the Commission's attention to such matters themselves by direct correspondence.

Where LSC funding is intact, this costs protection puts an assisted party in a powerful negotiating position at a mediation, since they face no adverse costs consequences if they lose. Defendants may be inclined to propose settlement even if they have a strong defence, as they face having to bear their own costs even if they win. If the LSC funded party wins, he will usually be entitled to an order for standard basis costs. If his solicitor is entitled to charge the assisted person for work done but cannot recover for that work as standard basis costs (for instance, where the defendant obtained a costs order against the claimant on an interim application), those irrecoverable costs will be deductible from the claimant's damages under what is termed the LSC's 'statutory charge'. LSC funded parties will therefore always seek to recover the maximum for costs at a mediation in order to minimise the impact of the statutory charge on agreed damages.

The statutory charge takes on greater significance if the LSC funded party loses to any extent. If for instance an LSC funded party is allowed to continue a claim after a Pt 36 offer has been made, but fails to beat that offer at trial, such reduced damages as were awarded will first be subject to the deduction of the defendant's costs since the Pt 36 offer. They will then have the LSC funded party's own solicitor's costs incurred since declining the Pt 36 offer deducted by virtue of the statutory charge. This can seriously deplete or exhaust the damages fund, and can put pressure on an LSC funded party to consider a compromise. If the case is lost altogether, with no damages available to reduce costs liability, the court will normally make a costs order 'not to be enforced without the court's permission'. So, if the LSC funded party receives a later financial windfall, the whole costs order might be successfully enforced later.

### 8.4.3  Legal expenses insurance

This is one of the main funding methods for private litigants. Legal expenses insurance may be purchased as a stand-alone policy, or more usually it is offered or purchased as an additional form of cover with a household or motor insurance policy. In effect, it indemnifies the policy-holder against liability for the legal costs of any claim brought or defended by the insured, whether payable to his own solicitor or to any opposing solicitor, up to a preset limit which may be as much as £50,000. If the claim involves defending a claim arising from a motor accident, however, a driver will normally be represented by his motor insurer and his defence funded under the motor policy. The insurer will often require their own panel solicitor to represent the claimant. These policies are sometimes called 'before-the-event' insurance or BEI policies, as the indemnity for costs is put in place before any claim has arisen.

Such an indemnity limit looks very substantial, but, with legal costs as high as they are, this can be rapidly expended on a substantial claim with complex and expensive evidential requirements. It must also be remembered that an opposing party can seek to transfer their costs liability by making a Pt 36 offer. Insurers require close monitoring and reporting by the insured's solicitor of any offers to settle which might impinge on the costs liabilities of the parties, so as to ensure that the litigation still has acceptable prospects of success.

If a claim funded by legal expenses insurance is lost, the insurer will be liable to pay both the insured's and the opponent's costs up to the indemnity limit under the policy, leaving the insured liable for any additional costs recoverable by the winning party unrecovered from the policy. Solicitors whose clients have to resort to their legal expenses policy to pay for representing the client may have to weigh their risks to their claims reputation or panel membership with that legal expenses insurer when considering recovery of their own costs.

### 8.4.4  Conditional fee agreements and after the event insurance

Conditional Fee Agreements were initially introduced to make it possible for a wide range of claimants to seek compensation for road traffic accidents and, to an extent, clinical negligence claims. Their scope has now been widened to most types of claim, most notably commercial claims and defamation, and occasionally the defence of claims. The principle behind the current law[8] is that a claimant can instruct a solicitor to pursue or defend a claim regardless of means, knowing that broadly speaking he will not have to pay his solicitor's costs of the claim if the case is lost. This has given rise to the over-simple tag 'no win-no fee' for such arrangements. The solicitor therefore agrees to handle the case based on his risk assessment as to success. If he is wrong, he will carry out the work on the case without charge. But if he is right and his client wins, he becomes entitled to claim a 'success fee' of up to 100 per cent of his normal costs on the case from the unsuccessful defendant. The riskier the case, the higher will be the percentage mark-up sought. When first introduced, the success fee was borne out of the claimant's own damages, but the 1999 Act has shifted the burden of success fees across to unsuccessful defendants. Barristers too can agree to act for clients on a conditional fee basis, so that if a case is lost, the claimant will have no liability for the fees of either his solicitor or his barrister.

However, if a claimant loses, the mere existence of a CFA between the claimant and his solicitor and barrister provides no protection against the defendant's claim for payment of costs, having defeated the claim. The claimant remains personally liable to pay any adverse costs order. However, it is possible for claimants to insure against potential liability for an opponent's costs in the event of losing the litigation. Such policies have come to be known as 'after-the-event' insurance (or AEI) policies, though this is a misnomer. They are of course taken out *after* the accident which led to the claim, but *before* the real insured event, which is the making of an adverse costs order at the end of the litigation. Premiums for such policies are rated in accordance with the likely costs to be incurred and the risks of failure. Rates can be very high indeed, especially in sectors where claims are hard to bring home successfully, such as clinical negligence.

A party who enters into a CFA must give notice of such a funding arrangement and also of the existence of a litigation protection policy as soon as it is signed or taken out.[9] No details of the percentage uplift or the premium level need be given, though, as this would disclose to the opposition the view as to risk taken by the claimant and his insurer. Funders of litigation for their members like trades unions are entitled to enter into Collective CFAs with their members, and such CCFAs, as they are called, take similar effect as individual CFAs.

Such policies are not compulsory when entering into a CFA, and many claims are run under a CFA without any such protection in place. In such circumstances, the claimant may risk bankruptcy if he loses, and the successful defendant then has to choose whether to enforce a costs

---

8 Set out in the Access to Justice Act 1999.
9 See generally CPR Pt 44.3A.

judgment against an often indigent claimant's assets or abandon recovery of the costs judgment. So a 'no win-no fee' arrangement can lead to serious financial consequences if things go wrong. But if such a policy is taken out and the case is won, the defendant will normally be required to pay the policy premium as well as the success fee mark-up on the successful party's costs, as part of the costs judgment on the standard basis. On detailed assessment by the court, a defendant can challenge the success fee percentage mark-up and/or the premium paid as being unreasonable. Some levels of success fee and insurance premiums have been agreed by both sides of the personal injury claims divide: details appear in CPR Pt 45, ss 2–5, dealing with fixed costs and mark-ups in road traffic, employers liability and industrial disease claims.

### 8.4.5 Contingency fee funding

Though commonplace in the United States, contingency fees involving remuneration of the claimant's lawyer by taking a percentage of *damages recovered* (as opposed to a mark-up on *chargeable costs*, as permitted by statute with CFAs) are not permitted in civil litigation in the United Kingdom. They may be used in certain types of cases outside the civil courts, particularly in employment tribunals. Strictly, CFAs are a particular type of contingency fee, the contingency being that the claimant's lawyer is not paid if a case is lost, but is paid on an enhanced basis if the case is won. Both can be characterised by the over-simplified label of 'no win-no fee'.

Contingency fees work in employment tribunal cases because adverse costs orders are very rarely made. Thus an applicant who is represented has very little prospect of obtaining an award of costs against his employer to pay his own lawyer, even if he wins. If the case is lost, the applicant will rarely be ordered to pay the respondent employer's costs of defending the case. Win or lose, he will remain liable for his own lawyer's costs, unless represented by a trades union through its membership services. The ban on contingency fees in civil claims applies to 'contentious business' only, a definition which oddly does not extend to tribunals, which involve technically 'non-contentious business'. So a solicitor can agree with a tribunal applicant client that he will not be charged fees if the application is lost, but if he wins, the lawyer will be paid by receiving a percentage of the winnings. A similar arrangement is possible in claims for compensation from the Criminal Injuries Compensation Authority – again non-contentious business – where claimants can agree to remunerate their legal representative by a percentage of the compensation recovered.

### 8.4.6 Wasted costs orders

Though hardly to be regarded as a mainstream means of funding litigation, wasted costs orders should be considered here for completeness, as such issues do occasionally arise at mediations. Where a lawyer involved in litigation has acted in a manner which has led to the waste of time and cost, it is open to the court, after hearing representations from the lawyer, to order that he should personally pay the costs wasted by such conduct.[10]

## 8.5 The status of the 'costs of the mediation' and 'mediation fees'

It will be remembered that we distinguished 'costs of the mediation' and 'mediation fees' as part of the costs of the claim.[11] Having now given an outline of how costs and funding work, we now examine how these fit into the costs regime.

Lawyers can incur appreciable costs in relation to a mediation. Thorough preparation is required, both of the client and in assembling the necessary paperwork and arguments. A case summary is usually needed to set out each party's position or alternatively a jointly drafted summary is circulated for all to agree and use. Counsel may be briefed to attend, and preparation falls only a little short of what is needed for trial, though the informality of the mediation process enables a rather less perfectionist approach to document bundles.

This is rarely wasted work if the mediation does not give rise to final settlement. But attendance at the mediation may involve anything from six hours upwards, and some mediations last for more than 12 hours. Whether the mediation fails or succeeds in engendering settlement, the work done in attending the mediation gives rise to very substantial legal costs. Are these recoverable?

This question needs to be considered before the mediation, as the wording of the mediation agreement is vital to the way costs may be treated later, whether the case settles or not at the mediation. In commercial cases, it has long been the tradition to provide that the mediation fees are shared equally between the parties, and that each party bears their own costs of the mediation, whatever the outcome of the mediation. Often this may be exactly what the parties wish, especially in a commercial dispute where the privacy of the process and its outcome may outweigh other considerations, and where there may be a rough equivalence of negotiating strength. But in claims by individuals against corporations such as insurance companies, banks, and Government departments, – thus embracing personal injury, clinical negligence, professional indemnity claims and many other types of claim – a successful claimant will normally expect to recover costs in the event of a favourable settlement. If this is accepted by both parties before the mediation, it is prudent to amend the terms of the mediation

---

10  See s 51(6) of the Supreme Court Act 1981 and CPR Pt 48.7.

11  See 8.1 above.

agreement providing for equal sharing of the mediation fees and each party bearing their own costs of the mediation, by making both heads of outlay 'costs in the claim'. This will mean that liability for these will be regarded as falling on whoever is liable for the costs of the claim generally. Parties are free to debate and agree such matters at the mediation, but in default of agreement to the contrary, the agreement to share mediation fees and bear their own costs will bind the parties and no court will have power to go behind that agreement.

This matters whether the mediation leads to settlement of the claim or not. When the subject of legal costs arises at a mediation, quite often the parties will agree a set figure for costs, or agree a global figure for compensation and costs, leaving client and lawyer to allocate the gross sum between them. If however a firm costs figure cannot be agreed, the parties will usually agree in the settlement agreement that one party's costs 'will be paid on the standard basis, subject to detailed assessment if not agreed'. Thereafter the lawyers for each party will try to agree a figure, with the option of commencing detailed assessment proceedings within three months of the agreement or the court order.[12] If agreement cannot be reached, the court will be bound by the default costs provisions in the mediation agreement, and neither the mediation fees nor the costs of the mediation may be regarded as costs in the case disposable by the costs judge. The same considerations apply if the mediation fails to settle the claim. Unless the parties have agreed that the mediation fees and the costs of the mediation are to be regarded as costs in the case, liability for these outlays may not follow the event but be governed by the overriding terms of the mediation agreement.

These questions were considered in the Supreme Court Costs Office in *National Westminster Bank Plc v Feeney and Feeney*,[13] a possession action resolved by a Tomlin Order agreed at mediation. The consent order provided for detailed assessment on the standard basis. The defendants sought to argue that the costs of the mediation and the mediation fees were to be included in the standard basis costs of the action. The Master held that they were both capable of being treated as such, as being 'work done in connection with negotiations with a view to settlement'.[14] However, the mediation agreement was not silent about this: it provided that each party should bear their own costs of preparation and attendance at the mediation, and for the mediator's and provider's fees to be shared. The Master held that

---

12 It would seem that the costs judge will be able to reduce costs on the grounds of reasonableness and/or proportionality; see *Finster v Arriva London and Booth* (unreported SCCO, 11 December 2006).
13 [2006] EWHC 90066 (Costs): appeal heard on 14 May 2007.
14 In *Chantrey Vellacott v The Convergence Group plc* [2007] EWHC 1774 (Ch) at para 227, Rimmer J found that mediation costs can be treated as part of the 'costs of and incidental to the proceedings within the meaning of the Supreme Court Act 1981, s 51'. He was not addressed as to the effect of the mediation agreement in relation to costs.

the parties' agreement over the costs of the mediation was paramount, and the later Tomlin Order did not alter that agreement. This view was upheld on appeal by Eady J sitting with Master O'Hare and another assessor.

## 8.6  Practical considerations for mediators on costs issues

It is hoped that the above outline survey will have equipped mediators and others at mediations with a number of ideas as to how the complex issue of costs can arise and might be handled. The following points summarise the key steps to be taken:

– Before the mediation, unless it is obvious, the way each party is funding a case needs to be clarified: parties operating under a CFA will not be likely to disclose to an opponent the actual percentage success fee or level of AEI premium, but they are under a duty to disclose to other parties the existence and general nature of a funding arrangement, and may be prepared to disclose details confidentially to the mediator.

– The mediator should be given details of any Pt 36 or other settlement offers made by any party, and any earlier costs orders on interim hearings.

– All parties should bring a reasonably accurate summary of their costs of the claim to date to the mediation, preferably apportioned before and after any material Pt 36 offer, and also a projection of costs of the claim from the mediation date to the end of trial.

– Parties should decide whether they wish to provide that the costs of the mediation and the mediation fees be shared, borne by each party in any event, or be treated as costs in the case.

– At the mediation, the mediator must ensure that the issue of costs is discussed, and preferably agreed at a precise figure or by inclusion in a global settlement figure. Such matters as reasonableness and proportionality may arise, both as to the base costs and also the success fee and (if any) the level of insurance premium.

– Failing agreement at the mediation as to the precise figure for costs, the settlement agreement should probably provide that costs will be paid 'on the standard basis subject to detailed assessment if not agreed'. The receiving party needs advice from their lawyer as to what (if anything) might be deducted from the damages to reflect the difference between standard basis costs and what the solicitor is entitled to charge his client, or (if in receipt of LSC funding) how much might be caught by the statutory charge.

*Chapter 9*

# Contracting in advance to use ADR

This chapter is of particular relevance to transactional lawyers, both in-house and external, in seeking to provide in advance that Alternative Dispute Resolution (ADR) is to be used as the primary means of resolving any disputes that may arise in the future in contractual terms and conditions. Mediation as a process is actually very much suited to transactional lawyers generally, they being used (unlike most litigation lawyers) to the cut and thrust of negotiation with their client at their side in order to achieve acceptable deals. But this area relates back to the original transactions themselves, and how they might provide for dispute resolution in case a deal breaks down.

This is an area that is not free from legal controversy, and the experience of other common law jurisdictions more advanced in ADR than the United Kingdom suggests that we can expect the law to develop and change in the future. Because there is still an absence of definitive Court of Appeal authority on the effectiveness of ADR contract clauses, we have set out the current position fully as we see it.

## 9.1   What is an ADR contract clause?

An ADR contract clause is a clause in a an agreement by which the contracting parties agree to attempt to resolve any disputes between them by the use of one or more ADR processes. It may be a very simple, short clause, or alternatively set out a lengthy and complex process. It may specify a particular ADR procedure, such as mediation; or leave the parties to agree on one as and when a particular dispute arises. Where it contemplates the use of a *non-binding* ADR procedure, such as mediation, executive tribunal, or early neutral evaluation, it can clearly only require the parties to *attempt* resolution. A clause requiring use of a *binding* ADR procedure, such as expert determination or adjudication can oblige the parties to abide by any award which results from it. Arbitration clauses, which we do not consider in their pure form here, were the earliest form of clause of this type, and these in effect sought to exclude or at least delay the involvement of the courts in determining a dispute.

## 9.2   What do ADR clauses aim to achieve?

The whole thrust of ADR tends towards a non-binding, 'without prejudice' approach, designed to provide an opportunity for the dispute to be discussed, and resolution explored, in a relatively risk-free and confidential environment. The use of a contract clause to *compel* parties to take part in, for example, mediation might therefore be regarded as contrary to the essential philosophy of ADR. After all, if the parties are only attending a mediation because they are contractually obliged to do so, it may be difficult to achieve settlement. Mediation presupposes some degree of willingness on the part of both or all parties at least to explore the various settlement options and to listen to the other side's arguments, whatever view is eventually taken. This may be absent among parties compelled to attempt ADR. Similar arguments arise in the debate over whether the courts should compel disputing parties into ADR by order.

However, the primary value of an ADR clause lies not in its element of compulsion, but in the fact that it puts ADR on the agenda. It is a reminder to the parties that, when they signed the agreement, ADR was viewed as a sensible step to take in the event of a dispute arising. It may even helpfully remind them that there was a time when relations between them were better! Most importantly, it overcomes any reluctance to suggest ADR when a dispute arises, for fear that such a suggestion may be viewed as an indication of weakness. ADR can be discussed and attempted merely because it is in the contract. It is difficult to overstate the importance of such clauses in enabling parties to set up an ADR procedure. There used to be a widespread assumption that the suggestion by one party of a willingness to use ADR will be perceived by the other(s) as a sign of weakness. Whatever the truth of this since the CPR were introduced, such a fear acts as a significant barrier to many disputes reaching mediation (or other ADR processes). ADR contract clauses constitute by far the most effective way of circumventing this fear. The existence of the clause provides ample justification for mediation to be suggested, discussed and entered upon freely and voluntarily and on an equal basis without any assumptions about the relative strength of each party's position. If ADR is not felt suitable, the parties can always agree to waive the requirement. Indeed, since some ADR clauses may not be enforceable as a matter of law (see **9.5** below), either party can often unilaterally avoid the obligation in any event.

In fact, the inclusion of ADR clauses in contracts is a vital element of good dispute systems design and management. It is an attempt to pre-empt future disputes by putting in place the appropriate resolution structure while the parties are still on good terms. At the very least, it provides yet another argument to deploy before the court in inviting the judge to refer a case to ADR, because the resistant party already signed up to its use before the dispute began.

For this reason it is important to note that consideration of ADR begins at the contractual, non-contentious stage. Those involved in drafting and preparing contract documentation need to be as informed and aware of the various ADR possibilities as those who will eventually handle the resulting disputes. Creative design and mobilisation of contractual dispute systems ought to be considered the responsibility of noncontentious lawyers and contracts managers.

## 9.3    Types of ADR clause

There is a wide variety of types of ADR clause, some examples of which are set out in Appendix C.[1] Although the precise wording of the clause may seem to matter less if it is unenforceable, the clause should nevertheless be the subject of considerable thought. If the parties do choose to implement it when the dispute arises, it will need to meet the demands of their situation effectively. The nature of the agreement in which the clause appears may well have a bearing on the choice and drafting of the clause. For example, a partnership agreement would suggest the use of a very flexible, facilitative process such as mediation, whereas a highly technical engineering contract might call for an expert determination, adjudication, or early neutral evaluation, at least if the resulting dispute is a technical one.

## 9.4    Drafting Considerations

There are a number of considerations to bear in mind. These include:

### 9.4.1    Length and detail

Essentially, the clause merely needs to stipulate that in the event of a dispute arising, the parties will attempt to resolve it by ADR. A very short form of clause can accomplish that with ease.[2] However, such a clause may beg as many questions as it answers, such as which ADR process will be used, who will the neutral be, is the ADR process a condition precedent to litigation or arbitration, what (if any) should the timetable be for carrying out the ADR process, and so on.

Surprisingly, this may in fact be of benefit. It leaves the details of the process open for the parties to decide at the time the dispute arises. The most appropriate type of ADR process might only become clear at that time, and the parties would not want to be restricted by reference to an earlier stipulation. Furthermore, some contracting parties might find it distasteful to draft too detailed a disputes clause at a time when no dispute exists between them. On the other hand, leaving the parties with a choice

---

1 Included in Appendix C are the CEDR and the ICC model clauses.
2 See the specimen in Appendix C.

when the dispute arises can also present problems. If they are unable, when a dispute does arise, to agree to the requisite details, the whole value of the clause may be lost. Furthermore, parties wanting some objective justification for not complying with a clause will find it easy to disagree on the details and hence prevent any progress.

The drafting of each clause should therefore be approached freshly each time, with thought given to the context in which disputes will arise, each party's likely attitude, the results which the clause is intended to achieve, and so on. In fact, the principle that contracting parties should discuss the resolution of any disputes *at the time of contracting* is a sound one, and is more likely to increase rather than diminish the trust between the parties, since the otherwise taboo subject will be brought out into the open. That discussion will serve as a much more solid base to which the parties may refer when any dispute does arise. Ideally, the drafting of ADR clauses should be much more than the reproduction of a standard form ADR clause, and in particular the parties themselves, and not just their advisors, should be drawn into discussion about the optimum dispute resolution structures.

Drafting should also be approached with imagination. There is no reason why each contractual context should not have its own custom-designed dispute resolution process. Parties will become increasingly aware of the approaches that prove most effective for them through a process of trial and experience.

### 9.4.2 Content

In terms of the detailed contents to be included in an ADR clause, the following points at least should be considered:

- Will the clause refer to an ADR process to be agreed, or stipulate a particular one (eg mediation)?
- Is there to be a timetable for compliance with the clause or with procedural stages within the clause (eg appointment of a mediator, exchange of case summaries etc.)?
- Is the ADR process intended to be a condition precedent to the commencement of litigation or arbitration proceedings, or not?
- Is the identity or discipline of the neutral or mediator to be spelled out in advance? If not, what provision should there be for appointment?
- Is an ADR organisation to be used to nominate or appoint a mediator and administer and supervise the process?
- How will any costs of the process be apportioned?

> – Is a tiered process to be used, e.g. direct negotiations, followed (if necessary) by mediation, followed (if necessary) by adjudication, arbitration or litigation?

### 9.4.3    Tiered or stepped clauses

ADR clauses present an opportunity for the use of a 'tiered' structure within the clause – that is, a series of steps in the overall dispute resolution process, each designed to handle the dispute if it has not been resolved by the previous step. These can be particularly effective. Indeed, this approach has already been widely used in the past, for example in the introduction of a negotiating phase as a prerequisite to the commencement of litigation or arbitration, and the 'engineer's decision' in some construction contracts. ADR techniques allow for this principle to be developed more extensively.

The principal strengths of a tiered structure are:

> – The dispute resolution mechanism in use at any particular stage of a dispute will be the one most likely to resolve it. For example, it may be that the issue of proceedings too early in a dispute will drive out certain settlement possibilities, which have not been achievable through initial direct negotiations. The introduction of a mediation phase between the negotiation and litigation phases may well provide a process more capable of teasing out a settlement in that particular environment.

> – The resolution processes can increase in formality and structure as it becomes clear that the dispute itself requires that. All the benefits of the litigation or arbitration processes remain available to the parties, but the formality and rigidity they bring is delayed until it is considered indispensable.

Some detailed examples of tiered ADR clauses are set out in the Appendix. In terms of drafting, the guiding principle should again be an attempt imaginatively to anticipate likely dispute scenarios, and to match them with relevant methods of resolution.

It is also worth noting that the choice of dispute clause can constitute a powerful form of policy statement to those with whom one deals. The tiered ADR clauses all anticipate mediation being attempted before litigation or arbitration has been commenced, but not thereafter. This reflects the policy approach not to commence litigation until other avenues have been exhausted, but equally not to use any ADR processes once proceedings have been commenced. Those advising government departments or their contractors clearly need to be aware of this approach.

## 9.5    Enforceability of ADR clauses

We suggested earlier that the primary value of an ADR clause does not necessarily lie in its enforceability as a matter of law, but rather in its role as a pretext for discussion of possible ADR solutions. Indeed, even before addressing the legal position on the enforceability of such clauses, there is considerable debate on whether it is appropriate or even desirable for ADR clauses to be enforceable and enforced. The arguments were neatly summarised by Giles J in the Australian case of *Hooper Bailie Associated Ltd v Natcon Group Pty Ltd*[3]

> 'Conciliation or mediation is essentially consensual, and the opponents of enforceability contend that it is futile to seek to enforce something which requires the consent of a party when co-operation and consent cannot be enforced; equally they say that there can be no loss to the other party if for want of co-operation and consent the consensual process would have led to no result. The proponents of enforceability contend that this mis-conceives the objectives of alternative dispute resolution, saying that the most fundamental resistance to compromise can wane and turn to co-operation and consent if the dispute is removed from the adversarial procedures of the Courts and exposed to procedures designed to promote compromise, in particular where a skilled conciliator or mediator is interposed between the parties. What is enforced is not co-operation or consent, but participation in a process from which co-operation and consent might come.'

## 9.6    The position under English law

Three decisions at first instance have now considered the enforceability of ADR clauses in English law: first, Judge Hegarty QC sitting as a High Court judge in Liverpool District Registry in *Cott (UK) Ltd v F E Barber Ltd*[4] then McKinnon J in *Halifax Financial Services Ltd v Intuitive Systems Ltd*,[5] and finally Colman J in *Cable & Wireless v IBM*.[6] So far no higher court has directly ruled on such clauses apart from the House of Lords in *Channel Tunnel Group Ltd v Balfour Beatty*,[7] dealing with a very narrow type of expert determination clause. Before we look at these recent cases, it may help to review the legal position from first principles.

---

3  Unreported, 12 April 1992, pp. 24–25.
4  [1997] 3 All ER 540.
5  [1999] 1 All ER Comm 303.
6  [2002] EWHC 2059 (Comm); [2002] 2 All ER Comm 1041.
7  [1993] 1 All ER 664. See also *DGT Steel and Cladding v Cubitt Building* [2007] EWHC 1584 (RC) as to a stay in compliance with an adjudication clause.

### 9.6.1 An agreement to negotiate is unenforceable

Until the decision of the House of Lords in *Walford v Miles*,[8] there was still some doubt about this proposition, stemming from the dictum of Lord Wright in *Hillas & Co v Arcos Ltd*.[9] However, the position following the *Walford* case is clear, namely that an agreement to negotiate is not enforceable in law. This case followed and endorsed the decision of the Court of Appeal in *Courtney & Fairbairn Ltd v Tolaini Brothers (Hotels) Ltd*.[10] It is worth looking at the *Walford case* in some detail.

The case concerned the sale of a photographic processing business, and the central issues were the enforceability of a contract to negotiate and the terms of a 'lock-out' agreement (ie an agreement not to negotiate with any other parties whilst negotiations were continuing with one party). In 1986 the vendors decided to sell the business and received an offer of £1.9 million from a third party. In the meantime new purchasers (the later claimant in this case) had entered into negotiations with the vendors and in March 1987 the vendors agreed in principle to sell the business and premises for £2 million. It was also further agreed in a telephone conversation that if the purchasers provided a comfort letter confirming that their bank had offered them loan facilities, the vendors would 'terminate negotiations with any third party or consideration of any alternative with a view to concluding agreements' with the purchasers, and that even if the vendors received a satisfactory proposal from any third party before that time they would 'not deal with that third party and would not give further consideration to any alternative'.

Subsequently, the vendors withdrew from negotiations and decided to sell to a third party. The proposed purchasers brought an action against the vendors for breach of the lock-out agreement under which the proposed purchasers had been given an exclusive opportunity to try to come to terms with the vendors and which was collateral to the 'subject to contract' negotiations which were proceeding for the purchase of the business and the premises. The proposed purchasers alleged that it was a term of the collateral agreement, necessarily to be implied to give business efficacy to it, that so long as the vendors continued to desire to sell the business and the premises, the vendors would continue to negotiate in good faith with the proposed purchasers. It was contended that the consideration for the collateral contract was the proposed purchasers' agreement to continue negotiations.

On appeal, the Court of Appeal held that the alleged collateral agreement was no more than an agreement to negotiate and was therefore

---

8  [1992] 1 All ER 453.
9  (1932) 38 Com Cases 23; [1932] All ER Rep 494.
10  [1975] 1 All ER 716.

unenforceable. On further appeal, the House of Lords held that a lock-out agreement, whereby one party for good consideration agreed for a limited specified time not to negotiate with anyone except the other party in relation to the sale of his property, could constitute an enforceable agreement. This was confirmed by the Court of Appeal in *Pitt v PHH Asset Management*,[11] where Sir Thomas Bingham MR's lead judgment found that a lock-out agreement for a period of two weeks relating to the sale of land was enforceable. However, an agreement to negotiate in good faith for an unspecified period was not enforceable, nor could a term to that effect be implied in a lock-out agreement for an unspecified period, since a vendor was not obliged under such an agreement to conclude a contract with a purchaser and he would not know when he was entitled to withdraw from the negotiations. Furthermore, the court could not be expected to decide whether, subjectively, a proper reason existed for the termination of the negotiations. It followed that the alleged collateral agreement was unenforceable.

Lord Ackner gave the lead judgment in the *Walford* case. In it he said (at 459):

> 'Mr Naughton accepted that as the law now stands and has stood for approaching 20 years an agreement to negotiate is not recognised as an enforceable contract. This was first decided in terms in Courtney & Fairbairn Limited v Tolaini Brothers where Lord Denning MR said:
>
> "If the law does not recognise a contract to enter into a contract (when there is a fundamental term yet to be agreed) it seems to me it cannot recognise a contract to negotiate. The reason is because it is too uncertain to have any binding force... It seems to me that a contract to negotiate, like a contract to enter into a contract, is not a contract known to the law... I think we must apply the general principle that when there is a fundamental matter left undecided and to the subject of negotiation, there is no contract."'

In the *Courtney* case Lord Denning had rejected the dictum of Lord Wright in the *Hillas* case as not well founded:

> 'There is no bargain except to negotiate, and negotiation may be fruitless and end without any contract ensuing: yet even then, in strict theory, there is a contract (if there is good consideration) to negotiate, though in the event of repudiation by one party the damages may be nominal, unless a jury thinks that the opportunity to negotiate was one of some appreciable value to the injured party.'

---

11  [1993] 4 All ER 961.

Having considered a proposition put forward by Bingham LJ in the Court of Appeal in the *Walford* case that there was an obligation upon the vendors not to deal with other parties which should continue to bind them 'for such time as is reasonable', Lord Ackner concluded:

> 'However, as Bingham LJ recognised, such a duty, if it existed, would indirectly impose upon the respondents a duty to negotiate in good faith. Such a duty, for the reasons which I have given above, cannot be imposed. That it should have been thought necessary to assert such a duty helps to explain the reason behind the amendments to para 5 and the insistence of Mr. Naughton that without the implied term the agreement, as originally pleaded, was unworkable – unworkable because there was no way of determining for how long the respondents were locked out from negotiating with any third party. Thus, even if, despite the way in which the Walford case was pleaded and argued, the severance favoured by Bingham LJ was permissible, the resultant agreement suffered from the same defect (although for different reasons) as the agreement contended for in the amended Statement of Claim, namely that it too lacked the necessary certainty and was thus unenforceable.'

In essence, then, the *Walford* case confirmed that a contract to negotiate is unenforceable, since a court cannot say with sufficient certainty what the obligations are that it is being asked to enforce, and in any meaningful way monitor or assess compliance.

### 9.6.2 A court can require compliance with certain procedures as a condition precedent to issue of litigation or arbitration proceedings

This general principle was established in the case of *Scott v Avery*.[12] Whilst the eventual jurisdiction of the court cannot be ousted, it can nevertheless be validly delayed or stayed, in that the parties can properly impose on themselves, by way of agreement, a series of intervening steps which have to be completed as a condition precedent to either party commencing litigation or arbitration.

This principle translates easily into the ADR arena. Many ADR clauses simply require parties to attempt resolution by an ADR process (see, for instance, the short-form clauses in the Appendix). However, it is equally possible (indeed, increasingly common) for the clause to express compliance with, and exhaustion of, the ADR phase as a condition precedent to the issue of any proceedings, usually with a specifically timed moratorium. Such a clause at least has the effect of introducing a slightly clearer, and

---

12  (1856) 5 HL Cas 811, 10 ER 1121.

therefore more certain, set of steps into the process, which arguably a court might find easier to enforce, though on the clause used in *Halifax Financial Services v Intuitive Systems*,[13] as we shall see, the court did not find that the steps specified were clear, or even whether they had been implemented or breached. Thus, unless drafted with great care, the uncertainty problems raised in the *Walford* case persist, since the court still has to determine whether compliance with that condition precedent has been achieved, so that proceedings could be validly issued. For example, would a party who attended a mediation but terminated it by leaving after an hour be said to have 'attempted to mediate'?

Whilst it may be difficult to produce a set of criteria or rules by which compliance can be judged in every situation, it is in practice often very clear to the parties whether they have attempted to settle a case through ADR or not. It is, of course, even clearer to the mediator, who is not in a position to confirm or deny compliance after the event, partly because of the contractual commitment to confidentiality and partly because his role during the mediation would be fatally compromised if the parties felt that the mediator could eventually pass judgment on their conduct.

The problem is, of course, exacerbated by a lack of comprehension of what ADR actually involves. Thus, the uncertainty argument is strengthened because it is assumed that ADR procedures are inherently either too unclear or too flexible to be able to require compliance. As ADR use has grown, however, this argument has lost some of its impact, since there is greater familiarity with ADR practice and the processes themselves have become more regularised. Indeed, although mediation is a very flexible and adaptable process, it is already possible to say with some consistency what constitutes, in procedural terms, a 'typical' mediation. It must also follow that the more detailed the ADR process is spelt out in an ADR clause, the greater the likelihood of it being enforceable. Thus, a simple commitment to attempt an ADR process leaves too many procedural issues unresolved (not least as to which ADR process will be used). Conversely, an agreement to use mediation, under the auspices of a particular ADR organisation, or using a certain individual mediator, where the procedural requirements for the process (e.g. timetable for submitting case summaries and holding the mediation, who will attend the mediation, etc) are spelt out in detail, must inherently be more capable of enforcement.

It is worth noting, however, that such detail may in fact be counter-productive. Mediation (of all the ADR processes) has a unique flexibility to respond to the very particular exigencies of a given situation. The greater the emphasis on a pre-arranged structure, the less the opportunity to

---

13 [1999] 1 All ER Comm 303.

adopt a particular approach and format of mediation which the situation demands. There is therefore some measure of balance to be achieved in the drafting of such a clause.

It is also important to distinguish between various kinds of ADR process. Some, such as early neutral evaluation, contain no element of negotiation about them. There, the parties simply make oral and/or written submissions to an agreed neutral, who makes a nonbinding evaluation, which the parties can then use to inform their negotiations. There is no reason in principle why the uncertainty objections raised in the *Walford* case should apply to such a process. Indeed, since the process is not inherently one of negotiation at all, the *Walford* case is not directly relevant to any assessment of it.

Finally, the uncertainty objections in the *Walford* case can be very largely minimised by the use of specific time periods, or 'lock-out' agreements. For example, rather than requiring the parties to mediate prior to issuing proceedings, an ADR clause may simply impose a time period between the dispute arising and proceedings being commenced during which proceedings may not be issued. Provided it follows the *Scott v Avevy* form, there is no objection to such a clause. During the intervening time period, the clause can either impose an obligation to use ADR, or simply offer it as an option, subject to the parties' consent at the time (see the long-form clauses in the Appendix). As a matter of law, this changes little. An obligation to use ADR would still be vulnerable to the uncertainty arguments and an option to use ADR is in fact no more than the parties already have in any event, even without such wording.

In practice, however, the position is very different. A specific breathing space is created, during which the parties are unable to issue proceedings. ADR is on the agenda during that period, whether by obligation or option, and there can therefore be little concern about raising it with the other side. Many parties, faced with an intervening period during which they may either negotiate and/or use ADR, or do nothing, will sense the value in trying to use all available means to resolve the dispute. If the breathing space were not imposed on them, it is likely that some of them would be tempted to miss out the ADR, and even the negotiation, phase, and a valuable settlement opportunity might be lost.

Finally, where there is a concern that the imposition of a breathing space may prejudice a party's position in the event that, for example, immediate injunctive relief is required, express provision for that can easily be made in a clause giving rights to bypass the ADR or negotiation phases in such circumstances (see the Appendix for examples).

161

### 9.6.3 Is ADR equivalent to negotiation, such that the law regarding agreements to negotiate applies equally to ADR?

So far in this section, we have assumed largely that ADR is a form of negotiation, and thus that the law regarding the enforceability of agreements to negotiate applies equally to agreements to use ADR. However, we have already drawn a clear distinction between ADR processes which involve a large element of negotiation (eg mediation, mini-trial, etc) and those which do not (eg judicial appraisal, early neutral evaluation, etc). Clearly, the latter category is exempt from any of the problems relating specifically to agreements to negotiate. The remainder of this section therefore applies to the former category of ADR processes.

On the face of it, those processes are extremely similar to negotiation. Indeed, their aims and objectives are almost indistinguishable from those of direct negotiations. Both seek a consensual result, with no ability to mandate any concession or change of position from the other side. Both can be abandoned by either party at any time. Neither requires or permits the imposition on the parties of any form of binding judgment. The outcome of both types of process is either a mutually acceptable agreement (which the parties can agree should have binding or nonbinding status) or no agreement at all. Following this rationale, the law applicable to negotiation should also apply to ADR.

However, whilst ADR and negotiation may share the same aims and objectives, there are fundamental differences of process. Anyone familiar with both will immediately appreciate this. The introduction of a third party (a neutral and independent mediator) fundamentally changes the terms and conditions of the negotiating process. The parties submit themselves to management by a third party in a process with an independent dynamic and momentum of its own, to a far greater degree than they do in direct negotiations. Indeed, the mere fact that the process has such a momentum and a structure beyond that generated by the parties themselves, distinguishes it very significantly from direct negotiations. The process elements of a mediation are to a large extent governed by the mediator's own input and perceptions of what will prove effective, even allowing for the fact that the parties must at least consent to any such process decisions.

It is therefore possible to say, at least to some extent, that ADR processes exist as structures independent of the parties themselves. The implication of this is highly significant. If it is possible to identify such processes or structures with sufficient clarity, the uncertainty objections raised in the *Walford* case begin to fall away. By agreeing to use ADR, the argument runs, the parties are not agreeing to negotiate, but rather to submit themselves to a series of objectively definable processes, the effect of which is likely to be greater on them than if they merely entered the direct negotiation process. To quote again from Giles J in the *Hooper Baillie* case,

'What is enforced is not co-operation and consent, but participation in a process from which co-operation and consent might come.'

If that rationale is adopted, it becomes much easier to countenance enforcement of an ADR clause.

To use an analogy, assume that a husband and wife have a particular problem in their marriage. They may agree between themselves to attempt to resolve it by discussion. Clearly, they cannot be compelled to resolve the problem. Realistically, neither can they be compelled to 'discuss it' since that is too vague an obligation to define effectively. How productive do discussions have to be in order to constitute compliance? If they set aside an hour to do so, and simply sit in silence, or scream at each other, have they complied? And for how long do the discussions need to continue? On the other hand, they might agree to attempt to resolve the matter by seeking the assistance of a counsellor. Even more expressly, they might commit to have 10 weekly sessions with the counsellor. This is an easy obligation to monitor. It contains no assumptions that they will succeed in reaching resolution but merely a commitment to submit themselves to a particular and definable process. Implicit in it is an assumption that the counselling process constitutes something independent of the parties, a pre-existing structure into which the parties will submit their differences.

Necessarily, the counselling process itself is not easy to define in advance, in terms of the detail of how a particular session will progress. But that does not mean that it does not have enough of a structure of its own to enable the parties to know in advance what obligations they will take on when they agree to use it. Exactly the same is true of, for example, the mediation process. Indeed, the only difference between the two (in terms of ensuring compliance) is that counselling is currently better known and more widely used than ADR and thus more easily permits an immediate and objective recognition of what is involved.

In summary then, we tend to the view that ADR is more than direct negotiation, in a way which tends to distinguish the two processes and therefore the law applicable to each. We can envisage circumstances in which an ADR clause requiring mediation might be enforceable. Perhaps with its new-found mainstream status under the CPR, the courts might confer that degree of authenticity on ADR as a separate entity over and beyond ordinary negotiation.

### 9.6.4 The practicality of enforcement

How then could a party enforce an ADR clause? Could a stay be obtained from the court to enforce such a clause? Subject to the arguments set out above, there happens to be one specific statutory provision that specifically provides for such a step to be taken, albeit by a side-wind.

The Arbitration Act 1996 made sweeping changes to the framework for arbitration. Section 9 of the Act provides:

'(1)    A party to an arbitration agreement against whom legal proceedings are brought (whether by way of claim or counterclaim) in respect of a matter which under the agreement is to be referred to arbitration may (upon notice to the other party to the proceedings) apply to the court in which the proceedings have been brought to stay the proceedings so far as they concern that matter.

(2)    An application may be made notwithstanding that the matter is to be referred to arbitration only after the exhaustion of **other dispute resolution procedures** [our emphasis].

(3)    An application may not be made by a person before taking the appropriate procedural step (if any) to acknowledge the legal proceedings against him or after he has taken any step in those proceedings to answer the substantive claim.

(4)    On an application under this section the court shall grant a stay unless satisfied that the arbitration agreement is null and void, inoperative, or incapable of being performed.

(5)    If the court refuses to stay the legal proceedings, any provision that an award is a condition precedent to the bringing of proceedings in respect of any matter is of no effect in relation to those proceedings.'

This provision was inserted to reflect the effect of the House of Lords decision in the *Channel Tunnel* case.[14] In theory, therefore, if a contract contains a stepped clause that provides for, say, mediation to be followed by arbitration, and one party issues proceedings without using either mediation or arbitration, a court would be bound to order a stay under s 9(4).

Enthusiasm about this provision was tempered by the decision of McKinnon J in *Halifax Financial Services v Intuitive Systems Ltd*,[15] in which he held that the stepped ADR/arbitration procedure devised for a contract between the claimant and a software designer did not make compliance with its procedures mandatory. More importantly, he held that it was doubtful whether such clauses were enforceable. He drew a distinction between determinative procedures such as arbitration or binding expert determination as against non-determinative procedures such as negotiation, mediation, expert appraisal and non-binding evaluations. This contract had a series of non-binding processes coupled with a series of moratoria on issue of proceedings, leading towards permission to issue proceedings unless arbitration was agreed. No mention was made of s 9 of the

14   [1993] 1 All ER 664.
15   [1999] 1 All ER Comm 303.

Arbitration Act 1996 in the judgment, but he distinguished the case before him from the *Channel Tunnel* case on the grounds that the *Channel Tunnel* case involved a clause which was 'nearly an immediate effective agreement to arbitrate, albeit not quite.' The *Halifax* clause could not be construed as anywhere close to being nearly an immediately effective agreement to arbitrate. He drew comfort from the judgment in the *Cott (UK)* case[16] on the basis that, although the judge had been prepared in principle to order a stay for ADR, the relevant clause required the case to be referred to an expert whose decision was to be final and binding, and was thus going to lead to a determinative rather than non-determinative outcome.

In truth, McKinnon J in the *Halifax* case felt that the stay sought by the defendant under the ADR clause was being used as a device to delay the start of proceedings and keep the claimant unjustifiably out of his claim. If the decision had gone to mere exercise of discretion as to whether to grant a stay or not, he would have found against the defendant, because he felt it was time for the claim to proceed. He found specifically that the claimant 'has not rushed to litigation or refused to consider a negotiated settlement'. If the claimant had rushed to issue, it is clear that the CPR gives ample grounds to a court to penalise such an approach.

This underlines what the true incentives and disincentives are for unreasonable parties since the CPR came into effect. A rogue party who issues court proceedings too early, especially in the face of a pre-agreed commitment to ADR, is going to face a serious risk of costs sanctions under CPR Pt 44.5, for ignoring the letter (where applicable) or the spirit of the pre-action protocols and the overriding objective in CPR Pt 1, extending as they do to unreasonable conduct pre-issue. Even where the aggressor 'wins', the party aggrieved simply needs to point out to the court that there was no good reason for failing to try ADR first, and a court should be prepared to be sympathetic over the costs order to be made.

The issue finally came before Colman J in the Commercial Court in the *Cable & Wireless* case.[17] He was being invited by the claimant to make a declaratory judgment about a contractual provision in a Global Framework Agreement for the provision of worldwide information technology, whereas the defendant wanted him to stay proceedings under an 'escalator' clause for dispute resolution which required the parties to enter stepped negotiation and then, if unsuccessful, 'to attempt in good faith to resolve the dispute or claim through an alternative dispute resolution procedure as recommended to the parties by CEDR', though this was not to preclude proceedings from being issued. *Halifax* seems not to have been cited, for it is not mentioned in the judgment. Colman J reviewed the *Courtney & Fairbairn* case and *Paul Smith Ltd v H&S International Holdings*

---

16 [1997] 3 All ER 540.
17 [2002] EWHC 2059 (Comm); [2002] 2 All ER Comm 1041.

*Inc*[18] as supporting the concept that an agreement to negotiate is not enforceable. But he observed that CEDR's procedure, as set out in its then published Model Mediation Procedure and Agreement, coupled with the freedom to withdraw from the process if unproductive, provided sufficient certainty for a judge to decide whether a party had complied with the terms of this clause for it to be enforceable. He said that courts should not be astute to accentuate uncertainty and therefore unenforceability in relation to references to ADR in contracts, and commented:

> 'For the courts now to decline to enforce contractual references to ADR on the grounds of intrinsic uncertainty would be to fly in the face of public policy as expressed in the CPR and as reflected in the judgment of the Court of Appeal in *Dunnett v Railtrack*.'

Of course one can point out that the clause in question did not itself incorporate CEDR's then published Model Mediation Procedure. CEDR could have chosen to recommend early neutral evaluation or mediation in any form of design, which hardly amounts to certainty of chosen process. A clause which merely delegates responsibility to advise to an apparently well-reputed service provider might be regarded as a slightly surprising way to satisfy a court that there was more than a mere agreement to negotiate. But a senior and well-respected judge has taken this view now and there has been little evidence of reluctance to distinguish or overrule it since. Perhaps the fact that costs sanctions await unreasonable pre-issue refusal to mediate, whether or not such an ADR clause exists, has tempered the need for such debate.

## 9.7 Areas of relevance

ADR clauses of different types are being used in a wide variety of contexts. Examples of these include general commercial contracts, partnership agreements, terms and conditions of business, construction contracts, development contracts, and so on. In each new application, thought should be given to the type of ADR process most likely to generate resolution.

It is also important to remember the value of ADR clauses in corporate policy statements. Thus, many large American companies have adopted a public corporate pledge, to use ADR processes in appropriate situations. Although not legally committing the company to the use of ADR in any particular dispute, this pledge has been used to send a powerful message to those with whom the company deals, and promote the company's public image. This is similar in concept, as we have noted, to accords, by which parties, insurers, lawyers, even governments, and others engaged in a particular area of dispute state their intention to use ADR when problems arise.

---

18  [1991] 2 Lloyds Rep 127.

# Chapter 10
# ADR and European law

## 10.1 The European dimension

The use of ADR has grown throughout Europe at a considerable pace, though not at the same pace in every jurisdiction. All the authors have been involved in various ways in training and consultancy initiatives in both the old and new Europe, as well as further afield. Details of where each country has reached are beyond the scope of this book, and readers are referred to *The EU Mediation Atlas*[1] for a helpful snapshot of most of the European landscape, though bearing in mind the speed of change.

The European Commission has been actively considering ADR from the policy perspective and in 2002 it circulated a Green Paper seeking to canvass the views of Member States on ADR in civil and commercial disputes. A summary of responses was published in early 2003, and these led to the drafting of two important documents, the EU Draft Directive and the European Code of Conduct for Mediators, both of which are to be found in full in Appendices D and E to this book. There were initial fears that the Commission would seek to go down the route of regulation of ADR, but in the event they were persuaded that its role was to encourage rather than control its use in what is still a relatively immature market.

Also reflecting the increasingly international nature of mediation practice, the ICC ADR Contract Clauses are set out in Appendix C, with references to the UNICITRAL Conciliation Rules and Model Law.

## 10.2 The EU Draft Directive on mediation

The title and scope of the Directive is worth noting, as its predecessor Green Paper was concerned with ADR in general. The Directive, however, issued in March 2004, is concerned only with mediation, the prime form of ADR in Europe.[2] Article 1 states its intention as being able:

> – to facilitate access to justice by promoting the use of mediation in civil and commercial disputes; and

---

1 Singer et al, *The EU Mediation Atlas: Practice and Regulation* (LexisNexis, 2004).
2 The text in the Appendix is that issued in October 2004. The European Parliament subsequently considered this text and has proposed a number of amendments, but these are yet to be confirmed. They do not substantially alter the effect of the original text. Where significant, they are footnoted below.

 –   to ensure a sound relationship between mediation and judicial
     proceedings.

The preamble spells out the thinking behind these twin themes in greater
detail. It emphasises that the Directive is not concerned with adjudicatory
processes, whether binding or not. It visualises that framework legislation
may be required of Member States to promote mediation and establish a
predictable legal framework.

There are 10 Articles. Article 1 sets out the objectives as noted above,[3] and
Article 2 defines 'mediation' and 'mediator', making it clear that neither
includes attempts by a judge to settle a dispute within the course of judicial
proceedings.[4]

Article 3 deals with referral to mediation, providing that courts may invite
parties to use mediation, or attend an information session on mediation,
but does not prevent countries making mediation compulsory, or subject to
incentives and sanctions, so long as the right of access to the judicial system
is not impeded. Certainly the regime in England and Wales permitting
ADR 'Orders' and the imposition of sanctions for unreasonable refusal
to mediate[5] would appear to comply with this Article, and there would
even be room for strengthening such approaches if it is accepted that
mediation does not in any way 'impede on the right of access to the judicial
system'. This issue is discussed more fully in **10.4** below in relation to the
European Convention on Human Rights.

Article 4 of the Directive deals with the promotion of Codes of Conduct for
mediators and providers, quality control of mediators and good training
standards so that parties can be offered effective mediators.

Article 5 reflects some of the differences in procedural approach between
Member States. It provides for parties to be able to request that a mediated
settlement can be recorded and confirmed in a formal judgment of a
court or public authority, so that it can be enforced as if it were a court
judgement, so long as it is not in any way illegal. In England and Wales,
mediated outcomes in cases where proceedings are afoot will almost
always be embodied in a consent order, as otherwise the proceedings will
not be brought to an end. But there is no provision for formally recording
settlement terms where proceedings have not started. Other jurisdictions
have such facilities. Whether such harmonisation is necessary when there

---

3 A new Article 1A is proposed which makes the Draft Directive directly applicable to
  cross-border disputes only. The amendments to the Preamble suggest that the Directive
  might cover national jurisdictions too.
4 The European Parliament amendments in 2007 propose that the Directive will cover
  mediations conducted by a judge who is not responsible for any judicial proceedings in
  that dispute. Judges do act as mediators in a number of European jurisdictions.
5 Discussed in **Chapters 5** and **6** above.

has been no practical difficulty over performance and enforcement of pre-issue settlement agreements is open for debate.

Article 6 deals with the admissibility of evidence from mediators and as to what happened at a mediation. As noted in **Chapter 7**, this is an area of doubt in English law, and clarification and certainty would be welcome. The Directive suggests that mediators and providers of mediation services shall not give evidence of:

- invitations to mediate or a party's unwillingness to mediate;
- offers to settle made in a mediation;
- statements or admissions made by a party during a mediation;
- mediator proposals, or a party's willingness to accept such a proposal (though, oddly, not a party's unwillingness to accept such a proposal);
- any document prepared solely for the purpose of a mediation.

These provisions are strengthened by proposing that a court should not be able to admit any such evidence except to enforce a settlement agreement reached as a direct result of a mediation, or overriding considerations of public policy or to prevent harm, or where the mediator and the parties agree. This would be an important provision if introduced, as it would confirm that the mediator has a veto on disclosure of mediation intelligence, not just the parties. Had such a provision been in force then, the course taken in *SITA v Watson Wyatt and Maxwell Batley*[6] might well have been different.

Article 7 proposes that any relevant limitation period is suspended from when the parties agree to use mediation, or mediation is ordered by a court or a statutory obligation to mediate arises. If the mediation fails to settle the claim, it will resume when one or both parties or the mediator declare it terminated or withdraw from it, with a minimum of a month's grace from termination. This is a difficult provision to apply, as the start and finish of a mediation may well be a matter of controversy. The English response to this proposal was to oppose it as impractical, but there may be Member States whose domestic limitation regime makes such a provision desirable.

Articles 8 and 9 require notifications to the Commission of data and require Member States to have legislation in place by September 2007 reflecting the contents of the Directive. After being stalled somewhat, it appears that the Directive has taken on a new life, though the exact extent of its likely effects on the domestic law of Member States is still far from clear, as is the question of whether its scope will be limited to cross-border disputes.

---

6 See the discussion in **Chapter 7.2** of this case.

## 10.3 The European Code of Conduct for Mediators

Having decided not to embark on a regulatory regime for mediation, the Commission developed a Code of Conduct to establish levels of expectation for service quality and to provide mediators in every European jurisdiction with a common standard. It is not compulsory, but is available for incorporation by reference into mediation agreements or terms of business. The text of both the EU Code and the CEDR Code are in the Appendix for comparison.

The topics covered by the EU code are what might be expected. They include a mix of ethical and administrative standards. Its style makes it read as instructions to the mediator rather than as undertakings given by the mediator to the parties. The key provisions cover:

- competence and continued training, with the mediator disclosing details of personal background to potential clients, satisfying himself that he is appropriate for a particular dispute;
- independence and neutrality of the mediator, with a duty to disclose any conflict of interest;
- the mediator must ensure that the parties understand the process and the mediation agreement, and also any settlement terms, and must conduct the process fairly, clarifying also the basis of remuneration;
- confidentiality about the process as a whole, including the fact of the mediation, and also as to keeping information given confidentially by one party from any other party, though always subject to any disclosure compelled by law.

By way of comparison, the CEDR Code of Conduct for mediators and other third-party neutrals reads as a form of undertaking given by CEDR about neutrals, which it nominates. It too covers impartiality and conflict of interest, confidentiality, transparency as to fees and circumstances justifying withdrawal. It also includes an undertaking to take out professional indemnity insurance.

## 10.4 The European Convention on Human Rights and ADR

The European Convention on Human Rights (ECHR) was adopted into English law as from 2 October 2000 as a result of the Human Rights Act 1998, having been implemented in Scotland in May 1999 as part of the devolution process.

Article 6 of the ECHR is by far the most significant provision in relation to ADR. Article 6(1) of the ECHR provides as follows:

'In the determination of his civil rights and obligations...everyone is entitled to a fair and public hearing within a reasonable time by an independent and impartial tribunal established by law.'

Its significance lies over whether court referral of claims to ADR or, by analogy, the enforceability of ADR clauses, are caught by this provision of the ECHR, by interfering with the citizen's right of access to a prompt fair trial. In making an ADR Order, or providing for mandatory mediation, or even in upholding the effect of an ADR contract clause so as to delay access to a public civil remedy, do judges risk attack under Article 6? The answer to this question goes to the heart of the true nature of mediation as a process.

The point is put into sharp focus by the position of arbitration, which certainly in the United States is regarded as ADR, though less so in the United Kingdom. Arbitration is distinguishable from non-binding ADR processes like mediation in two ways: first, it is statute-based; and secondly, it does indeed offer a *binding adjudicative process* for 'determination' of civil rights and obligations, but in an essentially private hearing before an arbitrator. Parties contract to go to arbitration and thus in effect exclude the jurisdiction of the courts. Bearing in mind that even a statutory provision must yield to the effect of the ECHR if it infringes it, could an arbitration be impeached for infringing the Article 6(1) requirement for public determination?

So far as *non-adjudicative* ADR is concerned, it is difficult to see how this could be regarded as anything approaching a 'determination'. By definition a decision is *not* made by the neutral in the process; the parties alone decide whether to settle. They remain at all times entirely free to withdraw from the process and return to the path which leads to actual determination of their civil rights and obligations by the independent and impartial tribunal established by law, namely the relevant court. Indeed, mediation agreements often specifically state that:

> 'The referral of the dispute to mediation does not affect any rights that may exist under Article 6 of the European Convention on Human Rights. If the dispute is not settled by the mediation, the parties' rights to a fair trial remain unaffected.'

It is evident that the European Court encourages parties to settle disputes extra-judicially, thus relieving the courts of excessive strains. Regarding submission to arbitration as compliant with Article 6 of the ECHR is just one way in which this encouragement is manifested, and other forms of ADR might be expected to prove to be another. In the case of arbitration, the European Court recognises the right of disputants to waive their rights under the ECHR by electing for arbitration. It is, however, clear from authority and commentary that the court might intervene to protect the

171

right to trial in a case where any undue pressure was put upon a party into a non-judicial adjudicative process such as arbitration, or where there was no real opportunity for a party truly to agree (or not) to such a term in a contract.

The leading case on such matters is *Deweer v Belgium*,[7] the facts of which provide rather a surprising entry-point into a debate about whether or not mandating mediation is permissible. Deweer's butchery business was found on inspection to be selling pork at more than a prescribed price limit. The inspector threatened provisional closure of his business, to last until the conclusion of criminal proceedings. However, by paying a 'friendly settlement' of 10,000 Belgian francs, Deweer could avoid such proceedings and his store could reopen immediately. Unsurprisingly, he chose settlement, but reserved his rights to challenge the proceeding. He then initiated a challenge, inviting consideration of the effect of Article 6 on whether taking the obvious temptation to pay a generously-discounted composition payment fettered his right to a fair public trial, at which he would have had arguable defences. The ECHR expressly approved the concept of waiver of Article 6 rights frequently found 'in civil matters, notably in the shape of arbitration clauses in contracts'. But settlements resulting from 'constraint' which effectively prevents access to the courts are impeachable. The court did not criticise the theory of composition of criminal liability, but concentrated its fire on the fact that unless he paid the composition, his business would have been closed until the end of criminal proceedings, resulting in substantial business losses. On the facts, Deweer was held to have waived his right to go to court only by reason of constraint, which vitiated his consent to paying the friendly settlement.

To the surprise of many, the Court of Appeal in *Halsey v Milton Keynes NHS Trust* launched into a discussion of the *Deweer* case. The surprise emanated from the fact that the conjoined appeals in the *Halsey* case and *Smith v Joys and Halliday*[8] were both about whether costs sanctions were to be imposed on parties who had declined proposals to mediate by their losing opponents. In neither case had an ADR Order been made by a judge, nor did the facts of either case require the Court to rule on whether mediation could or should be mandatory. Thus, its comments on Article 6 were strictly *obiter*. But the court quite often seeks to give guidance beyond the strict remit of the cases before it, and its views must be accorded respect. We discuss it now both because the point may perhaps arise again in later cases when entirely germane to their facts, and also because judges have subsequently referred to this portion of the judgment in support of their own decision.[9] It is also important because the view

---

7  (1980) 2 EHRR at [49].

8  See disscussion in **Chapters 5** and **6**.

9  For example, Pumfrey J in *Nokia v Interdigital Technology* [2005] EWHC Pat 2134 and Jack J in *Hickman v Blake Lapthorn* [2006] EWHC 12 (QB).

taken may betray a significant misunderstanding by some judges of what mediation truly is.

Dyson LJ sets out the argument pithily in paragraph 9 of his judgment in the *Halsey* case:

> 'We heard argument on the question whether the court has power to order parties to submit their disputes to mediation against their will. It is one thing to encourage the parties to agree to mediation, even to encourage them in the strongest terms. It is another to order them to do so. It seems to us that to oblige truly unwilling parties to refer their disputes to mediation would be to impose an unacceptable obstruction on their right of access to the court. The court in Strasbourg has said in relation to Article 6 that the right of access to a court may be waived, for example by means of an arbitration agreement, but such waiver should be subjected to "particularly careful review" to ensure that the claimant is not subject to "constraint": see *Deweer v Belgium*. If that is the approach of the ECHR to an **agreement** to arbitrate, it seems to us likely that **compulsion** of ADR would be regarded as an unacceptable constraint on the right of access to the court and, therefore, a violation of Article 6.'

As a precedent in the English sense, the *Deweer* case seems a strange bed-fellow with the *Halsey* case or indeed with mediation and ADR, generally. In the *Deweer* case, the mischief was for the Belgian authorities to have constrained M Deweer to avoid both criminal proceedings and concomitant closure of his business by paying a compromise settlement figure. Constraint to settle by feeling compelled to waive Article 6 rights was easy to discern. In mediations, no one is constrained to settle. Once arrived at the mediation, continued participation is entirely voluntary, and even an unreasonable disengagement from the process by one party cannot later be discussed or challenged before a judge because of confidentiality and 'without prejudice' privilege, at least under current English law and procedure.[10] Nor does anyone waive their rights of access to a public court by entering mediation. No one ever enters the mediation process on the basis that they *must* settle; or that if they do not, they cannot revert to seeking a remedy in a public court. They never participate in mediation on the basis that a binding outcome will be imposed on them. On the contrary, mediation is symbiotic with litigation: settlements in mediations are often predicated against the risks of failing to achieve the desired outcome through trial. Parties may choose or perhaps feel or (where a mandatory scheme exists) be compelled to mediate first for fear of penalty if they do not. Is this 'constraining a waiver' of Article 6 rights?

---

10 Though attempts have been made to do so in the US and Australia.

Part of the apparent misunderstanding of the status of mediation may relate to the umbrella title 'Alternative Dispute Resolution'. Superficially it sounds as if ADR and litigation are absolute alternatives; that a disputant must choose between one or the other, forfeiting their rights of access to one if choosing the other. Of course entering or (if permissible) being constrained – perhaps by a arbitration clause in a contract – to enter an adjudicative process like arbitration *does* deprive those disputants of access to a decision made at a public trial by a judge. But mediation is not equivalent to arbitration, in that it is entirely up to the parties as to whether they emerge from the mediation process with an agreed binding outcome, or revert to the public litigation process. If settlement is desirable to reduce the call by citizens on the courts, or to encourage them to make their own decisions as to where their best interests lie to improve social cohesion, then perhaps courts should encourage or even require engagement in proper settlement processes. Indeed, many jurisdictions with extremely strong sensitivities about human and constitutional rights to access to courts mandate mediation and indeed other settlement processes such as conciliation or settlement conferences chaired by judges. Perhaps the more integral that mediation is within the court process, the more acceptable it becomes to mandate it.

What other arguments might be deployed? An order to mediate, particularly if the litigation is stayed pending mediation, might be regarded as hindering a public hearing 'within a reasonable time'. However, in practice, a stay is not a necessary component of a court-referred mediation, and even if a stay were granted, it is highly unlikely that the kind of delay that this would create would be regarded in the general scheme of litigation progress as an infringement of such a right.[11] The cases decided by the European Court so far deal in much longer delays than is likely to be generated by a referral to ADR, particularly mediation, which often takes no more than a few weeks from initial referral to outcome.

Are there other instances where the court has approved delayed or denied access to the courts before a litigant can meet pre-conditions? The European court has held that Article 6 is not infringed by restricting court access to vexatious litigants, bankrupts, mental patients, those required to give security for costs or to pay a previous costs order before being allowed to start fresh proceedings, and those who cannot obtain legal aid on the merits of their case.[12] The CPR themselves impose a number of procedural requirements on parties before they can appear before a judge for the public trial required by Article 6. Before proceedings can be issued, disputants must comply with the Pre-action Protocols and their Practice

---

11 See *DGT Steel Cladding and Cubitt Building* [2007] EWHC 1584 (TEC) para 47, where Judge Coubon dismissed an argument that adjudication would seriously delay access to the court.

12 *Webb v UK* [1983] 6 EHRR 120; *McVicar v UK* [2002] NLJR 759.

Direction (which now require consideration of, but does not compel, ADR). Parties must then pay court fees at several stages, now very substantial. Indeed, in *R v Lord Chancellor ex parte Witham*,[13] withdrawal of a court fees exemption scheme for those on income support was deemed in breach of Article 6. Parties must also comply with procedural requirements as to allocation questionnaires, statements of case, disclosure, and evidence, all buttressed by statements of truth which, if untrue, are punishable as contempt and with possible imprisonment. It might be argued that these CPR requirements are breaches of Article 6. If they are not breaches, the question arises as to why ordering mediation should be a breach? It is one of the identified tools of active case management, so arguably it stands no different relationship to Article 6 than any other court rule. On these points, Article 6 is said to require that any restrictions on access to the courts are proportionate, certain, and in pursuit of a legitimate aim – see *Golder v UK*.[14] With ADR given approval in CPR Pt 1, a mediation is unlikely to be regarded as breaching such requirements.

The *Deweer* case makes it clear that encouraging settlement is a proper activity of any civil justice system and in no way infringes a party's Article 6 rights. However, encouragement to settle is one thing. The question is whether it is in breach of Article 6 for a civil justice system to *require* a party to participate in a settlement process before being able to have a day in court. There seems to be no authority on this point. It is however a far less draconian requirement than banning a party altogether from access to the courts, as in some of the above examples. From that perspective, requiring mediation is no more an inherent potential breach of Article 6 than any other aspect of implementation of the overriding objective through active case management as set out in CPR Pt 1, or any other compulsory procedural step. For instance, CPR Pt 26.4 already permits a stay of one month at allocation stage to explore settlement by ADR or any other means. No one suggests that this provision is in breach of Article 6.

The real issue may lie in the proportionality (a favourite European concept) of the remedy deployed when a breach occurs. If failure to comply with an ADR order meant that an otherwise valid claim would be permanently struck out, or committal to prison for contempt, Article 6 might well come into play. In England and Wales, the remedy for unreasonable conduct in relation to ADR, as any other manifestation, is to impose costs sanctions, even on an otherwise successful litigant. We suggest that Article 6 that it is unlikely that this will be found to infringe Article 6.

But even as a matter of principle, it is hard to see how such costs sanctions could remotely be classified as breaching Article 6. Judges often impose costs sanctions on what they regard as unreasonable litigation conduct.

---

13 [1997] 2 All ER 779.
14 1 EHRR 524.

If to do that is a breach of Article 6, the entire underpinning philosophy of the CPR, which has made such a positive difference to the litigation landscape would be jeopardised. Parties cannot expect unfettered access to courts on the basis of a financial indemnity against legal costs if they win. This did not happen under the old Rules of the Supreme Court, and is even less the case now under the CPR. In many jurisdictions without a costs jurisprudence, this does not happen at all. Certainly, proportionate orders for security for costs have been upheld as not being in breach of Article 6.[15]

Where issues of proportionality may prevail, including allotting to a case 'an appropriate share of the court's resources' and presumably no more, a much more pragmatic regime is possible, where one litigant may be denied excessive access to a judge on the grounds of disproportionate use of court resources. Regulating reasonableness of litigation conduct by costs sanctions is something clearly within the discretion of a given jurisdiction, which can use its own ways of regulation to suit it. No other EC country has quite the same mechanisms of costs controls as the United Kingdom, so others may use different models, loosely based around case management in its multifarious forms. The very fact that there is such a range of approaches over how judges are empowered to deal with litigant discipline (whether by costs sanctions or otherwise) emphasises the comparative marginality of such issues to human rights. It is to be hoped that some opportunity will arise to test out some these areas of uncertainty in greater depth.

---

15 For example, *Stevens v SOASS* (2001) The Times, 2 February though excessive court fees were regarded as in breach of Article 6 in *Kreuz v Poland* 11 BHRC 456.

*PART C*

# THE PRACTICAL FRAMEWORK OF MEDIATION

*Chapter 11*

# Advising on mediation – strategies and duties

The notion that there might be a 'duty' to consider mediation creates an unfortunate impression – namely, that one might do so only out of obligation. In reality, mediation constitutes one of the most dynamic and effective routes for parties in dispute to achieve an acceptable outcome, and the more pressing question is how those benefits can be secured and the process used to greatest effect. Considerations of strategy should outweigh those of duty. In this chapter, we will look at both.

## 11.1  Is there such a duty?

A client approaches a lawyer in the expectation of receiving advice on the best way of achieving what the client wishes. What duties are imposed upon a lawyer at that point? Rule 2.02 of the Solicitors Code of Conduct 2007 (replacing the provisions of the Solicitors Practice Rules and the Solicitors Costs Information and Client Care Code as from 1 July 2007) says that solicitors are to:

> '(a)  identify clearly the client's objectives in relation to the work to be done for the client;
>
> (a)  give the client a clear explanation of the issues involved and the options available to the client;
>
> (b)  agree with the client the next steps to be taken; and
>
> (c)  keep the client informed of progress, unless otherwise agreed.'

On most occasions, what the client wants above all is the resolution of a dispute by the quickest and most cost-effective means available and on the best terms available. Often this is achieved by engaging directly with the other side through correspondence and negotiation, and without resort to any more formal process, whether using the courts, tribunals or the arbitration process. Normal negotiation and settlement procedures often work perfectly well, so long as the client has obtained a satisfactory outcome.

But what happens if the settlement process does not work, breaks down or drags on? Perhaps the client becomes impatient with the rate of progress and feels that the issue of proceedings will concentrate the opponent's mind. At this stage another set of choices faces the client and lawyer. The solicitor must give advice to the client about the implications of starting litigation – the risk, the likely costs, the cost-benefit and risk, different tactical approaches, the forum, and so on. These duties are ongoing, and require updated information throughout the claim.[1]

Once the prospect of litigation or arbitration has loomed large, it is not uncommon for differing perceptions to arise in the mind of lawyer and client. The lawyer may tend to view the litigation in terms of the process itself, as a series of procedural steps and a timetable to be followed. By contrast, the client still has in mind those initial aims and priorities – to resolve the matter as quickly and cheaply as possible and on the best available terms. While these views will often co-exist comfortably, most lawyers (and many commercial clients too) will be no stranger to court actions which take on a life of their own. They acquire an inherent momentum focused on the next procedural step, often losing sight of the wider commercial or personal picture.

The lawyer's duty is always to safeguard and pursue the client's own priorities and aims. Litigation, or indeed any other legal process which a lawyer can offer to clients, is really only justified to the extent that it seeks to achieve that. Thus at all stages during litigation, procedural and tactical choices should be exercised in the light of the client's overriding goals. The process, be it litigation or anything else, is the means but never the end.

## 11.2   Other sources of the duty

There is now an additional overriding objective for a lawyer to bear in mind, as we have seen in **Chapter 4**, namely that of the civil court system itself. The CPR embody an overall framework for the conduct of litigation and spring from the philosophy enunciated in the overriding objective defined in CPR Pt 1. Thus, specific duties are now laid on the court, which parties and lawyers are required to help the court to discharge, to encourage the parties to co-operate with each other, to use ADR if appropriate and facilitate its use, to help the parties settle and to undertake cost benefit analysis.[2] It is a rash lawyer or party who fails to do this.

Non-compliance with (or mere lip service paid to) such obligations is almost certain to open a lawyer to valid criticism and probable costs sanctions from the court and thus from the client, even to the extent of wasted costs orders against the lawyer personally. This is amply illustrated by the cases discussed in **Chapter 6**.

---

1 See in particular the Solicitors Code of Conduct 2007 Rule 2.03(1).
2 See generally **Chapter 4**.

## 11.3   What is the scope of the duty?

As noted above, the Solicitors Code of Conduct 2007 has replaced the The Law Society's Guide to Professional Conduct of Solicitors and the Solicitors Practice Rules as the prime source for defining solicitors' duties and obligations to clients, though many of these are regarded as originating from the common law itself. Other sources of professional duty for UK lawyers are to be found in the Bar Standards Board Code of Conduct and the Council of the Bars and the Law Socieities of Europe (CCBE) Code of Conduct for EC lawyers. These all set out the classical requirements of independence, integrity, confidentiality and duty to the rule of law itself. The Bar and CCBE Codes are silent on the duty to advise lay clients about ADR, nor was there any specific professional obligation imposed by the former Solicitors Practice Rules to do so. The section in the former Guide to Professional Conduct dealing with ADR primarily covered the duty of solicitors acting as mediators to avoid conflicts of interest, and introduced Codes of Practice for solicitor mediators. This guidance is reproduced in simplified form in Rule 3.06 of the 2007 Code. The Bar Code of Conduct does not deal specifically with avoiding conflict of interest as a barrister mediator, but it does now permit barristers to pay reasonable fees for work referral from mediation provider organisations, and to enter a reasonable fee-sharing arrangement with such organisations on comparable terms to other mediators.[3]

However, the Guidance at Rule 2.02 of the 2007 Code very specifically deals with the duty to advise about ADR in the following terms:

> 15. *When considering the options available to the client (2.02(1)(b)[4],
> if the matter relates to a dispute between the client and a third
> party, you should discuss whether mediation or some other form
> of alternative dispute resolution (ADR) procedure may be more
> appropriate than litigation, arbitration or other formal processes.
> There may be costs sanctions if a party refuses ADR – see* Halsey v
> Milton Keynes NHS Trust and Steel v Joy [2004] EWCA Civ 576.
> *More information may be obtained from the Law Society's Practice
> Advice Service.*

It might be pointed out that choosing between litigation and mediation is not a final option to be made before litigation starts, but one that may properly arise after litigation or arbitration has started. But here for the first time is the articulation of an express professional duty to advise on ADR, based on a reading of *Halsey* about which there can be

---

3 Rule 307(e), introduced in July 2007. The only other reference to mediation in the Bar Code of Conduct is a rather touching requirement in Rule 307(c) that 'a barrister must not compromise his professional standards in order to please his client, the court or a third party, **including any mediator.**'

4 Quoted in full at 11.1 above.

no argument. Perhaps failure to do so could now amount to a basis for disciplinary proceedings against a solicitor. Whether or not this is so, there are many sanctions which a court might deploy, especially in relation to its jurisdiction to order penal interest and indemnity costs and wasted costs to make this almost an unnecessary refinement. The courts are well placed to police this area of advice-giving, as they represent the final venue for solving the problem, either if ADR is not tried or it is tried and does not lead to settlement.

This is even more the case given the existence of court-annexed mediation schemes, especially prevalent in the county of England and Wales, and with the development of the National Mediation Helpline, giving ready access to advice on ADR to all. Where the availability and existence of mediation is built into the fabric of the court system itself, even to the extent that the court of its own initiative offers mediation to the parties, it must follow inevitably that there is a duty to a advise a client on the implications of taking that option.

The duty clearly extends to giving full advice on ADR to one's own client. This advice should include:

- the full range of ADR techniques available;
- the legal and financial implications of each;
- whether the case is in any way unsuitable for ADR;
- whether it is ready for ADR yet;
- how best to approach the other side;
- when the best time to attempt it might be.

Similar considerations apply to meeting the requirements of the Commercial Court, Chancery, Queen's Bench, Technology & Construction Court and Mercantile Court Guides, also discussed in **Chapter 4**.

## 11.4 Implications of the duty

It is fair to say that the existence of the duty to advise on ADR has not yet been directly tested in the English courts in terms of an overt penalty imposed for frank breach of the duty to advise about ADR. Perhaps the clearest judicial pronouncement on the existence of a duty to advise is to be found in *Halsey v Milton Keynes NHS Trust*,[5] in which Dyson LJ said unequivocally,'All members of the legal profession who conduct litigation should now routinely consider with their clients whether their disputes are suitable for ADR.'[6]

---

5 [2004] 4 All ER 920, and discussed fully in **Chapters 5.4** and **6.5**.
6 At para 11.

This is a clear articulation of the Court of Appeal's expectation of all legal practitioners. The Court of Appeal went further in *Burchell v Bullard*,[7] where Ward LJ starkly warned the legal profession:

'The court has given its stamp of approval to mediation and it is now the legal profession which must become fully aware of and acknowledge its value. The profession can no longer with impunity shrug aside reasonable requests to mediate. The parties cannot ignore a proper request to mediate simply because it was made before the claim was issued. With court fees escalating it may be folly to do so.'

In his own short but important judgment in the *Burchell* case,[8] Rix LJ adds some useful glosses to this general statement by warning that a party 'may not be able to rely on its solicitors' or experts' advice where the result shown that mediation ought reasonably to have been attempted'.

This underlines the lawyer's duty to advise thoroughly and authoritatively and in a way that is judge-proof. Unsurprisingly, no party may shelter behind their lawyer's failure to advise: party and lawyer are, as usual, treated as one. Nor can a lawyer rely on a client's ignorance or prejudice or intransigence when exposed to later scrutiny by a judge making a costs order. The lawyer and client will need a very clear understanding as to where responsibility lies if mediation is declined, or else the client may well seek some comeback against the lawyer.

As Rix LJ again reminds practitioners:[9]

'Now that CPR 44.3 . . . has given to the courts such flexibility in the awarding of costs, litigants should be aware and should be made aware by the lawyers whom they consult, that there are considerable perils in adding to a good case other aspects or items of dubious merit.'

Of all the changes wrought by the CPR, it is this uncertainty on costs outcomes that has most modified the culture of litigation. Rix LJ warns that the implications of this remain solidly in place, both in terms of the risks of exaggeration and the risks of not mediating. Supposing a case takes the traditional course taken by at least 90 per cent of cases following the issue of proceedings, by settling, whether before or perhaps even at the door of the court. Even if the deal done there includes payment of costs on the standard basis to be assessed if not agreed, it is well known that recovery may not be more than two-thirds to three-quarters

---

7 [2005] EWCA Civ 358: discussed fully in **Chapter 6.7**.
8 At para 50.
9 In *Burchell v Bullard* at para 49.

of the costs expended by a winning party. Furthermore, it is impossible to recover anything to reflect the lost management time and sheer stress, strain and uncertainty of the case hanging over the parties' heads. If, following a settlement at the door of the court, a party were to learn for the first time that ADR might have been deployed earlier, would a claim in negligence succeed against a lawyer for failure to give advice about the option (subject of course to proof of causation and loss)? We shall have to see, but this is even more likely if the lawyer is shown to have been in breach of the Admiralty and Commercial Court Guide or any other duty to advise.

What still remains to be tested is whether judges themselves are going to remain prepared simply to accept and ratify court-door settlements. What if a judge enquired into why a case had only been settled that late, and insisted on operating on the assumption that cases settled then are almost always capable of earlier settlement through ADR? It is open to the court to apply the principle of proportionality as it affects other court users, to whom the facilities of a court-room and a properly prepared judge have been potentially denied by failure to address settlement earlier in the case before the court. In doing so, a judge could well be tempted to impose penalties on court users in the absence of proper justification for late settlement. Lost costs in those circumstances would undoubtedly be regarded by the client as something for which the lawyer should take responsibility, if adequate ADR advice had not been tendered earlier. Whether penalties based on non-return of court fees for trial charged on notional estimates for a judge's trial time at £ 200 per hour will be introduced is not yet clear. Certainly the reduction of court-door settlements has been regarded as a leading benchmark for the success of the CPR.

## 11.5 Developing strategies over mediation

But it is disappointing even to have to address the issue of a formal *duty*. Mediation, like other forms of ADR, is inherently a process in the client's interests, which should and increasingly does come naturally to many lawyers and parties. The developing attitude of the courts in favour of its use is consolidating that view. Mediation is increasingly being viewed as an effective route to achieving desired outcomes, and one which is adopted proactively and on its own merits, and not merely because of a duty to do so.

As part of that shift, lawyers and parties have become far more sophisticated in their approach to it, both in terms of their willingness to use it, their choice of situations in which to use it, and perhaps most importantly their approach to the conduct of the mediation itself. We touch on some key aspects of this in **Chapter 12**. For now we simply note that a strategic approach to mediation may be informed by answers to questions such as the following:

– How might mediation contribute to achieving our client's stated aims and priorities in this case?

– What could mediation add over and above direct negotiations with the other side?

– Why has this case not settled so far, and what would a mediation contribute to that?

– What impact do we wish to have on the other side and how might a mediation enable us to achieve that?

– Will a mediation enable us to negotiate with (or confront) the right people on the other side?

– How might a mediation affect the other side's (or indeed our) view of the case?

This list is by no means exhaustive. However it provides an indication of the kind of thinking which is required to generate a proper assessment of the likely relevance and contribution of mediation to a particular situation.

## 11.6   When to advise on mediation

It will be apparent from **11.5** above that ADR options can and should be considered at all stages of a dispute, before proceedings are issued, right through to immediately before trial. The most effective use of ADR will often depend on the client receiving advice on it as early as possible, ideally before any dispute has arisen, but certainly before proceedings are issued, as required by the spirit of the pre-action protocols and the CPR. Mediators have often heard parties say that they wished that they had come to this point years earlier.

### 11.6.1   Dispute system design

Bitter and costly experience of disputes has caused parties to give serious thought to putting into place a system designed to cope with and manage the breakdown in a relationship so as to avoid subsequent unnecessary and time-consuming confrontations. The particular strength of this is that the parties address the whole issue of dispute resolution before one arises, and thus at a time when they are able to approach the subject more dispassionately and indeed together. If an effective mechanism is put in place at that stage, much of the acrimony and defensive posturing so characteristic of disputes can be avoided. The growth of this area is reflected in the increased number of attempts to design dispute systems.

In the early 1980s, a major contract for the construction of the El Cahon dam in South America introduced a Disputes Review Panel. This consisted of two independent nominees, one chosen by the owner and one by the contractor, who together then chose a third neutral chairman. Members of the panel were sent the site minutes and all relevant contract documentation and viewed the construction site on a regular basis. Disputes arising under the contract were put to the panel which gave an interim adjudication. At the conclusion of the contract there were no outstanding claims. Building on this experience the American Society of Engineers introduced such a panel on a number of its underground sewage works projects. It was also used on some harbour projects, particularly in Boston.

In the United Kingdom, the first high profile use was on the Channel Tunnel. Decisions by the panel were binding on the parties unless they gave notice of arbitration within a certain period. The matter then became subject to arbitration in the normal way. This structure is to be seen set out in the report of *Channel Tunnel Group Ltd v Balfour Beatty Ltd*[10] and it was duly supported by the House of Lords. More recently, such hybrid schemes have been designed for the Hong Kong Airport and the Channel Tunnel Rail Link.

One of the problems with construction and other business disputes lies in allowing them to fester until the conclusion of the commercial venture. With the passage of time attitudes harden, positions become more entrenched and there is a general reluctance to back down from a position for fear of it being taken as a sign of weakness or considered as a loss of face. The introduction of an intermediate panel allows for an early determination of the dispute, thereby nipping any potential problems in the bud. The nature of such a panel can be flexible. In its simplest form it can consist of a nominated executive from each of the contracting parties: indeed such a version is commonly found in joint ventures and commercial shareholders' agreements.

Another notable example of mediation design in an entirely different context has been the retained organs litigation in England and Wales from 2002 onwards. Two Group Litigation Orders were made in relation to claims brought by parents against various National Health hospitals which had been found to have retained the organs of deceased child patients after post mortem examination without explaining this fully to the parents or expressly obtaining consent. The existence of such organ retention emerged during the Inquiry into paediatric cardiac treatment in Bristol. The Redfern Inquiry heavily criticised the practice in the context of what had happened over many years at Alder Hey Hospital Liverpool. The legal issues were largely novel, and the spectrum of factual issues and psychological reactions among claimants involved was

---

10 [1993] 1 All ER 664.

extremely wide-ranging. It was agreed to mediate these claims involving well over 2,500 claimants and a large number of hospitals, albeit that they had unified representation by the NHS. Two mediators consulted with each interested party over process design to produce a template for both process and documentation. Two different mediators then handled a three-day mediation in a residential setting, at which focus groups from the two main group actions attended with whom the claimant advisers worked. One of the cases relating to Alder Hey Hospital in Liverpool was settled. The second action involving hospitals nationwide was not settled, and proceeded to trial, but mediation was again used to resolve the amount of the claim once the judge had determined liability, finding that the claims of a large class of claimants who had been involved in the Liverpool settlement failed in law, and setting a difficult test in causation for those whose claims survived.[11] A different focus group of those surviving claimants attended a two-day mediation led by two further mediators (one having been involved with the initial design process and thus well known to all) which led to agreement over global damages, and two later separate mediation days dealt with the amount and apportionment of legal costs, an extremely difficult issue in view of the length and depth of the litigation.

Dispute systems design is an extensive and sophisticated topic in its own right, and we cannot begin to do justice to it here. It can be applied in a wide variety of contexts. Some of us have even used it to reform the system of social security claims against the State in Russia. It pushes the issues back up the chain from dispute resolution (which assumes the existence of the dispute) to dispute management and even prevention.

### 11.6.2  At the contract stage

There is a temptation amongst non-contentious lawyers to assume that ADR solely concerns litigation and is therefore not within their concern or province. It must be remembered that it is the non-contentious lawyers who are responsible for drawing up the commercial agreement. Often one of the few clauses that is not argued over is the disputes resolution clause. Many non-contentious lawyers put in such a clause, often choosing arbitration, without proper consultation with their litigation colleagues as to what would be the preferred method of dispute resolution. These days, a standard form arbitration clause is not always in the parties' best interests.

The introduction of an ADR clause into the contract at a time when the parties' relationships are at their best, with the hopes and aspirations of both sides looking towards a beneficial commercial agreement, is an effective way to introduce the concept of ADR. Most such clauses provide that in the event of any dispute the parties will attempt to resolve

---

11 For the full judgment, see *A v Leeds Teaching Hospital NHS Trust* [2004] EWHC 644 (QB): [2004]2 FLR 365.

their differences through mutual discussion, failing which, the parties will attempt to resolve their dispute through mediation or some other ADR means. A more detailed discussion of such clauses, together with some sample clauses, can be found in **Chapter 9** and the Appendix.

As noted in **Chapter 9**, it is difficult to exaggerate the value of an ADR clause. Its introduction into a contract overcomes one of the fundamental difficulties that one party faces when attempting to suggest ADR to the other – the fear that the suggestion of ADR will be regarded as indicating lack of confidence in their own case. If ADR arises contractually, no such fear need exist. As we also note in **Chapter 9**, the issue of whether such clauses do or do not create binding obligations is only their secondary value. Their primary value lies simply in putting ADR on the agenda between the parties without either of them having to raise it unilaterally once a dispute has arisen. Furthermore, if the *parties themselves* have negotiated use of such a process, and in doing so have considered the options between them, they are far more likely to buy into it when the time comes to use it. Encouraging clients to think seriously about, and actually to discuss with their proposed contractual counterparts, the possibility of a dispute arising between them and how they will deal with it, can have a much greater impact on the resolution of any subsequent dispute than they or their advisers might guess.

### 11.6.3 When a dispute arises

It has to be remembered that many disputes do not even get to the stage where proceedings are issued. Many disagreements are settled amicably between the contracting parties before even reaching an external lawyer. Lawyers only see the tip of the iceberg. Even then, of the claims that reach lawyers, whether for breach of contract or damages for some actionable wrong, many settle then through negotiation, long before any need to consider litigation may arise. Most lawyers find that negotiation is a key professional activity and skill throughout their careers, and spend much time engaged in it, be it discussing the terms of a conveyancing transaction, a commercial agreement or the settlement of a piece of litigation.

Yet, as we have seen, even the best negotiators may find it difficult to achieve agreement through direct talks or contact, often through no fault of their own. It may well be that before the next stage of the dispute resolution process is mobilised, the introduction of a third party facilitator could break what is otherwise a negotiating impasse. One of the recurrent themes of the ADR process is that the earlier it is introduced the better, and the greater the savings in time and cost. While many traditional litigators are reluctant to embark upon a full negotiation without many of what they perceive are the essential facts at their fingertips, nevertheless it must be remembered that the majority of commercial disputes settle prior to litigation, and without necessarily having assembled every last piece of information. Company executives and insurers repeatedly take decisions to settle matters often with only the information available from their own side. The introduction of a mediator may cause the parties to re-assess their positions and possibly widen the scope of the negotiations. Mediation itself very frequently provides a very efficient occasion for information exchange and clarification of positions in any event.

Mediations at this early stage can provide their own particular challenges, typically where there is insufficient information available to either side, or one or more of the parties is not yet psychologically disposed to consider settlement at such an early stage. We address these considerations in more detail in **11.7.2** below.

### 11.6.4   Entering the litigation or arbitration stage

The parties have failed to reach agreement through negotiations. There seems to be no other alternative but to issue proceedings. Especially where the lawyer consulted has not been involved in the contract or dispute negotiations hitherto, the range of options open to the client should be explored thoroughly at this stage more than any other. Few lawyers will ever advise their clients to issue proceedings solely in the hope that it will bring the opponents to the negotiating table. Very often, the issue of proceedings is the defining act in solidifying the dispute. Litigation should rarely be embarked upon unless there is willingness and ability to carry the matter through to its ultimate conclusion. Thus, quite apart from the implications of the CPR and the pre-action protocols, it makes considerable sense to try one final attempt to conclude matters by agreement before embarking upon the long and expensive litigation trail. The introduction of a neutral third party into the negotiation dynamic is usually a new idea and can easily be seen to be a worthwhile extension to what has been tried in negotiation hitherto. Especially if ADR has not been raised before, it should be discussed with the client at this stage.

Once the litigation process starts up, it is extremely difficult to stop the machinery from grinding remorselessly on. This is perhaps particularly so where the court is repeatedly imposing target dates by reason of its active case management responsibilities, let alone where the case is allocated to the county court fast track. There is also the temptation always to want to go on just to the next stage, be it sight of the opponent's defence, disclosure of documents, exchange of witness statements or expert's reports, before deciding that the moment is right to open or resume negotiations. All these sub-processes cost time and money. The sooner the suggestion of ADR is made and taken up, the better. The likening of litigation to dancing with a gorilla, whilst well aired among advocates of ADR, is nevertheless a neat metaphor of the experience – you only stop when the gorilla wants to stop.

### 11.6.5   During litigation or arbitration

The same rationale applies once litigation or arbitration is under way. Disputes change as they progress. Issues emerge or are clarified, positions are adjusted, expectations shift. If lawyers are truly to serve their clients' interests, they will need to revisit questions of settlement and settlement strategy on a regular basis. The use of ADR should always be part of that discussion.

## 11.7   When to use mediation

It is sometimes assumed that a case will *either* go to ADR *or* to litigation or arbitration, perhaps as a consequence of the word 'alternative' in the acronym. This is quite incorrect. Many if not most mediations concern disputes in which proceedings have already been commenced and in some cases trial is due very shortly. In other cases, the disputing parties may not even have consulted lawyers and may regard the use of ADR as a way of avoiding that altogether. It follows that there can be no universal right time to take a case to mediation. However, the following general principles should be borne in mind at least as a starting-point.

### 11.7.1   The earlier the better

As a general principle, this is true not just because the cost and time savings are at their greatest, but because parties tend to become more entrenched the longer the dispute lasts. The more they invest in the dispute, not just in terms of money, but in time and commitment to the outcome, the harder it is to focus on the underlying issues themselves. Expectations have been created, boards of directors briefed, claimants have mentally spent what they hope to recover, and bullish defendants have made little or no financial provision in their budget. Both sides increasingly lose sight of the scope for a genuinely constructive settlement, particularly one that involves ongoing relations. Meanwhile the recovery of escalating professional costs will increasingly distort the substantive issues.

In relation to the use of mediation prior to the issue of proceedings, it is of course important to remember the operation of any statutory time limits under the Limitation Acts. The use of mediation (or any other ADR procedure) will not of itself prevent these from running.[12] In circumstances where the period is about to expire, it would be prudent to issue proceedings as a protective measure, or to enter a binding agreement

---

12 The draft EU Directive on mediation, discussed in **Chapter 10, 10.2** above, would reverse this position. It would suspend the running of limitation periods for the duration of a mediation (though what such duration might be is not defined and is open to considerable debate and confusion). It is by no means clear that either the Directive as a whole, or this provision, will be passed into law.

to postpone their operation, then allowing attempts to be made to mediate the dispute before proceedings go any further.

### 11.7.2 Some disputes may have to run for a time before mediation

It is not unusual for some parties only to countenance mediation, or any settlement discussion, when they have fought for a period of time. This may stem from tactical considerations, perceptions of relative merits, or even pride or the desire for revenge. In terms of the timing of mediation, this needs to be borne in mind. Refusal to entertain mediation early in a case may well not equate with unwillingness to use it at all, though it is wise for parties to try to avoid even the impression of intransigence in the light of the possible costs penalties that might emerge from CPR Pt 44.5. In fact, as a case progresses, perceptions of merits and risks change, new information emerges, costs and delays increase, and the parties may have vented their initial spleen, all of which can increase readiness for settlement exploration.

### 11.7.3 Enough information needs to be available to permit a realistic risk assessment

This is dealt with in more detail in **11.7.4** and **11.7.6**. Suffice it to say here that unless sufficient information is available (or potentially available through a chosen ADR process) to enable parties to establish in their own minds the parameters for settlement, it may well be difficult and even imprudent to settle the case, by mediation or any other means. This may be their own information (counsel's opinion, medical or experts' reports and so on) or the other side's (available through disclosure of documents or exchange of evidence).

That said, three qualifications should be borne in mind:

(1) Many disputes are actually settled by the parties even before lawyers are consulted. The benefits of an early settlement must be weighed against the risks of doing so without (perhaps) all the information that litigation might produce, and a commercial judgment made. Neither option is objectively right. An early settlement may ultimately prove to be on less advantageous terms than would subsequently have been available (though how will this be discovered?), but with savings of time and cost and with relationships preserved. Conversely, litigation may provide an ultimate victory, but with loss of other commercial opportunities for the parties as a consequence, or maybe intervening financial failure by the unsuccessful party will render it a Pyrrhic victory. It falls to the lawyer and particularly the client to make this judgment in each set of circumstances.

(2) The question of available information usually centres on disclosure of documents. The argument is sometimes made that mediation should not be attempted before that stage because settlement discussions may otherwise be ill-founded. Sometimes this will be true. Often, however, disclosure does not reveal anything of sufficient importance materially to change the nature of a case. The desire to complete disclosure may reflect the lawyer's very understandable desire to keep immune from criticism (and an action for negligence) in relation to the terms of settlement. This needs careful advice from lawyer to client, but a decision can then be made by the client, who may be best placed to know if disclosure will or will not be helpful first. In many actions, the issues and relevant information are clear long before disclosure. Disclosure of relevant documentation is not, therefore, a prerequisite for mediation, but should reflect a reasonable assessment of what information is really needed for effective case evaluation and negotiation.

The same considerations apply in relation to expert evidence. Where a case turns substantially on what each party's expert says, a serious analysis of their position by each party and serious subsequent debate of the issues in a mediation may not be possible until the experts' views are tabled. Equally, however, parties are not driven solely by their experts' views: they have their own priorities for settlement. As noted in **Chapter 12**,[13] it may be possible to bring the experts to the mediation and test out their views there with all key decision-makers present to see how they perform.

(3) However, the above assumes that the production of information relevant to case analysis and settlement discussions can only be achieved by the litigation or arbitration processes. This is certainly not the case. There is no reason why early disclosure of key materials cannot be arranged in order to facilitate early settlement discussions. Quite apart from the duties imposed by the pre-action protocols and their CPR practice direction, voluntary disclosure can be built into the mediation process itself. It is a good example of the outcome dictating the process and not the other way around.

Additionally, the courts, especially the Technology and Construction Court, have begun to make directions early in the life of litigation which facilitate the production of information and expert evidence to enhance the prospects of early mediation.[14]

---

13 See **12.4.8** under point 5.
14 Although for technical reasons this was not found to have worked by the Court of Appeal in *Aird v Prime Meridian* [2006] EWCA Civ 1866, the principle of making supportive directions remains undisturbed.

### 11.7.4   Assessing case value and risk

Assessing case value from a risk management point of view is clearly a key element of dispute handling, and the assessments reached will necessarily affect the choice of dispute resolution process. The structure of litigation and arbitration tends to defer a detailed consideration of the case until much nearer to trial (and indeed many clients do not want to face the uncomfortable realities of their positions). Mediation necessitates a disciplined focus on the case whenever it takes place, often long before trial. Thus an assessment of case value is both a part of the decision about whether to take a case to mediation, and also a likely product of doing so.

The front loading of preparation and costs required by the CPR tends to encourage much earlier assessment than used to be the case, and perhaps this has been one factor behind the increased use of mediation since the CPR came into effect. There is certainly evidence that cases are being prepared earlier and not settled so late as formerly. The DCA reviews of the effect of the CPR have certainly noted fewer court-door settlements, though by no means have they disappeared altogether.

In litigation terms, risk management breaks down into two elements:

(1)   *A claim recovery analysis:* an assessment of one's own likely recovery and that of the other side.

(2)   *A cost risk analysis:* an assessment of the cost of pursuing the various options, and the attendant risks of each.

#### 11.7.4.1   Claim recovery analysis

It should be possible though a systematic and methodical approach to carry out a detailed analysis of each item of claim assessed against a degree of possibility and probability of success. The need for a high/low bracket is to allow for the uncertainties of litigation such as the ultimate performance of the witness in the box, the quality of the case presentation and the judge's reaction to it. Having assessed each and every claim in percentage terms, they can then collectively be averaged out.

Obviously, such an analysis would not be complete without carrying out a similar exercise upon any counterclaim. In addition, if a broader view is required, the exercise can be repeated based upon differing 'what if' scenarios.

#### 11.7.4.2   Cost risk analysis

A similarly detailed and methodical approach, coupled with a litigator's experience and a great deal of realism, can produce a reasonably likely forecast of the costs of an action. Indeed, summaries of future anticipated costs are now required by CPR to be produced for the court and the opponent at several key stages of any action. Inaccuracy in producing these may have an influence on whether costs are awarded in full or only in part once the action is determined. Each stage of the litigation (claim form, particulars of claim, defence, allocation, case management conference, disclosure, evidence exchange, pre-trial review and trial) needs to be analysed, and a calculation of the cost of each stage in terms of minima and maxima of work and cost produced. Figures for counsel, court and expert fees and other disbursements must be ascertained and included. The figure can then be worked through to the conclusion of the trial. This will be of great use both to the party (for cash-flow purposes) and his adviser. The likely shortfall between standard costs and solicitor and client or indemnity costs on detailed assessment even in the event of the client succeeding at trial needs to be borne in mind.

For such management information to be fully accurate and useful, this exercise and evaluation needs to be carried out on a regular basis through-out the course of the litigation. The discipline imposed by the CPR and Solicitors Practice Code para 2 will make it an ordinary part of case management and client care anyway. The factors to be taken into account will change and vary in the light of the experience gained during the conduct of the litigation. Lawyers are often criticised for inability or reluc-tance to give their clients accurate quotations for the cost of litigation. This can thus become a useful marketing tool for professional advisers, quite apart from assisting the client in evaluating the most cost-effective time to attempt to settle the case.

Clients in any complex action should ensure they receive a regular update on cost levels, predictions of success in the action and review of appropriateness of ADR, including potential cost-saving benefits.

If all the above seems obvious, it is still nevertheless a regular and depress-ing part of a UK mediator's experience to mediate disputes where there appears to have been little serious or informed risk analysis. Mediators will often go through a risk analysis with each party during a mediation, in front of their lawyers, and all too often the parties seem not to have grasped the true extent of the risks they face. Usually there has been a considerable focus on the potential upside of their case, and not enough of the possible downside. Mediators have no wish to embarrass lawyers in front of their client in conducting a risk analysis which should have been done thoroughly in private beforehand.

In any event, careful risk assessment is an absolute business requirement for successfully running claims on conditional fee agreements. In both this area and in the context of risk reappraisal generally, one useful tool is decision-tree analysis, when assessing the real value of claims in the light of their chances of success. Any detailed study of either area is beyond the scope of this book, but there is material now available in the United Kingdom which explains and its usefulness.[15]

### 11.7.5 Direct negotiations between the parties or their advisers are not succeeding

Direct negotiation between parties and their advisers is clearly the most efficient and effective method of resolving a dispute. Generally, parties should have attempted these before attempting mediation, not least because it is cheaper. The negotiations may take the form of direct talks or (usually less effective) an exchange of correspondence, perhaps including 'without prejudice' offers. However, it is important to remember that:

- Some direct talks may in fact drive the parties further apart, particularly if there is personal animosity between the protagonists.

- Some direct negotiations may not succeed after a couple of hours, whereas others may prove very effective if left to continue for several days, or even over a period of weeks or months. It is not always easy to assess when talks are not in fact producing results.

- Since most litigation cases settle before trial, on the basis of direct negotiations, it is tempting to assume that most settlement negotiations work. However, the crucial question is not whether they work (in the sense of ultimately producing a negotiated settlement), but whether they work well. It is not the hallmark of an efficient process if, in order to ... generate settlement, the negotiations have to take place over a number of years, whether or not against the back-cloth of expensive litigation, when a mediation might produce settlement in a few days. Mediation will usually concertina the negotiation process into a much tighter time-frame, because of the inherent nature of ADR processes.

### 11.7.6 Selecting individual cases

There have been long debates, often among those with little or no experience of ADR, as to how to assess whether a case is suitable for ADR in general and mediation in particular. The experience of ADR usage and practice built up in this jurisdiction alone for over ten years, let alone the much longer experience of other common law jurisdictions, has not identified a large tranche of cases which are inherently unsuitable. Indeed, some sophisticated repeat users of mediation in the United Kingdom have reversed the normal question and self-imposed onus of proof by asking

---

15 See for instance Chalk: *Risk Assessment in Litigation* (2001, Tottel Publishing).

'is this case **un**suitable for ADR?', and this may well be a much sounder approach. Very often the right question is not 'is it suitable?' but 'is it ready' for mediation. Section **11.8** sets out some reasons for not using mediation immediately in a given case, but here we set out a rule of thumb which can at least act as a starting-point for consideration of a given case.

The rule is that a case is, on the face of it, suitable for ADR if

- each party has sufficient information regarding the case to enable it to make a reasonable assessment of its position; and

- direct negotiations are not proving effective in generating a settlement; and

- none of the reasons set out in Section **11.8** applies.

It will be apparent from this that large numbers of disputes, perhaps even most disputes, will be suitable for resolution by mediation at some stage in their life-cycle. This counters the common perception that only the occasional dispute will be suitable. Perhaps the harder question, but one which can impact significantly on how likely the mediation is to produce a settlement, is determining the right moment to try mediation. While there is clearly no right answer, the following additional factors set out below should all be considered:

- The readiness of all parties to consider settlement (and all should beware the easy assumption that 'the other side are not interested in settlement'). Will these parties become more or less willing to contemplate settlement as the case progresses? Will delay harden or soften their position?

- Will some opportunities for settlement disappear with time – eg chances for the parties to co-operate in some way?

- Can or should over-investing in a case be avoided, before recovery of costs (whether time, money or emotion) become the driving force?

- If there may be insufficient information available for exchange, will it really only require litigation or arbitration to be commenced for it to be supplied?

### 11.7.7 Systematic case selection

Much current ADR use in the United Kingdom at present is on an essentially case-by-case basis. Parties and advisers discuss ADR in relation to a given case and in due course agreement is reached (or not) with the other side to use it.

From the point of view of a client with a large through-put of litigation (typically insurance companies, banks and some other large corporations), the real benefit of ADR is to be obtained through much more systematic use. Some insurers are choosing to use mediation in a consistent and planned way for their claims work, in an attempt to reduce their overall claims handling expenses by achieving earlier and better outcomes, thus minimising their exposure to legal costs. This is a lesson long since learned by many US carriers and large corporations with heavy involvement in claims settlement. Typically in such cases, no assumption is made that mediation will emerge as an option at some unspecified future point. Instead, a policy is implemented which imposes a formal requirement that the initial and regular subsequent reports on each case from its in-house or panel lawyers contain a proper review of mediation possibilities. It presumes that all cases within certain pre-selected criteria are suitable for ADR (usually mediation), unless specific justification is given to the contrary.

These might include:

- all claims over two years old which are not dormant or allegedly fraudulent;
- all new claims above a certain value;
- all multi-track claims;
- all fast-track cases where liability is significantly at issue;
- all cases where the difference in valuation between claimant and defendant exceeds a certain figure;
- all claims within a certain category of risk (professional indemnity, construction, brain damage); and
- any other criterion that fits the insurer's particular claims philosophy.

The use of a more systematic approach to case selection, whilst not removing the need for individual consideration of each case, has a number of benefits:

- it is likely to generate a much higher level of ADR use;
- it will therefore maximise the benefit delivered to the client;
- it transfers the onus of responsibility and judgment over case selection from individual case handlers to objectively established systematic criteria;
- it swiftly builds up data to form an empirical basis by which to measure the benefit that mediation is delivering to that company; and
- it may enhance that company's claims handling reputation in the market-place.

197

A number of such schemes are being developed in the United Kingdom, and have been in place for many years in other parts of the common law world. Essentially such approaches show a side of mediation too little considered. Its systematic use is fundamentally a strategic and financial management decision, not a legal one. It requires a broader view of the processes and performance of a business, a clear sense of where process improvements and efficiencies can be implemented for a business. There is little doubt that if more businesses approached the issue like that, mediation use would grow very significantly.

### 11.7.8 Common misconceptions about suitability

There are many misconceptions about the suitability of cases for mediation. Some of the more frequent are set out below:

- *There is no point mediating a strong case.* In practice, cases of all degrees of 'strength' or 'weakness' *are* regularly mediated. The misconception often rests on an assumption that mediated outcomes inevitably 'split it down the middle'. In fact, experience does not bear that out, and there is no reason why the inherent strength or weakness of a case should not be reflected in the agreement which resolves it. Mediations have been settled on the basis of claims being withdrawn in their entirety, or indeed being paid in full.

- *There are issues of law involved.* In practice, of course, many cases involving issues of law *are* successfully mediated. The assertion that such cases are unsuitable for mediation arises presumably from the notion that such issues could not be 'decided' by a mediator, and thus the matter could not be settled. In fact of course, parties regularly 'take a view' on such issues and the absence of a finding on them is no bar to settlement. Indeed were that not the case, no dispute involving issues of law could ever be resolved without a trial.

- *It's a multi-party dispute.* It is unclear quite why that should render a case unsuitable for mediation. In practice, multi-party disputes are regularly mediated, to great effect. In fact, the feature of multiple parties can often make settlement negotiations *without* a mediator particularly difficult, since party B will not commit to terms with A, until his position with C is resolved, and so on down the line. These structural difficulties can be avoided through mediation.

- *It's too complex to be addressed in mediation.* Again it is not entirely clear what is meant by this objection.[16] It is true that a

---

16 The scorn with which such an assertion made by a building surveyor was dismissed by Ward LJ in *Burchell v Bullard* [2005] EWCA Civ 358 is telling.

one or two day mediation cannot address in forensic detail all the complexities of a case, but then it does not attempt to do so. It is precisely the discipline (and it is a discipline) of each party having to take a *broader* view of settlement (albeit in the light its own previously ascertained detailed knowledge of the case) that makes mediation so effective at producing settlement.

- *The parties are too entrenched.* Mediation cannot guarantee an outcome. However it is striking how many cases are resolved in mediation where the parties or their advisers thought before-hand that settlement was highly unlikely.

## 11.8 When mediation might not be appropriate

It should be clear from the above that mediation is not a universally applicable process, nor is it intended to replace the litigation and arbitration systems in their entirety. The key to the successful use of mediation is to know when, and when not, to use it. Again, it is unwise to be too prescriptive, but the following general principles should be borne in mind in relation to when mediation may not be suitable.

### 11.8.1   Negotiations proving effective

If the negotiation process is already working there is no absolute necessity to introduce the agency of a third party. It should be remembered that even taking into account the vast number of litigated cases that settle prior to trial, the majority of disputes do not even reach the stage where pro-ceedings are issued. Countless commercial disputes are settled perfectly adequately without recourse to the courts.

There may be cases, such as clinical negligence claims, where a trial is very unlikely to occur because of earlier settlement, or not seen as providing an adequate opportunity for emotional issues to be handled properly, when the mediation process will be seen as offering a better settlement event than either trial or a mere bilateral negotiation, and be preferred for that reason as giving the chance for face-to-face contact across a table between the key parties. Negotiations are not necessarily effective simply because a resolution is reached. Questions of their efficiency, their inherent nature in delivering what clients need, and implications as to how long they take are all critical.

### 11.8.2   Need for court assistance/protection

If there is a need for an injunction or some other form of relief available only through the court procedure, such as a declaration, then mediation (and indeed any form of ADR) will not be appropriate. Clearly, the need to protect or seize assets will require a court-based approach. However, it may well be that once such protection or seizure is obtained, the underlying issues can be resolved through ADR.

### 11.8.3 The need to set (or try to avoid) a precedent

Mediation and other forms of ADR cannot deliver a decision with the force of precedent and in circumstances where that is required, mediation is clearly inappropriate. For example, an insurance company might litigate over the interpretation of a policy condition, and require the finality of a court decision in order to substantiate its stance towards all policy-holders. Similarly, a commercial precedent might be required for reasons of corporate policy or image. A company might wish to assert the primacy of a form of conduct – eg a firm commitment to dismissals for theft – or send a particular message to its market-place competitors. Equally, an employer might want not to be seen to be soft on certain types of claim, a situation which occurred in *Daniels v Commissioner for Metropolitan Police*,[17] a case where such a policy approach was held to justify refusal to negotiate or to make a Part 36 offer. In these circumstances, mediation or other types of ADR are unlikely to be used, except perhaps as an aid to streamlining the issues for trial.

It is important to remember, however, that a precedent can be a two-edged sword. If the insurance company litigating over a policy term is unsuccessful, it not only loses that action, but also publicly declares to other holders of a similar policy that they too have a right of redress against the company. Where such concerns exist, the privacy afforded by ADR can be attractive. The safest test for a litigant who wants a precedent is for the question to be asked whether the precedent will be valuable, *win or lose.* If losing a case, and thus setting an adverse precedent would be painful or dangerous, settlement by mediation or any other means may be preferable.

Furthermore procedures very often require a decision of the Court of Appeal, and the additional costs risks of prolonged litigation need to be weighed.

### 11.8.4 Publicity

Sometimes a party may perceive that one of the major benefits (perhaps the only benefit) of litigation is the publicity that it can attract. This can be used to apply commercial pressure or the pressure of public opinion, which can be a very powerful weapon. The public vindication of a reputation is often the primary objective of a libel action. The privacy and confidentiality of most ADR processes does not generally permit such publicity. However,

---

17 [2005] EWCA Civ 1312.

libel actions are themselves being mediated now, often involving a planned move from private negotiation to an agreed public declaration of outcome.

Interestingly, however, ADR techniques (primarily consensus-building) have been used to great effect in environmental disputes, where the publicity element is often regarded as very important, and provision for it can be made in the design of the process itself. This is a useful reminder that the flexibility of ADR techniques permits a matching of the chosen process with the priorities and aims of the parties.

### 11.8.5   Economic power

Litigation can be used by the commercially stronger party in an oppressive way. A party which is perceived to have limitless resources to pursue or resist litigation can often exploit its advantage, thereby forcing the weaker party into a compromise at a figure below that which they could reasonably expect in litigation. The weaker party either cannot wait or simply does not have the resources to take the matter right the way through to a conclusion. The risks involved are too great. Often, in addition, merely to sue invites a cessation of commercial relations. This is one reason why many large oil companies appear to have a relatively litigation-free existence. Some of their smaller suppliers simply do not dare issue proceedings. Economic power may therefore be used to prevent, inhibit or determine litigation outcomes. Whether this is an appropriate strategy is a wider issue than the question of ADR use. However, some companies have begun to set up schemes with distributors as a way of deflecting just such criticism. What it very clear is that the management of reputation, stakeholder opinion and supply chain relations is critical to many businesses. Increasingly, the investment being made in those areas is focusing on the effective resolution of contentious issues in ways that are not only fair and appropriate, but *perceived* to be such. ADR has an increasing role to play in that arena.

### 11.8.6   Summary judgment

Where summary judgment is available (whether to claimant or defendant, by virtue of CPR, Pt 24) and attainable, there is an argument for seeking it as an end in itself. Alternatively, it might be sought so that, should there be any subsequent negotiations, perhaps over enforcement or terms of payment, the claimant can operate from a position of strength. Thus, in a straightforward debt recovery action with no substantive defence, ADR is not often used. Similarly, if a defendant can dispose of an unmeritorious claim once and for all by using Pt 24, there is little point in considering ADR.

However, even in those situations, there are still valid arguments for using mediation in particular, for example the desire to maintain good commercial relations with customers or suppliers. In this context, mediation usage has to be viewed in the light of wider corporate policy or image, and not solely as a question for that particular dispute. Mediation (or some other ADR process) is sometimes used by a party who thinks that it has an unanswerable case simply to meet with the opposition to explain that view to them and to listen to any persuasion to the contrary. It is best to discover at the earliest possible time that a case thought to be cast iron, or a defence thought to be just plausible, is less so than hoped. If this can be done in a principled and respectful way, any possible future relationship may well be able to be preserved.

In any event, there are many actions where summary judgment is not obtainable or too risky an exercise in the view of the balance of merit. If a claimant, or indeed defendant, applies for it and fails, that may well be an appropriate juncture to try mediation. A wise mediator, faced at a mediation with a party who says they have an unanswerable case, may gently enquire why summary judgment was not sought. The answer may well be illuminating as to that party's true perception of the strength of their case.

### 11.8.7   No genuine interest in settlement

ADR processes are consensual, and to that extent require all parties to be interested at least in exploring settlement opportunities (though that is by no means tantamount to a willingness to settle on any terms). If one or more parties to a dispute can genuinely be said to have no interest in settlement, then manifestly mediation or any other ADR process is unlikely to work, except to the degree that such an attitude may itself change as a result of engagement in such a process.

However, it would be unwise to assume too readily that any party is genuinely uninterested in settlement. Very few parties litigate for the sake of inherent enjoyment of the process, unless perhaps motivated by a desire for vindication or revenge. Most parties are interested in the substantive outcome, not the process. If terms can be found that satisfy their demand (in the light of the strengths and weaknesses of their position) then settlement can be achieved. The question is simply which process will be more likely to generate such terms.

Therefore, great caution should be applied in interpreting the inevitable posturing of both the other side and indeed one's own client. Such behaviour is by no means necessarily inconsistent with a willingness to settle.

## 11.9   The benefits of ADR

Any advice to clients on whether or not to use mediation will need to contain an assessment of the benefits and risks of doing so. Although these are touched on in other parts of this book, it is useful to draw those strands together and summarise them. Clients for whom ADR in general, and mediation in particular, is new will almost certainly want to address these at some length.

### 11.9.1   Cost

It is self-evident from the informality and speed of ADR processes that the costs are likely to be significantly less than commencing or continuing with litigation or arbitration. The costs element is dealt with in more detail in **11.10.3**.

### 11.9.2   Speed

The speed with which ADR can achieve solutions is in marked contrast to litigation or arbitration. A typical mediation lasts one day. Infrequently, a mediation may extend to two days, and an exceptionally lengthy one might last up to five days. Moreover, mediations can be set up as quickly as the parties require, the only constraint being the availability of those who will attend. Especially since court-referred mediations, whether under a CPR, Pt 26.4 order or at case management conference, involving a stay for one month or more, have become increasingly common, the time from referral to mediation has been reduced as a matter of course from six to eight weeks to three weeks or even less.

The importance of speed cannot be underestimated. Commercial disputes take place in a commercial context, not a vacuum. The inability of business managers to plan for the future because of the uncertain outcome of a dispute, which in litigation may remain uncertain for many months and even years, can be a major problem, touching not only on cash-flow, but often on much wider issues of corporate planning and strategy. Similarly, lay claimants often find the slow nature of litigation incomprehensible, painful and unacceptable. Again, a straw poll of mediators will very likely indicate quite how often such considerations feature in the settlement considerations of one or more parties.

### 11.9.3   Control

Business people (and many lay people) are used to being involved in the negotiation process, in which they retain a large measure of control over both the process and the outcome. In litigation they can find they have very little, if any, control, and that in itself is immensely frustrating. The process is largely dictated by predetermined court procedures, and the outcome is dependent on the forensic presentation of their case, the performance of their witnesses, and the opinions of the judge, all of which are largely beyond their control.

Mediation in particular among ADR processes returns the element of control to the parties, in conjunction with their advisers. The shape of the process is not predetermined, but open to the parties to decide in response to the mediator's suggestions. Thus a process can be chosen or even designed to reflect their intentions and priorities, as well as the nature of the problem. The similarity of mediation to normal methods of direct negotiation means that many clients are instinctively familiar and at ease with the process. The outcome, too, remains entirely within their control, in the sense that terms cannot be imposed upon them, but only arrived at through negotiations. Furthermore, the informality of the process, and its similarity to direct negotiations, makes their active and confident participation far more likely, and compares very favourably to the experience of being in the witness box at a trial or arbitration hearing.

Court trial can be a very unpleasant environment for any party, whether the case involves commercial or personal issues. Control is in effect given over to the professionals. This is in marked contrast to the centrality of parties within mediations, both physically to the mediator in joint sessions and also at the heart of the discussion and decision-making process.

### 11.9.4   Relationships

The adversarial nature of litigation and arbitration forces parties into confrontation. Not only does confrontation not always generate results efficiently or effectively, it may drive the protagonists further apart. In some cases this may not matter, since the parties have no ongoing relationship to consider. In a commercial context, however, the adverse effect on business relations can be a major disincentive to, or a detrimental by-product of, litigation or arbitration.

By contrast, the mediation process is an approach far more likely to minimise the deterioration in relationships, and in some cases may even provide a forum for new and more creative future working relationships to be established. That is not to say that the atmosphere of a mediation is not a tough and often aggressive one, but rather that the process itself is potentiating, rather than destroying, the parties' relationship.

This can also have implications for a company's image or reputation. Consistent and fair use of mediation (where appropriate) may be used to send a significant message to business suppliers, customers, and others. The use of mediation should, at best, go far beyond consideration of individual cases, and inform a company's approach to its corporate image. A good example of this is the corporate ADR pledge, used to good effect by leading companies in the United States. This involves a public commitment to the use of mediation in appropriate cases. In reality, the discretion over mediation use is left entirely to the company, on a case-by-case basis, but the message sent to the market-place is an important one. Furthermore, it is much easier for a party in dispute with such a company to suggest ADR in the light of such a pledge.

Such an approach was taken by the UK government when it promulgated a pledge in March 2001 that it would agree to use ADR whenever sought by those with whom it was in dispute, in appropriate cases. Since then it has published periodic figures designed to demonstrate its compliance with its own pledge.

The practice of entering into non-binding statements of intent to mediate or use other forms of ADR has become more popular. For example, the Market ADR Commitment (MAC) is an accord which commits signatories, all of them significant participants in the professional indemnity insurance market, to utilise ADR where possible to resolve such disputes. Individual businesses have sought to demonstrate their credentials through other similar public commitments.

### 11.9.5   Creative and forward-looking solutions

Litigation and arbitration are historical exercises, based on an analysis of rights and obligations. The focus of any search for a solution, or the final judgment, tends to be based solely on what happened (historical facts) and what rights and obligations attach to the parties as a result (law).

These elements certainly feature in mediations, but other elements are also involved, especially in designing settlements within the process – in particular, appertaining to the parties' interests and needs. Necessarily, therefore, the scope for settlement is wider, generating more possibilities and making settlement more likely. Settlements reached in mediations will often reflect much more than a straightforward payment of damages. A typical example in a commercial dispute is terms of settlement including an agreement for A to supply B with certain products at discounted rates (say, cost price). B will then receive something with a value of, say, 100 units, which only costs A 50 units to supply.

Furthermore, it is entirely logical that a settlement should reflect not only the strict legal position (or rather the parties' perceptions of it), but where possible their personal or commercial interests and needs as well. There are often situations where the payment of damages, whilst always welcome, does not in itself address the underlying commercial problem. Such interests and needs are simply not relevant as far as a judge or arbitrator is concerned, in arriving at a decision, but are highly relevant in mediation.

Such innovative and wide-ranging solutions are particularly to be found in personal injury, clinical negligence and employment mediations. Those who bring such claims often labour under a major sense of grievance. They may want to know why a catastrophe (as they perceive it) happened to them, whether any changes have occurred to ensure that no one else goes through the same experience, or whether any disciplinary steps are to be taken against someone who discriminated against them. Even receiving an expression of regret can help.

More tangible outcomes can be negotiated, such as:

- – an assurance of future employment;
- – the restructuring of a department or of a hospital's procedures; and
- – compensation in kind, such as treatment or care or a written expression of regret for delay.

The list is potentially endless, and illustrates the scope for imagination in devising ways of meeting the true interests of those involved in disputes.

### 11.9.6   Confidentiality

There will often be situations where, for example, commercial considerations demand confidentiality. Litigation is almost always a public forum, and arbitration can become public on appeal. Alternative Dispute Resolution is a private process, and this is frequently cited by parties as a reason for using it. For example, a company may wish to settle with a certain litigant without that information becoming known to other litigants with similar claims. A charity might fear the effect on its donation income if it is seen to be involved in a bitter and costly dispute. A professional partnership may wish to deal with a negligence claim against it without knowledge that the claim was made entering the public domain, not least for reasons of professional reputation.

Equally, it is open to parties at a mediation to discuss and plan any necessary publicity for the outcome of the mediation. Mediation is now being used for defamation claims, the outcome of which might well require public statements as part of the settlement terms. The parties can therefore agree within the entirely confidential process which led to settlement precisely how retractions, apologies and agreed statements are to be given due circulation.

### 11.9.7   Discipline and focus

The CPR have injected the concept of active case management into the litigation process. This means that even the heaviest case will move from case management conference to case management conference with the court keeping an eye on progress. The whole jurisdiction of striking out cases for want of prosecution, so beloved of defendant lawyers, is largely irrelevant and defunct now. However, there is still no doubt that the time-scales at which litigation and arbitration move are much slower than mediation. While litigation and arbitration might not be able to drift along quite so much as they could before the CPR, it is still by no means rare that it is relatively late in the day that the case begins to be analysed in full. The pre-action protocols will help in advancing information exchange, of course, but there is always a temptation to want to extract yet more information (by disclosure, exchange of evidence, further expert opinion and so on) before the case can be properly and fully appraised. This can also be a symptom of an unwillingness, sometimes on the part of the lawyer and sometimes the client, properly to focus on the case, to address the issues and take decisions.

Ultimately, the only procedural step (in litigation or arbitration) that forces them to do so is the final hearing or trial; hence the tendency for such focused analysis to happen late, and probably the reason for many court door settlements. Mediation engenders the same effect, forcing the pace of rigorous analysis, debate and decision-making, but it can do so at any stage, though preferably sooner rather than later. It operates as an artificial court door, creating much of the atmosphere and focus associated with an imminent trial, but doing so much earlier and without all the expensive trappings of trial such as fully paginated bundles of evidence and attendant counsel and experts waiting to contribute. As we have seen, it is possible that settlement at the real court door may be made less attractive as the implications of the CPR and its costs sanction regime are worked through in judicial decisions.

### 11.9.8   Satisfaction and consequent compliance

Alternative Dispute Resolution processes are often more satisfying to the parties than a trial or hearing, for many reasons. First, the relief of reaching a settlement, and of doing so by consensus, coupled with all the other attendant benefits referred to in this section, tends to generate very high levels of satisfaction. Inevitably, some of this will reflect well on their advisers, and furthermore, the parties are much more likely to return to those advisers with future disputes if the whole experience has been a positive one.

Secondly, mediation is likely to provide a much more satisfying day in court than a real day in court. The informality means that parties can participate fully, rather than solely through their advocate, and there is none of the stress of cross-examination by the other side. They can, and often do, speak their minds, and indeed some element of venting of emotion may be vital in generating settlement.

Finally, since any settlement is reached by consensus, it follows that implementation or enforcement is much less likely to be a problem than it is where judgment is imposed.

### 11.9.9 Effectiveness

Finally, ADR processes in general, and mediation in particular, have a remarkable track record in generating settlements. Whatever the arguments, this fact alone suggests that the use of such processes should always be considered.

## 11.10 Answering common concerns about mediation

It is generally accepted that mediation is not, on the whole, a risky process. The fact that continued participation is voluntary, confidential and 'without prejudice' leaves little real scope for parties to be exposed or prejudiced as a result. However, such concerns as there are do need to be addressed, not least because clients may well wish to discuss them.

### 11.10.1 'I will have to disclose my hand'

The trend towards 'cards on the table' litigation was confirmed and consolidated by the CPR. The components of the overriding objective, embodying concepts of an equal footing between parties, fairness, proportionality, cost saving and so on mean that a party who endeavours to take an opponent by surprise at trial is likely to find such a tactic back-firing. A prime example of this is found in the case of *Ford v GKR Construction*,[18] a personal injury case in the Court of Appeal, where the claimant still received her full costs despite failing to beat a Pt 36 offer. During an adjournment of her trial for two months, the defendants obtained video evidence showing that she was capable of doing more than she claimed in her evidence. This was disclosed before the hearing was resumed some weeks later but the defendants declined to negotiate. The judge accepted the evidence of the film but was supported by the Court of Appeal in declining to give the defendants their costs from the date of the Pt 36 offer. They had chosen not to video her before and then refused to negotiate. The implication was that the continued trial had in effect been their fault. Thus a party conceals their true case in order to ambush their opponent at trial at their peril, at least in relation to costs orders.

All procedures within both the mainstream CPR and the specialist court jurisdictions now require exchange of witness statements and experts' reports well in advance of hearings. The pre-action protocols even require

---

18  [2000] 1 All ER 802.

a substantial degree of frankness about each party's position before proceedings can safely be issued at all. For instance, the Personal Injury Protocol calls for a detailed letter of claim setting out a full factual summary, the nature of any injuries suffered and financial loss incurred. The defendant must respond within three months: if liability is denied, reasons for doing so must be given, and a list of relevant documents sent. There is also provision for medical evidence to be obtained either jointly or separately. The Clinical Negligence Protocol additionally deals with disclosure of medical records. There are similar provisions in the other protocols. The same spirit of pre-action frankness is demanded of all litigants in whatever type of case by Practice Direction to the Protocols, para 4, which reads:

> '... the court will expect the parties, in accordance with the overriding objective ... to act reasonably in exchanging information and documents relevant to the claim and generally in trying to avoid the necessity for the start of proceedings.'

In such circumstances, it is unlikely that resort to an ADR process will have what is perceived to be the adverse effect of giving the other side early notice of one's 'clever points'. Furthermore, the reluctance to disclose one's hand contains an underlying logical flaw. The only way to make no disclosure at all is to have no contact with the other side (a risky omission in the light of the CPR anyway), by making no attempt to settle. This will virtually guarantee that the case will be tried. Refusal even to negotiate is readily penalised, as **Chapter 6** clarifies.[19] Perhaps it is only where one side intends to argue that an available document or a piece of evidence has much greater significance and effect on a dispute than an opponent seems to anticipate that legitimate reluctance over disclosing such a position arises.

Once it is accepted that some degree of communication and discussion, and therefore disclosure, is necessary, the argument is simply one of degree. All potential disclosures will be subjected to a cost-benefit analysis. What is the perceived or likely benefit of making this disclosure, in terms of generating movement towards settlement? What is the potential risk if settlement is not achieved? Those familiar with mediation will be aware that parties frequently conduct such an analysis during the mediation itself.

Furthermore, mediation contains a structural feature that enables, in effect, partial disclosure. A matter can be disclosed to the mediator, but without giving the mediator permission to disclose it to the other side. This enables hitherto highly secretive points or concerns to be raised for

---

19 See for instance *Virani v Manuel Revert* discussed in **Chapter 6, 6.3.** above.

discussion, and exposed to neutral third party input, without the risk of raising them directly with the other side. In addition, the mediator may well be in a position to assist that party in assessing the value of extending the disclosure to the other side, and is more likely to know how such a point would be received.

Finally, the following points are worth noting:

– If a party has a strong case, what is the point in keeping all those strengths hidden? If the intention is to encourage or force the other side to change its position, early disclosure is likely to assist.

– If a party has a weak case, how much advantage is there in prolonging the agony? Of course there will always be instances where, for tactical, financial or commercial reasons, one party perceives it necessary to prolong the litigation process for as long as possible. However, that has to be offset against the ultimate and far greater exposure of losing at trial. Furthermore, discounted terms may be available in exchange for a quick settlement.

– In practice, the majority of cases are not sufficiently strong or weak to be able actually to guarantee an outcome with certainty. If they are, an application for summary judgment is always available to the claimant or defendant. If either party seeks and fails to obtain summary judgment, there is almost by definition enough doubt about the outcome of the case to justify consideration of mediation.

### 11.10.2 'Mediation is merely a delaying tactic'

Another perceived risk is that mediation can be used merely as a delaying tactic by the other side. Some litigants try to use CPR Pt 26.4 to obtain a stay of proceedings, while ADR is explored but with the ulterior purpose of buying time. Some of the tactics experienced by mediation providers to delay by declining to agree on a mediator or making difficulties over finding a date are perhaps further illustrations of this.

However, ADR should not be allowed to delay the overall prosecution of a claim. The maximum compulsory stay provided for by CPR Pt 26.4 is for one month, and all parties must consent to that. Otherwise the court must consider a stay to be appropriate. The court has ample power to control, pressurise and if necessary penalise, tardy parties. If one party delays in agreeing for a mediator or a date or venue for mediation, applications back to the court have resulted in tough orders, on occasions conferring power on the ADR provider to nominate a mediator and to fix arrangements in default of agreement.[20] A party or lawyer may try to delay once or twice, but it will be difficult to escape a developing reputation for such tactics, against which opponents will take steps.

The defendant can therefore be made fully aware that the claimant has every intention of vigorously pursuing the claims timetable set by the court. If the litigation clock is still ticking and costs rising, this will provide useful concentration on the need to consider reaching a solution to the dispute. But in practice, it is rare for referrals to mediation to be delayed in this way, more so given the courts' case management powers to intervene.

### 11.10.3 'There are no real costs savings'

Another objection to mediation is that it can only be usefully deployed once the whole panoply of the various litigation steps have been completed (statements of case on each side, disclosure, exchange of lay and expert evidence). Thus, it is said, savings in cost and time will be minimal. It is often said that the primary factor which contributes to settlement at the door of the court (certainly in English procedure) is that it is only shortly before trial that the barrister who is to conduct the case is fully briefed with all the relevant information to hand. Counsel is thus in a position (some would say for the first time) to make a detailed and informed assessment of its merits. As we have seen, this may prove a dangerous approach under the CPR.

The question of what stage a case needs to reach before it can be referred to ADR is dealt with above. In this particular context, the following observations can be made:

- Even where a case is referred to ADR shortly before trial, the costs of doing so will frequently compare very favourably with the costs of trial itself. With counsel and experts often not required at a mediation, and nothing like the formality of preparation associated with a trial, major economies are available.

- Where a case does not settle at a mediation, on the face of it increased costs have been incurred. However, most cases do settle in mediations. Of those that do not, many settle shortly afterwards, as a result of participation in the process. In the remainder, much of the preparatory work for the mediation can be used at later stages. Finally, it may well be that following unsuccessful mediation, the resultant litigation is on narrower or more clearly-defined issues than before, thus making it cheaper to conduct.

- Finally, a company whose policy is to use mediation where possible will almost inevitably find overall cost-savings. Even if one particular case fails to settle in mediation, and thereby generates

---

20 See *Kinstreet v Balmargo*, noted at 5.2.3.

increased costs, others will settle and the overall result is likely to be a net saving, rather than a loss. Several repeat users of ADR have now given details of major savings to their claims costs accounts.

### 11.10.4 'There is too much pressure to settle'

Those who experience mediation for the first time often reflect that they had not appreciated how much the process builds up pressure to settle. The combined effects of the parties' thinking about settlement objectives and the structure of mediation, with the process reposed in a skilled and trusted mediator's hands, mean that a considerable momentum builds up towards settling the case. This is seen in the high percentage of cases which settle in mediation, which is normally regarded as a virtue of the process.

However, there may be cases where clients need to be advised that they can achieve better settlement terms, or even maybe a better result at trial, than those finally on offer in a mediation. This assumes that the advice is sustainable, and that 'better' takes into account the wider considerations of uncertainty, commercial risk, the stress of continued litigation, and so on. Alternatively, a period of reflection might be more appropriate than signing up to a late-night agreement.

The pressure or momentum built up during mediation is not so much a risk of the process, but rather a warning to parties to ensure that they are properly advised in relation to settlement proposals.

### 11.10.5 'I will give an impression of weakness on liability'

It is a common problem in many disputes that when each party has taken up its position, neither wishes to suggest any form of settlement discussion (including mediation) for fear of appearing weak or exposed. However, the CPR has done much to rid parties of any such fear. It is now entirely congruent with the thrust and purpose of the overriding objective that ADR be proposed by any party, weak or strong. Because ADR is recognised as a full component of active case management by the court, anyone proposing it is simply acting consistently with that duty to assist the court in achieving the overriding objective.

That being so, the sooner the problem is addressed the better, otherwise the parties may find themselves committed to a trial that neither they nor the judge may want.

## 11.11   Securing the involvement of other parties

ADR processes remain essentially consensual, and that is a key feature of their effectiveness. The chance to explore settlement in a consensual environment removes a level of pressure from the parties. The confidentiality, coupled with the inability of a mediator or the other side to impose an outcome, creates scope for a more open discussion of the issues, and these are a regular precursor to surprising settlements.

Equally, however, its consensual nature often means that disputes that might really benefit from it are not referred to mediation. Certainly, until the CPR came into force on 26 April 1999, it used to be true that one of the most difficult problems connected with ADR was to persuade an opponent into the process. This is still the case in a number of litigation sectors, notably in personal injury and clinical negligence, where mediation is used far less for dispute resolution than in other common law jurisdictions. There is after all a dispute. Commercial relationships have broken down. A serious injury has been caused, said to be the other party's fault. An insurer has declined to pay a claim promptly. Feelings for a variety of reasons are running high. In such circumstances, it is perhaps unsurprising that one party's suggestion of a conciliatory process will be viewed with considerable suspicion by the other. Even when relations are reasonably good, the common reaction amongst warring parties is that if one suggests something new, in all probability it is to their advantage, and therefore to the other's disadvantage.

Why should proposing mediation be any different? The problem is still exacerbated by the fact that knowledge and experience of ADR remains surprisingly limited even now. While a number of law firms and their clients have become sophisticated repeat users, a significant further number of law firms have still not been involved or undergone any training in ADR. Why should either party, or their lawyer, risk a process about which they know so little? Furthermore, there is no rule book, no formal Practice Guide, as there is for litigation. The absence of rules for a process not previously experienced may understandably provoke suspicion, insecurity and reluctance to engage in it.

However, mediation is now part of the mainstream of litigation practice, and these problems of unfamiliarity can be expected to continue to ease. There will still remain the question as to how and when best to suggest mediation to the other side, and considerable thought is still required to ensure the best approach. It is certainly true that there is no universally right method or time: each case will depend upon its particular facts, circumstances and personalities.

### 11.11.1  Methods of persuasion

Choosing between each of the following suggested methods for raising the ADR option with an opponent will turn on prior planning or on the assessment by lawyer and client as to which is the most likely to succeed.

### 11.11.1.1 Referral to an ADR contract clause

The problem is largely eradicated if there is a contract between the parties containing a clause referring the dispute to ADR. The importance of such clauses in promoting an effective dispute resolution avenue, and therefore in helping to ensure the smooth performance of the contract, cannot be over-emphasised. These clauses are dealt with in detail in **Chapter 9**. For the present, it is important only to note:

- It is largely irrelevant whether, as a matter of law, the clause is enforceable or not. The debate about enforceability is also set out in **Chapter 9**. The primary value of the clause does not lie in giving either party the right to mandate the other to attend a mediation. Indeed, one might readily conclude that a mediation taking place in such circumstances would have lost much of its potential for successful resolution (although experience of mandated or compulsory mediations in many countries suggests that there is still considerable value in it).

- The value of the clause is that it enables the subject of ADR to be raised without any fear of indicating a concern about the strength of one's own case.

- The clause also reminds the parties that, at the time the contract was signed and relations were better, ADR was generally perceived to be a sensible route to take. In practice, parties are generally content to follow the contractual route, which they themselves determined.

- The responsibility for the inclusion of these clauses rests with the non-contentious lawyers, being those charged with drafting the agreement in the first place. Alternative Dispute Resolution is not only a proper concern for litigators.

### 11.11.1.2 Court-related ADR

Mediation has become increasingly intertwined with the litigation process, and one aspect of this is the court's willingness to encourage or order cases into mediation, either of its own initiative or at the request of the parties. Mediations routinely take place pursuant to court orders. Many of these orders are agreed between the parties, and obtained at Case Management Conferences or other interlocutory hearings. We address these orders in more detail in **Chapter 5**.

For present purposes, it is important simply to note the importance of such orders as a route into mediation. Where the court takes the initiative, the parties are absolved from having to raise the subject themselves, with the (generally misplaced) fear that to do so would reflect a lack of conviction of confidence in their case. However the order arises, mediation pursuant to an order does provide a useful framework for the parties, setting a timetable within which it must be completed and making the parties answerable for any failures to comply. For those who fear that mediation will merely provide a pretext for delay, such a framework can be important.

Increasingly, too, court-annexed mediation schemes are being established. Many county courts throughout England and Wales now offer these. Essentially, they are systems established and operated by the courts themselves, whereby mediation is offered to parties directly by the court office. If the parties consent, mediations are set up by the court office. Some schemes operate by bringing in an external mediator while in others the court has its own full-time mediator at the premises. In smaller cases, the National Mediation Helpline may be a route into the process, or referral to a court which has an in-house small claims mediator may be possible. Again, where the court itself raises the possibility of mediation with the parties, they are freed from the perceived 'risk' of doing so themselves.

### 11.11.1.3 Persuasion

Assuming that there is no contractual or court-derived obligation to use mediation, the only route to the mediation table is through persuasion. This is a skill in itself, requiring considerable thought and diplomacy. There is almost certainly very little to be gained from a demanding or heavy-handed approach; a subtler approach is more likely to bear fruit. The opening approach can take place at various levels.

- **Party to party**

If parties to a dispute have not yet consulted lawyers, any suggestion of mediation will be made directly between them. If lawyers are already involved there may still be good reasons for introducing the subject party to party rather than lawyer to lawyer. Lawyers often discourage direct client-to-client contact when a case is in litigation so that rights are not prejudiced. However, a direct contact between clients may be one of the primary ways to help people restore negotiating momentum. It is the clients who can really take decisions to progress the dispute. One of the reasons third-party ADR methods are often successful is that the resultant meeting produces client contact, often for the first time in many months or even years.

Furthermore, where, for example, talks between lawyers have failed to produce agreement to go to mediation, a subsequent dialogue between chairmen of the disputing companies, or their managing directors, may offer a second chance. Indeed, disputes are not infrequently disposed of in their entirety at this level, after previous settlement negotiations have failed.

- **Lawyer to lawyer**

If litigation or arbitration is under way, the majority of formal contact between the parties (whether concerning settlement or not) will be directly between each side's lawyer. Thus, if the suggestion is to be made that mediation be used, it can very properly be made through the lawyers. This has the advantage of introducing mediation within the context of the litigation or arbitration process, and thus avoiding the (false) impression that it is not part of the mainstream, or an attempt to circumvent the norm. Furthermore, it enables the lawyer to whom the approach is made to feel that the process is not one which will exclude him, a common fear amongst some practitioners.

- **Good offices**

This expression is commonly used in international diplomacy where a third-party country intervenes to act as a channel for making contacts and re-opening discussions between parties. The same role in commercial disputes can be performed by contacts which are common to the parties involved, such as a business associate, an acquaintance, an industry association or other interested third party. A good example of this was in the dispute between Euro Tunnel and TML over claims towards the end of construction of the Channel Tunnel. There was pressure from the governments of Britain and France and shareholders for the two parties to negotiate a settlement, which they had failed to do. The Bank of England stepped in to 'hold the ring' while the parties met and ultimately achieved a settlement that at least allowed for completion of the Tunnel, although it did not resolve every disputed claim.

- **Formal approach by an ADR organisation**

One of the benefits of ADR organisations is that they can take over the task of reopening bridges or making contacts to facilitate further negotiations. If one party approaches an ADR organisation, most such organisations will offer to contact the other side. In some disputes they may even initiate contact with both parties in order to encourage a more beneficial settlement. Where neither party has invited this approach, it has the added advantage that neither loses face by agreeing to further discussions under the auspices of the organisation.

In the right circumstances, an indirect approach to the other side through an ADR organisation can succeed where a direct approach has failed, or is likely to fail. An ADR provider is often perceived as more independent or neutral. The party receiving the approach has the opportunity to discuss its misgivings or anxieties about ADR more openly, as well as to inform itself about the process in more detail. In short, some of the inherent strengths of the mediation process can be used even before the mediation itself formally takes place, in winning the consent of all parties to participate. In some cases, however, the involvement of any external party will not be welcomed and such approaches may be rebuffed.

To have any chance of success, such approaches through a neutral broker (whether an ADR organisation, an industry body, or an individual) should have certain key features:

(1) The broker must be, and be seen to be, genuinely independent of the parties and the issues in dispute.

(2) The broker should have no stake in the outcome of the parties' decision on whether to mediate – indeed to this extent, there is an argument that any subsequent mediation should be handled by people unconnected with the neutral broker.

(3) Any terms of engagement (eg remuneration for the broker's efforts) should be agreed that reflect and demonstrate the broker's neutrality. For example, this may extend to all parties paying equally for his services.

### 11.11.2   Choice of approach

Given the difficulties often experienced in getting other parties to the table, the choice of approach should be informed by the likelihood of success. A certain amount of forethought may be important and the following considerations may assist:

– Is there any objective information to refer to? For example, does the other side have any form of corporate pledge or public statement on its use of ADR? Is the other law firm a member of an ADR organisation and/or has it a track record of using ADR? In particular, it is worth noting that if a government department is involved in the dispute, the government's ADR pledge can be referred to. A copy can be found in the Appendix. This commits all government departments to the use of ADR in a wide variety of contexts.

– Is the suggestion most likely to be well received by the parties, their lawyers or other advisors? Are the lawyers likely to have to persuade their clients, or the reverse?

– Will the use of a third party approach make the suggestion seem more independent, and is that particularly important in this case?

- Does the other side and its lawyers understand what ADR is about? At all costs, avoid putting the other side or its lawyers in a position where they have to respond to the suggestion of ADR without having time to inform themselves. Ideally, once the suggestion has been made, they should be encouraged to discuss the matter with an ADR organisation, before giving a response.

- What factors would make ADR unattractive to you if you were advising the other side, and can they be met or addressed in any way?

- Offer 'talks about talks'. These can be very effective in obtaining unanimous consent to mediation. They will often consist of a meeting of all parties and advisers together with an ADR organisation if one has been engaged, or perhaps with some other neutral chairman, usually on a 'without prejudice' basis. Views can be canvassed as to the most appropriate ADR process (mediation, executive tribunal, expert or judicial appraisal, etc), the ground rules that would be acceptable, a proposed timetable, and so on. A standard form of mediation agreement makes a useful focal point for discussion. The mediation process can be explained and discussed with reference to each clause of the agreement. It soon becomes apparent that the nature of the obligations that the parties are being asked to accept under the agreement are not particularly onerous. The process then becomes much less intimidating. Furthermore, the mere fact of bringing parties together for discussions (albeit not of the substantive claim) creates a constructive momentum and opportunity to re-open settlement discussions which may lead to an agreement without further third-party intervention.

- Emphasise that the likelihood of both parties' gaining from the outcome is greater than in litigation, or at least that an effective review of each party's case will result.

- Emphasise that the offer of ADR should not be taken as a sign of weakness. Contrary to much expectation, the offer of ADR can in fact indicate, and be read as, a position of strength, especially since the CPR came into effect. What need is there to camouflage the factual and legal issues of the case behind the procedural technicalities of litigation? Surely a confident party will be willing to discuss the issues fully and frankly?

- Emphasise also a genuine willingness to hear the other side's arguments.

- Indicate, if your mind is not made up, that the approach does not pre-judge the nature of the ADR process to be used, nor does it commit to the selection of a particular mediator or neutral – these can all be the subject of genuine dialogue.

– Recognise in particular that parties reluctant to use ADR at first may agree to it months or even years later. Many disputes have their own momentum, and will only come to ADR (if at all) once that force has been spent.

– Be thick-skinned! If you want to use ADR, accept the fact that not all the offers you make will be accepted. This is not a flaw in the process, but simply a fact of life. Your position after a refusal is unlikely to be materially worse than if no offer was made. Indeed, it may even have bolstered your ultimate position on the question of costs.

– Consider the balance between a consensual and a threatening approach – a 'carrot or a stick'. Either may be more effective, depending on the context, personalities, disputes, timing, etc. The 'stick' approach tends to revolve around costs-related threats, such as 'I wish to engage with you voluntarily in mediation, as this is the best way. If however you decline, I will draw this letter to the court's attention at trial. Unless you have achieved something wholly beyond what mediation might have supplied, we will invite the judge to make no order as to costs from the date at which mediation might have resolved the case.' This power-play approach is probably only going to work if all else fails, and even then it may not allow the mediation to set off in an atmosphere of harmony. Furthermore, it may overlook some of the subtleties that inform parties choices about mediation. A 'carrot' approach may choose to emphasise the scope for a mutually acceptable resolution, the benefits and savings accruing to both parties, the chance to engage in meaningful dialogue, and so on.

– Since the Access to Justice Act 1999, Legal Services Commission (LSC) funding is likely to be relatively rarely encountered except in clinical negligence claims. However, if the opponent has LSC funding, a refusal to mediate following a proposal by the unassisted party can be referred to the Legal Services Commission, who have made it clear that they might in those circumstances require the LSC funded party to mediate before permitting further progress with litigation.

*Chapter 12*

# Setting up a mediation

Once all parties have agreed to participate, setting up a mediation is a relatively easy task. There are a number of issues to be dealt with, and these are set out below.

As with all approaches to ADR, flexibility is critical. It may be, for example, that many of these points need to be discussed and agreed before a party will give final consent to participating in the mediation. A rigid procedural approach should therefore be avoided. Whilst the various points below do need to be addressed, this can easily be done conditionally upon final consent to mediate being given. Indeed, receiving satisfactory answers to these points may be what finally brings a reluctant party to the mediation table.

## 12.1 Choosing a mediator

Mediator selection is an important and sometimes sensitive issue. Parties or their advisers may well have strong views on who should, or should not, be appointed. Their views may derive from previous experience of a given mediator (good or bad), a particular strategic view of what they want to achieve through mediation, or indeed their understanding (or misunderstanding) of precisely what a mediator's role is.

The fact that parties can generally choose their mediator is important. It brings with it an important sense of control, and makes it easier for them to invest the required trust in the chosen mediator. It also gives them a chance to reflect in the choice of mediator their own priorities and concerns about the way in which the mediation should be conducted.

At the same time, it is important not to over-complicate the issue of mediator selection. In reality many mediators could mediate the same dispute equally well, albeit differently. Parties should not become paralysed in choosing a mediator for fear that there is only one correct choice, since that in very unlikely to reflect the reality on the ground. Indeed, some parties adopt the view that, where possible and assuming that the mediator concerned is appropriately qualified and experienced, they will accept the other party's choice of mediator. The rationale for this is that they want the mediator to be able to have an impact on the other side's decision making, and this is more likely to be achieved by someone whom they themselves have chosen.

Whatever the underlying theory or intention, there are some important factors to bear in mind in mediator selection.

### 12.1.1 Mediator qualities and personality

The personality and qualities of a mediator are central to the way in which they perform their role. Parties should seek a mediator with whom they can engage effectively, someone they feel they can work with well. Much of this is a question of personality and therefore individual preference, and cannot be reduced to a formula. But it is no less valid a consideration for that.

Advisers choosing (or at least recommending) mediators will also have in mind someone with whom their clients can work, and who will engender respect and confidence.

### 12.1.2 Subject-matter expertise or effective mediation skills?

A common debate in mediator selection concerns the extent to which mediators require some expertise in the underlying subject matter of the dispute in order to be effective. Experienced mediators generally take the view that this is rarely necessary, and so do many experienced users of the mediation process.

It is possible that in the context of a highly technical dispute there may be some advantage in it. Equally, however, it is important to focus on the purpose of a mediation, which is to find a solution which the parties can live with. The risk associated with a mediator who has expertise in the subject matter is that a rigorous focus on resolution may be sacrificed in favour of a pre-occupation with the issues which divide the parties.

That said, it is true that some familiarity (as distinct from expertise) with the subject matter of a dispute can help. The parties may gain confidence from a mediator who speaks their language, or who understands the way in which their industry typically deals with a particular technical issue. If the expertise in question is legal expertise, parties may want a mediator who is comfortable with the legal issues under consideration.

Whatever the underlying technical expertise of a mediator, however, what is unquestionable is the importance of good mediator skills. The fundamental contribution of a mediator lies in the effective exercise of mediation skills, and not in deploying any underlying technical expertise they may have. Good mediators achieve this because they are good mediators, not good technicians. To the extent that technical points need to be debated in a mediation (and that can be an important aspect of progress towards settlement), the mediator's role lies primarily in enabling the parties (or more typically their respective experts) to debate those points in a meaningful and constructive way, and to ensure that their conclusions are factored in to their thinking about settlement. It does not generally lie in second-guessing the 'correct' answer.

More importantly, there are many further aspects of effective mediator practice which underlie the importance of having good mediation skills and experience as the prime determining factor in choosing a mediator. Mediator training books are full of them, and it is not the function of this book to describe them in detail. What is perhaps most revealing, however, is that experienced users of mediation will almost invariably assert the primacy of mediation skills above any technical subject-matter knowledge and expertise.

### 12.1.3   Facilitative or evaluative mediators?

Linked with the above, there has long been a debate amongst mediators and mediation users about the relative merits of 'facilitative' or 'evaluative' mediators. Very broadly, 'evaluative' mediators are considered to be those who if asked will offer an opinion on the relative merits of each party's case. 'Facilitative' mediators are those whose role does not extend that far. As is often the case, these stereotypes are misleading and mask a subtler series of considerations.

First, there are not simply two types of mediator – 'facilitative' and 'evaluative'. Rather, there is a wide spectrum of interventions which a mediator can legitimately and usefully employ, and which may be more 'facilitative' or 'evaluative' in nature. All effective mediators should be able to deploy those interventions as the case demands. When and how they elect to do so is an inherent part of any mediator's skill. It is true that mediators will usually, by dint of personality and experience, instinctively gravitate towards a particular position on the spectrum, where they will feel more comfortable exercising their skills. But this should not affect their willingness to adopt a different approach as and when the situation demands.

Secondly, it is often assumed that evaluative mediators are somehow more robust than facilitative ones, presumably because of their willingness to express a view. This also betrays a misunderstanding of these concepts. In particular, an *effective* mediator (whatever label might be attached to them) should be able to explore with parties the underlying strengths and weaknesses of a given position in such a way as to influence that party's thinking, but without necessarily offering a personal view. Indeed, such reality-testing is at the heart of a mediator's skills. According to the terminology, that is a facilitative approach, but the experience for the parties may be no less robust than if the mediator had offered a view.

### 12.1.4   Combined expertise

Notwithstanding the above, it is sometimes the case that a combination of mediation process skills and subject-matter expertise, or even facilitative and evaluative input, is required by the parties. There are a number of ways of achieving this.

#### 12.1.4.1   The use of experts

A good process mediator can be selected to lead the mediation, assisted by a subject-matter expert in whom all the parties have confidence, who will provide specific expert input. This method has been used to great effect in a number of mediations in which we have been involved. It has similarities with the ADR processes of early neutral evaluation and expert appraisal, referred to in **Chapter 3**, but with the additional benefit of a mediator present to negotiate with the input provided by the parties and the neutral expert. However, there are obvious cost implications of having an additional professional on the mediation team.

#### 12.1.4.2   The use of co-mediators

Two mediators may be able to work together effectively on a dispute, by bringing to it a combination of differing skills and personalities. This can be a useful way of resolving a dispute between the parties as to the kind of mediator each wants, although great care has to be taken to ensure that the co-mediators can establish a realistic joint working method in advance of the mediation itself. That is particularly the case in mediation, where each mediator tends to have his own style and approach, which may not be shared by the other, and of course their ability to work together is central to their effectiveness. Again, there are cost implications.

#### 12.1.4.3   The use of assistant mediators

Some mediation organisations offer 'assistant' mediators to work alongside the appointed mediators. These are trained but inexperienced mediators who work with more experienced mediators for a number of cases, in order to gain experience. The prime rationale is for the assistant mediator to gain experience. However, it can also be a useful way of combining different professional expertise in the mediation, in all probability without the cost implications of formal co-mediators. Some care should be exercised, however, since assistant mediators are not generally familiar with the mediation environment, and any contribution they make may not be with the same skill and impartiality as an experienced mediator.

Mediators with some experience may also have a supervisory mentor at the mediation who is there to give additional feedback and advanced training, as well as offering input to the process. Such an arrangement should always be disclosed to the parties in advance and requires their consent.

### 12.1.5  Professional background

Professional background is another factor in mediator selection. In practice, the majority of civil and commercial mediators in the United Kingdom have a legal background. This probably reflects two particular features of that field. First, most such disputes are already at least 'in the shadow of the law', if not already the subject of court proceedings; and secondly, mediator selection is heavily influenced by the parties' respective lawyers, particularly if their clients are new to the process.

That is not to say that a legal background need be an important or even relevant pre-requisite for an effective mediator. Many excellent mediators come from other professional backgrounds. Accountants (eg, in share valuation or business interruption cases) and construction industry professionals (eg, in construction or engineering disputes) are often used.

Most importantly, however, the considerations that we discussed in relation to subject matter expertise apply equally to professional background, and the primary focus should always be on mediator skills.

### 12.1.6  Track record

Experience is often the best teacher, and this is no less true of mediators. A mediator's past record (as a mediator, rather than in any other capacity) is an important indicator of ability. Parties will often want to enquire whether a mediator has previous experience of mediating a particular type of case – e.g. professional negligence, IT, personal injury, shipping, or defamation.

They may also be tempted to enquire about a mediator's 'success rate'. Usually, they have in mind the percentage of that mediator's mediations which have resulted in settlement. Whilst a very low rate might indicate some cause for concern, in general this can be a very misleading indicator of 'success'. Success may be more accurately determined by factors other than settlement – for example, that the parties were brought significantly closer than before; that relations have been built through the mediation process which will allow for more effective settlement discussions in future; or that a key point of principle has been agreed, even though the case has not fully settled. Moreover, a good mediator will most likely be called upon to mediate more difficult cases.

### 12.1.7  References

There is no substitute for first-hand experience of how a particular mediator works, and so a more accurate guide to mediator performance and approach comes from parties themselves. If parties have not used a particular mediator before, then an informal discussion with those who have can offer valuable insights. The mediation market would do well to encourage the free flow of information on mediator performance, styles and approaches, and wherever possible mediators should be willing to refer potential parties to referees for feedback.

### 12.1.8　Interviews and 'beauty parades'

In some cases, mainly larger ones, parties may wish to conduct a series of interviews or 'beauty parades' with prospective mediators. This can provide a useful opportunity to meet the mediators and discuss with them their approach to mediation.

### 12.1.9　Useful questions to consider

The value of thinking about mediator selection is that is tends to reveal to parties what they think about the mediation process itself. When assessing possible mediators, it can therefore be very useful to consider some of the following:

- What do we want to achieve through mediation? What mediator input is most necessary in order to achieve that?

- What is standing in the way of settlement? What mediator input will most effectively enable progress past that point?

- What kind of person will we and our client team find it easiest to work with?

- What kind of mediator does the *other* side need? How can their views best be influenced through the mediation process?

- Does this particular mediation require a detailed discussion over the merits, or a technical issue, in order to generate settlement? If so, how will this affect the choice of mediator?

- Do we have any instinct towards a primarily facilitative or primarily evaluative mediator? Why? What primary input does that suggest that we are looking for from the mediator? Is that likely to be necessary in resolving this dispute?

- How vital is subject-matter expertise of the mediator? Are we looking primarily for an answer to a technical question or a negotiating opportunity?

- Are we looking for someone who will exert significant pressure to settle, or might that be inappropriate in that particular case?

- What other factors might suggest the importance of strong process skills? For example, are there strong or difficult personalities involved which need to be handled well?

This kind of thought process can be very helpful not only in considering mediator selection, but also in thinking more broadly about how to extract maximum value from the opportunity which mediation affords. It can also help clients who are unfamiliar with mediation to have a clearer view of what the process entails, which is itself central to them benefiting from it.

### 12.1.10   Sources of mediators

In the United Kingdom, there are two primary options for appointing a mediator: either to refer the case directly to the mediator, or to refer it to an ADR organisation which will itself nominate or appoint a mediator. Each has advantages and disadvantages, although the majority of appointments are now made direct to mediators.

An ADR organisation can have a useful role in recommending mediators where the parties cannot otherwise reach agreement on whom to appoint, and in providing feedback on mediators to potential parties. Such feedback is possibly their most important contribution, since the confidential nature of the mediation process makes it harder for such information otherwise to enter into wider circulation. ADR organisations can also assist with administering the mediation, by arranging venues and exchange of papers, briefing parties who are new to the mediation process, and generally providing suitable auspices under which the process can occur. ADR organisations generally charge for these services.

Many mediation appointments, however, are made direct with mediators, particularly where the parties (or more usually their advisers) are not new to mediation. It gives the benefit of early direct contact with the mediator, and such administrative tasks as there are can be dealt with by the lawyers involved.

## 12.2   Establishing the ground rules

Whilst the flexibility of mediation is rightly emphasised, there are never-theless some fundamental ground rules, which should govern the process. These are designed to provide a necessary level of protection for the parties, in terms of confidentiality and the 'without prejudice' nature of the process, so as to give the parties confidence in it and generate an environment for frank discussion.

### 12.2.1   The mediation agreement

The terms on which the mediation is to take place should be agreed in writing between the parties and the mediator. A short mediation agreement is the most common format. CEDR's standard form mediation agreement is set out in the Appendix, and discussed in detail in **Chapter 7**.

*Setting up a mediation*

The mediation agreement will typically aim to:

–   confirm the legal framework within which the mediation is taking place – without prejudice, confidentiality, mediator immunity, and so on;

–   confirm the relevant administrative and procedural details – the parties' names, who are attending on behalf of each party, the date, venue, time of the mediation, and so on.

It is worth noting that there is currently no Mediation Act or similar legislation in England and Wales, Scotland or Northern Ireland. One implication of this is that the primary legal framework for a civil/commercial mediation is provided by the mediation agreement itself. This contrasts with many other European, US and Australian jurisdictions, where mediation legislation provides an applicable legal structure for mediation in any event.[1] The terms of the agreement are therefore very important.

### 12.2.2   Codes of conduct

In addition to the mediation agreement, many mediators operate under written codes of conduct, and indeed ought to do so. These govern the ethical position of the mediator in various situations. As examples, the European Code of Conduct for Mediators and the CEDR Code of Conduct are set out in the Appendix.

The neutral and confidential position of the mediator is one which may create difficult ethical scenarios for him and it is as well to have thought those through and be able to rely on a written code of conduct should the need arise. Indeed, some mediation agreements incorporate an ethical code of conduct into their terms by reference. It is also important that the parties have the opportunity to consider the terms of any code prior to appointment of the mediator, so that their consent to its terms is obtained.

An example of the kind of ethical problem that might arise is the situation where one party discloses to the mediator, in a confidential private session, that the bridge which it has built (the final account for which is the subject of the mediation) may have a design fault. Although the chances are very slim, it is conceivable that the bridge may collapse in certain circumstances. The mediator is instructed not to divulge this information to the other side. What does he do? Clearly, he has a contractual and tortious duty of confidentiality to the disclosing party. But what kind of duties does he have to the other party and to third parties and members of the public? At what point, if at all, is he released from his duty of confidentiality? Should

---

1   An exception to this is employment-related mediations or conciliations carried out through ACAS, for which there is some statutory provision.

he merely resign from the mediation and inform no one? These matters are discussed in **Chapter 7**.[2]

Another important issue would be in relation to conflicts of interest. In view of the importance of the mediator's neutrality, mediators should also operate under a duty not to act in circumstances where any conflict might arise. For example, if in the past a mediator has acted as an adviser to one party, is he prevented from ever mediating a case in which they are involved? Or is this merely for a period of time, and if so for how long? And at what point should he be influenced if his firm has acted for one of the parties in a related matter? These are all issues that a code of conduct will try to cover.

## 12.3   Costs of the mediation

### 12.3.1   Who pays?

The costs of a mediation can be divided into two elements: what we have called in **Chapter 8** as the 'mediation fees' (including the fees and expenses of the mediator, and any mediation provider, plus venue hire, refreshments, etc) and the 'costs of the mediation' (each party's legal costs for preparation and legal or other representation during, the mediation).

The usual position has been for the mediation fees to be shared equally between the parties, and for each party bears its own costs of the mediation. This reflects the fact that parties to a mediation are, in essence, buying a negotiating opportunity, and that opportunity applies equally to both or all parties. There is value too in each party investing financially in the mediation as well as in terms of time and effort. Experience and common sense tend to show that those who have invested their own money in the process will approach it with a greater commitment to making it work than those who have not.

### 12.3.2   Variations on who pays

As is typical of ADR, flexibility is the key. If one party simply cannot afford the cost of a mediation, or is unwilling to because it is not convinced of the likelihood of success, it may be worth the other party paying all the fees in any event. This is more common a practice than one might imagine, usually where the paying party has previous experience of mediation and therefore of its value, and the non-paying party does not. It is an indication too of the perceived value of the process that one party is prepared to pay both sides' fees simply to get them to the table to talk. A variation of this is for one party to pay the other side's fees (as well as its own), but with the proviso for reimbursement in the event that settlement terms are (or alternatively

---

2 See **7.5**.

are not) reached in the mediation. If the settlement terms involve any payment being made, the reimbursement can easily be built into it.

In sectors such as personal injury and clinical negligence, where there is a normal expectation that if a claimant wins, costs will be paid in addition, largely because of funding and power imbalance issues, the mediation agreement is often amended to provide that both the costs of the mediation and the mediation fees are to be regarded as costs in the case. This will mean that, whether or not settlement is reached, the costs of the mediation and the mediation fees will be treated on detailed assessment (where necessary) as following their normal litigation destination. So, if a mediation leads to settlement beyond any Pt 36 offer made prior to it, the claimant will receive the costs of the mediation and his share of the mediation fees as part of the costs in the case. If the mediation does not settle the case and the claimant receives less than a Pt 36 offer made prior to the mediation, the defendant will be able to argue that the mediation costs and fees should not be recoverable by the claimant.

The relative informality of ADR means that the negotiations can include a wide range of matters, including costs. The starting-point for setting up a mediation may have been that each party has paid its own share of the mediation fees. However, there is no reason why the terms of settlement reached should not include, for example, reimbursement by one party of the other's mediation fees (and indeed of their legal costs of preparation for and representation during the mediation). This is purely a matter of negotiation.

### 12.3.3  Costs of the litigation or arbitration

If a dispute has been in litigation or arbitration for some time, each party may have incurred very substantial legal and other professional fees, and the question of who eventually pays for these will usually be a substantive part of the terms of any settlement negotiated through mediation.

As an entirely separate question, the costs implications of agreeing or declining to mediate, together with other costs issues, are dealt with in **Chapters 6** and **8**.

### 12.3.4  How much?

Most mediation fees are usually charged on a similar basis to any other professional fees, that is an amount per hour, per day, or for the whole mediation. However, the very short time periods required for a mediation (often only one day) mean that the costs are never likely to be that high, certainly relative to the value which parties can expect to gain from the process.

The advantage of a daily, as opposed to hourly, rate is that it frees parties from the pressure of watching costs rise as each hour of the mediation passes. Some take the view, however, that such pressure is effective in terms of making the parties, and therefore the whole mediation process, more focused on their priorities and negotiating stances, and preventing it from dragging on.

Whatever the amount and basis of charging, fees should be agreed (and will often be settled) in advance of the mediation. Fee arrangements should also be transparent to the parties. As noted above, fees may also vary depending on whether the dispute is referred to mediation through an ADR organisation or referred directly to a mediator.

### 12.3.5   Success fees and other fee arrangements

Occasionally, a mediator may agree to accept payment (or higher payment) only if the process achieves a settlement during the mediation (or within a defined period after the mediation). This is, however, not a common practice in the United Kingdom, and most mediators would consider that any such financial involvement in the fact or terms of settlement would entail an unacceptable compromise of their neutral position.

Public funding and conditional fee agreements are dealt with more fully in **Chapter 8**.

## 12.4   Who should attend the mediation?

The effectiveness of a mediation can be considerably enhanced or reduced by the choice of who attends, and careful thought should be given to this question. It applies to which parties attend, as well as to which of their representatives and advisers accompany them. As with the process of mediator selection, a party's choice of who should attend a mediation can reveal much about their views of the mediation process. The following points should be borne in mind when considering who should attend.

### 12.4.1   Authority to settle the dispute

Since the primary purpose of a mediation is to reach a final resolution of the issues in dispute, it follows that those with authority to agree settlement terms and bind their respective parties should attend. So central is this premise that many mediation agreements contain an express provision that those attending should have such authority.

In practice, however, authority to settle a dispute has two distinct components, both of which are important:

- Legal authority – i.e. the legal capacity and authority of a person to bind the party they represent; and

- Practical authority – i.e. the willingness to make settlement decisions in a mediation, and be accountable for them.

Pre-mediation assurances sought or received concerning a party's authority to settle often focus on the first component and omit the second, not least because in practice it is very difficult to ensure. However it is no less important for that, and its absence may jeopardise the prospects of a successful mediation. Mediation is an intense negotiating environment, requiring parties to make sometimes difficult decisions about settlement. It presupposes and requires a willingness on their part to engage fully in that process, and to exercise their own judgment about settlement options. For decision-makers, it lacks the safety of a judicially imposed 'right answer' and it may also require them to justify their decisions afterwards to fellow directors, shareholders, partners or others. A willingness to take such responsibility is just as much a feature of authority to settle as legal capacity to sign a settlement agreement.

In practice, of course, it is not so simple. Even those attending a mediation who claim to be armed with 'full authority' from their organisation will very likely have had some limit imposed on their negotiating freedom. For example, a director may have a mandate from his board to settle up (or down) to a pre-determined level. An insurer may attend with instructions from the senior claims manager to settle up to a particular sum, but not beyond, or may bound by a previously fixed reserve.

Furthermore, mediation is a process in which the parties seek to have an impact on each other's thinking and understanding of the case. If that has been successfully achieved, it should be no surprise if a party finds that it wishes to go beyond its previously agreed mandate, and has therefore not in fact come with sufficient authority, notwithstanding its efforts to do so. This need not be an indication of bad faith, but rather of the effectiveness of the mediation process.

There are also instances where it is not possible for someone with full settlement authority to attend a mediation. For example, the structure of decision-making authority in some public bodies may prevent any single individual from exercising sole discretion over settlement terms. In such instances (typically with government departments, local authorities or regulators) those attending the mediation may only have power to negotiate and then recommend settlement terms to the relevant committee. They may, however, be prepared to commit to make such recommendations and procure an answer within a specified (and short) period of time.

These considerations all highlight the need for flexibility in practice over questions of settlement authority. If there is a genuine willingness amongst the parties to seek a resolution, questions of authority can usually be resolved. Fresh representatives can be brought in, or at least telephoned, or adjournments to the mediation agreed whilst approval is sought.

### 12.4.2 Knowledge of the dispute, and detachment from it

To the extent that aspects of the detail or history of a dispute are to be discussed in a mediation, it will be important to have present those with the relevant information. First-hand knowledge of the situation can often shed useful light on a debate.

Equally, however, where such people have been involved in the dispute from the outset they may have positions to defend which cloud their approach to settlement. Involvement may bring knowledge and information, but can also bring partiality and a lack of detachment. Equally important at a mediation is someone who can take a more detached and dispassionate view of the dispute and the settlement options.

### 12.4.3 Ability to negotiate effectively

Mediation is at heart a process of negotiation, and parties should choose their representatives accordingly. This book is not a negotiation manual, but suffice it to say that effective negotiation is much more than the ability to say 'no'. A willingness and ability to engage fully with the other side over the issues, to present views and arguments with clarity, to judge when to hold out and when to concede – these are all crucial to maximising the value which a mediation offers.

### 12.4.4 Ability to make 'connections' with the other side

Effective communication between parties is vital to successful mediation. It is not unusual to find that a particular person on one side can in some way 'connect' better with someone on the other side. This may derive from a shared level of seniority, a respect for the other's abilities, previous experience of working together (even on opposite sides of a dispute), better communication skills, or simply their personalities. Whatever the reason, such connections can afford a useful opportunity in mediation, and parties should think about how to make and develop them.

### 12.4.5 Sending a message to the other side

Each party's choice of representatives can send a message to the other about their attitude or intentions coming into the mediation. For example, the absence of a sufficiently senior person from one side may be read by the other party as dismissive and disrespectful. It may even prejudice the chances of the mediation taking place. By contrast, the presence of a senior person, or someone who has travelled a significant distance to attend, is likely to build confidence. The presence of a large technical team may indicate an intention to approach the mediation from that perspective, and so on.

### 12.4.6   So who should attend?

In the light of the above considerations, who then should attend a mediation?

#### 12.4.6.1   Parties

Clearly parties ought to be present at the mediation. They will very likely be signatories to the mediation agreement and should play an active role in the process. This is of immense importance. Mediation provides the parties with an opportunity to take control of, and 'own' their dispute and any solutions reached. It is these elements of control and ownership that are so often squeezed out by the formal litigation process. The temptation to think that the legal advisers alone can attend the mediation, and then report back to the clients by phone for final approval of the terms of settlement, should generally be resisted. Settlement terms emerge during a mediation, and in order to be acceptable to parties, they will often need to have seen them emerge, and to understand them in the context of all the discussions in the mediation. Full participation by the parties is essential for successful mediation.

The rationale is no different in multi-party mediations, and it is important for all parties to take part in the mediation. Indeed, resolution of the dispute may only be possible if all do (eg, because the terms on which A settles with B may depend on the terms which B can agree with C and so on).

Similarly, a first defendant may only agree to pay the claimant £ X if the second and third defendants also accept a proportion of the liability. In fact, mediation can often be particularly effective in multi-party disputes because the process is one in which all the various permutations of settlement can be explored with all the parties present.

However, if some, but not all, parties in a multi-party dispute want to mediate, and the remaining one(s) cannot be persuaded to take part, the willing parties can still use the mediation process to great effect. This feature is often overlooked. For example, three defendants to an action might easily mediate as between themselves on the question of how any settlement with the claimant will be apportioned amongst them. This may then put each of them in a much stronger position with the claimant, focusing all their attention on defending or negotiating the question of liability to the claimant, rather than defending their positions with each other as well.

The same logic applies to the issues which parties wish to address in mediation. Most mediations aim to achieve permanent and binding settlement of all the issues in dispute between the parties. However, many disputes contain an array of different issues. If agreement cannot be reached to attempt mediation in respect of all of them, it is entirely valid to agree to attempt resolution of only some.

In class action litigation, with hundreds or sometimes thousands of claimants or defendants, the presence of an objectively selected focus group can be invaluable at the mediation process, however extensively represented that class of litigant may be. Their views will anchor the mediation in reality, and provide an immediacy of opinion about issues and proposals as they arise which later polling of that class will not match on its own.

### 12.4.6.2   Groups or associated companies

Mediated settlements can be wide-ranging in nature, sometimes touching on new commercial arrangements in their terms. Where a subsidiary company in a group is involved in a mediation, it is worth bearing in mind the possibility that another group company might ultimately be involved in any terms of settlement, and that representation of that company at the mediation (with appropriate settlement authority) might therefore be useful. However, that may be difficult to predict.

### 12.4.6.3   Insurers

Where a defendant is indemnified by an insurer in respect of any liability in a claim, it is the insurer who will in effect conduct the litigation by subrogation. The defendant may still have some interest by virtue of an excess or deductible, but the more the insurer has a financial stake in the outcome of a claim, the more important it is to be at a mediation to agree the terms of settlement. Where risks are shared between insurers or re-insurers, each may wish to be represented.

### 12.4.6.4   Legal advisers

Lawyers can, and usually do, play a very important role in the mediation process. Of course it is always open to sophisticated parties to choose to dispense with lawyers. If a mediation is to be in effect a business negotiation with a purely commercial interest-based objective, the process is likely to be essentially non-legal, at least until settlement terms are reached, when lawyers might well be required to check the legal implications or draft a legally effective agreement. But given that most mediations take place either during, or at least 'in the shadow of' litigation or arbitration, it is certainly unusual for commercial parties not to have lawyers present; sometimes in-house, sometimes external, and sometimes both. Some insurers choose to represent their insured at mediations using claims staff and dispensing with lawyers, particularly in cases before issue of proceedings.

Individuals unused to litigation, like claimants in personal injury or professional negligence claims, should certainly have a legal adviser present at a mediation, and indeed the general guidance should always be for any party to have such advice available at a mediation. Usually, the purpose of a mediation is to try to settle a claim which, if not already well into litigation mode, is likely to switch into litigation mode very quickly. The legal adviser is there to help assess the best choices to be made, advise on whether terms on offer might be bettered at trial and generally to keep the whole picture clear for the client. The mediator cannot fulfil the role of giving objective advice in the sole interests of each individual party: indeed it would be wrong for a mediator to do so, especially to an unrepresented party where this can give rise to real difficulties in mediations, as we shall see below.

Normally, the lawyers who attend mediations are solicitors, but in heavy cases a party might choose to have a barrister present also. Concern is sometimes expressed about the presence of barristers at mediation. The important point is not the qualifications of the individual (be they solicitor or barrister), but the role which they adopt in the mediation. Mediation is an informal forum, with very limited opportunity for forensic advocacy. One of its main virtues for lay participants is its very informality, and the centrality given to parties themselves. The more lawyers there are to get involved, the higher the risk that the parties will be marginalised in just the same way as occurs in litigation or arbitration.

If the case is sufficiently complex in terms of legal issues, then a barrister's presence might be warranted, but the days of solicitors feeling the need to take counsel's opinion as a kind of insurance policy to protect themselves ought to be over. Such a view is in any event bad law: solicitors must take responsibility for the totality of advice given to a client and are not protected from liability in negligence by counsel's opinion. Furthermore, there is now no distinction between a lawyer's preparatory and advocacy roles in terms of exposure to claims for negligence, since the House of Lords in *Arthur J S Hall & Co (a firm) v Simons*[3] reversed the principle of advocate immunity from suit for negligence or breach of contract.

---

3  [2000] 3 All ER 673.

Mediation is a forum to which a solicitor's skills ought to be well adapted. While an ability to advise authoritatively on the litigation alternative is of importance, it may prove just as important in a complex commercial case to have a non-contentious commercial lawyer at a mediation to help with constructing and drafting a workable commercial outcome.

In one circumstance, it is particularly useful to have counsel for a party at a mediation. This is where the interests of a party who is under a disability are involved, so that any settlement could only be provisional and subject to the approval of the court. Most typically this will involve children and adult claimants lacking legal capacity in personal injury claims. It will be counsel who will advise the litigation friend as to whether what is proposed is acceptable, and will have to take responsibility for persuading the court to approve the settlement. In such cases, there may have been an appreciable discount from the sums claimed to reflect a real litigation risk. It is much better for counsel to have taken an integral part in the debate, which led to such concessions, so that a convincing case can be put to the court to give approval.

### 12.4.6.5 Expert and factual witnesses

It is important to note how often cases which at trial would turn on testing out and resolving differences in expert evidence are mediated successfully without the experts being at the mediation. The truth is that parties and lawyers are always taking a view on the strengths and weaknesses of expert evidence when they settle cases before trial, and very much the same happens at mediations. Besides the expense factor of having an expert witness present, when the debate turns to commercial and personal interests and away from legal rights and the prospects of success at trial, the details of the likely trial evidence, expert or lay, can become less significant.

That said, there are circumstances where the involvement of expert witnesses can be useful. A highly technical dispute, for example one involving computer software or a complex clinical negligence claim, might well benefit from the presence of each side's expert, and this approach is relatively common. The only question is whether the experts themselves are prepared to adopt a constructive and open approach to the discussions, or whether they are themselves part of the problem in being too partisan or losing sight of their clients' commercial agenda. Of course experts who are going to give evidence at trial will have to guard against such partisanship, and are under an overriding duty to the court.[4] A mediation could provide a safe forum for finding out whether they will approach their role appropriately if a trial takes place. A similar approach can be taken with lay witnesses.

---

4  See CPR Pt 35.

A further alternative is to have an expert available at the end of a telephone to confer over any points that might arise, either throughout the day or at a specific time. While there should be no difficulty over confidentiality, especially where an expert has already had a report disclosed as part of the claim, it may be wise to clear such an approach with the mediator at least and probably also with the other side.

In theory, it would be perfectly open to the parties to agree to have a trial cross-examination of expert or lay witnesses at a mediation. Mediation practice is flexible enough to allow for any such sub-process if the parties and the mediator see that it would help. As an alternative, it can be useful to have witnesses attend at a mediation to test their evidence out in private against whatever emerges to challenge that witness's evidence, and thus decide in private whether it will be persuasive at trial.

A further option in cases where there is a dispute between experts seen as crucial to the outcome of litigation already commenced is to hold the CPR Pt 35 meeting of experts at the same time as, or shortly before, the mediation. The results of that meeting can then be fed into the mainstream of the mediation and processed with great efficiency and convenience into each party's risk analysis and decision-making at the mediation.

### 12.4.6.6   Unrepresented parties

Having an unrepresented party, or one who is not sufficiently sophisticated to appraise their rights, obligations or negotiating position, can present considerable difficulties to a mediator. Every effort should be made to encourage such a party to have legal advice available to them. Such a problem quite often arises where the claim is for professional negligence against one or more former solicitors. For entirely understandable (even if misguided) reasons, a claimant suing a former solicitor may well have no wish whatsoever to trust yet another lawyer as a representative and adviser. Sometimes such a party can be persuaded to use counsel instead.[5]

With a mediator's obligation to be impartial and not to advise, it can be very frustrating and puzzling for an unrepresented party when the mediator declines to help with such problems. It can be very difficult for a party to make sound decisions, especially with such difficult issues as causation of damage to disentangle. There is also the very real problem of how to ensure that a settlement is not unfair to the unrepresented party in terms of how it reflects their actual rights and obligations in the dispute.

---

5 The Bar Free Representation Unit or the Solicitors Pro Bono Group (now called Law-Works) or specialist not-for-profit organisations in certain fields (such as AvMA in clinical negligence claims) may well be able to provide free representation at a mediation, if cost is the main problem for a party.

It is not the mediator's responsibility to determine or impose fairness, though that responsibility certainly extends to guarding the parties against the adverse effects that can arise from a significant imbalance of power. Even a friend who is not legally qualified can help to add perspective for an unrepresented party. Ultimately it may be wise for a mediator to suggest that a cooling-off period is written into a settlement agreement, for the protection of both parties. Even with a neutral mediator, there is still perhaps the risk that an obviously unfair agreement proposed by a strong party and accepted by a weak party might be set aside as unconscionable. However, it must be remembered that what might appear to be unfair to one party may yet be acceptable to that party because of other factors of which the mediator is unaware.

## 12.5   Other practical arrangements

### 12.5.1   Dates and length of mediation

A date or dates need to be agreed for the mediation. Most UK mediations of commercial and civil disputes take one day, sometimes two, very occasionally three. It is not always easy to judge the appropriate time to allow, and in doing so the following considerations may be useful:

- Mediations generally expand to fill the available time. There is therefore some benefit in establishing a confined period (say one day) in which decisions have to be made, since this focuses the thinking of those present.

- Conversely, some disputes (and some parties) require a fuller debate of the issues as a basis for then moving to settlement discussions. This is particularly true of disputes that are complex and/or have not been running for long. The parties may well need time to explore some of issues more fully before considering settlement and this inevitably takes time.

- Multi-party or multi-issue disputes may require a longer mediation.

- If parties are attending from abroad, then it may be wise to allow slightly more time for the mediation. Few things are as destructive of delicately balanced settlement negotiations as the need to leave to catch a flight home.

- Parties often have different expectations about how quickly settlement discussions will move. These may derive from their personal negotiation 'styles', previous experiences, or indeed cultural differences. It is important to recognise that a party who wishes to progress more slowly towards settlement may be no less committed to it.

239

## 12.5.2   Case documentation

It is typical in civil and commercial mediations in the United Kingdom for each party to provide a certain amount of paperwork to the mediator and the other parties in advance of the mediation. The purpose of this is usually:

– to brief the mediator on the key issues in the dispute; and

– to ensure each side understands the other's position/views.

This documentation usually consists of:

### 12.5.2.1   Case Summaries

The importance of case summaries is often underestimated. In particular, they provide a useful opportunity to:

– Set a clear agenda for the mediation discussions. This is extremely important in complex, multi-issue cases, and can help focus the discussions.

– Impact on the other side's thinking. This particularly applies to parties, as opposed to lawyers. The fact that they have seen the pleadings and received advice on the case does not always mean that they have fully appreciated the arguments. A clear and succinct summary of the issues, in plain English rather than the language of pleadings, can have a significant impact. It may well engender a greater appreciation of the risks.

– Clarify the decisions that need to be made. Faced with complex and long-running disputes, parties can lose sight of the key decisions they need to make. A short, focused case summary can restore clarity.

– Establish any further information that is required (or at least will assist) in order to progress settlement negotiations.

– Set an appropriate tone for the ensuring negotiations.

– Articulate any commercial or personal priorities relating to settlement.

Much of the above cannot be achieved through simply reading the material generated by litigation – such as the pleadings – the more so if the dispute has been running for some considerable time.

### 12.5.2.2   Other materials

That said, it can still be useful for a mediator to see the underlying material, such as the pleadings, any contract or document which is the subject of the dispute, expert's reports, summaries of issues or skeleton arguments, and particular any correspondence relating to settlement offers or discussions.

Where possible, a joint bundle of these documents should be agreed between the parties.

In addition, there may be materials which a party wishes to disclose to the mediator, but not to the other side, for example, an expert's report still in draft, or a counsel's opinion. Parties should be encouraged to do this.

Parties should always disclose to the mediator (and a wise mediator always seeks) details of previous offers made to settle, whether informal or in accordance with CPR, Pt 36. The requirement not to disclose such details to a judge does not apply to a mediator, who is working in a 'without prejudice' environment with the parties, and who needs to know where the parties have previously been prepared to pitch their case off the record.

'Less is generally more', and this certainly applies to mediation paperwork. The paperwork must serve the mediation, and not be an end in itself. As a general guideline, case summaries should aim to be no more than 10 pages, and supporting documentation only that which is really necessary to enable the mediator to understand the issues (bearing in mind that the parties will already be familiar with the latter). It is surprising how possible it is to reduce a complex and long-running dispute to a short précis of the key issues, without losing its core, but gaining significant clarity as a result.

Furthermore, if there are documents which parties consider may or may not be important for a mediator to see at some point, they can always be brought to the mediation and provided if necessary, rather than supplied in advance. The kind of perfection in terms of comprehensiveness and accuracy of numbering and copying which typifies trial bundles is not required in a mediation.

### 12.5.3   Venue

Venue is perhaps more important a topic than might be imagined. A normal mediation is potentially going to last from six to twelve hours or more, during which time there will be a mix of hard work interspersed with periods when not much seems to be happening. There will almost certainly be times of tension and emotion. Each party and their team will spend a good deal of the day in their own room, at times working with the mediator, or reworking figures or arguments on their own, or waiting for the mediator to return with news of the next stage in the process. The venue must be geared to coping with a possible late finish. Another consideration is the documentation. If there are a number of parties each with quantities of documentation which they want at least to have available for reference at the mediation, the convenience of being able to drive to an out-of-town location with bulky documents parked close to the mediation suite is considerable.

Thus the more comfortable the surroundings are, the better participants will be able to cope with the varying pressures that a mediation imposes. Rooms with natural light, suitable furniture, perhaps with easy access to a garden area or the outside – all can ease and enhance the process. There are a number of purpose-designed mediation suites and some mediation providers hold mediations at their offices.

Parties frequently use the offices of one of the parties' solicitors, and very often these meet the necessary comfort criteria, as well as minimising expense. If they do not offer the necessary comfort and out-of-hours servicing, serious consideration should be given to using, say, a hotel or a mediation suite. It is wise for the mediator to check whether the party who is, in effect, a visitor to an opposing solicitor's offices or barrister's chambers is in any way intimidated by their not being overtly neutral ground.

Mediators should inspect location arrangements before parties arrive to confirm that room layout is appropriate and to confirm or amend any requirements set out in preparation for the mediation. The following points should be remembered:

- Rooms should be of appropriate size for joint and private meetings (remembering that parties sometimes bring along additional unexpected participants).

- The layout of the main room should be suited to round-table negotiations rather than courtroom advocacy (and of appropriate size to avoid too much or too little distance between parties).

- There should be reasonably comfortable separate private rooms for each party (or coalition of parties).

- Soundproofing must ensure privacy for each party's discussions. It may be wise to have the private rooms separated by the joint meeting room or some other baffle for sound. Few party walls can exclude every sound, and to hear laughter or raised voices from someone else's private meeting can be unfortunate.

- Flip charts should be available in rooms and any audio-visual aids requested by the parties.

- Catering arrangements should be checked (buffet-style refreshments, preferably in an open setting between rooms, can assist parties to make informal contacts between sessions). Evening refreshments may be needed in a long mediation.

- Telephone, fax facilities and other business services need to be available, with effective reception for mobile phones.

- Overnight arrangements for rooms to be locked or other document storage facilities must be made where the mediation is to last longer than a day.

- Rooms should be available for discussions to continue late into the night.

## 12.6 Preparation for the mediation

Effective preparation for mediation is vital, and there is little doubt that it can and often does affect the end result. As noted above, mediation constitutes an opportunity for the parties to settle their differences. How well they use that opportunity is partly down to preparation.

The bulk of the responsibility for preparation will rest with the lawyers. We have already noted the practical considerations relating to paperwork, choice of venue, and so on. Once these are complete (or sometimes as part of dealing with them), substantive preparations will need to be made for how to approach the day itself. To maximise the opportunity which mediation affords, the following should be borne in mind:

### 12.6.1 Plenary or opening meetings

Mediation may well offer an opportunity for each side to address the other side directly, so:

- What key messages or points need to be conveyed?
- What impact might this have on the other party (ies) and on the rest of the mediation?
- Who can most effectively make those points? Such points may come with more force from the parties than from their advisers, or from a combination of the two.

### 12.6.2 Priorities

What priorities (commercial, personal or other) does the client have? Once the mediation is under way, it is easy to lose sight of these in the heat of the moment. A clear articulation of them in advance can provide an important benchmark for the client.

### 12.6.3 Blockages

What is currently standing in the way of settlement, and what might be done in mediation to remove it? Does the other side need further information? If the parties are divided solely by differing legal analyses, are they both in a position to debate the issue meaningfully at the mediation? If technical issues need to be addressed, is each side able to do so?

### 12.6.4   Risk analysis

A party will almost certainly be faced in mediation with a series of decisions about settlement. To make those decisions effectively, he will need to know what all the options are, and what risks attach to each. This presupposes that some clear risk analysis work has been done, ideally well in advance of the mediation (and in any event as part of the litigation process) but certainly during the mediation itself. Whole books are written on the subject, and this book is not one of them. But suffice it to say that parties should not be put in the position of having to decide on settlement terms without a clear and effective risk analysis.

### 12.6.5   Wider implications

Effective risk assessment should address not only the likelihoods of winning or losing at trial on particular issues, but also the wider implications of either settling or not settling – for example, the personal effect on the parties, the commercial ramifications, the time commitment and opportunity costs of litigation, reputational issues, and so on.

### 12.6.6   Costs

Parties should attend mediation with a clear understanding of the costs (legal, technical, and other) which they have incurred thus far, and which they are likely to incur if the case proceeds to trial (and indeed to appeal, if that is considered likely).

### 12.6.7   Parties

Some parties are well accustomed to the cut and thrust of commercial negotiations, whether through a mediator or otherwise. For others, the intensity of the process will come as a considerable surprise, even a shock. Lawyers should ensure that their clients are well prepared for the intensity, the likely (or at least typical) pattern of events, and the fact that they will need to make some decisions.

### 12.6.8   Those not attending

Will input be required from anyone who will not be physically present at the mediation? If so, what arrangements have been made for them to be contactable during the mediation?

### 12.6.9 Wider settlement advice

Whilst it is hard to predict in advance the outcome of a mediation, it may well be that settlement is reasonably likely to be confined to a number of potential structures. For example, in a shareholders' dispute, potential outcomes might include one shareholder buying or selling his shares from or to the others, or the company buying its own shares. Parties considering such outcomes (at least in theory) would be well advised to consider before the mediation issues such as the tax consequences of such deals, if only to know whether they are possible.

All that being said, however, full preparation does not and should not imply rigid positions. Flexibility is key within a mediation. There is an ebb and flow to the discussions as points are debated and negotiated, new factors or emphases emerge, and possibilities for resolution appear or disappear. It is vital that parties have the flexibility to factor such issues into their thinking as the mediation progresses.

The above preparation will involve parties as well as their lawyers. Parties should be fully immersed in preparatory discussions with their advisers, not least so that they can make as full and confident a contribution as possible in the mediation itself.

## 12.7 Preliminary meetings and mediator contact

Once appointed, mediators approach their task in their own ways. Most like a significant degree of contact with the parties (or at least with their advisers) beforehand, others less so. To some extent, therefore, the issue is in the hands of the mediator rather than the parties. However, it is always open to parties to request some pre-mediation contact, and so it is worth addressing the issue here.

Pre-mediation contact may take the form of a meeting(s) or just telephone calls, either separately with each side or jointly, and either with lawyers only or with clients as well. Such contact can be invaluable for the mediator, and may also serve a number of purposes for the parties and their advisers. These include:

- Conveying to the mediator a party's priorities for the mediation, and discussing how these might be met. These could well be matters of process, such as a party's desire to meet with his opposite number for face to face discussions during the meeting, or indeed an unwillingness to do so, and it is very helpful for the mediator to be aware of such matters in advance.
- Enabling the mediator, as a consequence, to think more about the structure of the mediation.

- It may also throw up unrealistic expectations held by the parties, and again knowing that in advance is important.
- Building the parties' confidence in the process and indeed the mediator.
- Ensuring that parties/advisers are ready and willing to address the main areas of contention – in terms of available information, understanding of each other's positions, and so on.
- Ensuring that the parties/advisers fully understand the nature of the process which they are engaging in.
- Creating a sense of momentum in the negotiations, which can enable all concerned to hit the ground running at the mediation itself.
- In addition, in a dispute with multiple defendants, there may well be merit in them meeting as a group with the mediator, to discuss the extent to which they will adopt a joint approach to the claim during the mediation. The same of course applies to multiple claimants.

Lengthy pre-mediation meetings will, of course, have cost implications for the parties, and may not be felt to be justifiable in smaller cases. At the very least, though, some pre-mediation telephone contact with the mediator is advisable.

## 12.8   Process design

Most civil and commercial mediations in the United Kingdom involve a typical model, built around a 1–2 day set-piece negotiation process. To some extent, that has been useful in engendering understanding, confidence and demand for mediation. However, it should not be allowed to mask the fact that mediation is a very flexible process, and can be designed to accommodate the needs of the parties. Provided that the basics remain intact (a neutral mediator, a confidential process) there is great scope for parties to build a process around their own particular needs.

Longer and more complex cases, those with parties in many jurisdictions, those with multiple issues which need resolving sequentially, or those which raise public policy issues which cannot be signed off in a single session, may all require a different process structure. Good mediators will be able to work with parties and their advisers to address these aspects. The field has an inherent scope for creativity which remains under-used. Some of the possible options open have been discussed in **Chapters 3** and **11**.[6]

---

6  See 3.5 and 11.6.1.

*Chapter 13*

# What happens at a typical mediation

## 13.1 Duration: the practicalities

The duration chosen for a mediation has to be a matter of experience and intuition. What do the parties feel comfortable with in terms of time commitments and potential cost, set against the perceived need for a long or short enough period? Where the case can be quickly moved into settlement offers over a few central issues, a short time-scale can be proposed. If the case demands that the mediator and parties work through a range of information and case investigation before settlement discussion can sensibly occur, then a longer time-span will have to be set. Parties used solely to working with litigation will normally expect the mediation to take longer than it need, although mediators should not brush aside party expectations. At the same time, setting aside only a day or two for mediation can be a useful discipline on both the parties and the mediator. It will focus their objectives primarily on mediation as a settlement process rather than an investigation process and avoid concerns that mediation may be used as a deliberate time-wasting exercise.

Typical commercial cases can often be mediated within a day, albeit a day which can sometimes stretch well into the evening before settlement is achieved. Very high value, complex or multiparty cases may need two to three days set aside, and even more complex cases or cases with many parties may require between a week or several months (usually in a series of separate meetings rather than continuous mediation). In such cases it may be unrealistic or inadvisable to keep all parties together for the length of the mediation, but care should be taken with this, as a sense of meeting together at some stage helps settlement momentum.

The key objective for mediators, whatever the case duration set, will be to ensure that parties feel that the process continues to make or promise progress towards settlement. Open-ended timescales should be avoided. Setting a deadline for the mediation to be completed helps to discipline the parties into making realistic decisions on settlement. ADR contract clauses, with mediation as a stage prior to arbitration or litigation proceedings, generally set time limits from initiation of the mediation. Parties can always agree to extend a deadline if they are satisfied progress can, or is likely to be, achieved.

Two further models need mention. Certain County Courts operate the use of three-hour *time – limited* mediations, taking place on court premises between 4.30 and 7.30 pm. ADR providers are now increasingly offering time-limited mediations as an option. In order to be effective, these call for a high degree of skilled time management and careful but brisk focus on the issues by the mediator. However, if all parties accept responsibility for using the time as productively as possible, this short-form process can work well if the ground to be covered is not simply too extensive. Repeat users of mediation can take much of the process framework for granted, but a lay party new not only to mediation but to making a claim at all may well need time and space to adapt to its demands and possibilities.

At the other end of the scale is what has been termed *strategic or project mediation.* A dispute resolution structure is made available to be used whenever disputes arise during, for instance, a lengthy civil engineering project. A mediator will be appointed from a panel well versed in the general structure of the contract who is thus able to intervene effectively and speedily.

In strategic mediation, the same idea is applied to a complex personal injury case which is almost certain to be long-running. Typically, the mediator is appointed very early in the life of the claim and will assist the parties in sorting out both the issue of liability and, where liability is likely to be established, provision for rehabilitative treatment. Sympathy and regret can also be expressed at a time before positions have hardened. This early contact also means that a sensible working relationship, moderated by the mediator, can infuse the quality of all subsequent negotiations. The mediator, armed with full knowledge of the dispute from the outset, remains available to mediate in a formal way with parties on any large issues that later prove difficult to settle. The fact that the parties have learned to work well together from the beginning will probably minimise the need for such later intervention.

A similar type of process has been called *pathfinder mediation,* where the mediator is in effect assisting the parties to design their own process for resolving their dispute. Mediation can be used to address purely procedural questions, ignoring substantive ones, at least at the outset. For instance, in one mediation the parties sought to address only the disagreement between them over the extent of disclosure of documents which should take place, and not the substantive claims and counterclaims. Rather than argue their respective cases at an interim hearing, they chose to bring the matter to mediation. In fact, once the mediation was under way they chose to address the substantive issues as well and were able to settle the matter in its entirety.

## 13.2   Documentation: the practicalities

As discussed in **Chapter 12**, the parties should have exchanged and copied to the mediator a brief case summary (and the objectives they seek, if felt appropriate) before the mediation, together with essential supporting documentation. These might include the relevant contract or leases, expert witness reports to be used to substantiate their positions, the pleadings, schedules of losses claimed and counter-schedules etc. An agreed bundle should be produced if possible. The mediation agreement will be signed at the beginning of the mediation, if not previously done. Many mediators use a simple notebook to take with them from meeting to meeting to emphasise the informality of discussions, though a ring binder with separate tabs may be more helpful with blank sheets of paper behind each tab. This can serve as a model for a lawyer's mediation file, adjusted for the different role. It might take the following shape:

– seating chart with name and occupational details of each person attending for easy reminder;

– mediation agreement and notes of any other agreed details on procedure;

– personal memory-jogger list of key mediation tactics;

– separate tabs for each party's statements and any essential documents;

– chronology of significant dates and a list of issues;

– damages data and calculations;

– section for recording key points made in the opening joint meeting;

– separate sections for each private meeting (the mediator must be careful not to leave pages open which reveal notes of private discussions with the other party);

– section for offers, counter-offers or statements that the mediator has permission to reveal to the other party;

– draft of a settlement agreement with blank schedule for details of terms (it is quite usual for the mediator to encourage the lawyers to prepare these in advance, bringing the outline of a possible agreement with standard clauses to be completed in the event of settlement in electronic form);

– address details of any ADR organisation administering the case, of parties' contact details, details of any other parties involved but not present (for example, insurance company, government department, etc).

A lap-top computer and printer, with a form of settlement agreement in blank on disk which can be built up during the day, can be extremely time-saving at the end of a mediation.

## 13.3   Arrivals

The mediator should show the parties to their private rooms or make suitable arrangements for this to happen. Meeting the parties as early as possible gives the earliest opportunity for the mediator to begin the process of building rapport. Making the geography clear over where the main meeting room is, where the toilets and telephones are, and how to contact the mediator during the day, all help parties to settle into an often unfamiliar environment. In general it is helpful to allow parties a short time alone with their team for a final briefing. The mediator should call into each room in order to:

- allow for informal introductions;
- check if everyone will be ready to move into the opening meeting and to deal with any final queries on procedure which parties may have;
- explain to those unfamiliar with mediation about the privacy of discussions in the party's private room and what to expect about the suggested process during the day;
- ensure that the mediation agreement is signed, with any modification agreed; and
- confirm that there are no problems with authority to settle (though it is wise to have done so before the mediation day also).

There are cases where it is particularly important that the opening joint session is handled sensitively. In a clinical negligence case, for instance, a patient and the allegedly negligent doctor may be facing each other for the first time since things went wrong; or in a fierce family company feud, where there is deep animosity between directors. If pre-mediation contacts have been unable to deal fully with these issues, it may well be wise for the mediator to use private sessions with each party at some length to prepare them for the opening joint meeting. Both party and representative need to be sure of the wisdom of what they are planning to say, and also to prepare to receive comments that may be very difficult to hear. Careful preparation which makes sure that each party is approaching the impending joint meeting in a sound and respectful way is vital for its success.

## 13.4   The mediator's opening at the joint meeting

Most mediators have their own style and approach to their opening remarks. However, in every case mediators should be looking to establish their authority, win the parties' confidence, set an appropriate tone for discussions (in terms of formality or informality), and begin to create momentum. This is particularly important where the parties or their advisors have not previously met the mediator. First impressions can be vital in terms of the mediator's effectiveness during the mediation itself.

The length of the opening remarks should also be thought through beforehand. If they last too long, it may frustrate parties who are keen to get to grips with the issues, and may tend to over-formalise the process. If they are too short, it may lead to key points being omitted, depriving the parties of understanding or clarity about the process.

In general, mediators will normally deal with the following points:

- seating the parties according to a pre-arranged seating plan, perhaps placed between their advisers and the mediator to encourage them to contribute;
- formal introductions;
- outlining the purpose of the mediation;
- reviewing the key legal points of the mediation agreement; authority to settle, confidentiality, without prejudice, etc (this can be done where appropriate by directing attention to the mediation agreement provisions) and arranging for it to be signed, if not already done;
- outlining the structure of the day, describing briefly the nature of opening statements and their duration, questions, private meetings, possibility of further joint meetings or of occasions where the mediator may want to meet only principals or advisers to assist in achieving progress towards a settlement;
- dealing with the fact that any settlement must be reduced to writing and signed by the parties for it to be binding;
- suggesting and agreeing any other ground rules;
- confirming that parties must have full authority to settle, in order to emphasise again the purpose behind the meeting. This should normally have been confirmed, however, at a preparatory stage. Mediators should not generally labour this issue in a joint meeting, as it may spark off early destructive arguments. In some cases parties will only have authority up to certain limits and may have to refer back if the mediation moves them potentially beyond those limits. It is of great comfort to lay claimants to meet, usually for the first time, a person representing an insurer or a bank who tells the party face to face that they have come with authority to settle their case.

The dispute, and particularly the hitherto faceless opponent, is suddenly humanised, and this in itself often makes settlement feel much more possible. Conversely, if an institutional party later claims not to have authority or only to have a limited authority, this can have a seriously demoralising and indeed inflammatory effect on the other party. They may legitimately feel that perhaps the opponent has not taken the amount of the claim with adequate seriousness, or that the right person could not be bothered to attend;

- dealing with the estimated time-scale of the process;
- checking each party's time constraints for the day: whether they are available if the mediation runs into the evening or not;
- if not previously done, explaining any previous contacts with parties or advisors;
- checking for any questions or problems;
- inviting one of the parties to make their presentation first, because ... (they are making the claim or they called for the mediation or they are first alphabetically – mediators should have a reason for selecting the first party, to prevent arguments or uncertainty).

## 13.5 Opening statements by each party

The opening statement at a joint meeting is a crucial tool in the mediation process. Its context bears review. In many cases, this is the first time that all the parties and their advisers have sat around a table to discuss the issues since the dispute began. They may have been together in court corridors before procedural hearings, but usually then in separate huddles. For the first time too, the opposing parties and not just their lawyers are there to hear what the other party has to say about the dispute. They have declared that they have authority to settle the case. Now therefore, is the opportunity for each party to explain both the strengths of their own case to the other party or to their key negotiator personally, and why the opposing case might be less strong than they believe.

### 13.5.1 Conciseness

The opening statement should therefore be concise, yet firmly should take advantage of the context in which it is made. The presentation should be made, not with the mediator in mind, but the other party. The mediator is not there to make an award or to judge the merits. It can sometimes be useful to appear to address the mediator, especially if very difficult things have to be said. If possible, however, the opening statement should be made to the other team, maintaining eye contact as much as possible with the other party or key negotiator, this being the person that really needs to be persuaded. It is tempting, particularly for lawyers, to concentrate on the strengths of their case and the weakness of the others, as they would if making submissions to a judge. They should remind themselves that the purpose of mediation is to achieve a resolution. Part of their presentation should therefore explore possible avenues for settlement, or at least express a commitment to endeavour to achieve a settlement.

### 13.5.2 Courtesy

Conciseness and firmness should not be at the expense of courtesy and human sensitivity. It is a matter of judgment in each case as to what is the right tone to adopt. In preparing effectively, it is essential to test out in advance what is proposed to be said to the opposing team by asking how it would feel to receive such a presentation. If a party has undergone a terrible experience that has led to the claim, it is vital to acknowledge and express sympathy with that, even if compelled in the next sentence to say that in law there is arguably no liability for what occurred. The occasion is without prejudice, so it is possible to express regret, and sympathy, even an apology, without in any way compromising arguments on liability that may be mobilised, whether during the mediation or in any subsequent litigation if no settlement is achieved.

### 13.5.3 Cogency

There is a slightly different, yet very important reason, why an opening presentation needs also to be cogent and easily understood by the mediator. In private sessions, the mediator will be testing out with each party the strengths and weaknesses of each case. A party whose opening presentation, coupled with the written submission, provides clear material with which the mediator can test out the other side's case, can be sure that the mediator, clothed with the strength of neutrality, will be equipped to reality-test effectively in the privacy of the other team's room. The same must of course be expected in return.

### 13.5.4 Key points

Thus, when planning an opening statement a party should:

- stress their alternatives to settlement and their credibility;
- aim to highlight and emphasise only the key parts of their written submission: say something new or different to reflect the fact that this is a face-to-face occasion, and to acknowledge that the mediator and the other participants will have read the submission, even if they have not yet done so properly, they

253

will be able to refer back to it during the day, whereas an oral presentation is deliverable only once;

- identify any fair or objective standards by which they seek to have the strength of their case or any weakness in the other side's case measured and approved;

- respond to any new points made by the other side's written submission or oral statement;

- involve other members of their team to corroborate key claims or assertions, to vent their sense of grievance or determination to secure a just outcome, or to establish their credibility as a potential witness;

- acknowledge the other side's just grievances, apologise where appropriate, though not necessarily concede legal liability;

- while addressing the other party or key negotiator, a party should not ignore or demean the lawyers or their role, as this may antagonise them and jeopardise their commitment to the process and even compromise the mediator's ability to reality-test that parties case with them;

- make concessions where possible, either for all time or (as is perfectly possible) for the purposes of the mediation only, reserving the right to withdraw that concession if the case does not settle; and

- end on what it is hoped can be achieved by the mediation.

### 13.5.5   Willingness to move

It is sometimes said that it is always necessary for a party to come to a mediation prepared to move from their opening and public position to achieve settlement. *Being prepared to move* is almost certainly a wise approach. It by no means follows that a party *has to move* from their prestated position if no reason emerges to justify such a move, so long as such a possible course of action is flagged up clearly in advance. It is perfectly justifiable to come to a mediation and open it by saying something like:

'We have come to this mediation believing that our case is unanswerable and that you have no prospect of success. We believe in the mediation process [and have paid for it/paid our contribution towards its cost] as providing us with the earliest possible face-to-face occasion on which we can tell you our view. We want to be sure that we are right, and want to give you the best possible opportunity to present your best arguments to suggest that we are wrong. We have come to listen carefully to those arguments, and will take them fully into account. We ask you to do the same with our arguments. If

we are persuaded by you at the end of the day, we are open to
moving [and the decision-maker with authority to do so is here].
If, however, we are not persuaded, we shall tell you and invite
you to withdraw your claim/defence so as to save any additional
unnecessary costs risks.'

Mediations do, on occasion, end effectively by withdrawal of the entire
claim or defence by one party, and the above illustrates a perfectly
respectful way in which to frame that possibility. It should not be overplayed
nor used as a tactic, as that might undermine the good faith approach that
should characterise participation in mediation and that party may have to
deal with the same lawyer or party in a future mediation. This approach
might especially be considered where proceedings have not been issued:
thereafter, either side can apply for summary judgment under CPR Pt 24
if they prefer.

### 13.5.6 The impact of opening statements on each side

The importance of the opening statements in terms of making an impression on the other party or parties should not be underestimated. It may
well be the first time that a senior decision-maker on the other side has
heard the opposing case put in a succinct and cogent manner. Even more
importantly, it will probably be the first time that the case has been put
without being filtered through legal advisers, such filtering having perhaps modified or diminished its impact. The impression created by a short,
cogent, articulate, polite and eminently reasonable presentation can have
a significant effect on the settlement position which that decision-maker
will ultimately adopt.

Equally, it is wise to listen carefully to the other side's presentation. It
may well contain hints about their true aspirations, and in any event
attentiveness will demonstrate a good, faith approach to the mediation.
Interruption will also have an adverse impact on the whole atmosphere of
co-operation, which should imbue the mediation process.

### 13.5.7 Division of labour

A party should give considerable thought to how much of the presentation
should be made by advisers, and how much by the parties themselves. It
may be instinctive to assume that advisers will make them, and indeed that
may be appropriate, particularly if, for example, complex legal arguments
are to feature. However, the presentation phase of a mediation is the closest
that the process comes to providing a 'day in court'. A party may well want
the opportunity to speak to the other party directly, to convey the depth of
feeling and the importance with which the dispute is regarded. Indeed, a
vital factor to the success of the mediation may depend on enabling that

party to express strong emotion properly, being able thereafter to move on to discuss specific settlement proposals. That kind of party contribution is made easier by the informal environment of a mediation. At the very least, if advisers are to make the opening statement, then parties should be asked if they wish to add anything.

### 13.5.8 The length of opening statements

The length of time given to opening statements should be considered in advance. The intention is generally to provide a short succinct summary, and therefore brevity is usually regarded as important. However, in complex mediation cases it may also be important to spend time conveying to the other side the exact nature of a detailed argument, and if the opening statement is too short, this may not be achieved. The mediator should have formed a sense of what will be appropriate from reading the case summaries and from initial pre-mediation discussions with each party and may well have discussed the length of the opening statements with the parties. It can be useful to agree a specific timetable for opening statements, so that each side knows how to prepare its statement, and so that the issue does not become too contentious within the mediation. However, as with any mediation procedure, an agreed timetable will need to be flexible enough not to impose a rigid structure on the mediation, and the responsibility for handling these situations will effectively rest with the mediator.

## 13.6 Questions, clarification and information exchange

It entirely depends on the way the opening presentations have been made and received as to whether the mediator immediately breaks into private sessions, or whether the joint session continues for a short or an extended period. The following points may be helpful.

### 13.6.1 Considerations for advisers:

- Encourage an early sense of adopting a constructive approach to the process and to negotiation, especially if it is felt that previous contacts have not led to an effective relationship for negotiation.
- Avoid antagonistic or provocative questions or comments.
- Limit any questioning simply to seeking clarification of what their team genuinely do not understand, trying to use open questions and receiving the answers without comment unless they themselves require clarification.
- Use the opportunity if the atmosphere is right to seek and exchange information about areas of factual doubt, so that subsequent negotiations and discussions are founded on a full

appreciation of what each party's assertions actually are, trying to minimise any misunderstandings.

– Stress willingness to search for settlement if it meets the client's understanding of the merits of the case (maybe later settlement terms will be revisited which reflect the client's personal or commercial interests: it is very rare for these to be openly debated at the joint meeting stage).

### 13.6.2   Considerations for mediators:

- Ensure no interruptions from other parties (preferably by restating this ground rule just before the opening presentations, rather than by quelling later interruption) and stress that there will be plenty of opportunity for each party to put its case and to respond to comments.

- Ask silent team members at the end of each presentation if they wish to add anything (to encourage involvement in the settlement process).

- Keep this period short if the parties are clearly antagonistic or going over well-trodden ground or repeating themselves.

- Ask neutral questions for general clarification.

- Avoid questions in an open session that might imply an early view of the merits or predisposition to one side.

- Avoid questions that may require parties to touch on sensitive areas in front of the other parties – these can be left to the private sessions if they have not been raised by other parties already (eg it is unwise to ask if they wish to continue in a business relationship in a joint session).

- Expect some venting of emotions if there are strong feelings in the case and the parties have not had any real opportunity to have such a 'day in court' before; the mediator needs to judge when and how to move beyond such emotional contributions to further questions, information exchange or indeed private meetings.

- Thank the parties for their contributions.

- Explain the next stage and underline that:
  – private sessions are confidential: nothing said to the mediator will be conveyed to other parties without express authority;
  – nothing should be read into the time the mediator may be taking with each side as to whether support or criticism of their case is implied;

- when the mediator is absent, this is an opportunity for each party to reflect further on the case or on any requests for further work the mediator may leave with them, or to make contact with their office or to relax;

- it may help each party if at the right moment you reality-test their case with them, and that this is something that you will do with each party – emphasising that to ask such awkward questions privately in this way later does not mean that the mediator has formed a view or taken sides; no answers are required but, if given, will be treated with complete confidentiality;

• undertake to provide, for the parties not meeting with you, an estimate of the time you will take with the other party (and keep to it), and to give rough estimates of the minimum time before expecting to finish each private session and move to the next or other party, trying to stick to the estimate or send messages about any slippage as the mediation proceeds.

## 13.7   Private meetings

In the United Kingdom, the description 'private meetings' is used for meetings with one party's team privately and without any representative of the other party present, instead of the imported American term 'caucus', where it means a confidential meeting of a small political group, but has been used widely in mediation terminology. The use of the word 'caucus' has declined in UK mediation practice in favour of 'private meeting'.

### 13.7.1   Their purpose

These meetings between the mediator and the individual parties are usually vital to progress in a commercial mediation. They are an opportunity for the mediator and each party and their advisers to explore frankly and in confidence the issues in the case, and options for settlement. A mediator should always seek authority to convey to another party anything specific said during such private meetings.

In addition to ensuring an easier setting for open discussion, private meetings:

- give the mediator an effective forum for making progress and the opportunity to build good relationships with the parties;

- prevent a party becoming locked into positions and judgments stated in front of the opposing party;

- allow for deeper, sustained discussion on issues without arguments or interruptions or the necessity for posturing;

- give more time and space for offers or counter-offers to be thoroughly examined and analysed rather than requiring an immediate reaction that tends to be demanded in face-to-face negotiations;
- make it easier for mediators to discuss a proposal's strengths and weaknesses without appearing to take sides;
- allow the parties to build up more trust in the mediator.

Generally, the mediator will first meet privately with the claimant or the party who most recently declined to respond to an offer, or where the emotion is highest. Mediators should beware of simply becoming locked into the private meeting mode of shuttling back and forth until agreement. In some mediation settings, such as family and neighbourhood disputes, private meetings are less common. They work well in commercial mediations, but mediators should remember that there are other options.

Private meetings may, for example, be mixed with further joint meetings on particular areas of disagreement. This helps to build up relationships across the parties and to encourage the parties to feel that the mediation is a joint venture and a more fluid and dynamic process. The more time spent on private meetings with the mediator, the more the mediator will tend to be a shuttle negotiator. Finally, the more the settlement is likely to involve parties working together afterwards, the more the mediator might be advised to structure joint meetings to help this new phase get started on an appropriate note. The mediator may also encourage meetings between principals only (perhaps on commercial issues or to see if a figure can be struck), or legal advisors or experts only to establish points of agreement or differences and their implications in terms of further information requirements and such matters. The mediator may or may not choose to attend these meetings, depending on his judgment as to the likely progress. On the whole a mediator's instinct will be to sit in on the meetings, first to get a sense of how the negotiations progress, and secondly so as to encourage and enable the parties to move forward constructively, rather than retreat into well-rehearsed positions. Sometimes what the parties or principals need is simply space to adjust their positions.

### 13.7.2 Issues to consider in private meetings

Since the aim of the process is to achieve agreement between the parties, the mediator will endeavour to leave each private meeting (with the possible exception of the first meetings with each side) with permission to convey something new. It might be a change of offer or counteroffer to put to the other party, or some new issues or emphases that need to be explored, a new factual concession or waiver of a position for the purposes of the mediation only. If there is no real change by either party after some early private sessions, the mediator may begin to consider ways of changing the dynamics of the meetings or identifying new information that needs to be researched.

In early private meetings, there should be an emphasis by the mediator on the use of open questions seeking clarification of what parties would ideally like from a settlement. There will then often be a series of private meetings discussing the gap between the parties and searching for options to overcome their remaining differences.

The pattern of private sessions is often similar to the core phases of the negotiating process, namely, *'Discussion – Problem-solving – Closing the deal';* or *'Exploration – Bargaining – Settlement'*.

The choice of issues to raise in private meetings will depend on the case and the mediator's judgment. It is a useful principle to follow that the mediator should allow the parties to lead with their agenda at the start of early private meetings. Subject to that, a mediator will generally wish to cover the following:

- **Ventilation of grievances and self-justification**
  Parties will often feel freer to sound off in private session. This is an important phase. By letting off steam, parties can 'have their day in court'. Mediators should acknowledge that they recognise parties have these strong feelings without necessarily sympathising or agreeing. Such ventilation should not be cut off or suppressed but should after an appropriate period be diverted into more positive issues.

- **Strengths and weaknesses on both sides**
  Where a settlement will be primarily geared to the outcome of a future possible trial, the mediator will need to discuss with each party the strengths and weaknesses of their claims, again avoiding any appearance of personal judgment or evaluation (unless explicitly part of his requested role). Thus, for example:

  - What do you feel are your strongest points?
  - Are there any areas where you think you might be vulnerable on the facts/principles/expert testimony/costs/rules/real chances of recovery?
  - What about the other side? How do you see their case?
  - How do you think they see things?

  A good understanding of the issues helps the mediator challenge each side's claims, using material from the other party as the basis of the challenge rather than the mediator's own views. In this context, there may well be a temptation for legal advisers to want to focus exclusively on the legal arguments in a dispute, and to address the mediator on those points. Certainly, the legal issues in a case are generally important, and will inform the negotiating stance that a party is willing to take. However, legal arguments in private meetings are usually most valuably dealt with by an open discussion of the strengths and weaknesses of a given argument, followed by discussions on the degree to which it should alter a party's current position. Legal advisers in particular need to remember the shift from advocate to negotiator, which the majority of their role in mediation entails. There will almost always be important commercial and personal interests underpinning each party's position, which the lawyers may not necessarily know.

- **BATNA and WATNA**
  The importance of any party to a dispute being clear about the concept of their BATNA (Best Alternative To a Negotiated Agreement) is emphasised in *Getting to Yes* by Fisher and Ury, discussed in **Chapter 2**. The mediator may well seek to remind each party of the need to be clear about this:

  - What is your BATNA if you fail to settle?
  - What is your Worst Alternative (WATNA)?
  - How confident are you? Where are you vulnerable?
  - What else would make a difference in terms of these alternatives?

  This area will generally involve a mediator in testing the advice being given to the client on likely trial outcomes, and the costs and time elements associated with that, and in exploring the commercial context of the conflict.

- **What do you need? What do they need?**
  Even where no future relationship is likely, and the mediation merely involves an early attempt to settle damages, one of the mediator's tasks is to help parties to start thinking about the present and the future. What are the risks of not achieving the desired objectives in the claim or the defence? What are their needs and wants? What lies behind these that might be met by other means than currently claimed? In other words, what are their true interests? What would they ideally like to see in an agreement at the end of today? Similarly, how do they see the other side's true interests? Is there a way to help them say yes to a deal that both parties would like? What price is it worth paying for certainty?

- **What has been on the table?**
  The history of settlement negotiations should be reviewed to establish how close the parties have been in the past and the

261

obstacles to settlement then. It may be that a previous offer is now acceptable under changed circumstances or can be made acceptable with sufficient adjustment or with new elements.

- What else could be relevant?
  The mediator should explore all possible settlement options in terms of:
  - figures (and how they could be amended, where they come from and how they might be justified to colleagues);
  - time-scale of payments;
  - future services;
  - future business relationship possibilities;
  - performance criteria and guarantees;
  - apologies, explanations and reassurance of changed practice.

- What other information or comfort do the parties need to settle the dispute?
  The mediator should keep searching for options.

- What are the parties willing to offer?
  This ensures that a specific settlement momentum can be established. Sometimes parties will be unwilling to be specific about proposals unless the mediator reassures them on confidentiality. The mediator can say in confidence that something is needed to encourage the other party to show willingness to move also. The parties may be closer together than they think.

- Is there anything else?
  This is always a valuable question for a mediator to ask, to ensure that a team has revealed all that they want to reveal at that stage.

### 13.7.3  Disclosure of information

The instinct to conceal information from the other side is pervasive in disputes. Within mediation, there are two issues to consider – disclosures to the other side and disclosures to the mediator.

*Disclosures to the other side*

If a mediation is to be effective in generating movement from entrenched positions, much of this will come from a fresh assessment of the respective merits, facts, risks and other circumstances of each party. Such an assessment will be prompted, though not delivered, by the mediator, testing out each case in private. That in turn will often flow from fresh information brought to bear on the discussions. It follows, therefore, that the disclosure of information can be important in generating movement. Indeed, the failure to disclose may well only serve to make settlement impossible until a later date, and much of it will come out at trial in any event.

On the other hand, the possibility that the dispute may not settle in mediation, leading to the commencement or continuation of proceedings, will often act as a check on the willingness of parties to make disclosures to each other.

In mediation, a balance has to be achieved between these two competing priorities – sealed lips may prevent settlement, but an over-willing tongue may prejudice a position. This balance is something which parties and their advisers should discuss at length. Although there are no fixed rules, a useful guideline is to have to justify each non-disclosure, rather than each disclosure.

Much, though not all, of the problem is resolved by the confidential and 'without prejudice' nature of the proceedings. Thus, offers and admissions made in the context of a mediation may not be referred to in subsequent proceedings relating to the same dispute. The implications of these concepts are discussed fully in **Chapter 7**.

The rest is a matter of judgment for the parties and their advisers. In fact, such judgments, and the considerations on which they will be based, are exactly the same whether the parties are in direct negotiations or in mediation.

## Disclosures to the mediator

The structure of mediation is designed to generate an environment in which frank and open debate is possible, so as to increase the likelihood of settlement. Recognising that such debate is unlikely to take place directly between parties who are instinctively protective of their positions, the private meeting becomes the primary tool for the mediator. As we have observed several times, all discussions between the party, their advisers and the mediator which take place in private meetings are confidential between them and may not be discussed with other parties without the disclosing party's consent. If the mediator feels that disclosure to another party would assist settlement, permission may be sought to make the disclosure, but if this is not forthcoming, the mediator remains bound not to disclose it. It is the parties themselves who control the outflow of information from them to the other side, irrespective of what is discussed in private meetings with the mediator. This structure should, and does, encourage parties to be frank with the mediator. There is in fact little to be gained from hiding information from the mediator.

Some parties are prone to negotiate with the mediator, as well as with the other side. For example, they might only partially disclose their position on a given issue to the mediator, hoping by so doing to affect the way it is then presented to the other side. In practice, however, the net result is likely to be that the mediator's task is harder and settlement less likely or at least that the whole process will take considerably longer than necessary. Mediators need to be alive to this happening. Parties should be encouraged where possible to avoid it.

Parties will also often ask the mediator to leave the private meeting while they discuss a possible change of position or a revised offer without the mediator there. This may be the result of a positional approach to negotiation and is symptomatic of feeling uncomfortable in sharing a sense of weakness with the mediator. However, wise mediators will not object. Parties need, at times, to protect themselves against apparent loss of face by changing a previously asserted position. Indeed, mediators spend much of their time helping parties gently to accept or avoid loss of face in moving towards settlement.

### 13.7.4 At the end of the private meeting

It is a useful practice for mediators at the end of private meetings to summarise or clarify the points of information or offers checking that they are able to reveal to the other side, anything else being confidential. It can also be important to leave behind some questions for the party and their adviser to consider or work on until they see the mediator next. This can help generate further evaluation or movement. The mediator will make it clear that the parties have time to call the office or attend to other matters. The mediator will explain that the amount of time spent with the other side has no special significance as to where the case is going.

In a multi-party case, this may also be a good time to suggest that some of the parties seek to work together towards agreement on some of the issues while the mediator caucuses with another.

### 13.7.5 Between private meetings

The mediator does not have to shuttle directly from one room to another. In a complex case or where a private session has been particularly tough, it is wise for the mediator to spend a little time reflecting on the case, reviewing the issues raised in the previous meeting or where to go on the next one. Representatives can use the time to review negotiating strategy with their clients, to do some recalculation of figures involved, or to research further information relevant to discussions with the mediator. Merely because the mediator is not with one party does not necessarily mean that he is with the other.

## 13.8 Further joint meetings

Whether these should be convened is a matter of judgment for the mediator as the custodian of the process. There is also a range of practice and preference among mediators. Some prefer to keep parties separate for the whole mediation, from the end of the opening until the final meeting, at which either the settlement agreement is signed or regret expressed that no deal was done. Conversely, some mediators see strength in keeping the parties together to work on the problems for as long as possible after the opening. This is so, especially where there is almost certain to be a continuing business or employment relationship which needs to be tested out and in effect modelled at the mediation to see how possible it is or whether redefinition is necessary.

A middle course is for the mediator to derive as much as possible from the opening joint meeting and thereafter in confidential private meetings with the parties, but to keep open the possibility of a further joint meeting or meetings. These have the incidental value of reassuring those who attend a later joint meeting that the other party is still there and still engaged in the mediation process. This can be lost sight of when there is only contact with the mediator in a party's own room. More substantive practical reasons for such meetings are:

–   To avoid misunderstanding about issues which are likely to be key to the success of one party's case and which have either to be accepted or rejected by the other party for them to formulate their negotiating position. It is often better for such key points to be conveyed party to party rather than risk that the strength of feeling behind the message, or even its precise contents, may not be faithfully conveyed.

–   To remedy past failed communication between the parties by giving them a chance to say and hear what perhaps should have been said and heard long ago.

–   To review the issues together and the stage reached by that point in the mediation (the mediator being careful not to breach confidentiality in that review) and to plan for the next stage of the process.

–   To try to advance understanding and agreement over highly technical issues relating to the substance of the dispute itself, or to matters of law or expert opinion, which might best be addressed by joint meetings of the technical, legal or expert members of each team, with or without the mediator.

–   To check that exploration is complete and suggest a move into bargaining.

## 13.9 Moving from facilitation to evaluation

As discussed in **Chapters 3** and **12**, this is a delicate area, but one that needs to be considered. A distinction must be drawn between the following uses of the word 'evaluation':

–   Formal evaluation towards the end of a mediation in which settlement seems unlikely to be achieved at the mediation; and

–   The evaluation implicitly underpinning any reality-testing with parties (often based upon the mediator's expertise in the subject area in dispute) to help them assess the strengths and weaknesses of their case. It is not easy for the mediator to avoid giving the impression of having formed an opinion when reality-testing, but experienced mediators would not attempt to start doing so until a degree of trust with each party has been established;

–   A form of evaluation quite often deployed by a mediator, by expressing views privately to each party as to whether a certain level of settlement is either realistic or likely to meet with favour. Where deadlock occurs, a mediator might be persuaded to give an objective assessment to both sides as to the terms on which both parties might give consideration to settling if they want a deal. This will not breach confidentiality, as it is a mutual exercise, but each side will learn whether there is room for movement. The reaction to such a proposal can be given privately, so that neither side actually hears the other's reaction, but if the proposal is acceptable, then a deal is done.

When approaching the possibility of evaluation towards the end of a mediation, a balance must be struck in relation to how the parties see the future. At one end, if the amount or the issues in dispute are of sufficient importance to justify a BATNA of going to court trial or arbitration, the parties are unlikely to invite the mediator to give even a non-binding view to resolve their differences. Again, if the process has brought the parties much closer, but with still an appreciable margin in dispute, the mediator may well be of much more value to them by continuing in a neutral role available to facilitate further discussions, once the parties have had time to reflect after the mediation.

Where the gap between the parties is such that they are content in effect to let the mediator suggest how to close it on what has been heard, then such an invitation can be issued. The reasons why this needs a health warning are:

–   The mediator may be making a settlement recommendation in the light of confidential information received in private meetings from each party: if that is the case, reasons for the recommendation may not be able to be given. This may ultimately prove more frustrating for the parties the impression than closing the gap (or not) themselves.

- If at all possible the mediator should explain the basis for his recommendation, so as not to give the parties the impression that he has plucked a figure out of the air, or merely split the difference down the middle.

- The parties may have chosen mediation as a means of *retaining* control over the outcome: to pass any degree of responsibility to another, even a trusted mediator, will derogate from that. It is thus important that parties are clear that this is what they really want to do.

Thus evaluations should only be given if all the parties request it, and only after the implications have been fully considered. The mediator should discuss these in a joint meeting, so that all can hear the advice and can also discuss and contribute to the way the mediator suggests that the evaluation should be done.

Evaluations can really only be made (and respected by the parties) if they are given either by a mediator valued as possessing relevant expertise; or if in the form of a general view expressed in terms of commercial common sense from the viewpoint of a detached observer. They are always best given in private session with each party, and should be given consistently between each party, as they have the choice at a later stage to exchange them. Also, mediators might otherwise be tempted to tell both parties that they have a bad case in order to generate pressure to settle.

Advisors might want to consider inviting a mediator to give an evaluation if they are uncertain of the real strength of their case or perhaps have differences with their client over assessment of the strength of the case. They may, however, find that a mediator will resist accepting ultimate responsibility for undertaking what is really a task for the lawyer, however difficult: namely to form a clear a view of what advice to give to a client, and also to give the client bad news about the claim and adjust any unrealistic expectations.

There is further general discussion about these issues in the following section. Parties can also sign up in advance to 'med-arb', a process where the mediator changes role from mediator to arbitrator if mediation does not produce a settlement.

## 13.10    No agreement at the end of the mediation

If a scheduled time for ending a mediation is approaching (at the end of the first or subsequent agreed days), the mediator must determine whether to continue in the hope of reaching a settlement that day, whether to suggest an adjournment of the mediation to a future date, or whether to terminate the mediation. As well as the question of whether the days set aside for the mediation are coming to an end, there may be an issue of time limits in a contractual ADR procedure.

If a mediator has a strong sense that there is sufficient momentum to achieve an agreement, it is usually worth pressing on, even late into the night. If undecided, it is still worth consulting with the parties (privately) if they wish to press on. Otherwise, the mediator should encourage an adjournment. A week or two will help the parties reflect, unless it is obvious that the gap between the parties gives no grounds for belief that a settlement is achievable. This last position should rarely be adopted and only when at least one party tends to agree with it. Mediation experience suggests solutions are very often achievable with sufficient patience and persistence. A final suggestion from the mediator on a new proposal can be tested privately with each side.

Where the mediation is being terminated without settlement, the mediator's role remains one of doing what can be done to create an atmosphere for future settlement or cost effective outcomes. After consulting privately, the mediator may reconvene a joint meeting, and thank all parties for the efforts they put into trying to achieve a settlement, reminding them of the advantages of settlement over litigation. The hope can be expressed that the process will have at least brought them closer, clarified the issues dividing them and enabled them to have a further meeting more easily or to reconvene in a further mediation. He can point out that most such cases end up settling within a few weeks or months after mediation. Indeed, if the case merits it, the mediator should have explored in the final private sessions whether the parties might consider another cost-effective dispute resolution procedure, with a view to clinching settlement. For example, if the parties are effectively arguing about a reduced gap between them on a few items, a 'pendulum' or final offer arbitration might be acceptable as the next stage. An alternative process is an arbitration that can award only between agreed limits ('high-low' arbitration) after summary presentations (or the mediator may have suggested in private a final 'splitting the difference' proposal as a last resort).

It is important here to distinguish the process from the substantive dispute. Where no agreement is reached on the latter, the mediator still has responsibility for the former. The closing stages of a mediation that has not (yet) settled can be valuably used to steer parties into a discussion of the way forward in terms of process. A framework can then be established which may well lead to agreement on the substantive issues, albeit weeks or months later. Parties will often be too focused on the substantive disputes to have a sense of what process options still exist.

Often it is helpful for the mediator to remind the parties, perhaps by letter or e-mail the day after as to the amount of progress that *has been* made, as it is easy for disappointed parties to lose sight of this. Thus, if the parties started £1,000,000 apart and ended up £100,000 apart, real progress has been made.

As we have suggested, the mediator should not normally take on the role of arbitrator unless both parties are enthusiastic about this and clear on the potential procedural and legal pitfalls of 'med-arb' (see **Chapter 3**).

Where settlement is not reached at the mediation, parties sometimes cannot even bear to meet again, though it is broadly a good idea for the mediator to encourage this out of respect for each other. By virtue of the absence of settlement, the parties are likely to meet again, if only at court.

## 13.11 Reaching a settlement

In a substantial majority of cases, the parties reach agreement through mediation, even despite the fact that an appreciable number of cases are court-referred. In the final private sessions, the details of this agreement will have been hammered out, so that the mediator should have a clear summary that has been confirmed with the parties. Alternatively, the last sessions may have involved joint meetings, meetings to resolve commercial details between principals, or meetings between legal or other professional advisers. The mediator should help confirm all the elements agreed in a final joint session and deal with any final uncertainties or demands. It can be a mistake at times to bring parties together prematurely when key items have not been agreed in private.

It can also create problems to allow parties to leave after an oral agreement without ensuring they sign up to a formal agreement in writing. A signed memorandum (even if not legally binding) ensures greater commitment with less chance of rescinding. A written signed settlement is usually required by the mediation agreement for its terms to be binding.

The commitment to settlement terms engendered by a written and signed document still holds even where an agreement is expressed to be not binding in law. If parties are all legally represented it may be simplest to ask the advisers to work together in order to agree a draft, ensuring that the clients stay around to sign this. It is essential that mediator remains in attendance as points can emerge during the drafting process, which require the mediator's help to resolve. The waiting period is a good opportunity to end on a personal and amicable note, again reinforcing commitment to the implementation of the agreement. We consider the practical issues relating to settlement agreements in **Chapter 14**.

*Chapter 14*

# Settlement at mediation and beyond

It is late. Hours of hard negotiation have eventually resulted in a mutually agreeable set of terms on which the dispute can be settled. The parties, the lawyers and the mediator are relieved and pleased. What remains to be done? We consider the answers to these questions.

## 14.1 The settlement agreement

The following considerations arise, coupled with the legal questions discussed in **Chapter 7**.

### 14.1.1 Written or oral?

It is vital that the agreed terms should be reduced to writing and that the parties should indicate their consent to these terms. First of all, this ensures that the terms of agreement are commonly understood by all concerned. All who have attended a mediation or indeed a protracted negotiation will be well aware of the difficulties that arise in translating an apparently agreed oral position into an agreed written one!

Secondly, it gives the opportunity for further detail on the agreed points, and indeed further substantive points, to emerge. Although hearts may sink if they do, it is far better to have this happen during the mediation than a few days later.

Thirdly, most mediation agreements (including those in the Appendix) provide that no agreement reached between the parties during the mediation will be binding unless and until it is reduced to writing and signed. This helps to create a freer atmosphere for debate and consideration of offers during the mediation, but obviously imposes a need for any binding settlement agreement to be in writing. The importance of this is emphasised by the decision in *Brown v Rice and Patel,* discussed in **Chapter 7**.[1]

---

1 See **Chapter 7.8**.

### 14.1.2 Binding or non-binding?

The settlement agreement, whether oral or written, can be made binding or non-binding in law. This is a matter for agreement between the parties. Most agreements are likely to be legally binding subject to normal contractual principles, in the absence of this point being explicit in the agreement itself. In most cases, particularly where the dispute is in litigation, the parties will opt for a binding agreement. An agreed and executed binding document will commit the parties to the outcome they have agreed in the mediation. Considerable momentum should have been generated during the mediation, and parties may have arrived at a different view of the dispute from that with which they began the mediation. It is important to harness that momentum in the form of a written commitment.

Inevitably, that leaves mediation open to the charge that parties, worn out by the process, will commit to terms which in the cold light of day they would reject. If this is an overriding concern, then of course they are free to conclude some form of non-binding memorandum of understanding or 'gentleman's agreement'. They might agree to implement a cooling-off period during which the terms can on reflection be rejected. In practice, however, the agreement will reflect terms at which they have freely arrived, albeit in a tough negotiating environment. There is no reason why the agreement should not be binding. Furthermore, if those of their colleagues not present at the mediation find it hard to understand why such terms were accepted, that is more than likely a reflection of the fact that they were not present to hear the arguments, participate in the discussions with the mediator, and watch the positions emerge. It is not necessarily an indication that the terms agreed were unfavourable or wrong in any objective sense.

In some disputes, however, a non-binding agreement might more accurately reflect the agreed terms and the nature of the future relationship which the parties are trying to create. For instance, in employment disputes, parties may seek to agree an action plan to regulate future relationships between employees. A cooling-off period may also be appropriate in consumer cases or where one party is not legally represented.

### 14.1.3 Detailed agreement or heads of terms?

The question of how much detail to put into a settlement agreement at the end of a mediation will often arise. Where the nature of the dispute is relatively simple, the drafting of a document incorporating all the relevant detail should not pose a problem. If, however, the dispute has been highly complex, the settlement agreement may itself need to be a lengthy document. In addition, the terms of settlement reached may contemplate a new contractual arrangement between the parties, such as a new distribution agreement, which may itself require detailed drafting.

Further formalities may also be required to implement any agreement reached, for example, to transfer land from one party to another.

A balance needs to be achieved in the drafting process. Clearly, detail is more likely to provide clarity and less scope for future argument. On the other hand, it may simply be unrealistic for the parties to be able to produce a highly detailed document during the mediation itself. If that is the case, heads of agreement which set out the main points will often be prepared. These themselves contemplate a further, more detailed, agreement being drafted over the coming weeks. The only note of caution which needs to be sounded is as to the degree to which such heads can be made binding, prior to the signing of the more detailed agreement. They will need to contain sufficient detail to avoid being unenforceable, assuming that this is the parties' intention (see **14.2**).

### 14.1.4   Commonly used terms of settlement

Much of the substance of a settlement agreement, whether a contract or a consent order, will be fairly standard 'boiler-plate' drafting, including the identity and addresses of the parties, the recitals and even some of the substantive clauses. This, coupled with the fact that in many mediations the drafting of agreed terms will take place after many hours of arduous negotiations, leads some mediators to suggest standard form settlement agreements. An example of this is to be found in the Appendix.

Clearly, the content of any settlement agreement will need to be agreed between the parties and much of the detail cannot be prejudged. However, as an outline structure, a standard form can be a valuable skeleton on which to hang the flesh of the agreement. This is particularly so where the substantive terms of the agreement can simply be inserted as a schedule, or as one clause of the existing outline agreement. Mediators often suggest that the parties bring with them to the mediation possible draft terms of settlement which can be filled in as the process progressively moves towards settlement.

It also serves as a checklist for the parties as to some of the clauses they may want to consider including in any settlement. Thus, for example, the specimen agreement in the Appendix includes:

- a warranty by each signatory of his/her authority to sign the agreement;
- a checklist, at clause 2, of issues which might need to be considered in relation to the substantive terms of agreement;
- consideration of the effect that breaches of the settlement agreement will have on the remainder of its terms;
- provision for dealing with disputes arising out of the settlement agreement (see also **14.3**);

–  provision for dealing with matters still in dispute, if the mediation
has only resolved part of the dispute;

–  consideration of which elements of the mediation agreement
remain in force following settlement, such as confidentiality of
the outcome, and how those should be addressed.

Parties and their advisers may conclude that many of these provisions are
not in fact required in their particular case, but at least the points will have
been raised and considered.

Mediators vary in their practice as to the extent to which they are involved
in the drafting of the settlement. If lawyers are present, most mediators will
leave the drafting to the lawyers. The situation is more difficult when one
or both the parties are unrepresented. If the mediator becomes involved
in the drafting process, there is a danger of straying from a position of
neutrality into the role of an adviser.

However, it is important for the mediator to be present for a number of
reasons. First, points of detail can arise which have either been overlooked
or not discussed and which need to be resolved (sometimes with the
assistance of the mediator). The mediator can also assist in cross-checking
and ensuring that all the constituent strands of the settlement are recorded.
The parties are more likely to negotiate constructively in the presence of
the mediator. Sometimes (though not normally, as the mediator should not
be put in the position of needing to be a witness to anything) the mediator's
signature is required. The mediator also has a continuing role of ensuring
that the terms are workable. Finally, the mediator offers another pair of
eyes to proofread the document.

## 14.2   Enforceability: some practical considerations

Many parties, and their advisors, will want to be sure that an agreement
reached in mediation will be enforceable, should the need arise. Sceptics
who criticise the process for having no teeth forget that most mediated
agreements are, in fact, binding and enforceable. In addition the terms of
agreement reached in mediation are likely to be simpler and clearer for
the purposes of enforcement, probably by summary judgment, than the
original matters in dispute.

There are several traps, however. One is the problem of uncertainty of
terms. If it is decided to use heads of agreement rather than set out all
the details of the agreed terms in the settlement document, care must be
taken not to omit any significant term which might lead a court to construe
the 'agreement' as void for uncertainty. Another trap would be to draft a
settlement 'agreement' which is a mere agreement to agree, and thus not
binding in contract law. A third is to draft the settlement agreement in

terms making it a conditional contract which is only enforceable if a certain condition is met. That might even be a condition that a consent order is drawn up and filed. If there is no enforceable duty to conclude such an order or fulfil the outstanding condition, the contract may never become legally enforceable because that condition is never met. There is not normally any problem over consideration for settlement agreements, because most involve the payment of money or the compromise of litigation, with the exchange of promises as to future conduct, representing valid executory consideration. If there is any doubt as to the validity of consideration to support a settlement contract, the parties can always opt to embody the terms in a formal deed, for which consideration is not necessary.

Assuming that the agreement itself is intended to be binding, the following options exist.

### 14.2.1  Contract

The settlement agreement can take effect between the parties as a contract and bind them under normal contractual principles. Thus there will need to be the usual contractual elements of an offer and acceptance, consideration and intention to create legal relations. In practice, these are very likely to feature in any event. Furthermore, any relevant contractual formalities, such as those governing the transfer of an interest in land, will need to be observed.

Assuming that the correct content and formalities exist, the agreement can be enforced in the same way as any other contract. The court will be able to look at its terms if and when invited to enforce it, as it always has been able to do. This is so even when the contract is negotiated through 'without prejudice' negotiations (albeit here within the mediation process) as was made clear in *Tomlin v Standard Telephones and Cables.*[2]

### 14.2.2  Consent or Tomlin Order

If litigation proceedings have been commenced, terms of settlement reached between parties can be given the force of a court order by using a Consent Order, usually in 'Tomlin' Order form, which imposes a stay on the proceedings, except for the purposes of enforcing the agreed terms of settlement. This procedure applies whether the agreed terms have been arrived at through mediation or direct negotiation and is a relatively straightforward formality to implement. A model Tomlin Order is set out in the Appendix.

The advantage of such an order is that, depending on the way it is phrased, its terms can be enforced through the court as if it were a judgment without

---

2  [1969] 3 All ER 201 (CA).

any need to start a fresh action. The enforcement of the kind of contract referred to in **14.2.1** would require the issue of proceedings based on the alleged breach of the settlement contract. A Tomlin Order properly drawn can permit immediate application to enforce the settlement terms in the existing proceedings. Tomlin Orders also have the advantage of permitting the terms of the settlement to be kept off the face of the Order lodged with the court. It is perfectly permissible to refer in the Schedule to the Tomlin Order to terms set out in an identified document, for instance the written settlement agreement signed at the mediation. Thus the order kept on the court file will not have on its face (and so preserved from possible public access) such terms as the parties might prefer to remain entirely confidential.

## 14.3 The mediator's continuing role after settlement

Some settlement agreements can be performed almost immediately, for example by the payment of cash, release of goods, or the signing of documents. Others, however, by their very nature, will be performed or implemented over a period of time following agreement. Where this is the case, parties may well welcome the idea of the mediator (or ADR organisation) continuing to perform some overseeing role. A mediator who has performed effectively will be seen by the parties to be impartial, committed to resolution of the dispute and informed as to its detail, and thus ideally placed to contribute in an on-going way in one or more of the following roles.

### 14.3.1 As a mediator

It is not uncommon for a settlement agreement arrived at in mediation to provide that any disputes arising out of the agreement will be referred, in the first instance, to mediation, perhaps with the same mediator. The fact that mediation is stipulated at all suggests that the parties have been relatively satisfied with the process thus far, and of course the use of the same mediator will be cheaper and more efficient, being already familiar with the issues. This approach is particularly effective where the agreement envisages the performance of various future events, and there is concern about whether and how that will occur.

### 14.3.2 As an adjudicator or arbitrator

If the settlement agreement involves, for example, the subsequent sale of assets, the parties may choose to appoint the mediator to adjudicate on the valuation of those assets. This appointment can be included as a term of the settlement agreement.

### 14.3.3   As an overseer

The future role of a mediator might be less formal than that of mediator or arbitrator. For example, if a partnership dispute is settled on terms that provide for the future management of the partnership to be conducted according to certain general principles, the parties might appoint the mediator as an overseer of their conduct or of performance of agreed terms. This role, in essence, would be to assist the parties in the practical implementation of their agreed principles, and to be available to discuss and resolve with the parties any problems which might arise.

## 14.4   Where the dispute does not settle at mediation

It is an interesting feature of mediation that in the small percentage of disputes that do not settle in the mediation itself, the parties nonetheless often express themselves satisfied with the process. Furthermore, a high proportion of such disputes do then proceed to settlement in the immediate aftermath of the mediation. It is therefore often inappropriate to talk in terms of the mediation having failed, but rather that discussions have been adjourned, since manifestly the process may well have played a pivotal role in generating settlement. Very often, the parties to a mediation which does not lead to immediate settlement will comment that they now understand both their own and the other side's case more fully, and that the gap between their respective positions, although not closed, is significantly narrower than before. If nothing else, this may make a subsequent trial quicker and cheaper, because only some of the original issues may remain to be decided.

### 14.4.1   Partial settlement

Mediation may result in a partial settlement, where some but not all of the issues in dispute have been resolved. In this situation, it can be very valuable to draft a document which is not legally binding, but which sets out those matters that have been agreed, and the parties' positions in respect of those that have not. This has the effect both of encapsulating, and therefore in some way preserving, the progress that has been made, and at the same time reminding the parties that it is only the remaining issues which have so far prevented final agreement being reached. If the issues are separable, it may even be possible to reach a binding agreement on some without resolution of the others.

If offers are to be left open for a set period after the conclusion of the mediation day, this fact should be recorded in writing as a formal option agreement and signed by the parties, to ensure that if one party denies such an agreement or exchanges their mind, such an option is enforceable. If it is intended that a decision about an outstanding offer is the only term unagreed, all the other terms of the potential settlement agreement, including those relating to implementation, need to be recorded in writing and signed as well.[3]

### 14.4.2  Further mediation

Further mediation should not be ruled out. Some mediations have lasted up to five days or more, sometimes spread across several months. The adjournments provide important time for reflection, so that parties are not pushed too fast into settlement. Further information can be gathered, without which the decisions about settlement may not be capable of being made. The opportunity is given for reassessment of positions and perhaps the generation of further options for settlement.

Mediation should never be seen as a fixed, one-session process. One of its great strengths is its flexibility. Mediators, parties and advisers should be alive to the possibility of adjournments and reconvening where necessary. Thus, for example, the parties might send in a fresh negotiator or negotiating team, or add some additional experts to the old team. The presence of fresh minds (perhaps with wider settlement authority) may help break the log-jam. The parties may even elect to appoint a new mediator, or an additional expert to advise the mediator. It is often the case that a subsequent mediation session, perhaps with time for reflection in the interim, can bring a change of approach.

If they do not wish to meet each other, the parties may nonetheless be prepared for the mediator to continue discussions with each of them in private. This could be done by visiting each of them in turn as a 'shuttle diplomat', or indeed by continuing the mediation more informally over the telephone, or via telephone conference calls or video conferencing.

### 14.4.3  Further direct negotiation

It may well be that the mediation has brought the parties to the point where they can manage to hold further direct talks without the assistance of the mediator. By coming to mediation in the first place they have indicated a willingness to talk. The mediation process may well have encouraged the perception that, although settlement has not (yet) been reached, further talks may make progress. It may even be that, at the end of the mediation, the parties will be prepared to sign a declaration of intent to have further talks and even to commit themselves to a date.

Care must be taken to clarify whether the mediation is at an end or merely adjourned. If negotiations are to continue, it needs to be clarified whether these are under the umbrella of the mediation agreement or outside it. In

---

3 For an instance of where this went wrong, see *Brown v Rice and Patel,* [2007] EWHC 625(Ch) discussed in **Chapter 7.4** above, and in **14.4.3** below.

the *Brown* case,[4] an issue arose as to whether an offer that was made at the end of the mediation was open for acceptance by mid-day the following day. When one party sought to accept the offer, there then arose a dispute as to whether there had been an offer in the mediation in the first place. In the event, the judge held that, regardless of whether there had been a valid offer or not, there had not been a binding acceptance. Furthermore, the mediation agreement contained a standard clause recording that any settlement would not be legally binding until it had been reduced to writing and signed, which had not happened, nor was any agreement sufficiently full to be enforceable.

### 14.4.4   Using a different ADR process

The reason that many different ADR processes exist is that each can play a different role in generating resolution. What is applicable for one situation may not be for another. It may well be that, during a mediation, problems emerge which might best be dealt with through a different ADR process.

Typically, for example, one element of a dispute may prove hard to settle in a mediation because the parties had, and have maintained, a genuine good faith disagreement about a particular point of law, or technical issue. Depending on the view they take, they can come up with diametrically opposing views on the implications, and the whole settlement is put in jeopardy. Even a highly effective and trusted mediator may be unable to break this impasse through mediation. One option would be for the parties to submit the particular issue to, for example, a judicial appraisal or neutral evaluation. This would provide a non-binding but authoritative view to the parties jointly on the issue in question. Armed with that, they may well be in a position to return to the mediation and progress beyond the earlier obstacle.

Similarly, a mediation might have settled five out of six issues dividing the parties. They might therefore agree to commit to settlement of those on condition that the sixth issue be referred to some form of short-form binding adjudication process, perhaps binding judicial appraisal, documents-only arbitration or expert determination.

Combining processes such as these exemplifies the way in which ADR can, with a little imagination and flexibility, be used to provide a settlement forum designed to address the particular problems of a given situation.

### 14.4.5   Proceeding to trial

This always remains an option, whether or not proceedings have been issued by the time of the mediation. The question may arise as to whether

---

4  [2007] EWHC 625(Ch).

the court is going to explore why mediation failed and try to make a costs order which reflects its interpretation of which party should take responsibility for the failure of the mediation.

The topic of costs sanctions for refusing ADR is discussed in **Chapter 6**. The confidentiality of the process is discussed in **7.3** and the ability of the party to bring an opponent's behaviour in the mediation into any subsequent trial is set out in **7.4**.

Having concluded this analysis of the mediation process, we finally consider in the next chapter some of the more personal and stylistic issues relating to those who participate in the process.

# Chapter 15

# The roles of mediator, lawyer and party

The previous chapters have studied in a roughly chronological way the anatomy of a mediation, with a number of ideas as to what to expect and how to prepare for the process. This chapter concludes this study of mediation by looking at the roles of each of the major participants in a mediation to ensure that all concerned fully understand what is going to happen from a human as well as technical viewpoint, what their own role is likely to be, and the different perspectives which the other party is likely to have during the process.

## 15.1   The role of the mediator

In clarifying the role of the mediator, it is vital to distinguish between the two fundamental elements of a mediation, or indeed any dispute resolution process, and where responsibility for each lies. These are *process* and *outcome*.

### 15.1.1   Responsibilities for process and outcome

As should be clear from the description of the mediation process throughout Part C, responsibility for *process* in mediation lies with the mediator, just as it lies with the court in litigation. This encompasses the nature of the event, whether all of its possible component parts are used in a given case, and if so in what order and involving which participants.

Responsibility for the *outcome* of mediation and indeed the outcome of the dispute rests always with the parties, as advised by their lawyers. The mediator is not a judge or arbitrator and makes no findings as such. The parties are free to negotiate or not, make offers or not, or settle or not. It is their dispute and it needs to be their solution. This very control over the outcome is what makes mediation an attractive process for many who ultimately might feel they would prefer not to confer responsibility for making a major business or personal decision on their behalf on a third party stranger. Whether that stranger is a judge or an arbitrator, the person who decides the case has absolutely no personal or legal responsibility for any later consequences of that decision, subject only to any right of appeal.

Of course, parties have a contribution to make to decisions about process and the mediator to discussions about outcome. The mediator will obviously consult with the parties to make sure that decisions about the order of joint and private meetings, opening presentations and so on are made as far as possible to suit the particular needs of participants. Ultimately though, it is for the mediator to determine these issues, being confidentially armed with information about attitudes and emotions in each room which can influence the mediator's advice as to what will work and what will not.

The mediator will also stimulate debate and analysis of the issues and possible solutions too, and may perhaps suggest the order in which issues are discussed. But this will not normally involve crossing the boundary into expressing a view on the merits unless clearly asked to do so, and (after reflecting on that invitation) agreeing to do so with the mutual agreement of all.

These parameters explain differences in approach of mediators on various matters and at various stages within the mediation process. A mediator may well be firm and authoritative (but not domineering or autocratic) in managing the process, but much less assertive when it comes to dealing with the issues at stake in the dispute. Especially with parties and (perhaps even more) lawyers who are inexperienced with the mediation process, there is a need for careful handling and explanation of procedural decisions. Even if a lawyer has explained the mediation process to the client, it will be rare for a mediator not to do the same to some degree, enabling the client to gauge the mediator (having usually never met or spoken with each other before this moment) as a person and as a process manager in whom trust can be reposed.

Trust is a key requirement. It can be unsettling for those new to mediation to engage in conversation with the mediator early in the day, perhaps giving an indication of feelings or even of confidential thinking on relevant issues, to find the mediator departing for conversation with the opposing team with whom the lawyer and client have been in often acrimonious dispute over a lengthy period. A mediator really has to earn trust over confidential handling of the issues.

The relative informality of the process can help lay parties to settle in. Mediators will quite often work in shirt-sleeves and invite use of first names by all in a way that is very different from a court room. But even this can be a little unsettling at first, and a wise mediator will bed parties and lawyers down gently and carefully at the beginning of a mediation day and seek to win their confidence as to the process to be adopted.

In novel or complex cases, or where issues of public accountability arise, there is a similar need for mediators to consult and guide over what steps to take and what order of events should be followed. The skilled mediator must take responsibility for ensuring a fair unbiased process and if this is not secured, a party who perceives apparent disadvantage may well quickly object.

A mediator is unlikely to bring the same style when dealing with the substantive issues in the dispute. Mediators will probably avoid arguments with parties and advisers, and should not give approval to one or other party on the merits of their case. The aim is to establish a working atmosphere in which the parties sense that the mediator is working alongside them in a joint problem-solving venture with each side. This may well involve testing reality in a direct and probing way at the right time, but this should be challenging rather than confrontational or judgmental. The key is for the mediator to be able to discuss the issues with each party in an analytical and objective way, which will help that party to reach a better understanding of the strengths and weaknesses of their position. They should feel that the mediator has not judged them or 'come down in favour of the other side'.

It is not for mediators to ensure that the outcome is what *they* consider to be just. It is always for the parties to decide what is fair for them, though they are free to seek as much perspective from the mediator on what is fair as they wish.

A mediator will almost always seek to explore the interests of each party (in other words, what that party really needs and is looking to achieve from the situation of dispute) as well debating the pure legal rights which underpin the dispute, and on which doubtless their position in the dispute is based. In most mediations, settlement is reached without determining or reaching a final decision as to what the purely legal rights are. Indeed, very often, the final outcome falls somewhere between two diametrically opposed outcomes, in which one party wins and the other loses, which is all that a court could decide.

Gaining the trust of all present at a mediation is very important for what is likely to occur in the later stages of a mediation. Until there is a good level of rapport between mediator and party or advisers, any venture even into entirely objective reality-testing may be viewed suspiciously as evidence of the mediator having taken the other side's view. This means that a mediator may even need to spend some time on apparently inconsequential or marginally related topics with a party, if that necessary degree of confidence in the relationship has still not been established.

Mediators will also seek to judge the balance to be struck between dwelling on the strict legal position and investigating and mobilising interests. Parties may well need the occasion provided by the mediation to give vent to their feelings about what has happened, both to the other party and to the mediator. Such catharsis may well prove fundamental to that party's ability to move on from the past in order to find a solution to the present and future. A skilled mediator will allow just enough of that to happen to be effective without its becoming destructive.

The mediator must assess:

- how much the legal issues themselves are really responsible for the deadlock in negotiations, rather than lack of information about the other side's case or unrealistic negotiating positions: this can be a function of excessive lawyer control over the content and balance of the dispute and might as a result need reassessment with the party direct; and

- the strength of feeling the parties have about them: if strong, more time for review may be needed until the party feels they have been given due respect and attention, and even just a chance (often denied them by settlement before trial, and even by the trial process itself) to articulate their strong feelings, before turning to what might be a sensible or commercial way of trying to solve the problems.

### 15.1.2 Mediator intervention

Mediators undoubtedly influence party thinking over outcomes, perhaps when expressing views as to where the zone for settlement might (or might not) lie, or in the areas where they choose to reality-test positions. The following are instances of where a mediator might well make a more positive intervention over influencing the outcome, in part to preserve the integrity and reputation of the process:

#### 15.1.2.1 *The need for a workable agreement*

The terms of agreement emerging seem to be acceptable, but the mediator may have a strong sense that it will break down soon afterwards or that the draft agreement or order has omitted a crucial term or consideration. This needs to be carefully tested out in private sessions first: it is possible, for example, that one party does not expect workability but is using mediation to achieve a simple agreement on which to sue for summary judgment.

#### 15.1.2.2 *Protection of unrepresented parties*

Unrepresented parties can present a significant challenge for a mediator, unless they are obviously sophisticated enough not to need representation. There is a temptation for mediators to be drawn into advising them, albeit informally, and so to depart from a purely neutral role. Mediators will have their own views in dealing with this, but as a general rule should confine themselves to ensuring fairness of process, not outcome. A degree of imbalance of power between parties is almost always manifested at a mediation. However, a mediator ought to intervene where power is obviously being abused or undue influence exercised by a strong party against an unrepresented party. In any event, an unconscionable bargain can sometimes be set aside by a court on established legal principles. The fact that such a bargain was struck at mediation will probably not of itself legitimise it. A mediator will therefore want to ensure that the good faith approach inherent in the mediation process is not subverted.

### 15.1.2.3   Unethical conduct

A mediator should not *aid* a party to lie or make misrepresentations in negotiating with the other side. No mediator expects to be told everything by a party or for that party to be entirely frank with either the other side or the mediator, but that does not go so far as in effect colluding with a party who reveals an intention to mislead. Equally, mediators will not convey something which they are told is untrue, and will usually strongly test out whether it is good sense for a party to try to do so. Untruths or misrepresentations can easily emerge later, and will shatter the reputation of a party who has represented themselves as acting in good faith within a consensual process.

### 15.1.2.4   Protection of third party safety or property

It is theoretically possible that information may emerge during a private meeting in a mediation which indicates imminent danger to the health, lives or property of third parties (for example disclosure of a defect in new vehicle equipment). In such instances, mediators arguably may be under a legal or moral duty, higher than their duty of confidentiality to that party, to ensure that appropriate third-party agencies are informed by the party or themselves. This is one of the most difficult ethical situations for a mediator to face, and fortunately likely to be a very rare occurrence. Mediator codes of ethics may address this concern, and it may be incorporated as a term in the mediation agreement. Mediator codes of conduct usually deal with such matters. The legal arguments relating to this conflict of duty are set out in **Chapter 7**.[1]

### 15.1.3   Some role models for mediators

Mediators may undertake a wide variety of roles in a single mediation process. These will vary in balance and intensity according to the needs of the parties and the context of the dispute. Some of the more usual ones are set out here, with brief critiques. Some will be more surprising than others.

---

1 See **7.5**.

- ### Process manager

We have looked at this role above. Exercising this role effectively frees the parties and their advisers to concentrate on the problems at issue and finding acceptable solutions for them. A well-managed process will increase the chances of a resolution.

- ### Facilitator

There is always an important job to be done in easing communications by defusing a hostile or provocative atmosphere, channelling exchanges into a constructive mode, clarifying complex points and allowing or discouraging discussion of sensitive areas.

- ### Problem-solver

This is not to suggest that the mediator will wave a wand and produce solutions for the parties which relieve them of any obligation to solve their dispute themselves. That is the role of an adjudicative neutral such as a judge or an arbitrator, and if such a means of reaching an outcome is desired, the parties should go to an adjudicative tribunal. But as someone with no stake in the outcome, the mediator can assist the parties to explore potential areas for solution, and to review obstacles and options for overcoming them. The mediator can help identify where expert advice may be worth calling in, review previous proposals for settlement and discover if adjustments can be made to make these more acceptable. Occasionally a mediator may suggest other options for ending disagreement to set against those which the parties and their advisers propose. But more often, the mediator seeks to help parties shift their perspective, perhaps to look at matters through the eyes of the other party, or to see what is common ground that importantly joins the parties rather than to dwell on the problems that separate them; or to turn from a past focus to a future focus. Such reframing of language and perspective is very typical of a skilled mediator's activities.

- ### Information-gatherer

There is much that can be achieved at a mediation by way of filling gaps in knowledge in a way that improves the parties' assessment of risk. Mediators may well be used for this process through private sessions, or may convene a joint meeting as a more efficient and responsive method of information exchange.

- ### Reality-tester

The mediator's neutrality is very important. It allows each party to have someone independent reflect on their case, in the sense of holding up a mirror to it so that parties and advisers can check the way it looks. While generally avoiding the expression of opinions on the merits or likely outcome at trial, the mediator can help shift party positions by questioning and reviewing their evidence and arguments in a non-partisan manner as a 'devil's advocate'. This can bring a greater sense of perspective to the existing views of clients or advisors. Mediators chosen for their expertise in a field may be expected to adopt an even clearer role of case assessment and evaluation and have more licence to challenge each party's case. But they should be scrupulous to do so in an even-handed way and to avoid doing so until they have a good sense of the issues from both parties, and should preferably acknowledge that any views they express are based on the limited evidence presented to them.

- *Scapegoat/lightning conductor/sponge*

Mediation gives aggrieved clients and their advisers their 'day in court' more frequently than settlement negotiations within traditional litigation. It arguably even provides a more satisfying 'day in court' for lay parties than a court hearing (so often forestalled by settlement at the court door), since the informality of the process allows for a much freer and franker exchange in the parties' own words. There is a neutral third party to listen to the expression of the problems and damage caused by the other side. The mediator may create the environment in which a party with strong feelings is able to express them in a joint meeting to the other side. But even if too embarrassed or reluctant to go that far, a party can tell the mediator about what they feel in private meetings, which can have a similarly cathartic effect. By acting as a lightning conductor for feelings which permeate even the driest of commercial disputes, let alone personal injury, clinical negligence or employment disputes, the skilled mediator will provide a useful safe outlet, capable of allowing and acknowledging the strength of views and feelings held in an empathetic way, but not adopting them or lining up at the barricades next to the party with strong emotions.

- *Observer and witness*

This is not a witness for the sake of any future litigation, as the parties contract not to use the mediator as a witness in any subsequent litigation. But the mediator is someone who is able to watch parties as they deal directly with each other when together, or exchanges between party and legal team in a private meeting, and who is able to control and step in if matters go wrong, and also to reflect back to each party in later sessions what went on during that meeting.

- *Messenger*

This tends to be a less welcome role for mediators. Whilst there will be messages to be conveyed from one room to another, mediators who limit their role to this are unlikely to be very effective. If the mediator feels, from what has been learned of the views of the recipient of the proposed message, that the message or bid to be conveyed will be misunderstood or counter-productive, he will probably say so and seek to persuade the party to adopt an approach which is more likely to be conducive to progress. Furthermore, responsibility for the contents of messages lies with parties sending them, and a mediator may feel it more appropriate for a message to be conveyed by the sender direct. The mediator should arrange a carefully prepared environment for this to take place, perhaps a joint meeting with a limited agenda.

- ### Negotiation coach

This role arises out of our comments above on the 'messenger' role. One of the most helpful things that a mediator can provide to a party's team at a mediation, where there have been several private meetings with each side, is some sense of what is and is not likely to work in terms of the acceptability of offers. It may be that one party intends to send an insult by way of a nuisance value offer to the other side, but if their real intention was to propose something credible, the mediator may well be able to give guidance, even if bound by confidentiality over matters of detail. But the coaching role may need to go further than that. Sadly, mediators frequently find that the way the parties seek to negotiate with each other is rather unsophisticated and clumsy. Every bid of a sum of money incorporates that side's discounts for risk on the merits, so every sum exchanged in bidding is as important for the message it sends as for the sum of money as an inherent figure. Mediators will often try to assist by suggesting that a bid might best be for slightly more or less than suggested by the party, so as to convey the right impression or to appeal psychologically to the recipient, and to convey the underlying message accurately and in accordance with what the party really intends to convey.

- ### Deal-maker

Having acted in a coaching role, the mediator is then able effectively to convey or make suggestions for, offers and counter-offers, concessions, or settlement package components that represent party negotiations chan-nelled through the mediator. In sensitive or difficult negotiations, the mediator will almost certainly be much better placed to do this than the parties could in direct face-to-face negotiations.

- ### Post-breakdown resource

If a mediation fails to produce a settlement, the mediator remains available to broker discussions or continue directly to participate in or facilitate further discussions if these would be helpful.

## 15.2 The role of the legal representative

In this section, we look at the role of the lawyer who attends at a mediation to represent the client's interests, in an attempt to help lawyers establish clearer guidelines for themselves within the process. Such a role may vary according to the nature of each dispute, the relative power relationship between each party, and the composition of the team attending. It is important to grasp the beneficial effect which well-judged professional advice and representation can have on the mediation process.

The fundamental role of any lawyer at any time is that of the skilled adviser. Classically, the lawyer is the well-informed champion of the client, advising on law and procedure, articulating the client's views to others and pursuing the client's best interests. Most lawyers are used to the requirements of such a role in litigation, but fewer have grasped the different, and subtler, application of that role in mediation. Let us look at some of these components.

### 15.2.1 Preparation

The amount of preparation needed to be effective at a mediation is easily underestimated by lawyers, if the observations of many experienced mediators are to be believed. Putting it another way, like most spheres of endeavour, the better-prepared participant will almost always do better than the less well-prepared.[2]

It is vital to have a session with the client before the mediation day to prepare in detail, going over the facts carefully, discussing and analysing the risk factors playing on the case honestly and openly. This session must also involve any or all of the following:

- a thorough investigation and understanding of the client's and the opposing party's position, motivation and imperatives, financial, technical and legal, so as to be able to deal with them in terms that they understand;
- thinking of as many concessions as possible which will be of value to the other side but which do not involve great cost to one's own client, such as regret, empathy, apology, or services of marginal cost to the client which are of much greater value to the opponent, in effect equivalent to money;
- deciding how best to demonstrate to the other party that the case being presented has substance, is being run competently, and needs to be respected as such and taken seriously;
- thinking through a series of stepped concessions in advance, costing honestly what each option will mean in terms of management time, public and internal relations, as well as money;

---

2 See also the section on preparation for a mediation in **Chapter 12**, particularly **12.7**.

- testing each proposition against what the best or worst alternative is;
- assessing the risk factor for each possible outcome and valuing them realistically, in order to reach a composite approach to chances of success which can be set against what emerges as being on offer;
- taking the client through their part in presenting the best case both in joint sessions with the opposing team and in private with the mediator, rehearsing all the likely questions and issues that might emerge and how to respond to them;
- endeavouring to define the provisional 'bottom line' point below which negotiations within the mediation are simply not worth continuing because the chances of bettering the proffered outcome by continuing the litigation are clearly better;
- trying to define what factors would make a difference to the decision about bottom line and which would cause a change of approach.

These are what a sophisticated mediator will expect party advisers to have done previously, and to have available at the mediation, and it is as well to do most of the thinking in advance.

That said, much of the impact of mediation is in the parties' revising previously held views in response to what they hear. The value of detailed preparation is to give the parties a clearly thought-out platform from which to negotiate.

### 15.2.2 Diplomacy with client and opponent

The lawyer will often be responsible for selecting the team to attend the mediation. Everyone who attends should be necessary and have a clear role to play. If they do not, then they should not be there. We have already emphasised that a vital aspect of this is to be able to ensure that a person with sufficient authority to concede the worst case attends the mediation, however much either lawyer or client expects or merely hopes to improve upon that authority or reserve. It is impossible to predict what might emerge at a mediation to alter advance thinking. If parties are truly going to attend a mediation to listen, ready to change their mind in the face of persuasive argument, it is extremely hard having to explain the niceties of this to someone more senior by telephone, often outside office hours, who has not been involved in the debate. Even if a more senior person needed to give that higher level of authority is reluctant to attend, it is essential that every effort be made to bring about a change of mind. There may be situations with a company, a trust or public corporation where authority can only be obtained by referral back to committee or Board. This must be flagged in advance with mediator and opponent. The mediator may be able to add weight to such a discussion in advance of the mediation.

Diplomacy is required too in handling relations with the other team, with whom there will almost certainly be face-to-face contact, not only during the opening joint meeting, but also in side meetings with members of teams, perhaps lawyer to lawyer, later in the day, quite apart from casual encounters in corridors and at lunch. Litigation has often been conducted fiercely up to the mediation day, with acrimonious correspondence and exchanges. If these have characterised matters up to that point of the dispute, the mediation process gives an opportunity to park that kind of approach on the shelf for a day and to see if dealing with each other in a respectful and diplomatic way might be as good if not better a way to make progress towards settlement in each client's interests. A wise mediator will facilitate such a change of atmosphere.

Diplomacy is also required when contemplating how to address the lay party on the other side of the table at a joint meeting. The privilege of having the ear of the other party in person, unfiltered through that party's legal team, is a considerable one, but to strike the right balance between frankness without unnecessarily or destructively offending either the party or legal adviser requires considerable judgment. There are careful choices to be made, for instance, in explaining convincingly and respectfully to a badly injured or bereaved claimant on behalf of an insurance company just why there are difficulties in paying their claim fully or even in part. It may be best to look that person directly in the eye and talk to them in accessible language and in a friendly way, even if the message is likely to be an uncomfortable one to receive. It is wise to enlist the mediator's help if possible in gauging what approach is best likely to work. Certainly a careful check should be made of how any given communication is likely to be received, to ensure so far as possible a match between intent and effect. If objectives are thoughtfully agreed by each team in advance as to both the mediation as a whole and any given encounter, problems should be minimised. In some cases, a gentle approach may be most effective: in others, a firm and uncompromising approach may work best. What is needed is a range of presentational skills and discernment in selecting the ones to suit each given set of people and circumstances.

### 15.2.3  Professionalism and detachment

Lawyers should never over-impose themselves on their client's case. Some clients will never allow that to happen, particularly the more sophisticated or commercial clients. The risk is greater with apparently less sophisticated clients with little previous experience of the law in action. It is easy to forget whose case it is with such clients. It is also easy to over-identify with the client in a determination to act the role of knight-errant. Loss of objectivity in the approach to advising a client can be extremely dangerous in skewing and depriving the client of their proper control. This is no less dangerous than the lawyer who runs a case for the lawyer's own financial benefit rather than the client's. Lawyers have no business (literally) to run a case to satisfy their own emotional or material needs.

### 15.2.4 Presentation skills

Key decisions have to be made about what may more effectively be expressed in the pre-mediation written submission as opposed to oral presentation at the mediation, and how to mobilise the client to best effect at the mediation. This is as much a question of presentation as content, and needs to be approached in that light. While there may be an element of advocacy involved, consideration should always be given as to whether or not to involve the client in the presentation, to demonstrate credibility as a witness, or even to conceal lack thereof. This calls for considerable perception and sensitivity to the client's needs and capacities.

The role for the courtroom style of forensic advocacy is however limited. At the opening session, the presentation is not to the mediator but to the other parties and their advisers, and it is made in an informal and non-technical setting, with no rules of procedure or evidence to observe or circumvent. The process is much more like a negotiation than a trial. Lawyers, whether barristers or solicitors, need to make judgments as to how to make effective presentations in this different environment. There are many counsel, both senior and junior, with plenty of experience of attending mediations, and considerable skill in the way they participate in presenting and advising. It is legitimate to ask of their clerks about the extent of counsel's mediation experience when instructing them to attend.

### 15.2.5 Process skills

Mediations can present problems for those who have not been through the process before. Undoubtedly any client's case will benefit from being represented by someone with a good understanding of the dynamics of mediation, even if they have no previous direct experience. Role-play is a very effective learning tool and recreates with surprising faithfulness what a mediation is like. It is poor client care to have to admit neither prior experience nor training in an area where the client is instructing a lawyer to look after their interests in a significant dispute within a well-recognised dispute resolution process. Mediation requires new considerations, strategies and tactics to be taken into account and deployed. For instance, there is the question of how to harness the neutrality of the mediator to convey your case effectively to the other party in private sessions with them. Might the mediator (subject to confidentiality) be able to bring back and share useful information about the opponent's thinking and negotiating stance for the benefit of your client? These skills require insight, forethought and practice.

### 15.2.6    Negotiation skills

A good understanding of the range of negotiation theory and technique is always going to single out the best lawyers at mediations. There will be times for a combative negotiation style, but also (and perhaps more frequently) for co-operative or principled negotiation techniques, which are still perhaps less well understood and practised. Any chosen approach must however be founded on sound risk assessment. As the mediation process continues, a flexible approach is essential, open to the need for reappraisal of an earlier risk assessment in the light of new information or insights. A hard-line stance can simply have the (perhaps unintended) effect of suggesting to the other party an absence of good faith in seeking an outcome, which may result in driving them away from the mediation. Undue negativity or aggression may simply waste the opportunity created by mediation to reach settlement. A constructive problem-solving approach will at least ensure that every option is explored at the mediation without jeopardy to each party's previous public position in the dispute, even if agreement cannot ultimately be reached.

### 15.2.7    Knowledge of law and procedure

It is sometimes assumed that sufficient knowledge will repose sufficiently in a single lawyer. It is asking quite a lot for one person to combine all the essential skills needed. On the one hand, the lawyer must understand the law in a given area, the commercial implications behind the topic and the pitfalls in trying to draft a new commercial relationship, plus sufficient knowledge of the procedural alternatives through litigation or arbitration. On the other, the lawyer needs sufficient knowledge and practical experience of mediation or whatever ADR process is being used. A team approach may on occasions be needed. Bearing in mind that complex commercial cases which settle may well require sophisticated drafting and foresight as to what is required, this might justify having a transactional lawyer in attendance with the litigation specialist, who is there (and vitally so) to advise on what the litigation alternative might hold if the dispute does not settle.

### 15.2.8    Understanding the commercial or personal options and realities

This is a vital aspect of a lawyer's job, linked with the need to retain a professional objectivity about the client's control of the case. It is easy for both lawyers and clients to lose sight of the commercial or personal realities that hide behind the legal issues. The prospect of a solution which does not irreparably damage an existing commercial relationship, however strained by the dispute in issue, should not be forgotten.

## 15.2.9   Self-confidence, candour and courage

A mediator cannot necessarily be expected to solve all a lawyer's problems. One of the most frequently encountered reasons for non-settlement at mediation is that the lawyer has frankly found it impossible to get the client to accept the lawyer's risk assessment, or has been compelled to revise downwards the prospects of success to a level unpalatable to the client. This leads in turn to worries that the client may withdraw instructions, blame the lawyer or refuse to pay their bill in full in the event of 'failure', according to the client's definition of failure. Sometimes both lawyers may have difficult clients and tacitly or even expressly concede as much to each other. The temptation then is to advise the clients to go to mediation and hope that the mediator can somehow resolve the matter for them. It should never be assumed that this will succeed, though doubtless it happens.

Mediators do indeed use their independence as neutrals to reality-test with difficult parties. It is undoubtedly one of their most useful roles. But if such parties suddenly start to get an unacceptable message by this route that things look less good than had been hoped, at least from one perspective, they might well want someone to blame other than themselves. This could be the mediator or (if the case proceeds to trial) the judge, or their opponent or even a malign fate, but they might just as probably turn on their legal adviser. Mediations are undoubtedly harder where either or both of the lawyers hope to mobilise the mediator to discipline a difficult client. There is no substitute for good and fearless legal advice from the outset, giving an honest appraisal of the risks of losing.

Mediators can and do help intransigent parties to change their minds. Their strength in being able to do so lies in their neutrality. But the client may respond badly to mixed messages from lawyer and mediator about prospects, probably by an angry retreat into an entrenched position. A lawyer who wants a mediator to perform this role must tell the mediator and then give full support to the undertaking, otherwise it will probably fail. The mediator can help the lawyer over trying to avoid loss of face if earlier advice has been unrealistically optimistic, or the client has been wholly unrealistic in expectation despite the advice tendered, which is just a tricky a situation for the lawyer.

In the final analysis, wholly unreasonable parties may deserve an appointment with a trial judge with the authority ultimately to make a binding order to resolve it, and to make penal costs and interest orders against such parties. In cases like this, one or other party is almost certainly going to lose badly. The lawyer can only (and must) advise the client fearlessly of the risks and consequences of failure, placing responsibility for decision-making on the client.

On occasions, a lawyer has informally explored with the opposing lawyer a level at which settlement might be advised but without telling the client in advance or immediately afterwards. This must be dealt with openly by the lawyer with both client and mediator, as it will have raised expectations of the settlement range for the opposing team, and neither client nor opponent will understand the negotiation parameter expected by the opponent unless this is honestly disclosed.

## 15.3  The role of the party

Although dealt with briefly here, the party occupies the most important role of any of those involved in a dispute. For too long, many parties have felt marginalised by the litigation and arbitration processes. By taking a problem to a technician – a lawyer – the person whose problem it is will, in the absence of great determination or sophistication on the part of the lawyer, feel that they have lost a measure of control over the resolution process. Indeed, what usually happens is the solution is made subordinate to the process. Litigation has always been a process, and it remains so even in the CPR, however improved. It is circumscribed by several features:

– *the legal principles* it promulgates (based largely on retrospective precedent);

– *the remedies* it offers (again usually retrospective, to put the wronged party into the position they would have been in if the contract or the tortious duty had not been breached);

– *the procedures* it lays down to reflect those elements, which are technical and still not particularly accessible without the use of an expert.

The problem which gave rise to the claim was the party's before the lawyer was consulted and the outcome will be the party's after the final bill has been paid and the lawyer ceases to act. How involved can the party or client be in the process which leads from one to the other?

Proponents of ADR say that party involvement should be both encouraged and ensured by the process of exploration and settlement, though at all times with proper and full advice from a lawyer to assist proper assessment of prospects and options. Thus the lawyer, whether in-house and effectively integral to the client, or an external consultant, is vital to the process. But the party is the owner of the dispute and needs to preserve that final primacy.

### 15.3.1  Litigation and the removal of client control

It is perhaps too harsh to contrast the way that mediation deals differently with parties as compared with litigation or indeed much direct negotiation.

295

Parties often attend negotiations to resolve commercial disputes, sitting beside their lawyers as a deal is worked out. However, they are much less often sitting at the table during settlement discussions between lawyers of personal injury and clinical negligence claims or employment disputes. Such cases are usually settled by telephone negotiation or in writing, perhaps by acceptance of a Pt 36 offer. Of course the client gives instructions to accept or reject, but it is the quality of the settlement event that gives rise to questions.

There is an increasing use of settlement conferences or joint meetings, perhaps with counsel present as well as solicitor and client. Even these are likely to be under the control of the competing lawyers and may not have an independent chair. As a result, counsel may go off and negotiate privately, just as occurs at the door of the court. Again the control and input of the party may be reduced to a minimum, though probably to nowhere near as limited an extent as occurs in a trial.

The very layout of a court-room emphasises the way that parties are marginalised by the litigation process. Usually they will sit two or sometimes three rows back behind their advocate. The general flow of communication on behalf of each party is from the advocate (facing away from the party) to the judge, who is usually an appreciable distance from the parties. Parties attend essentially as witnesses and have no control at all of the proceedings, which are highly technical. Communication between party and advocate is usually conducted by scribbled note during the hearing or out-of-court conversation, which will often be too late, or at least seem to be so.

Once in the witness box, the party normally may not discuss the case with their lawyers during breaks. Now that examination-in-chief has largely been replaced by the prior reading of witness statements, there is no real opportunity for a party to tell their story to the court, or in that sense to have a hearing at all in a personal sense. The party's case is presented for the client by the hired technician – the advocate – but only to the extent that it has not already been presented on paper. The first questions of a less than formal nature for a party to answer are now more or less hostile cross-examination on behalf of the opposing party: indeed, the majority of testimony heard in trials now is what is elicited by cross-examination. Each party will thus spend the majority of their time compelled to defend their position without having any real opportunity to assert it free from challenge.

### 15.3.2 Mediation and the restoration of client control

Mediation restores control and centrality to each party. Each will usually sit next to the mediator in joint sessions, be offered the opportunity to speak, and will certainly be drawn into discussions in private session as a principal in the dispute. Parties should be encouraged and permitted to take this greater role if they want it, though there will of course be those who do not. They should also be allowed to develop an increasing role through the course of a mediation if they choose. After all, inexperienced clients may learn as much about mediation, growing in confidence over their role as the process unfolds, as inexperienced lawyers. Each party can strengthen the credibility of their case by active participation in joint and private sessions.

On a more negative note, a lawyer having difficulty with one layer of management in taking a reasonable line on the dispute may be able to involve a more senior layer. This might be done perhaps by reference to the need for adequate authority to settle, compelling the case to be taken seriously by the client at an earlier, safer and less expensive stage than trial. The client must clearly be prepared to engage with the dispute, and at least the forum offered by mediation makes it easier and in most cases quicker and more economical in management time terms for the party to do so. It is no more sensible for a client to dump a dispute on a lawyer than it is for the lawyer to snatch it away and exclude the client from the process of resolving it.

Teamwork is the key to success at mediation. Lawyers should, as experienced participants in the mediation and litigation processes, mobilise clients as effectively as possible and give them the central role that so often is not offered by the dispute resolution process. At the end of the day, having been thoroughly and wisely helped to look at all the legal, commercial, personal and financial issues that surround any dispute, clients can, and should be allowed to, make up their minds as to whether to settle on terms offered, taking into account all their interests and properly assessed risks as well as their legal rights and obligations. The skilled mediator is there to facilitate all those processes.

## 15.4   In conclusion

This book has endeavoured to make ADR in general and mediation in particular more accessible. We are alive to the possibility that in doing so we have made it seem more of a challenge and more demanding a process than it really is. Its essence is really practical and intuitive. Any of those with a role to play at a mediation, whether mediator (who will almost certainly have built up appreciable skill and experience), lawyer (who should have done so) or client (who will probably not have done so unless a repeat institutional litigant) need not fear the process. It is less technical and more flexible than litigation or arbitration, and both these features make it inherently accessible. It is not an unrealistic or soft process. Tough negotiation and difficult conversations characterise it, for which thorough and imaginative preparation are necessary. But as a means of assisting those in dispute to find satisfying outcomes in a tolerable and humane way, it has much to offer.

ADR theorists talk of 'win-win' as a feature of the process and its outcomes. There are occasions when this might emerge at the end of a long day. All most experienced users of mediation really aspire to is the wish to avoid the 'win-lose' that adjudicated outcomes almost inevitably deliver. What often does emerge is a sense of shared contribution to a fair settlement. Neither party has achieved everything that they hoped for, but certainty and a conclusion have been achieved, and each party has both given and received something in order to reach that outcome. While it is rare for both parties to descend the court-room steps with a broad smile, it is relatively rare for a settlement at mediation not to engender at least a watery smile of satisfaction on the faces of all.

# The ADR Practice Guide – Appendix Table of Contents

# Model Mediation Agreements

## 1 CEDR SOLVE MODEL MEDIATION PROCEDURE AND AGREEMENT (EDITION 9A)[1]

CEDR Solve publishes its Model Mediation Procedure and Agreement for use as a standard document for anyone needing a basic precedent. The procedure itself earned authoritative approval from Colman J in *Cable & Wireless v IBM* (see Chapter 7). The 10th edition is due to be published in early 2008. The latest edition is always available on the CEDR website at www.cedr.com/library/documents.

*Parties*

_____ ("Party A")
_____ ("Party B")

[_____ ("Party C")
etc.]

(jointly "the Parties")       *Add full names and addresses*
_____ ("the Mediator")

("the Mediator")

Centre for Effective Dispute Resolution Limited, Exchange Tower, 70 Fleet Street, London EC4Y 1EU ("CEDR Solve")

*Dispute ("the Dispute")*
  *Add brief description of the Dispute.*

*Participation in the Mediation*
  1     The Parties will attempt to settle the Dispute by mediation ("the Mediation"). The CEDR Model Mediation Procedure ("the

---

1  For further information please contact CEDR on +44 (0)20 7536 6000 or visit *www.cedr.co.uk*

Model Procedure") [as varied by this agreement] will determine the conduct of the Mediation and is incorporated into, and forms part of, this agreement. The definitions in the Model Procedure are used in this agreement.

*The Mediator*

**2** The Mediator[s] will be _____

If an Assistant Mediator is appointed by CEDR Solve, he/she will be bound by the terms of this agreement. The Mediator and Assistant Mediator will be referred to individually and jointly as "the Mediator".

*Participants*

**3** At least one attendee on behalf of each Party at the Mediation will have full authority to settle at the Mediation as set out in paragraph 6 of the Model Procedure ("the Lead Negotiator").

**4** Each representative in signing this agreement is deemed to be agreeing to the provisions of this agreement on behalf of the Party he/she represents and all other persons present on that Party's behalf at the Mediation.

*Place and time*

**5** The Mediation will take place on _____

*Confidentiality*

**6** Each Party to the Mediation and all persons attending the Mediation will be bound by the confidentiality provisions of the Model Procedure (paragraphs 16–20).

*Mediation fee*

**7** The person signing this agreement on behalf of the Party he/she represents is agreeing on behalf of that Party, to proceed on the basis of CEDR Solve's standard terms and conditions including the mediation fee as previously agreed by the Parties and CEDR Solve.

*Law and jurisdiction*

**8** This agreement shall be governed by, construed and take effect in accordance with, English law. The courts of England shall have exclusive jurisdiction to settle any claim, dispute or matter of difference which may arise out of, or in connection with, the Mediation.

*Human Rights*

   **9**    The referral of the Dispute to mediation does not affect any rights that may exist under Article 6 of the European Convention on Human Rights. If the Dispute is not settled by the Mediation, the Parties' rights to a fair trial remain unaffected.

*Model Procedure amendments*

   **10**  *Set out amendments (if any) to the Model Procedure -*

*Signed*

On behalf of Party A _____ Date _____

On behalf of Party B _____ Date _____

On behalf of Party C _____ Date _____

On behalf of the Mediator _____ Date _____

On behalf of CEDR Solve _____ Date _____

# Model Procedure

*Mediation Agreement*

   **1**    The parties ("the Parties") to the dispute in question ("the Dispute"), the Mediator and the Centre for Effective Dispute Resolution ("CEDR Solve") will enter into an agreement ("the Mediation Agreement") based on the CEDR Model Mediation Agreement in relation to the conduct of the Mediation. This procedure ("the Model Procedure") will be incorporated into, form part of, and may be varied by, the Mediation Agreement.

*The Mediator*

   **2**    CEDR Solve will, subject to the agreement of the Parties or any court order, nominate an independent third party(ies) ("the Mediator"). The Mediator, after consultation with the Parties where appropriate, will:

- attend any meetings with any or all of the Parties preceding the mediation, if requested or if the Mediator decides this is appropriate and the Parties agree;

- read before the Mediation each Case Summary and all the Documents sent to him/her (see paragraph 7 below);

- chair, and determine the procedure for, the Mediation;

- facilitate the drawing up of any settlement agreement; and
- abide by the terms of the Model Procedure and the Mediation Agreement.

3    The Mediator (and any member of the Mediator's firm or company) will not act for any of the Parties individually in connection with the Dispute in any capacity either during the currency of this agreement or at any time thereafter. The Parties accept that in relation to the Dispute neither the Mediator nor CEDR Solve is an agent of, or acting in any capacity for, any of the Parties. The Parties and the Mediator accept that the Mediator (unless an employee of CEDR Solve) is acting as an independent contractor and not as an agent or employee of CEDR Solve.

*Optional/additional wording*
4    CEDR Solve, in conjunction with the Mediator, will make the necessary arrangements for the Mediation including, as necessary:

- nominating, and obtaining the agreement of the Parties to, the Mediator;
- drawing up the Mediation Agreement;
- organising a suitable venue and dates;
- organising exchange of the Case Summaries and Documents;
- meeting with any or all of the Parties (and the Mediator if appointed), either together or separately, to discuss any matters or concerns relating to the Mediation; and
- general administration in relation to the Mediation.

5    If there is any issue about the conduct of the Mediation (including as to the nomination of the Mediator) upon which the Parties cannot agree within a reasonable time, CEDR Solve will, at the request of any Party, decide the issue for the Parties, having consulted with them.

*Participants*
6    The Lead Negotiators must be sufficiently senior and have the full authority of their respective Parties to settle the Dispute, without having to refer to anybody else. If there is any restriction on that authority, this should be discussed with CEDR Solve and/or the Mediator before the Mediation.

Parties should inform CEDR Solve prior to the date of Mediation of all persons attending the mediation on behalf of each Party.

*Exchange of information*

**7**  Each Party will prepare for the other Party(ies), the Mediator and Assistant Mediator sufficient copies of:

- a concise summary ("the Case Summary") of its case in the Dispute; and

- all the documents to which the Summary refers and any others to which it may want to refer in the Mediation ("the Documents").

The Parties will exchange the Case Summary and Documents with each other at least two weeks before the Mediation, or such other date as may be agreed between the Parties and CEDR Solve, and send copies directly to the Mediator and Assistant Mediator on the same date. Each Party will send a copy of the Case Summary to CEDR Solve.

In addition, each Party may send to the Mediator (through CEDR Solve) and/or bring to the Mediation further documentation which it wishes to disclose in confidence to the Mediator but not to any other Party, clearly stating in writing that such documentation is confidential to the Mediator and CEDR Solve.

**8**  The Parties should try to agree:

- the maximum number of pages of each Case Summary; and

- a joint set of Documents or the maximum length of each set of Documents.

*The Mediation*

**9**  The Mediation will take place at the arranged place and time stated in the Mediation Agreement.

**10**  The Mediator will chair, and determine the procedure at, the Mediation.

**11**  No recording or transcript of the Mediation will be made.

**12**  If the Parties are unable to reach a settlement in the negotiations at the Mediation, and only if all the Parties so request and the Mediator agrees, the Mediator will produce for the Parties a non-binding recommendation on terms of settlement. This will not attempt to anticipate what a court might order but will set out what the Mediator suggests are appropriate settlement terms in all of the circumstances.

*Settlement agreement*

**13**  Any settlement reached in the Mediation will not be legally binding until it has been reduced to writing and signed by, or on behalf of, the Parties.

*Termination*

**14** Any of the Parties may withdraw from the Mediation at any time and shall immediately inform the Mediator and the other representatives in writing. The Mediation will terminate when:

- a Party withdraws from the Mediation; or

- the Mediator, at his/her discretion, withdraws from the mediation; or

- a written settlement agreement is concluded.

The mediator may also adjourn the mediation in order to allow parties to consider specific proposals, get further information or for any other reason, which the mediator considers helpful in furthering the mediation process. The mediation will then reconvene with the agreement of the parties.

*Stay of proceedings*

**15** Any litigation or arbitration in relation to the Dispute may be commenced or continued notwithstanding the Mediation unless the Parties agree otherwise or a court so orders.

*Confidentiality etc*

**16** Every person involved in the Mediation will keep confidential and not use for any collateral or ulterior purpose all information (whether given orally, in writing or otherwise) arising out of, or in connection with, the Mediation, including the fact of any settlement and its terms, save for the fact that the mediation is to take place or has taken place.

**17** All information (whether oral, in writing or otherwise) arising out of, or in connection with, the Mediation will be without prejudice, privileged and not admissible as evidence or disclosable in any current or subsequent litigation or other proceedings whatsoever. This does not apply to any information, which would in any event have been admissible or disclosable in any such proceedings.

**18** The Mediator will not disclose to any other Party any information given to him by a Party in confidence without the express consent of that Party.

**19** Paragraphs 16–18 shall not apply if, and to the extent that:

- all Parties consent to the disclosure; or

- the Mediator is required under the general law to make disclosure; or

306

- the Mediator reasonably considers that there is a serious risk of significant harm to the life or safety of any person if the information in question is not disclosed; or

- the Mediator reasonably considers that there is a serious risk of his/her being subject to criminal proceedings unless the information in question is disclosed.

20  None of the Parties to the Mediation Agreement will call the Mediator or CEDR Solve (or any employee, consultant, officer or representative of CEDR Solve) as a witness, consultant, arbitrator or expert in any litigation or other proceedings whatsoever arising from, or in connection with, the matters in issue in the Mediation. The Mediator and CEDR Solve will not voluntarily act in any such capacity without the written agreement of all the Parties.

*Fees, expenses and costs*

21  CEDR Solve's fees (which include the Mediator's fees) and the other expenses of the Mediation will be borne equally by the Parties. Payment of these fees and expenses will be made to CEDR Solve in accordance with its fee schedule and terms and conditions of business.

22  Each Party will bear its own costs and expenses of its participation in the Mediation.

*Exclusion of liability*

23  Neither the Mediator nor CEDR Solve shall be liable to the Parties for any act or omission in connection with the services provided by them in, or in relation to, the Mediation, unless the act or omission is shown to have been in bad faith.

## Guidance notes

The paragraph numbers and headings in these notes refer to the paragraphs and headings in the Model Procedure.

The same terms ("the Parties" etc) are used in the Model Procedure and the Model Agreement.

*Introduction*

The essence of mediation is that it:

- involves a neutral third party to facilitate negotiations;

- is quick and inexpensive, without prejudice and confidential;
- enables the Parties to devise solutions which are not possible in an adjudicative process, such as litigation or arbitration, and which may be to the benefit of both/all Parties, particularly if there is a continuing business relationship;
- involves representatives of the Parties who have sufficient authority to settle. In some cases, there may be an advantage in the representatives being individuals who have not been directly involved in the events leading up to the dispute and in the dispute itself.

The procedure for the mediation is flexible and this Model Procedure can be adapted (with or without the assistance of CEDR Solve) to suit the Parties.

A mediation can be used:

- in both domestic and international disputes;
- whether or not litigation or arbitration has been commenced; and
- in two-party and multi-party disputes.

Rules or rigid procedures in the context of a consensual and adaptable process, which is the essence of ADR, are generally inappropriate. The Model Procedure and the Model Agreement and this Guidance note should be sufficient to enable parties to conduct a mediation.

In some cases the agreement to conduct a mediation will be as a result of an "ADR clause" (such as one of the CEDR Model Contract Clauses) to that effect in a commercial agreement between the Parties, or a court order. Where that is the case the Model Procedure and Mediation Agreement may need to be adapted accordingly.

The Model Agreement, which has been kept short and simple, incorporates the Model Procedure (see paragraph 1).

The Mediation Agreement can vary the Model Procedure; the variations can be set out in the body of the Mediation Agreement, or the Mediation Agreement can state that variations made in manuscript (or otherwise) on the Model Procedure are to be incorporated.

### Mediation Agreement – paragraph 1

If CEDR Solve is asked to do so by a Party wishing to initiate a mediation, it will approach the other Party (ies) to a Dispute to seek to persuade it/them to participate.

Alternatively, the Party who has taken the initiative in proposing the mediation may wish to send a draft agreement based on the Model Agreement to the other Party (ies).

Representatives of the Parties (and the Mediator if he/she has been nominated) and CEDR Solve may meet to discuss and finalise the terms of the Mediation Agreement.

### The Mediator – paragraphs 2–3

The success of the Mediation will, to a considerable extent, depend on the skill of the Mediator. CEDR Solve believes it is very important for the Mediator to have had specific training and experience. CEDR Solve will propose mediators suitable for the particular matter.

In some cases it may be useful to have more than one Mediator, or to have an independent expert who can advise the Mediator on technical issues. All should sign the Mediation Agreement, which should be amended as appropriate.

It is CEDR Solve's practice, as part of its mediator development programme, to have an assistant mediator ("the Assistant Mediator") attend most mediations. The Assistant Mediator signs the Mediation Agreement and falls within the definition "the Mediator" in the Model Procedure and the Model Agreement.

It is advisable, but not essential, to involve the Mediator in any preliminary meeting between the Parties.

### CEDR Solve – paragraphs 4–5

The Model Procedure envisages the involvement of CEDR Solve because in most cases this is likely to benefit the Parties and the Mediator and generally to facilitate the setting up and conduct of the Mediation. The Model Procedure, however, can be amended if CEDR Solve is not to be involved.

### Participants – paragraph 6

The lead role in the mediation is usually taken by the Lead Negotiators, because the commercial or other interests of the Parties will often take the negotiations beyond strict legal issues.

The Lead Negotiator must have full authority to settle the Dispute, as detailed in the text of paragraph 6. Full authority means they are able to negotiate freely without restriction or limits on their authority and that the representative does not need to refer to anyone outside the mediation when negotiating and agreeing a settlement. If negotiating authority is less than full, this fact should be disclosed to the other Party and to the Mediator at least two weeks before the Mediation.

The Lead Negotiator should be at the Mediation throughout the whole day. It is easy to forget that the mediation sessions often go well into the evening.

In certain cases, for example claims involving public bodies and class actions, the Lead Negotiator may only have the power to make a recommendation. In these circumstances the following clause should be substituted:

> *"the Lead Negotiator(s) [for Party] will have full authority to make recommendations on terms of settlement on behalf of its Party".*

Professional advisers, particularly lawyers, can, and usually do, attend the Mediation. The advisers play an important role in the exchange of information, in supporting their clients (particularly individuals) in the negotiations, advising their clients on the legal implications of a settlement and in drawing up the settlement agreement.

## Exchange of information – paragraphs 7–8

Documentation which a Party wants the Mediator to keep confidential from the other Party(ies) (eg a counsel's opinion, an expert report not yet exchanged) must be clearly marked as such. It can be disclosed confidentially to the Mediator by the Party before or during the Mediation. It will not be disclosed by the Mediator or CEDR Solve without the express consent of the Party.

One of the advantages of ADR is that it can avoid the excessive disclosure process (including witness statements) which often blights litigation and arbitration. The Documents should be kept to the minimum necessary to understand the Party's case and to give the Mediator a good grasp of the issues. The Summaries should be similarly brief.

Should the Parties require CEDR Solve to conduct a simultaneous exchange of Case Summaries and Documents, the following wording is suggested:

> *"Each party will send to CEDR Solve at least two weeks before the Mediation, or such other date as may be agreed between the Parties and CEDR Solve, sufficient copies of:*

- *a concise summary ("the Case Summary") of its case in the Dispute; and*

- *all documents to which the Summary refers and any others to which it may want to refer in the Mediation ("the Documents"), which CEDR Solve will send simultaneously to the other Party(ies), the Mediator and Assistant Mediator."*

### The Mediation – paragraphs 9–12

The intention of paragraph 12 is that the Mediator will cease to play an entirely facilitative role only if the negotiations in the Mediation are deadlocked. Giving a settlement recommendation may be perceived by a Party as undermining the Mediator's neutrality and for this reason the Mediator may not agree to this course of action. Any recommendation will be without prejudice and will not be binding unless the Parties agree otherwise.

### Settlement agreement – paragraph 13

If no agreement is reached, it is nonetheless open to the Parties to adjourn the Mediation to another time and place. Experience shows that even where no agreement is reached during the Mediation itself, the Parties will often reach a settlement shortly after, as a result of the progress made during that Mediation.

### Termination – paragraph 14

A mediator may withdraw from the mediation at any time if, in their view, there is not a reasonable likelihood of the parties achieving a workable settlement; or if in their discretion there is any other reason that it would be inappropriate to continue with the mediation.

### Stay of proceedings – paragraph 15

Although a stay may engender a better climate for settlement, it is not essential that any proceedings relating to the Dispute be stayed. If they are stayed, it is the responsibility of the Parties and their legal advisers to consider and, if necessary, deal with the effect of any stay on limitation periods. Suggested wording for a stay, which can be incorporated into the Mediation Agreement, is:

*"No litigation or arbitration in relation to the Dispute is to be commenced [Any existing litigation or arbitration in relation to the Dispute is to be stayed] from the date of this agreement until the termination of the Mediation."*

*Confidentiality – paragraphs 16–20*

Documents which would in any event be disclosable will not become privileged by reason of having been referred to in the Mediation and will therefore still be disclosable. The position on this may depend on the relevant jurisdiction and it is the responsibility of the Parties and their legal advisers to consider and, if necessary, deal with this.

If either Party wishes to keep confidential the fact the Mediation is taking place or has taken place, paragraph 16 can be amended by replacing the wording *"save for the fact that the Mediation is to take place or has taken place"* with the wording*"including the fact that the Mediation is to take place or has taken place".*

*[Paragraph 19 provides an exception to the general requirement for confidentiality where all Parties consent to disclosure or where the Mediator reasonably considers that there are public interest or similar reasons that would require disclosure to be made; this would include any circumstances arising under the Proceeds of Crime Act 2002 or any similar legislation.]*

*Fees, expenses and costs – paragraphs 21–22*

The usual arrangement is for the Parties to share equally the fees and expenses of the procedure, but other arrangements are possible. A Party to a Dispute, which is reluctant to participate in mediation, may be persuaded to participate if the other Party(ies) agree to bear that Party's expenses. Parties may also amend the agreement to identify that the costs of mediation may be taken into account in any court orders if there is no settlement at the Mediation.

*International disputes – language and governing law/jurisdiction*

The Model Agreement can be easily adapted for international cross-border disputes by the addition in the Mediation Agreement of wording along the following lines:

**"Language**

*The language of the Mediation will be [English] . . . Any Party producing documents or participating in the Mediation in any other language will provide the necessary translations and interpretation facilities."*

**Governing law and jurisdiction**

*The Mediation Agreement shall be governed by, construed and take effect in accordance with, [English] law.*

*The courts of [England] shall have exclusive jurisdiction to settle any claim, dispute or matter of difference which may arise out of, or in connection with, the Mediation."*

Where the law is not English or the jurisdiction not England, the Mediation Agreement may need to be amended to ensure the structure, rights and obligations necessary for a mediation are applicable.

## 2 INDEPENDENT MEDIATOR AGREEMENT

*This format of agreement is used by Independent Mediators, a group of experienced commercial mediators operating as a centrally managed practice in London. Their website is www.independentmediators.co.uk.*

Mediation Number:

Date of Agreement:

THE PARTIES:

    A.  ("Party A")

    B.  ("Party B")

collectively referred to as "The Parties"

THE MEDIATOR:

("the Mediator")

THE DISPUTE:

IT IS AGREED THAT:

1.    The Mediation will take place on xxx; at xxx; commencing at 9.30am; and scheduled to finish at 5.30pm.

2.    The Parties will be represented at the Mediation:

    (a)  for Party A, by xxx and accompanied by those shown on the attached Mediation Details;

    (b)  for Party B, by xxx and accompanied by those shown on the attached Mediation Details.

3. The Parties will:

    (a) inform the Mediator and each other immediately if there is any change to their representatives and advisers or attendees at the Mediation;

    (b) ensure that their representatives have full and unlimited authority to negotiate, compromise and settle the Dispute on their behalf;

    (c) attempt to agree a bundle of relevant documents and supply the Mediator with all documents by the date shown on the attached Mediation Details;

    (d) exchange with each other and supply the Mediator with a confidential Mediation Statement by the date shown on the attached Mediation Details;

    (e) pay their respective share of the mediators fees within 14 days following the issue of an invoice by the Mediator following the Mediation. If the Parties agree to continue the Mediation at some other place or time, a further fee shall be payable.

4. The legal representatives are liable for their respective client's share of the costs of the Mediator and the Mediation in the same way as they are liable for the disbursements incurred in the course of litigation.

5. The Mediator will:

    (a) assist the Parties to compromise and resolve the Dispute during the Mediation;

    (b) determine procedure at the Mediation, in consultation with the Parties;

    (c) assist (if requested) in drawing up any settlement agreement;

    (d) decline hereafter to act for any Party in any capacity in connection with the Dispute;

    (e) maintain and respect the confidentiality of all information provided to him by the Parties, saveas may be required by law, whether under the Proceeds of Crime Act 2002 and/or any Regulations relating thereto or otherwise.

6. The Parties accept and agree that the Mediator acts as an independent contractor and not as an agent of or in any capacity for any Party, and that the Mediator has no personal or financial interest in the subject matter of the dispute.

7. No formal record or transcript of the Mediation shall be made.

8. If the Parties are unable to reach settlement during the Mediation, then if the Parties jointly request (and the Mediator agrees) the Mediator may provide a recommendation of possible terms of settlement, which shall not be binding upon the Parties. In making any such recommendation, the Mediator may take into account such matters as he considers appropriate in the circumstances.

9. No settlement agreement reached between the Parties as a result of the Mediation shall be legally binding until it has been reduced to writing and signed by or on behalf of the Parties.

10. The Mediation shall terminate when:

    (a) a written settlement agreement is executed by the Parties, or

    (b) written notice of withdrawal is given by any Party, or

    (c) the time set for the Mediation has expired without agreement for continuation or resumption, or

    (d) the Mediator decides that continuing the Mediation is unlikely to result in a settlement, or is undesirable or inappropriate for any other reason.

11. Everyone involved in any manner in the Mediation shall keep confidential and shall not use for any collateral or ulterior purpose any or all information of any nature produced for or arising in connection with the Mediation save as may be necessary to implement and/or enforce any settlement agreement.

12. All documents, correspondence or information (in any format) produced for or arising in connection with the Mediation will be treated as privileged, and shall not be admissible as evidence or be disclosable in any proceedings connected in any way with the subject matter of the Dispute, UNLESS such documents or information would have been admissible or disclosable in any event.

13. It is agreed that in no circumstances shall any Party or their advisers or representatives require the Mediator either to act as a witness in any proceedings connected in any way with the Mediation or the subject matter of the Dispute, or to disclose any documents or notes he may have prepared in connection with the Mediation, nor shall any steps be taken by any Party in any jurisdiction to compel the Mediator either to act in any such capacity or to disclose such documents or notes.

14. (a) Unless otherwise agreed in the Mediation, each Party shall bear its own costs and expenses arising out of the Mediation and each Party will pay its share of the expenses

and/or costs payable to the Mediator and to the Mediation Venue.

(b) These provisions are without prejudice to the rights of either party to seek to recover their costs of the mediation and their share of the Mediator's fees and expenses from the other party in the proceedings, as appropriate, if there is no resolution at the Mediation.

(c) In the event that one or other of the Parties cancels the mediation, the following proportion of the agreed fees will be payable:-

(1) If the cancellation is made less than twenty four hours before the date of the mediation, the full fees will be due and payable by each party, without prejudice to a Party's right to recover such sums from any Party it may consider to be at fault for the cancellation.

(2) If the cancellation is made less than four working days before the date of the mediation, half the fees will be due and payable by each party, without prejudice to a Party's right to recover such sums from any party it may consider to be at fault for the cancellation.

15. The Mediator shall not be liable to any Party or their representatives or advisers for any view expressed by him during or in connection with the mediation or for any act or omission in connection with his conduct of the Mediation.

16. The Mediation and this Agreement shall be governed by and construed in accordance with English law, and the Parties agree that the High Court of Justice, London shall have exclusive jurisdiction to settle any claim, dispute or matter of difference which may arise out of or in connection with the Mediation and/or this Agreement.

**SIGNED:**

**Party A**

**Party B**

**Mediator**

# Model Settlement Agreement & Tomlin Order

## Model Settlement Agreement

**Date**

**Parties**

_____ ("Party A")

[Address]¹_____

_____ ("Party B")

[Address]²_____

[_____ ("Party C") etc.]
(jointly "the Parties")

### [Background]³

The Parties have agreed to settle "the Dispute" which:

- is being litigated/arbitrated [court/arbitration reference] ("the Action")⁴

- has been the subject of a CEDR Solve mediation today ("the Mediation").

---

For further information please contact CEDR on +44 (0)20 7536 6000 or visit *www.cedr.co.uk*

1 Not strictly necessary.
2 Not strictly necessary.
3 Not strictly necessary but may be useful for setting up definitions.
4 Omit this wording and para 4 if there are no court proceedings.

**Terms**

It is agreed as follows:

(1) [A will deliver . . . . . . . . to B at . . . . . . . . by not later than 4 o'clock on 25 December . . .]⁵

(2) [B will pay £ . . . . . . . . to A by not later than 4 o'clock on 25 December . . . by direct bank transfer to . . . . bank sort code . . . account number . . . . . .]

(3) . . . . . . . . . . . . . . . . . . . . . . . . . . . . . . . . . . . . . . . . . . . . .

(4a) The Action will be stayed and the parties will consent to an order in the terms of the attached Tomlin Order precedent [see attachment].

OR

(4b) The Action will be dismissed with no order as to costs.

(5) This Agreement is in full and final settlement of any causes of action whatsoever which the Parties [and any subsidiaries . . . . of the Parties] have against each other.

(6) This agreement supersedes all previous agreements between the parties [in respect of matters the subject of the Mediation].⁶

(7) If any dispute arises out of this Agreement, the Parties will attempt to settle it by mediation⁷ before resorting to any other means of dispute resolution. To institute any such mediation a party must give notice to the mediator of the Mediation. Insofar as possible the terms of the Mediation Agreement will apply to any such further mediation. If no legally binding settlement of this dispute is reached within [28] days from the date of the notice to the Mediator, either party may [institute court proceedings/refer the dispute to arbitration under the rules of . . .].

(8) The Parties will keep confidential and not use for any collateral or ulterior purpose the terms of this Agreement [except insofar as is necessary to implement and enforce any of its terms].

(9) This Agreement shall be governed by, construed and take effect in accordance with [English] law. The courts of [England] shall have exclusive jurisdiction to settle any claim,

---

5 Be as specific as possible, for example, how, by when, etc.

6 Only necessary if there have been previous agreements.

7 Alternatively, negotiation at Chief Executive level, followed by mediation if negotiations do not result in settlement within a specified time.

dispute or matter of difference which may arise out of, or in connection with this agreement.[8]

**Signed**

_____

for and on behalf of[9]_____

_____

for and on behalf of[10]_____

Note: This Model Agreement and attached precedent order is for guidance only. Any agreement based on it will need to adapted to the particular circumstances and legal requirements of the settlement to which it relates. Wherever possible any such agreement should be drafted/approved by each party's lawyer. Although the mediator is likely to be involved in help-ing the parties to draft acceptable terms, the mediator is not responsible for the drafting of the agreement and does not need to be a party to it. [See also provisions of mediation agreement which, if it is based on the CEDR Model Mediation Agreement, will deal with mediator liability, confidentially etc. and should not need to be repeated in this agreement.]

## Attachment to Model Settlement Agreement: Tomlin Order

[Action heading]

UPON hearing . . . . . .

**By consent**

**IT IS ORDERED** that all further proceedings in this case be stayed upon the terms set out in the Schedule to this Order the Settlement Agreement between Parties dated . . . , an original of which is held by each of the Parties' solicitors [*or* CEDR Solve/the Mediator] except for the purpose of enforcing the terms of that Agreement as set out below.

**AND IT IS FURTHER ORDERED** that either Party/any of the Parties may apply to the court to enforce the terms of the said Agreement [or to claim for breach of it] without the need to commence new proceedings.

---

8 Usually not necessary where parties are located in same country and subject matter of agreement relates to one country.

9 Not necessary where the party signing is an individual.

10 Not necessary where the party signing is an individual.

**AND IT IS FURTHER ORDERED** that [each Party bear its own costs].

**WE CONSENT** to an order in these terms

_____[Black & White], Claimant's Solicitors

_____[Red & Green], Defendant's Solicitors

[SCHEDULE OF TERMS OF AGREEMENT]

1.

2.

# Model ADR Contract Clauses

## 1 CEDR Model ADR Contract Clauses

*The full CEDR guide to drafting ADR contract clauses can be found on the CEDR website at www.cedr.com/library/documents/contractclauses.*

The clauses are also available on the CEDR website in the following languages: in French, German, Italian, Mandarin, Russian and Spanish. These can be found at *www.cedr.co.uk/internationalclauses.*

1

### 1.1 Simple core mediation clause

*Core wording*

*'If any dispute arises in connection with this agreement, the parties will attempt to settle it by mediation in accordance with the CEDR Model Mediation Procedure. Unless otherwise agreed between the parties, the mediator will be nominated by CEDR.'*

*Notes*

This clause by itself should be sufficient to give the parties the opportunity to attempt to settle any dispute by mediation. The CEDR Model Mediation Procedure provides clear guidelines on the conduct of the mediation and requires the parties to enter into an agreement based on the Model Mediation Agreement in relation to its conduct. This will deal with points such as the nature of the dispute, the identity of the mediator and where and when the mediation is to take place. If an ADR/mediation clause is sufficiently certain and clear as to the process to be used it should be enforceable. The reference in the clause to a model mediation procedure should give it that necessary certainty: *Cable & Wireless Plc v IBM United Kingdom Ltd* [2002] EWHC Ch 2059.

---

1  For further information please contact CEDR on +44 (0) 20 7536 6000 or visit *www.cedr.co.uk*

## 1.2 Simple core mediation clause including time and notification

*Core wording*

*'If any dispute arises in connection with this agreement, the parties will attempt to settle it by mediation in accordance with the CEDR Model Mediation Procedure. Unless otherwise agreed between the parties, the mediator will be nominated by CEDR. To initiate the mediation a party must give notice in writing ('ADR notice') to the other party[ies] to the dispute requesting a mediation. A copy of the request should be sent to CEDR.*

The mediation will start not later than [ ] days after the date of the ADR notice.'

*Notes*

This wording is to address the concern that mediation should provide a quick solution rather than delay an outcome. It evidences intention that a mediation should happen quickly and provides a trigger for commencement of the mediation with the service of the notice, including a copy to CEDR so that it can assist the parties to move the process as quickly as possible.

## 1.3 Simple core mediation clause including time, plus reference to court proceedings in parallel

*Core wording*

*'If any dispute arises in connection with this agreement, the parties will attempt to settle it by mediation in accordance with the CEDR Model Mediation Procedure. Unless otherwise agreed between the parties, the mediator will be nominated by CEDR. To initiate the mediation a party must give notice in writing ('ADR notice') to the other party[ies] to the dispute requesting a mediation. A copy of the request should be sent to CEDR. The mediation will start not later than [ ] days after the date of the ADR notice. The commencement of a mediation will not prevent the parties commencing or continuing court proceedings/an arbitration.'*

*Notes*

Strictly this wording is not necessary as nothing in the core mediation wording prevents the issuance of court proceedings. Further, CEDR's Model Mediation Procedure, Clause 15, provides that litigation or arbitration may commence or continue unless the parties are otherwise agreed. The inclusion of this wording in the contract clause may however allay the concern if a party wishes to retain the ability to resort to court proceedings.

## 1.4 Simple core mediation clause including time, plus reference to no court or arbitration proceedings until mediation terminated

*Core wording*

'*If any dispute arises in connection with this agreement, the parties will attempt to settle it by mediation in accordance with the CEDR Model Mediation Procedure. Unless otherwise agreed between the parties, the mediator will be nominated by CEDR. To initiate the mediation a party must give notice in writing ('ADR notice') to the other party [ies] to the dispute requesting a mediation. A copy of the request should be sent to CEDR. The mediation will start not later than [ ] days after the date of the ADR notice. No party may commence any court proceedings/arbitration in relation to any dispute arising out of this agreement until it has attempted to settle the dispute by mediation and either the mediation has terminated or the other party has failed to participate in the mediation, provided that the right to issue proceedings is not prejudiced by a delay.*'

*Notes*

The rationale for this wording is that an ADR contract clause is intended to curtail court proceedings, etc, and that for them to run in parallel may not be conducive to any attempt to settle. The prospects of settlement may be higher before the lines of battle have been drawn by the hostile steps of commencing court proceedings/arbitration. Bear in mind that, under the English jurisdiction, the courts always retain the ability to issue interim relief but they will stay proceedings to allow parties to honour an agreement to mediate.

## 1.5 Multi-tiered process

*Core wording*

'*If any dispute arises in connection with this agreement, directors or other senior representatives of the parties with authority to settle the dispute will, within [ ] days of a written request from one party to the other, meet in a good faith effort to resolve the dispute.*

*If the dispute is not resolved at that meeting, the parties will attempt to settle it by mediation in accordance with the CEDR Model Mediation Procedure. Unless otherwise agreed between the parties, the mediator will be nominated by CEDR. To initiate the mediation a party must give notice in writing ('ADR notice') to the other party(ies) to the dispute requesting a mediation.*

*A copy of the request should be sent to CEDR Solve. The mediation will start not later than [ ] days after the date of the ADR notice.'*

[The draftsperson has the choice to add Version 1, referring to court proceedings in parallel, or Version 2, no court proceedings until the mediation is completed.]

Version 1: 'The commencement of a mediation will not prevent the parties commencing or continuing court proceedings/an arbitration.' Version 2: 'No party may commence any court proceedings/arbitration in relation to any dispute arising out of this agreement until it has attempted to settle the dispute by mediation and either the mediation has terminated or the other party has failed to participate in the mediation, provided that the right to issue proceedings is not prejudiced by a delay.'

*Notes*

This adds an extra step providing for negotiations before mediation and the choice is then to have arbitration or litigation in parallel or deferred until after the mediation has effectively terminated.

## 1.6 International core mediation clause

*Core wording*

*"If any dispute arises in connection with this agreement, the parties will attempt to settle it by mediation in accordance with the CEDR Model Mediation Procedure. Unless otherwise agreed between the parties, the mediator will be nominated by CEDR. The mediation will take place in [city/country of neither/none of the parties] and the language of the mediation will be [ ]. The Mediation Agreement referred to in the Model Procedure shall be governed by, and construed and take effect in accordance with the substantive law of [England and Wales]. The courts of [England] shall have exclusive jurisdiction to settle any claim, dispute or matter of difference which may arise out of, or in connection with, the mediation. If the dispute is not settled by mediation within [ ] days of commencement of the mediation or within such further period as the parties may agree in writing, the dispute shall be referred to and finally resolved by arbitration. CEDR shall be the appointing body and administer the arbitration. CEDR shall apply the UNCITRAL rules in force at the time arbitration is initiated. In any arbitration commenced pursuant to this clause, the number of arbitrators shall be [1–3] and the seat or legal place of arbitration shall be [London, England]."*

*Notes*

This model clause should be suitable for international contracts, ie contracts between parties in different jurisdictions, but consideration should be given to including provisions relating to the location/language of the mediation, as well as the governing law and jurisdiction applicable to the mediation agreement along the lines of this paragraph. The clause refers to arbitration under CEDR's auspices if mediation does not resolve the dispute, but another arbitral institution and its rules may be identified where parties agree.

The clause can be amended to refer to 'CEDR, London' if the draftsperson believes this will specify more clearly where to find CEDR for international parties.

# 2 ICC (International Chamber & Commerce) ADR draft clauses

The ICC's ADR Rules are set out in full on the ICC's website at http://www.iccwbo.org/court/arbitration/id4199/index.html.

Also of interest may be the UNCITRAL (UN Commission on International Trade) Conciliation Rules 1980, and the 2002 UNCITRAL Model Law on International Conciliation, with a Guide to enactment and use, adopted in 2002 by the UN General Assembly, both available on the UNCITRAL website www.uncitral.org.

# Suggested International Chamber of Commerce (ICC) ADR clauses

Four alternative ADR clauses are suggested by ICC. They are not model clauses, but suggestions, which parties may adapt to their needs, if required. Their enforceability under the law applicable to the contract should be evaluated.

## 2.1 Optional ADR

"The parties may at any time, without prejudice to any other proceedings, seek to settle any dispute arising out of or in connection with the present contract in accordance with the ICC ADR Rules."

## 2.2 Obligation to consider ADR

"In the event of any dispute arising out of or in connection with the present contract, the parties agree in the first instance to discuss and consider submitting the matter to settlement proceedings under the ICC ADR Rules."

## 2.3 Obligation to submit dispute to ADR with an automatic expiration mechanism

"In the event of any dispute arising out of or in connection with the present contract, the parties agree to submit the matter to settlement proceedings under the ICC ADR Rules. If the dispute has not been settled pursuant to the said Rules within 45 days following the filing of a Request for ADR or within such other period as the parties may agree in writing, the parties shall have no further obligations under this paragraph."

## 2.4 Obligation to submit dispute to ADR, followed by ICC arbitration as required

"In the event of any dispute arising out of or in connection with the present contract, the parties agree to submit the matter to settlement proceedings under the ICC ADR Rules. If the dispute has not been settled pursuant to the said Rules within 45 days following the filing of a Request for ADR or within such other period as the parties may agree in writing, such dispute shall be finally settled under the Rules of Arbitration of the International Chamber of Commerce by one or more arbitrators appointed in accordance with the said Rules of Arbitration."

# EU Directive 2004/251

Brussels, 22.10.2004
COM(2004) 718 final

2004/0251 (COD)

Proposal for a

## DIRECTIVE OF THE EUROPEAN PARLIAMENT AND OF THE COUNCIL

## on certain aspects of mediation in civil and commercial matters {SEC(2004) 1314}

(presented by the Commission)
### EXPLANATORY MEMORANDUM

## 1  SCOPE AND OBJECTIVES OF THE PROPOSAL

### 1.1  Objective

*1.1.1  Ensuring better access to justice*

Better access to justice is one of the key objectives of the EU's policy to establish an area of freedom, security and justice, where individuals and businesses should not be prevented or discouraged from exercising their rights by the incompatibility or complexity of legal and administrative systems in the Member States. The concept of access to justice should, in this context, include promoting access to adequate dispute resolution processes for individuals and business, and not just access to the judicial system.

The proposed directive contributes to this objective by facilitating access to dispute resolution through two types of provisions: first, provisions that aim at ensuring a sound relationship between mediation and judicial proceedings, by establishing minimum common rules in the Community on a number of key aspects of civil procedure. Secondly, by providing the necessary tools for the courts of the Member States to actively promote the use of mediation, without nevertheless making mediation compulsory or subject to specific sanctions.

Provisions touching the mediation process or the appointment or accreditation of mediators have been excluded from the proposed directive. Having regard to the reactions to the Green paper of 2002 and current developments at national level, it is not clear that legislation is the preferred policy option as regards this type of provision. While excluding regulatory measures concerning the mediation procedure itself from this proposal the Commission has instead sought to encourage self-regulatory initiatives and is seeking to continue to do so through the proposed directive also.

In the consultations on the preliminary draft of this proposal most respondents endorsed the overall approach of the draft concerning the issues covered as well as the issues excluded from it. Compared to the preliminary draft certain changes, mainly of a technical nature, have been made to specific provisions and are further explained in the annex.

### 1.1.2   A sound relationship between mediation and civil proceedings

What have been retained for this proposal are essentially matters which cannot be adequately addressed through market-based solutions. This concerns notably civil procedural rules which may impact on the use of mediation as well as on its effectiveness. The interaction between mediation and traditional civil proceedings can take place at several occasions, for example:

- The parties consider use of mediation immediately after the dispute has arisen, as an alternative to launching civil proceedings; if the parties do chose to use mediation and fail to reach a settlement agreement, civil proceedings are launched after the termination of the mediation;
- If a settlement agreement is reached through mediation, one of the parties may fail to honour the agreement, calling for civil proceedings to be launched anyway;
- The parties launch civil proceedings immediately after the dispute has arisen, without having (yet) considered the possibility of mediation.

At present the interaction between mediation and civil proceedings presents a number of uncertain elements, due to the absence of or discrepancies between national procedural laws, elements which make themselves known with particular force in situations involving cross-border elements. Even if mediation may be the most suitable form of dispute resolution in a given case the parties may therefore opt for traditional civil proceedings in view of these uncertainties. A stable and predictable legal framework should contribute to putting mediation on an equal footing with judicial proceedings where factors related to the specific dispute play the most significant role for the parties in determining their choice of dispute resolution method. Such a framework should also help to preserve the possibility for the parties to solve their dispute through judicial proceedings even if mediation is attempted.

### 1.1.3    Promoting the use of mediation

The value of increasing the use of mediation rests principally in the advantages of the dispute resolution mechanism itself: a quicker, simpler and more cost-efficient way to solve disputes, which allows for taking into account a wider range of interests of the parties, with a greater chance of reaching an agreement which will be voluntarily respected, and which preserves an amicable and sustainable relationship between them. The Commission believes that mediation holds an untapped potential as a dispute resolution method and as a means of providing access to justice for individuals and business.

The role of the Community in directly promoting mediation is however by necessity limited and the only concrete measure to promote mediation contained in the proposal is the obligation for Member States to allow courts to suggest mediation to the parties. Ensuring a sound relationship between mediation and judicial proceedings will however indirectly contribute to promoting mediation also.

The pursuit of the objectives of this proposal can not take in place in isolation without regard to the very provision of mediation services. The question of quality of mediation services must therefore be addressed together with, and as a function of, the other provisions of the proposed directive which must operate with a sufficient level of mutual trust between the Member States in cross-border situations.

### 1.1.4    The relationship with the organisation of the judicial systems of the Member States

One of the often quoted benefits of mediation is that its increased use can offload pressure on the court system, thereby reducing what are often long delays in case-handling and possibly allowing for savings of public resources. As the proposed directive seeks to promote the use of mediation, it could indeed have a positive impact in this sense. This is however not pursued as an independent objective, for several reasons. First, the organisation of the judicial system is the sole competence of the Member States. Secondly, and most importantly, mediation has a value in itself as a dispute resolution method, to which citizens and business should have easy access and which deserves to be promoted independently of its value in off-loading pressure on the court system. The Commission does not see mediation as an alternative to court proceedings; it is rather one

329

of several dispute resolution methods available in a modern society and which may be the most suited for some, but certainly not all, disputes. Moreover, it should be stressed that the availability of ADRs in general can not in any way detract from the obligation of Member States to maintain an effective and fair legal system that meets the requirements of the European Convention of Human Rights, which forms one of the central pillars of a democratic society.

### 1.1.5 Impact assessment

A preliminary impact assessment of this proposal was carried out in the context of the Commission's annual policy strategy for 2004. The proposal has not been selected for an extended impact assessment. The proposed directive aims at increasing the use of mediation in the EU, which will have beneficial economic effects by lowering transaction costs for individuals and business, through a quicker and more cost-efficient resolution of disputes. Mediation can also contribute to more sustainable economic and social trends in preserving the relationship between the parties after the dispute has been solved, in contrast to the often disruptive effects of solving a dispute through an adjudicatory process. The consultation process and other preparatory steps are described in the annex. In terms of alternative policy options the proposed directive contains mainly rules on civil procedure, and the results can not be achieved using another policy instrument.

### 1.2 Legal basis

The objective and content of this proposed directive fall squarely within the scope of Article 65 TEC since it concerns civil procedural rules, where the provision on quality and training in Article 4 is ancillary to the other provisions. The proposed directive is necessary for the proper functioning of the internal market in view of the need to ensure access to dispute resolution mechanisms for individuals and business exercising the four freedoms and in view of the need to ensure the freedom to provide and to receive mediation services.

As has been stressed in the description of the objectives of the proposal the need for Community action in this field stems from the need to ensure legal certainty throughout the duration of a dispute regardless of the presence of cross-border elements at one stage or another. To ensure a coherent legal framework it is therefore necessary to address key aspects of the whole chain of possible events that can follow after the dispute has arisen, having regard to any possible scenario (success/failure of the mediation, settlement agreement followed by both parties or not, etc).

In the context of ADR the impact of cross-border elements is potentially greater than when considering measures relating to civil proceedings in isolation, since it is necessary to have regard to relevant factors at the time of the mediation as well as at the time of any subsequent civil proceedings, including the circumstance that these factors may change in the meantime. For example, cross-border elements may come from the domicile or place of business of one or both of the parties, the place of the mediation, or the place of the competent court. The agreement to mediate may in itself be governed by a different law than that which governs the original legal or contractual relationship between the parties, and an ensuing settlement agreement may be governed by the law of yet another third country. The settlement agreement may have to be enforced in yet another Member State depending on, for example, the location of the debtor's assets at the time when enforcement is sought.

However, it would not be feasible to restrict the scope of the proposal so as to only aim at removing obstacles created by cross-border elements or to ease the resolution of only those disputes displaying a cross-border element, however defined.

In assessing the suitability of mediation as a dispute resolution method for a given dispute, cross-border elements make up for only one of several relevant circumstances to be taken into account. Other circumstances include the nature of the dispute and the merits of the case as well as factors related to costs, delay and prospects of success. Promoting mediation in relation to those disputes that display a cross-border element only would therefore be arbitrary and create a risk of discriminatory effects, since the courts would suggest mediation to some parties only depending on their place of residence. A restriction of this type will undoubtedly entail a substantial reduction in the practical impact of the proposed directive also. Making the applicability of the civil procedural rules contained in the proposed directive subject to the presence of cross-border elements would rather lead to increased legal uncertainty. Alternatively such a restriction in scope may leave the applicability of the directive in the hands of the parties, who could introduce cross-border elements through their choice of mediator or court for the dispute in order to benefit from the rules laid down by the directive.

The proposed directive will form an important part of the legal framework for mediation services in the Community, as concerns the freedom to provide services in another Member State as well as the freedom to receive services. A limitation in scope to cross-border situations would lead to the creation of two parallel legal regimes, possibly even different standards as concern the provision and receipt of mediation services, with a risk of discriminatory effects for users as well as providers of mediation services. Such effects run counter to the principles of the internal market as well as the efforts of the Community to simplify the regulatory framework for individuals and business.

In conclusion the Commission considers that introducing an explicit condition of cross-border implications would invalidate the objectives of the proposed directive and be counterproductive to the proper functioning of the internal market. The directive must therefore apply to all situations regardless of the presence of cross-border elements at the time of the mediation or at the time of the judicial proceedings.

## 1.3 Subsidiarity and proportionality

In view of the need for legal certainty and predictability in situations involving the relationship between mediation and civil proceedings in situations displaying a cross-border element and the need to ensure the proper functioning of the internal market for the provision of and receipt of mediation services the objectives of this proposal cannot be sufficiently accomplished by the Member States. Measures taken at Community level will be more effective compared to individual initiatives taken by each Member State, for reasons of coherence and reasons of providing certain basic uniform rules applicable in cross-border situations as well as in domestic cases.

The provisions of the proposal are strictly limited to what is necessary to reach the objectives. A directive has been chosen as the most appropriate instrument since the provisions are designed to achieve certain specific objectives while leaving the means for how to reach those objectives to Member States' discretion. The proposal also confines itself to issues which can only be solved through legislation while inversely issues where market-based solutions are feasible have been excluded from the scope.

## 2  BACKGROUND TO THE PROPOSAL, CONSULTATION WITH INTERESTED PARTIES, AND COMMENTS ON MAIN PROVISIONS

The staff working paper annexed to this proposal provides further information on these issues.

2004/0251 (COD)

Proposal for a

## DIRECTIVE OF THE EUROPEAN PARLIAMENT AND OF THE COUNCIL

### on certain aspects of mediation in civil and commercial matters

THE EUROPEAN PARLIAMENT AND THE COUNCIL
OF THE EUROPEAN UNION,

Having regard to the Treaty establishing the European Community, and in particular Article 61 (c) and the second indent of Article 67(5) thereof,

Having regard to the proposal from the Commission,

Having regard to the opinion of the European Economic and Social Committee,

Acting in accordance with the procedure laid down in Article 251 of the Treaty,

Whereas:
(1)    The Community has set itself the objective of maintaining and developing an area of freedom, security and justice, in which the free movement of persons is ensured. To this end, the Community is to adopt, inter alia, measures in the field of judicial cooperation in civil matters that are necessary for the proper functioning of the internal market.

(2)    The European Council meeting in Tampere on 15 and 16 October 1999 called for, in relation to better access to justice in Europe, for alternative, extra-judicial procedures to be created by Member States.

(3)    The Council adopted conclusions on alternative methods of settling disputes under civil and commercial law in 2000, stating that the establishment of basic principles in this area is an essential step towards enabling the appropriate development and operation of extrajudicial procedures for the settlement of disputes in civil and commercial matters so as to simplify and improve access to justice.

(4)    The European Commission presented a Green paper in 2002, taking stock of the existing situation as concerns ADRs in Europe and initiating wide-spread consultations with Member States and interested parties on possible measures to promote the use of mediation.

(5)  The objective of ensuring better access to justice, as part of the policy of the European Union to establish an area of freedom, security and justice should encompass access to judicial as well as extra-judicial dispute resolution methods. This directive should contribute to the proper functioning of the internal market, in particular as concerns the provision and receipt of mediation services.

(6)  Mediation can provide a cost-efficient and quick extra-judicial resolution of disputes in civil and commercial matters through processes tailored to the needs of the parties. Settlement agreements reached through mediation are more likely to be enforced voluntarily and are more likely to preserve an amicable and sustainable relationship between the parties. These benefits become even more pronounced in situations displaying cross-border elements.

(7)  Framework legislation, addressing key aspects of civil procedure in particular, is therefore necessary to promote the further use of mediation and to ensure that parties having recourse to mediation can rely on a predictable legal framework.

(8)  This directive should cover processes where two or more parties to a dispute are assisted by a mediator to reach an amicable agreement on the settlement of the dispute, but exclude processes of an adjudicatory nature such as arbitration, ombudsmen schemes, consumer complaint schemes, expert determination or processes administered by bodies issuing a formal recommendation, be it legally binding or not, as to the resolution of the dispute.

(9)  A minimum degree of compatibility of civil procedural rules is necessary as concerns the effect of mediation on limitation periods and how the confidentiality of the mediator will be protected in any subsequent judicial proceedings. The possibility for the court to refer the parties to mediation should also be covered, while retaining the principle that mediation is a voluntary process.

(10) Mediation should not be regarded as a poorer alternative to judicial proceedings in the sense that settlement agreements are dependant on the good will of the parties for their enforcement. It is therefore necessary to ensure that all Member States provide for a procedure whereby a settlement agreement can be confirmed in a judgment, decision or authentic instrument by a court or public authority.

(11) Such a possibility will allow for a settlement agreement to be recognised and enforced across the Union, under the conditions

laid down by Community instruments on mutual recognition and enforcement of judgments and decisions.

(12) To ensure the necessary trust between the Member States in the respect of confidentiality, suspension of limitation periods, and recognition and enforcement of settlement agreements, effective quality control mechanisms must be put in place concerning the provision of mediation services and training of mediators.

(13) These mechanisms and measures, which shall be defined by the Member States and may include having recourse to market-based solutions, should aim at preserving the flexibility of the mediation process and the private autonomy of the parties. The Commission shall encourage self-regulatory measures at Community level through, for example, development of a European code of conduct addressing key aspects of the mediation process.

(14) In the field of consumer protection, the Commission adopted in 2001 a formal recommendation which establishes minimum quality criteria that out-of-court bodies involved in the consensual resolution of consumer disputes should offer to their users. It is advisable that any mediators or organisation concerned by the recommendation respect its principles. In order to ensure the dissemination of information concerning these bodies, the Commission is setting up a database of out-of-court schemes that Member States consider as respecting the principles of the recommendation.

(15) This directive respects the fundamental rights and observes the principles recognised in particular by the Charter of Fundamental Rights of the European Union. In particular, it seeks to ensure full respect for the right to a fair trial as recognised in Article 47 of the Charter.

(16) Since the objectives of this directive cannot be sufficiently achieved by the Member States and can therefore, by reason of the scale of effects of the action, be better achieved at Community level, the Community may adopt measures in accordance with the principle of subsidiarity as set out in Article 5 of the Treaty. In accordance with the principle of proportionality, as set out in that Article, this Directive does not go beyond what is necessary in order to achieve those objectives.

(17) [In accordance with Article 3 of the Protocol on the position of the United Kingdom and Ireland, annexed to the Treaty on European Union and the Treaty establishing the European Community, the United Kingdom and Ireland have notified their wish to take part in the adoption and application of this

Directive./In accordance with Articles 1 and 2 of the Protocol on the position of the United Kingdom and Ireland, annexed to the Treaty on European Union and the Treaty establishing the European Community, the United Kingdom and Ireland do not take part in the adoption of this Directive, which is therefore not binding on those Member States.]

(18) In accordance with Articles 1 and 2 of the Protocol on the position of Denmark annexed to the Treaty on European Union and the Treaty establishing the European Community, Denmark does not take part in the adoption of this Directive, and is therefore not bound by it or subject to its application.

HAVE ADOPTED THIS DIRECTIVE:

*Article 1 – Objective and scope*

1. The objective of this directive is to facilitate access to dispute resolution by promoting the use of mediation and by ensuring a sound relationship between mediation and judicial proceedings.

2. This directive shall apply in civil and commercial matters.

3. In this directive, "Member State" shall mean Member States with the exception of Denmark.

*Article 2 – Definitions*

For the purposes of this Directive the following definitions shall apply:

(a) "Mediation" shall mean any process, however named or referred to, where two or more parties to a dispute are assisted by a third party to reach an agreement on the settlement of the dispute, and regardless of whether the process is initiated by the parties, suggested or ordered by a court or prescribed by the national law of a Member State.
It shall not include attempts made by the judge to settle a dispute within the course of judicial proceedings concerning that dispute.

(b) "Mediator" shall mean any third party conducting a mediation, regardless of the denomination or profession of that third party in the Member State concerned and of the way the third party has been appointed or requested to conduct the mediation.

*Article 3 – Referral to mediation*

1. A court before which an action is brought may, when appropriate and having regard to all circumstances of the case, invite the

parties to use mediation in order to settle the dispute. The court may in any event require the parties to attend an information session on the use of mediation.

2. This directive is without prejudice to national legislation making the use of mediation compulsory or subject to incentives or sanctions, whether before or after judicial proceedings have started, provided that such legislation does not impede on the right of access to the judicial system, in particular in situations where one of the parties is resident in a Member State other than that of the court.

### Article 4 – Ensuring the quality of mediation

1. The Commission and the Member States shall promote and encourage the development of and adherence to voluntary codes of conduct by mediators and organisations providing mediation services, at Community as well as at national level, as well as other effective quality control mechanisms concerning the provision of mediation services.

2. Member States shall promote and encourage the training of mediators in order to allow parties in dispute to choose a mediator who will be able to effectively conduct a mediation in the manner expected by the parties.

### Article 5 – Enforcement of settlement agreements

1. Member States shall ensure that, upon request of the parties, a settlement agreement reached as a result of a mediation can be confirmed in a judgment, decision, authentic instrument or any other form by a court or public authority that renders the agreement enforceable in a similar manner as a judgment under national law, provided that the agreement is not contrary to European law or to national law in the Member State where the request is made.

2. Member States shall inform the Commission of the courts or public authorities that are competent for receiving a request in accordance with paragraph 1.

### Article 6 – Admissibility of evidence in civil judicial proceedings

1. Mediators, as well as any person involved in the administration of mediation services, shall not in civil judicial proceedings give testimony or evidence regarding any of the following:

   (a) An invitation by a party to engage in mediation or the fact that a party was willing to participate in mediation;

(b) Views expressed or suggestions made by a party in a mediation in respect of a possible settlement of the dispute;

(c) Statements or admissions made by a party in the course of the mediation;

(d) Proposals made by the mediator;

(e) The fact that a party had indicated its willingness to accept a proposal for a settlement made by the mediator;

(f) A document prepared solely for purposes of the mediation.

2. Paragraph 1 shall apply irrespective of the form of the information or evidence referred to therein.

3. The disclosure of the information referred to in paragraph 1 shall not be ordered by a court or other judicial authority in civil judicial proceedings and, if such information is offered as evidence in contravention of paragraph 1, that evidence shall be treated as inadmissible. Nevertheless, such information may be disclosed or admitted in evidence

(a) to the extent required for the purposes of implementation or enforcement of a settlement agreement reached as a direct result of the mediation,

(b) for overriding considerations of public policy, in particular when required to ensure the protection of children or to prevent harm to the physical or psychological integrity of a person, or

(c) if the mediator and the parties agree thereto.

4. The provisions of paragraphs 1, 2 and 3 shall apply whether or not the judicial proceedings relate to the dispute that is or was the subject matter of the mediation.

5. Subject to paragraph 1, evidence that is otherwise admissible in judicial proceedings does not become inadmissible as a consequence of having been used in a mediation.

*Article 7 – Suspension of limitation periods*

1. The running of any period of prescription or limitation regarding the claim that is the subject matter of the mediation shall be suspended as of when, after the dispute has arisen:

(a) the parties agree to use mediation,

(b) the use of mediation is ordered by a court, or

(c) an obligation to use mediation arises under the national law of a Member State.

2. Where the mediation has ended without a settlement agreement, the period resumes running from the time the mediation ended without a settlement agreement, counting from the date when one or both of the parties or the mediator declares that the mediation is terminated or effectively withdraws from it. The period shall in any event extend for at least one month from the date when it resumes running, except when it concerns a period within which an action must be brought to prevent that a provisional or similar measure ceases to have effect or is revoked.

### *Article 8 – Implementing provisions*

The Commission shall publish information on the competent courts and authorities communicated by the Member States pursuant to Article 5(2).

### *Article 9 – Transposition*

1. Member States shall bring into force the laws, regulations and administrative provisions necessary to comply with this Directive by 1 September 2007 at the latest. They shall forthwith inform the Commission thereof.

2. When Member States adopt those provisions, they shall contain a reference to this Directive or be accompanied by such a reference on the occasion of their official publication. Member States shall determine how such reference is to be made.

### *Article 10 – Entry into force*

This Directive shall enter into force on the twentieth day following that of its publication in the *Official Journal of the European Union*.

### *Article 11 - Addressees*

This Directive is addressed to the Member States.

Done at Brussels,

*For the European Parliament*          *For the Council*
*The President*                        *The President*

339

*Appendix E*

# European Code of Conduct for Mediators

*This code of conduct sets out a number of principles to which individual mediators can voluntarily decide to commit, under their own responsibility. It is intended to be applicable to all kinds of mediation in civil and commercial matters.*

*Organisations providing mediation services can also make such a commitment, by asking mediators acting under the auspices of their organisation to respect the code. Organisations have the opportunity to make available information on the measures they are taking to support the respect of the code by individual mediators through, for example, training, evaluation and monitoring.*

*For the purposes of the code mediation is defined as any process where two or more parties agree to the appointment of a third-party – hereinafter "the mediator" – to help the parties to solve a dispute by reaching an agreement without adjudication and regardless of how that process may be called or commonly referred to in each Member State.*

*Adherence to the code is without prejudice to national legislation or rules regulating individual professions.*

*Organisations providing mediation services may wish to develop more detailed codes adapted to their specific context or the types of mediation services they offer, as well as with regard to specific areas such as family mediation or consumer mediation.*

## 1  COMPETENCE AND APPOINTMENT OF MEDIATORS

### 1.1  Competence

Mediators shall be competent and knowledgeable in the process of mediation. Relevant factors shall include proper training and continuous updating of their education and practice in mediation skills, having regard to any relevant standards or accreditation schemes.

---

© European Commission. For further information please visit *www.ec.europa.eu*

### 1.2 Appointment

The mediator will confer with the parties regarding suitable dates on which the mediation may take place. The mediator shall satisfy him/herself as to his/her background and competence to conduct the mediation before accepting the appointment and, upon request, disclose information concerning his/her background and experience to the parties.

### 1.3 Advertising/promotion of the mediator's services

Mediators may promote their practice, in a professional, truthful and dignified way.

## 2 INDEPENDENCE AND IMPARTIALITY

### 2.1 Independence and neutrality

The mediator must not act, or, having started to do so, continue to act, before having disclosed any circumstances that may, or may be seen to, affect his or her independence or conflict of interests. The duty to disclose is a continuing obligation throughout the process.

Such circumstances shall include

- any personal or business relationship with one of the parties,
- any financial or other interest, direct or indirect, in the outcome of the mediation, or – the mediator, or a member of his or her firm, having acted in any capacity other than mediator for one of the parties.

In such cases the mediator may only accept or continue the mediation provided that he/she is certain of being able to carry out the mediation with full independence and neutrality in order to guarantee full impartiality and that the parties explicitly consent.

### 2.2 Impartiality

The mediator shall at all times act, and endeavour to be seen to act, with impartiality towards the parties and be committed to serve all parties equally with respect to the process of mediation.

## 3 THE MEDIATION AGREEMENT, PROCESS, SETTLEMENT AND FEES

### 3.1 Procedure

The mediator shall satisfy himself/herself that the parties to the mediation understand the characteristics of the mediation process and the role of the mediator and the parties in it.

The mediator shall in particular ensure that prior to commencement of the mediation the parties have understood and expressly agreed the terms and conditions of the mediation agreement including in particular any applicable provisions relating to obligations of confidentiality on the mediator and on the parties.

The mediation agreement shall, upon request of the parties, be drawn up in writing.

The mediator shall conduct the proceedings in an appropriate manner, taking into account the circumstances of the case, including possible power imbalances and the rule of law, any wishes the parties may express and the need for a prompt settlement of the dispute. The parties shall be free to agree with the mediator, by reference to a set of rules or otherwise, on the manner in which the mediation is to be conducted.

The mediator, if he/she deems it useful, may hear the parties separately.

### 3.2 Fairness of the process

The mediator shall ensure that all parties have adequate opportunities to be involved in the process.

The mediator if appropriate shall inform the parties, and may terminate the mediation, if: – a settlement is being reached that for the mediator appears unenforceable or illegal, having regard to the circumstances of the case and the competence of the mediator for making such an assessment, or – the mediator considers that continuing the mediation is unlikely to result in a settlement.

### 3.3 The end of the process

The mediator shall take all appropriate measures to ensure that any understanding is reached by all parties through knowing and informed consent, and that all parties understand the terms of the agreement.

The parties may withdraw from the mediation at any time without giving any justification.

The mediator may, upon request of the parties and within the limits of his or her competence, inform the parties as to how they may formalise the agreement and as to the possibilities for making the agreement enforceable.

### 3.4 Fees

Where not already provided, the mediator must always supply the parties with complete information on the mode of remuneration which he intends to apply. He/she shall not accept a mediation before the principles of his/her remuneration have been accepted by all parties concerned.

# 4 CONFIDENTIALITY

The mediator shall keep confidential all information, arising out of or in connection with the mediation, including the fact that the mediation is to take place or has taken place, unless compelled by law or public policy grounds. Any information disclosed in confidence to mediators by one of the parties shall not be disclosed to the other parties without permission or unless compelled by law.

# CEDR Code of Conduct for mediators and other third party neutrals[1]

## Introduction

1    This Code applies to any person who acts as a neutral third party ('the Mediator') in an ADR procedure (such as mediation or executive tribunal – 'Mediation') under the auspices of the Centre for Effective Dispute Resolution ('CEDR Solve').

## Impartiality and conflict of interest

2    The Mediator will at all times act, and endeavour to be seen to act, fairly and with complete impartiality towards the Parties in the Mediation without any bias in favour of any Party or any discrimination against any Party.

3    Any matter of which the Mediator is aware, which could be regarded as involving a conflict of interest (whether apparent, potential or actual) in the Mediation, will be disclosed to the Parties. This disclosure will be made in writing to all the Parties as soon as the Mediator becomes aware of it, whether the matter occurs prior to or during the Mediation. In these circumstances the Mediator will not act (or continue to act) in the Mediation unless all the Parties specifically acknowledge the disclosure and agree, in writing, to the Mediator acting or continuing to act as Mediator.

4    Information of the type which the Mediator should disclose includes:

- having acted in any capacity for any of the Parties (other than as Mediator in other ADR procedures);
- the Mediator's firm (if applicable) having acted in any capacity for any of the Parties;

---

1  For further information please contact CEDR on +44 (0) 20 7536 6000 or visit *www.cedr.co.uk*

- having any financial or other interest (whether direct or indirect) in any of the Parties or in the subject matter or outcome of the Mediation; or

- having any confidential information about any of the Parties or in the subject matter of the Mediation.

5   The Mediator (and any member of the Mediator's firm or company) will not act for any of the Parties individually in connection with the dispute which is the subject of the Mediation while acting as the Mediator or at any time thereafter, without the written consent of all the other Parties.

## Confidentiality

6   Subject to paragraph 8 below, the Mediator will keep confidential and not use for any collateral or ulterior purpose:

- the fact that a mediation is to take place or has taken place; and

- all information (whether given orally, in writing or otherwise) arising out of, or in connection with, the Mediation, including the fact of any settlement and its terms.

7   Subject to paragraph 8 below, if the Mediator is given information by any Party which is implicitly confidential or is expressly stated to be confidential (and which is not already public), the Mediator shall maintain the confidentiality of that information from all other Parties, except to the extent that disclosure has been specifically authorised.

© CEDR 2001

Centre for Effective Dispute Resolution International Dispute Resolution Centre 70 Fleet Street London EC4 Y 1 EU Tel +44 (0)20 7536 6000 Fax +44 (0)20 7536 6001 E-mail info@cedr.co.uk www.cedr.co.uk

Registered in England as Centre for Effective Dispute Resolution Limited number 2422813 Registered Charity number 1060369

8   The duty of confidentiality in paragraphs 6 and 7 above will not apply if, and to the extent that:

- all parties consent to disclosure;

- the Mediator is required under the general law to make disclosure;

- the Mediator reasonably considers that there is serious risk of significant harm to the life or safety of any person if the information in question is not disclosed; or

- the Mediator wishes to seek guidance in confidence from any senior officer of CEDR Solve on any ethical or other serious question arising out of the Mediation.

## Commitment and availability

9  Before accepting an appointment, the Mediator must be satisfied that he/she has time available to ensure that the Mediation can proceed in an expeditious manner.

## Fees

10  CEDR Solve will inform the Parties before the Mediation begins of the fees and expenses which will be charged for the Mediation or, if not accurately known at that stage, of the basis of charging and will not make any additional charges other than in exceptional circumstances.

## Parties' agreement

11  The Mediator will act in accordance with the agreement (whether written or oral) made between the Parties in relation to the Mediation ('the Mediation Agreement') (except where to do so would cause a breach of this Code) and will use his/her best endeavours to ensure that the Mediation proceeds in accordance with the terms of the Mediation Agreement.

## Insurance

12  The Mediator will take out professional indemnity insurance in an adequate amount with a responsible insurer.

## Withdrawal of Mediator

13  The Mediator will withdraw from the Mediation if he/she:

- is requested to do so by any of the Parties (unless the Parties have agreed to a procedure involving binding ADR);
- is in breach of this Code; or
- is required by the Parties to do something which would be in material breach of this Code.

14  The Mediator may withdraw form the Mediation at his/her own discretion if:

- any of the Parties is acting in breach of the Mediation Agreement;
- any of the Parties is, in the Mediator's opinion, acting in an unconscionable or criminal manner;
- the Mediator decides that continuing the mediation is unlikely to result in a settlement; or
- any of the Parties alleges that the Mediator is in material breach of this code.

*Appendix G*

# The Government's commitment to using Alternative Dispute Resolution

July 2002

**The Pledge**

Under the terms of the **ADR Pledge**, all Government Departments and Agencies have made the following commitments:

- Alternative Dispute Resolution will be considered and used in *all* suitable cases wherever the other party accepts it.

- In future, Departments will provide appropriate clauses in their standard procurement contracts on the use of ADR techniques to settle their disputes. The precise method of settlement would be tailored to the details of individual cases.

- Central Government will produce procurement guidance on the different options available for ADR in Government disputes and how they might be best deployed in different circumstances. This will spread best practice and ensure consistency across Government.

- Departments will improve flexibility in reaching agreement on financial compensation, including using an independent assessment of a possible settlement figure.

- Government Departments will put in place performance measures to monitor the effectiveness of this undertaking.

# Index

*[references are to paragraph numbers and appendices]*

351

*Index*

**Mediation** – *contd*
evidence, general
  inadmissibility     7.2, 7.4
  EC law aspects     10.2
facilitative and evaluative
  distinguished
     1.3.3, 3.3.2.2, 12.1.3
  moving between     13.9
fees, *see* COSTS
flexibility of *see also* FLEXIBILITY 12.8,
     14.4.2,
  further     14.4.2
information, exchange of, *see*
  INFORMATION EXCHANGE
initiating, manager to be
  alert to     3.2.5
legal framework    7.1 *et seq*, 12.2.1
legal representatives, *see* BARRISTER;
  SOLICITOR
mediator, choice etc, *see* mediator
meetings     12.6.1
  arrangements for    13.3, 13.4
  BATNA and WATNA
     2.2.2, 2.3.1.3, 13.7.2
  further joint     13.8
  further private     14.4.2
  joint    3.3.1.2, 3.3.1.4, 3.3.2.1,
     13.4, 13.5
  key points    13.5.4, 13.5.5
  mediator's role
     13.4, 13.6.2, 13.7.2
  opening    13.4, 13.5
  preliminary     12.7
  private    3.3.1.3, 3.3.2.1, 7.3,
     13.7–13.7.5
  questions and information
    exchange    13.6, 13.7.3
  showing willingness to move
    position     13.5.5
  statements by parties and
    advisers, opening
     13.5–13.5.8
National Mediation telephone
  helpline   1.5, 4.4.1, 11.11.1.2
negotiation, interaction with 11.7.5
no agreement reached at end
     13.10, 14.4, 15.1.3
order for, *see* ORDER FOR ADR
parties
  responsibilities     15.1.1
  roles     15.3

**Mediation** – *contd*
'pathfinder'     13.1
phases     12.8
  concluding joint session   3.3.1.4
  opening joint session   3.3.1.2
  preparation and agreement
     3.3.1.1
  private meetings    3.3.1.3
pilot schemes    4.4.1, 4.4.2
pre-action protocol encouragement
  of     5.6
pre-mediation contact between
  parties     12.7
preparation    12.6, 12.7, 13.2
  client's priorities, as to   12.6.2
  parties, of     12.6.7
  responsibility for     12.6
  settlement structures, advising
    parties of possible   12.6.9
  solicitor or legal representative ,
    by     15.2.1
privilege    7.2, 7.3, 7.9
procedure    3.3.1, 13.1 *et seq*
  arrival of parties, introductions
    etc     13.3
  opening of meetings   13.4, 13.5
  meetings, at    13.3–13.8
  processes    3.3, 12.8
  publicity statement after   11.9.8
refusal, *see* COSTS SANCTIONS
reluctance to use
  approach, forethought as to
     11.11.2
  carrot or stick approaches
    distinguished    11.11.2
  persuasion methods
     11.11.1.1–11.11.1.3
responsibilities as to     15.1
  process and outcome
    distinguished    15.1.1
risk assessment   11.10–11.10.5
selection of cases for  11.7.6, 11.7.7
settlement    14.1 *et seq*
  authority for   7.6–7.6.4, 12.4.1
  draft     13.2
  enforceability     7.7
  formalities    7.7, 7.8
  reaching     13.11
  *see also* SETTLEMENT
strategic approach to     11.5
  dispute systems design   11.6.1

358